Contemporary Perspectives on Mathematics in Early Childhood Education

A volume in
Contemporary Perspectives in Early Childhood Education
Olivia N. Saracho and Bernard Spodek, *Series Editors*

Contemporary Perspectives on Mathematics in Early Childhood Education

Contemporary Perspectives on Mathematics in Early Childhood Education

Edited by

Olivia N. Saracho
and
Bernard Spodek

≡**IAP**

INFORMATION AGE PUBLISHING, INC.
Charlotte, NC • www.infoagepub.com

Library of Congress Cataloging-in-Publication Data

Contemporary perspectives on mathematics in early childhood
  education / edited by Olivia N. Saracho and Bernard Spodek
      p. cm. – (Contemporary perspectives in early childhood education)
  Includes bibliographical references.
  ISBN-13: 978-1-59311-637-8 (pbk.) ISBN-13: 978-1-59311-638-5 (hardcover)
  1. Mathematics–Study and teaching (Early childhood) 2. Early childhood education.
I. Saracho, Olivia N. II. Spodek, Bernard.
  QA135.6.C659 2008
  372.7–dc22   2007037393

Copyright © 2008 Information Age Publishing Inc.

Printed in the United States of America

CONTENTS

INTRODUCTION

TRENDS IN EARLY CHILDHOOD MATHEMATICS RESEARCH

Olivia N. Saracho and Bernard Spodek

INTRODUCTION

The development of school mathematics curriculum and instruction are based on society's knowledge of the phenomenon and functions of mathematics. They are also based on the interpretation of research studies (Dossey, 1992). The mathematics reform movement (American Association for the Advancement of Science, 1990; Mathematical Science Education Board, 1990; National Council of Teachers of Mathematics, 1989) describes mathematics as a dynamic, growing field of study. On the other hand, many perceive and characterize mathematics as a passive discipline, concerned with being aware of a set of concepts, principles and skills (Fisher, 1990). According to Steen (1988):

> Many educated persons, especially scientists and engineers, harbor an image of mathematics as akin to a tree of knowledge: formulas, theorems, and results hang like ripe fruits to be plucked by passing scientists to nourish their theories. Mathematicians, in contrast, see their field as a rapidly growing rain forest, nourished and shaped by forces outside mathematics, while

contributing to human civilization a rich and ever-changing variety of intellectual flora and fauna. These differences in perception are due primarily to
the steep and harsh terrain of abstract language that separate the mathematical rain forest from the domain of ordinary human activity. (p. 611)

Recently research studies in the area of mathematics education have
proliferated. The results of these studies have contributed to the rapid
growth of new approaches to teaching mathematics. Scholars have meshed
a rich mosaic of mathematics concepts that range from axiomatic structures to generalized heuristics for solving problems. Their different perceptions have modified society's perceptions of mathematics and the way
mathematics effects peoples' daily lives (Dossey, 1992). In addition, these
perceptions have also attracted the attention of early childhood and mathematics education researchers.

Recognition of the increasing importance of mathematics to society and
to children's development has led to a dramatic increase in attention to the
mathematics education of young children. History shows that opportunities to learn mathematics were provided in influential early childhood education programs, although they were often later diluted by those who
misunderstood the children's interest in and capacity for engagement in
mathematical thinking. Children do build considerable informal knowledge of mathematics before entering school and can extend their knowledge if provided appropriate experiences at all ages. A growing body of
research and expert opinion provide detailed guidelines concerning what
children can and should learn about the five major mathematical topics:
number and arithmetic, geometry, measurement, patterning and algebraic
thinking, and data and graphing (Sarama & Clements, in this volume).
Thus, scholarly work in mathematics for young children has also emerged.
This volume provides a comprehensive critical analysis of the research in
mathematics education for young children. The researchers who conducted the critical analysis focused on the relationship between (1) mathematics learning in the early years and domain specific approaches to
cognitive development, (2) the children's social learning and their developing understanding of math, and (3) the children's learning in a natural
context and their understanding of mathematics concepts. The work of
these scholars can help guide those researchers who are interested in pursuing studies in early childhood mathematics in a specific area of study.
This volume will facilitate the research conducted by both novice and
expert researchers. The volume has accomplished its major goals, which
consists of critically analyzing important research in a specific area that
would be most useful in advancing the field and provide recommendations
for both researchers and educators.

In the first chapter, *History of Mathematics Research in Early Childhood*, Olivia N. Saracho and Bernard Spodek present the history of research in mathematics education that has surfaced over the last several centuries. They also discuss how research in mathematics has strenuously made attempts to gain its own identity. Throughout history researchers have identified mathematics issues, addressed them, defined the field, and generated a cadre of mathematics researchers. Saracho and Spodek follow the chronological history to discuss the history of early childhood mathematics in early childhood education and its impact of research on mathematics for young children.

The pervasive assumption that counting is the starting point for mathematical thinking and learning is contrasted with an alternative account based on the concept of number itself, which depends on other concepts (among them the concepts of equivalence and unit). This analysis leads to the claim that mathematical thinking begins not with counting but with comparisons of unenumerated quantities, on which children develop the concepts on which an understanding of number depends. Three lines of developmental research that bear on the contrast between counting-based accounts of early numerical development and the comparison-of-quantities position are summarized which consist of:

1. Research on infants' ability to discriminate between different numerical quantities;
2. Research on preschool children's reasoning about numerical relations between quantities; and
3. Research on children's reasoning about continuous quantities, particularly lengths.

An important instructional implication of the comparison-of-quantities position is that difficulties students experience with relatively advanced topics such as fractions are likely to stem from an inadequate grasp of much more basic concepts, notably the concept of unit. In order to forestall such difficulties, it is important that the design of early childhood mathematics instruction take into account the interrelations between basic numerical concepts and more advanced mathematical material. In her chapter titled, *Rethinking the Starting Point for Mathematics Learning*, Catherine Sophian considers the theoretical and empirical justification for, and the developmental and instructional ramifications of, a diverse perspective: That mathematical thinking begins with comparisons of quantities, which are the foundation for basic mathematical ideas that are essential to an understanding of number. This view has at its core that the recognition that children's knowledge about numbers is closely integrated with their understanding of very general properties of quantities (continuous as well as discrete). This view is supported by Piaget's (1952) analysis of the development of number concepts, which holds that children will achieve a meaningful understanding of numbers after they know more general quantitative concepts, such as conservation, seriation, and class inclusion, reflects this idea, as does the work of the influential Russian psychologist and educator, V. V. Davydov (1975).

The National Council of Teachers of Mathematics (NCTM) and the National Association for the Education of Young Children (NAEYC) recommend the implementation of a sequenced curriculum in early childhood mathematics. Yet doing so poses many challenges. Research suggest that teachers need to have a deep understanding of the mathematical content to teach it and also to interpret and to guide the students' thinking. However, Herbert P. Ginsburg and Barbrina Ertle (in this volume) believe that early childhood educators often lack the knowledge needed for solid mathematics teaching. In the next chapter, *Knowing the Mathematics in Early Childhood Mathematics*, Herbert P. Ginsburg and Barbrina Ertle explore the role of mathematical knowledge in early childhood education. They also provide a discussion of seven key factors and the challenges these factors pose for effective mathematics instruction, which consist of the following.

- First, the mathematics entails broad and deep mathematical ideas.
- Second, the everyday thinking that children use to assimilate what is taught is often complex and abstract.
- Third, experience with *Big Math for Little Kids* demonstrates that content knowledge and understanding of children's thinking are required to implement an early childhood mathematics curriculum effectively in a flexible, meaningful way.
- Fourth, implementing a complex preschool curriculum like *Big Math for Little Kids* requires the teacher to make many decisions that should be based upon deep knowledge of content and of children's thinking. Implementing a mathematics curriculum cannot be done in a rigid, scripted fashion; it requires flexibility, which in turn must be informed both by knowledge of content and of children.
- Fifth, exploiting teachable moments, which lies at the heart of some curricula, requires deep mathematical knowledge.

Ginsburg and Ertle also explain the reasons they believe that early childhood educators often do not possess adequate mathematical knowledge. Finally, they discuss the implications for teacher educators and in-service professional development.

Views of young children's mathematics have differed widely throughout history up to and including the present day. In this period of increased focus on the mathematics education of young children, both history and empirical research provide valuable perspectives. In the chapter titled,

Mathematics in Early Childhood, Julie Sarama and Douglas H. Clements begin with a brief consideration of the history of mathematics in early childhood and then turn to the question of what children know before entering school. The remainder of the chapter examines what children can and should learn about the five major mathematical topics: Number and arithmetic, geometry, measurement, patterning and algebraic thinking, and data and graphing.

In the next chapter, *Mathematics Education in the Early Years,* Ann Anderson, Jim Anderson, and Carolyn Thauberge review the research conducted over the past 10 years that focuses on children's mathematics learning in the early years (birth to eight years of age). They briefly examine the influence of the Piagetian and more recently, the Vygotskian theoretical underpinnings of this research. They synthesize the research that investigated infants', pre-schoolers' and primary children's mathematical knowledge and development. Ann Anderson, Jim Anderson, and Carolyn Thauberge also report on studies that examine the children's everyday experiences prior to school. They identify intervention studies that are designed for the primary school years. Comparative studies involving young children from various countries and/or cultural backgrounds are presented as well. In addition, they use the research on teachers' knowledge and practice to help them illustrate the close connection such studies have to research on young children's mathematical thinking. They stress a number of curriculum issues and examine some examples of appropriate curriculum for mathematics in these early years. Anderson, Anderson, and Thauberge conclude with an overview of the major findings of their review and make suggestions for future research.

During the last decade, mathematics education has undergone a major reform throughout the world. The principle stimulus for these reforms was the publication of the Third International Mathematics and Science Study [TIMSS] (Garden, 1996, 1997; National Center for Educational Statistics, n.d.; Mullis, Martin, Beaton, Gonzales, Kelly, & Smith, 1997). International comparisons of mathematics achievement indicated that students from many western countries performed less well than those from Asian countries (i.e., Korea, Singapore, Japan, & Hong Kong). These disappointing results have impelled some educators to create a radically different approach to mathematics education (British Columbia Ministry of Education, 2003; Commonwealth of Australia, 2000; Department for Education and Employment, 1999; Ministry of Education, 2001; National Council of Teachers of Mathematics, 2000–2004c). In the chapter titled, *The Development of Children's Mathematical Thinking in the Early School Years,* Jennifer M. Young-Loveridge explores the development of children's mathematical thinking as a result of initiatives designed to improve the teaching and learning of mathematics in the early school years. The first part of the chapter focuses on numeracy initiatives developed in New Zealand, Australia, England, the United States, and Canada. This section presents an overview of common features shared by many of the numeracy initiatives, including professional development programs for teachers, developmental learning frameworks, individual diagnostic interviews, a strong emphasis on mathematical thinking and reasoning, and a constructivist/socioconstructivist approach to the learning and teaching of mathematics. The second part of the chapter focuses on New Zealand's numeracy initiative, and examines its impact on the teachers and their students. The magnitude of the project's impact on the students' mathematical learning is explored using effect sizes calculated using slightly older students (from the adjacent age-group) as a "control" group with which to compare the "treatment" group. Data on students' perspectives provide an alternative view of the impact of the project. The final part of the chapter considers some of the challenges of implementing a numeracy initiative, using New Zealand's numeracy initiative as an example.

Learning mathematics is definitely necessary. Mathematics is a prerequisite in mastering any science or technology. It is a discipline that is basic to science, technology, engineering. In turn scientists and engineers are responsible for our modern technological societies and for maintaining modern technological societies. Evidently, learning mathematics is generally an essential educational objective worldwide and developmental psychologists are interested in the central topic of mathematical reasoning (Bart, Yuzawa, & Yuzawa, in this volume). In the chapter, *The Development of Mathematical Reasoning among Young Children: How Do Children Understand Area and Length?* William M. Bart, Masamichi Yuzawa, and Miki Yuzawa provide a review of the research literature on the development of the concepts of area and length mainly during the preschool years. Preceding the review, they provide a brief commentary on research on the development of mathematical reasoning. They provide a discussion in that initial commentary of the contributions of Piagetian (1952) research, the insights offered in the approach of Vygotsky (1978) to mathematical reasoning, and the relevant findings of the research of Robert Siegler (1976, 1991, 1996). After the review, Bart, Yuzawa, and Yuzawa offer suggestions for future research and suggestions for educational practices with young children. One such suggestion is that carefully formulated sequences of instructional activities be identified, formulated, and implemented to boost the intellectual resources of students. Such sequences of instructional activities are termed "cognitive enhancers" and some cognitive enhancers are appropriate for early childhood educational programs. With more research and development regarding mathematical educational programs that are developmentally appropriate for young learners, early childhood education programs could be developed and implemented to contribute to the development of mathematical reasoning among young learners.

Young children have an impressive understanding of mathematics at an early age. According to Baroody, Lai, and Mix (2006), the children's development of a sense of number in "mathematical learning begins early, very early" (p. 196). Many researchers still debate the exact age when mathematics learning is initiated (e. g., Baroody, 2004; Mix, Huttenlocher, & Levine, 2002; Starkey, Spelke, & Gelman, 1990; Wynn, 1998). Nevertheless, it is assumed that three- and four-year-olds have encountered many mathematical experiences (for reviews, see Baroody et al., 2006; Ginsburg, Cannon, Eisenband, & Pappas, 2006; Ginsburg, Klein, & Starkey, 1998). Ginsburg and his colleagues (1998) stated that researchers have "a rich understanding of the ways in which children construct an informal knowledge of mathematics in the everyday environment" (pp. 401–402).

In relation to number, Hannula (2005) indicated that "nearly all our knowledge of young children's number recognition skills is based on studies that explicitly direct children's attention to the aspect of number" (p. 11). Similarly, other mathematics areas have insufficient research on how much, and under what conditions, young children play with mathematical shapes, talk about time, estimate distance, and so on, in the course of their everyday activities. Both Piaget (1952) and Vygotsky (1978) showed that children, early in life, develop an informal understanding of mathematics in the course of their everyday lives, and there is a good deal of evidence that by the age of three children have had a good deal of mathematical experience. Most of our knowledge of children's understanding comes from experimental work, however, with comparatively little research into the extent and nature of these mathematical experiences. The research that has been conducted primarily relies on one of four different methods: (1) parents' reports of their children's engagement in daily activities (not always with a specific focus on mathematics), either via time-use diaries or during interviews; (2) live observations in the home, preschool setting, or both; (3) transcripts of audiotapes recorded in the home, preschool, or both; and (4) videotapes of naturally-occurring activities at home or preschool. In the chapter titled, *The Impact of Method on Assessing Young Children's Everyday Mathematical Experiences*, Jonathan Tudge, LinLin Li, and Tiffany Kinney show that the methods are clearly implicated in judgments of how much children engage in mathematics; only by using videotapes it is possible to see the full extent and variety of that engagement. Drawing on Piaget's (1952) and Vygotsky's (1978) insights, they suggest that parents and early childhood educators do not need to teach more mathematics but could do far more to respond to and extend their children's engagement in and understanding of their everyday mathematics. The focus in this chapter is on this type of informal mathematics that occurs during the course of the preschool-aged children's typical everyday activities rather than what can be seen in laboratory or other controlled conditions. They also describe the methods to use in assessing the children's involvement in everyday mathematics which heavily influence the apparent extent of their involvement.

Research examining young children's statistical thinking is in its infancy. Current research generally falls into two categories: the examination of understandings related to specific statistical concepts, or the development of models of the children's statistical thinking. In the chapter on *An Examination of the Role of Statistical Investigation in Supporting the Development of Young Children's Statistical Reasoning*, Aisling Leavy (1) identifies common themes emerging from both strands of inquiry, (2) determines the obstacles that young children face when engaging in data analysis, and (3) proposes factors to account for disparities in some of the research findings. She places particular attention on how efforts to engage young children in statistical investigation may provide meaningful contexts which support children in statistical reasoning.

The National Council of Teachers of Mathematics (2000–2004c) has stressed the critical role of developing "spatial sense" as well as "number sense" from the start of young children's formal mathematics learning. In their chapter, *Research on the Development of Block-Building Skills in Girls and Boys: The Relationship to Spatial Skills and Mathematics Learning*, Joanne Kersh, Beth M. Casey, and Jessica Mercer Young present an overview of the evidence documenting the importance of spatial skills for later mathematics achievement and discuss why this relationship is particularly critical for girls. Based on this framework, they review the research on gender differences in spatial and math skills, specifically addressing early childhood research. Block building is a fundamental spatial component of the early learning environment. In the last section of their chapter, Kersh, Casey, and Young review the evidence supporting the relationships between mathematics and spatial skills as well as the research on gender differences in block building. At the end of the chapter, they make recommendations for research related to block building and suggest ways to foster spatial skills within early childhood classrooms by establishing block building as a systematic, planned component of the early childhood mathematics curriculum.

For many years mathematical learning and development was not addressed in early childhood education due to theoretical misconceptions about the origins and early development of mathematical knowledge. Research has now found that mathematical competence originates and undergoes considerable development during the early childhood period. Cross-cultural and cross-socioeconomic research has revealed that sociocultural variables in young children's home and preschool learning environments influence early mathematical development. By three years of age differences in the extent of the children's mathematical knowledge are present in the children from different cultures and different socioeconomic circumstances. If preschool programs do not provide adequate enrichment in mathematics, some children, especially economically challenged children, will enter school without adequate preparation for mathematics. Both cross-cultural and intervention research have demonstrated that quality mathematics activities provided through preschool curricula can significantly close the socioeconomic-related gap in mathematical knowledge in young children. These findings have implications for early childhood education policy, particularly for economically challenged children. There is now ample evidence that close attention should be paid to children's early learning and development of mathematics. In their chapter, *Sociocultural Influences on Young Children's Mathematical Knowledge*, Prentice Starkey and Alice Klein first examine early theories of mathematical learning and development that support that mathematical knowledge initially develops during the elementary school years. They then review research that fundamentally challenge these theories. Mathematical competence is present from an early point in life and rapidly develops in the early years.

Recent theories of mathematical learning and development have acknowledged that a form of mathematical knowledge is present during these early years, but many theories assume that this knowledge develops naturally with little intervention by society and that this early development has little influence on mathematics achievement that occurs during the elementary school years or beyond. In the chapter, *Sociocultural Influences on Young Children's Mathematical Knowledge*, Prentice Starkey and Alice Klein argue that recent theories of mathematical learning and development (1) have underestimated the importance of the informal mathematical knowledge that develops in the early years, and (2) are incorrect in assuming that this early form of mathematical knowledge will naturally and fully develop without deliberate support. To the contrary, some cross-cultural and within-cultural differences in mathematics achievement stem from the foundation of informal mathematical knowledge children develop during early childhood. In some other countries, early childhood education programs use a systematic approach to support mathematical development in very young children. Starkey and Klein insist that preschool programs in the United States should likewise take a more deliberate mathematics approach to develop a good foundation of informal mathematical knowledge with young children, particularly those who are economically challenged.

Research conducted within a sociocultural perspective has demonstrated that parents often support the children's play at a more complex level than they would achieve on their own, by providing guidance within a zone of proximal development. The connections between play and emergent literacy have been examined frequently in early child development research, but seldom have connections between numeracy and parent-child play have been the focus of investigations. In her chapter, *Parental Guidance of Numeracy Development in Early Childhood,* Maureen Vandermaas-Peeler examines parent-child interactions during play within a sociocultural context and reviews the extent research on parent-child activities that support preschoolers' emergent numeracy. The findings indicate that parents supporte numeracy-related concepts in free play and in structured activities, and that parental support and teaching related to math activities at home islinked to the children's achievement in school. Vandermaas-Peeler recommends that researchers place greater emphasis and focus on parent-child interactions related to numeracy at home in both research and practice. She also suggests that more research be conducted within a sociocultural perspective to investigate parental motivation and efficacy for guiding emergent numeracy.

The following chapter, "Do Parents Count?: The Socialization of Children's Numeracy," by Joan P. Benigno and Shari Ellis examines the role that the culture of the family environment plays in promoting the children's mathematical cognition. The authors outline relevant research illustrating the role of family members, particularly parents, in socially constructing children's numerical knowledge. The studies reviewed suggest that parents engage in number activities with their children. Moreover, the frequency and types of number activities vary widely across families and the complexity of the activities increases as children grow older. Furthermore, the nature of parental involvement shifts once their children make the transition into formal schooling. Benigno and Ellis also discuss implications for evidence-based practice and directions for future research.

In the final chapter, "Research Perspectives in Early Childhood Mathematics," Olivia N. Saracho and Bernard Spodek discuss the current research and other developments that have impelled those involved directly and indirectly with young children to focus their attention on mathematics in early childhood education. These explanations are the results of the vast increase in mathematics research in early childhood education. In the *Before It's Too Late: A Report to the Nation from the National Commission on Mathematics and Science Teaching for the 21st Century,* the Glen Commission (2000) reported:

> at the daybreak of this new century and millennium ... the future well-being of our nation and people depends not just on how well we educate our children generally, but on how well we educate them in mathematics and science specifically. (p. 6)

To assure a quality mathematics early childhood education program, a set of guidelines and standards have been developed based on extensive knowledge of young children's mathematical knowledge, which includes acting, thinking, and learning (Clements, 2004). The National Council of Teachers of Mathematics (2000–2004a, 2000–2004b, 2000–2004c) responded by developing and publishing the *Principles and Standards for School Mathematics*, which included standards for children who were in pre-school through the twelfth grade. Although each of these Standards relates to all grades, Saracho and Spodek only focus on those *Principles and Standards* for preschool through second grade children. Since researchers are emphasizing young children's competence in their mathematical thinking, Ginsburg and Golbeck. (2004) have warned researchers that a strong emphasis on competence can (1) Reduce the limits on young children's mathematical understanding, (2) Over estimate young children's mathematical competence, and (3) Ignore the complexity of young children's competence. Educators need to assess the young children's early competence including their actions, abilities, and environment (Ginsburg & Golbeck, 2004). In addition, mathematical research and instruction need to be based on extensive knowledge of young children's mathematical acting, thinking, and learning (Clements, 2004).

Communication among researchers, educators, and policy makers is essential to understand mathematics that is developmentally appropriate for young children. Early communication was initiated to develop standards for preschool and kindergarten mathematics education in *The Conference on Standards for Prekindergarten and Kindergarten Mathematics Education* (Clements, 2004). In their chapter, Saracho and Spodek share the assumptions and recommendations that were developed in this conference by Clements (2004) and the conference participants who included a range of experts in the diverse fields such as representatives who were developing standards for young children's mathematics in almost every state; federal government officials; mathematicians, mathematics educators, researchers from mathematics education, researchers from early childhood education, and psychology researchers; curriculum developers; teachers; policy makers; and representatives from national organizations such as the National Council of Teachers of Mathematics (NCTM) and the National Association for the Education of Young Children (NAEYC). In addition, Saracho and Spodek share the recommendations in the use of technology in the learning and teaching of mathematics. These recommendations are derived (1) from the book, *Principles and standards for school mathematics*, published by the National Council of Teachers of Mathematics (2000–2004c), (2) from the National Council of Teachers of Mathematics October 2003 position statement in technology, and (3) from those selected by Masalski and Elliot (2005). As a result of research studies and developmental trends, researchers from a variety of disciplines focused on research related to different perspectives in mathematics. Currently, there is a recognizable body of research that extends beyond the mathematics realm. Studies differ in the degree to which they explore and are sensitive to the area of mathematics education. Nevertheless, sufficient data are available to characterize research on mathematics education as a research field and to identify those researchers who focus on the mathematics education research community. This volume has provided a synthesis and reconceptualization of past research, recommended guidelines for future research, and identified educational implications.

CONCLUSION

Over the turn of the century, mathematics research in early childhood education have surfaced. Presently, researchers have contributed to a concrete body of research that integrates the realm of mathematics in early childhood education with the nature of the mathematics domain. Current researchers consider all factors of mathematics study including formulating research questions, selecting the type of inquiry, developing measures, gathering data, interpreting results, and providing recommendations for future research and practice. Studies range in their degree of focus in mathematics research and responsiveness to each of the facets of the mathematics area. Nevertheless, sufficient research outcomes exist to identify research on mathematics education as a research field and to recognize those researchers from the mathematics research community (Grouws, 1992).

REFERENCES

American Association for the Advancement of Science (AAAS). (1990). *Project 2061: Science for all Americans.* Washington, DC: Author.

Baroody, A. J. (2004). The developmental bases for early childhood number and operations standards. In D. H. Clements, J. Sarama, & A.-M. Dibiase (Eds.), *Engaging young children in mathematics: Standards for early childhood mathematics education* (pp. 173–219). Mahwah, NJ: Erlbaum.

Baroody, A. J., Lai., M., & Mix, K. S. (2006). The development of young children's early number and operation sense and its implications for early childhood education. In B. Spodek & O. N. Saracho (Eds.), *Handbook of research on the education of young children* (2nd ed., pp. 187–221). Mahwah, NJ: Erlbaum.

British Columbia Ministry of Education. (2003). *Supporting early numeracy: BC early numeracy project (K–1).* Province of British Columbia: Author.

Clements, D. H. (2004). Major themes and recommendations. In D. H. Clements, J. Sarama, & A-M. DiBiase (Eds.). *Engaging young children in mathematics: Standards for early childhood mathematics education* (pp. 7–72). Mahwah, NJ: Erlbaum.

Commonwealth of Australia. (2000). *Numeracy, a priority for all: Challenges for Australian schools: Commonwealth numeracy policies for Australian schools.* Author.

Davydov, V. V. (1975). Logical and psychological problems of elementary mathematics as an academic subject. In L. P. Steffe (Ed.), *Children's capacity for learning mathematics. Soviet Studies in the Psychology of Learning and Teaching Mathematics, Vol. VII* (pp. 55–107). Chicago: University of Chicago.

Department for Education and Employment. (1999). *The National Numeracy Strategy: Framework for teaching mathematics from reception to year 6.* London: Author.

Dossey, J. A. (1992). The nature of mathematics: Its role and influence. In D. A. Grouws (Ed.), *Handbook of research on mathematics teaching and learning* (pp. 39–48). New York: Macmillan.

Fisher, C. (1990). The research agenda project as prologue. *Journal of Research in Mathematics Education, 21,* 81–89.

Garden, R. A. (1996). *Mathematics performance of New Zealand Form 2 and Form 3 students: National results from New Zealand's participation in the Third International Mathematics and Science Study.* Wellington: Ministry of Education.

Garden, R. A. (1997). *Mathematics and science performance in middle primary school: Results from New Zealand's participation in the Third International Mathematics and Science Study.* Wellington: Ministry of Education.

Ginsburg, H. P., Cannon, J., Eisenband, J., & Pappas, S. (2006). Mathematical thinking and learning. In K. McCartney & D. Phillips (Eds.), *Blackwell handbook on early childhood development* (pp. 208–230). Malden, MA: Blackwell.

Ginsburg, H. P., & Golbeck, S. L. (2004). Thoughts on the future of research on mathematics and science learning and education. *Early Childhood Research Quarterly, 19,* 190–200.

Ginsburg, H. P., Klein, A., & Starkey, P. (1998). The development of children's mathematical thinking: Connecting research with practice. In I. E. Sigel & K. A. Renninger (Volume Eds.) and W. Damon (Series Ed.), *Handbook of child psychology, Volume 4: Child psychology in practice* (pp. 401–476). New York: Wiley.

Glen Commission. (2000). *Before it's too late: A report to the nation from the National Commission on Mathematics and Science Teaching for the 21st century.* Washington, DC: United States Department of Education.

Grouws, D. A. (Ed.). (1992). *Handbook of research on mathematics teaching and learning.* New York: Macmillan.

Hannula, M. M., Mattinen, A., & Lehtinen, E. (2005). Does social interaction influence 3-year-old children's tendency to focus on numerosity? A quasi-experimental study in day care. In L. Verschaffel, E. De Corte, G. Kanselaar, & M. Valcke (Eds.), *Powerful learning environments for promoting deep conceptual and strategic learning* (pp. 63–80). Studia Paedagogica. Leuven: Leuven University Press.

Masalski, W. J., & Elliot, P. C. (2005). Prologue NCTM position paper on technology. The use of technology in the learning and teaching of mathematics. In W. J. Masalski & P. C. Elliot (Eds.) *Technology-supported: mathematics learning environments.* (pp. 1–2). Reston, VA: National Council of Teachers of Mathematics.

Mathematical Science Education Board (MSEB). (1990). *Everybody counts.* Washington, DC: National Academy Press.

Ministry of Education. (2001). New Zealand Numeracy Project material. Retrieved from http://www.nzmaths.co.nz/Numeracy/project_material.htm on November 24, 2006

Mix, K. S., Huttenlocher, J., & Levine, S. C. (2002). *Quantitative development in infancy and early childhood.* New York: Oxford University Press.

Mullis, I. V. S., Martin, M. O., Beaton, A. E., Gonzales, E. J., Kelly, D. L., & Smith, T. A. (1997). *Mathematics achievement in the primary school years: IEA's third international mathematics and science study (TIMSS).* Chestnut Hill, MA: Center for the Study of Testing, Evaluation, and Educational Policy, Boston College.

National Center for Educational Statistics. (n.d.). *TIMSS results.* Retrieved from http://nces.ed.gov/timss/results.asp on November 24, 2006

National Council of Teachers of Mathematics (NCTM). (1989). *Curriculum and evaluation standards for school mathematics.* Reston, VA: Author.

National Council of Teachers of Mathematics. (2000–2004a). *Overview: Prekindergarten through grade 2.* Retrieved from http://standards.nctm.org/document/chapter4/index.htm on November 21, 2006.

National Council of Teachers of Mathematics. (2000–2004b). *Overview: Standards for school mathematics: Prekindergarten through grade 12.* Retrieved from http://standards.nctm.org/document/chapter3/index.htm on November 21, 2006.

National Council of Teachers of Mathematics. (2000–2004c). *Principles and standards for school mathematics.* Reston, VA: National Council of Teachers of Mathematics.

Piaget, J. (1952). *The child's conception of number.* New York: Norton.

Siegler, R. (1976). Three aspects of cognitive development. *Cognitive Psychology, 8,* 481–520.

Siegler, R. (1991). *Children's thinking* (2nd ed.). Englewood Cliffs, NJ: Prentice-Hall.

Siegler, R. (1996). *Emerging minds: The process of change in children's thinking.* New York: Oxford University Press.

Starkey, P., Spelke, E. S., & Gelman, R. (1990). Numerical abstraction by human infants. *Cognition, 36,* 97–127.

Steen, L. (1988). The science of patterns. *Science, 240,* 611–616.

Vygotsky, L. S. (1978). *Mind in society: The development of higher psychological processes.* Cambridge, MA: Harvard University Press.

Wynn, K. (1998). Psychological foundations of number: Numerical competence in human infants. *Trends in Cognitive Sciences, 2,* 296–303.

CHAPTER 1

HISTORY OF MATHEMATICS IN EARLY CHILDHOOD EDUCATION

Olivia N. Saracho and Bernard Spodek

Early childhood mathematics education includes more than arithmetic or "numeracy." It covers a broad range of ideas, as Ginsberg and Ertle, in this volume, have indicated. Besides number, it includes geometry, measurement, and algebra, as well as patterns. This is far beyond the arithmetic that was exclusively taught in the kindergarten programs and elementary schools a half a century ago. The change has its roots in the curriculum reform movement of the 1960s and 1970s, which was responsible for the creation of the "New Math." It is also rooted in the history of mathematics itself, which stretches across centuries as well as in the history of developmental psychology and of early childhood education. The purpose of this chapter is to describe the foundation for mathematics in early childhood education.

HISTORICAL FOUNDATIONS THAT INFLUENCED EARLY CHILDHOOD EDUCATION

Current day mathematics can trace its history to Ancient Greek civilization. Most literate Americans are familiar with the names of Plato, Pythag-

Contemporary Perspectives on Mathematics in Early Childhood Education, pages 1–20
Copyright © 2008 by Information Age Publishing
All rights of reproduction in any form reserved.

oras, and Euclid, a few of the pioneers of mathematics of that time. Plato assumed that the objects of mathematics existed on their own—beyond the mind—in the outside world. He distinguished between the concepts of the mind and those perceived by the senses. This led Plato to differentiate between arithmetic and the theory of numbers and logistics. On the other hand, Aristotle's (Plato's student) perception of mathematics disregarded the idea of an external, independent, and unobservable body of knowledge. Instead, he depended on experienced reality as the basis of mathematics. He believed that mathematical knowledge is acquired through experimentation, observation, and abstraction, which represents the current mathematical position. Aristotle separated mathematical knowledge into three taxonomic groups (Dossey, 1992): the physical, the mathematical, and the theological. According to Ptolemy (1952), the Greek mathematician,

> [Mathematics is the one] which shows up quality with respect to forms and local motions, seeking figure number and magnitude, and also place, time and similar things.... Such an essence falls, as it were between the other two, not only because it can be conceived both through the senses and without the senses. (p. 5)

Thus, Plato's and Aristotle's works and concepts represent the two principle opposing themes regarding mathematics (Dossey, 1992), which later had an impact in early childhood education mathematics.

During the nineteenth and twentieth centuries, different viewpoints on the study of real number and the theory of sets emerged. Experimentation and perception in mathematics research were disregarded, which led to new difficulties. Three new perspectives in mathematics appeared to solve these difficulties.

1. *School of logicism*, which was founded by the German mathematician Gottlob Frege in 1884, based on the Platonic school that the mathematics concept is a subset of the ideas of logic. The advocates of logicism referred to mathematical statements as interpretations of logic instead of depending on a given contextual environment for interpretations (Dossey, 1992).

2. *Intuitionism* is based on L. E. J. Brouwer's (1975), the Dutch mathematician, philosophy of mind. Brouwer (1975) believed that mathematics is an activity without language, since language merely describes a mathematical activity after the fact. His belief disregards axiomatic approaches to any foundational function in mathematics. In addition, he interpreted logic as the study of patterns in linguistic performances of a mathematical activity; thus, logic depends on mathematics (as the study of patterns) and not vice versa. He used

these determining factors to distinguish between mathematics and metamathematics, which he refers to as "second order mathematics" (van Atten, 2004, 2005). Brouwer's (1975) thoughts delineated mathematics as resulting from "valid" demonstrations. The human minds were the only ones who were able to create mathematical concepts, which was within the Aristotelian orientation. The intuitionists' work evolved into a set of theorems and conceptions that differed from those of classical mathematics (Dossey, 1992).

3. *Formalism*, which emerged toward the twentieth century, was shaped by the German mathematician David Hilbert. He introduced the difference between real and ideal formulas. He assumed that formulas and proofs should be syntactically manipulated, while the properties and relationships of formulas and proofs must be equivalently based in a logic-free intuitive capacity to guarantee that syntactic operations are used to obtain the knowledge about formulas and proofs (Zach, 2003). Hilbert and Ackermann (1928) stated, "This formula game is carried out according to certain definite rules, in which the technique of our thinking is expressed.... The fundamental idea of my proof theory is none other than to describe the activity of our understanding, to make a protocol of the rules according to which our thinking actually proceeds" (Hilbert & Ackermann, 1928, p. 475). Weyl (1925) stressed that Hilbert's proof theory would protect mathematics from becoming a meaningless game of symbols, but it would evolve into a theoretical science which systematizes scientific (mathematical) practice (Mancosu, 1998).

The aforementioned principle schools of thought focused on varying conceptualizations of mathematics toward the end of the nineteenth century and stimulated communication about mathematics. All schools of thought perceived the contents of mathematics as products. In *logicism*, the contents were the elements in classical mathematics, its definition, its postulates, and its theorems. In *intuitionists*, the contents were the theorems derived from the first principles via "valid" patterns of reasoning. In *formalism*, the contents were the formal axiomatic structures to eliminate the weak points in classical mathematics. Platonic and Aristotelian concepts contributed to the development of these theories. The source of the "product" continued to be problematic whether it is a pre-existing external object or an object developed through experience using sense perceptions of experimentation (Dossey, 1992).

A mathematics philosophy requires ideas that can assist mathematicians, educators, and students to participate in the invention of mathematics. It needs to provide opportunities for the mathematization or modeling of concepts and circumstances. An innovative philosophy is developed through mathematical dialogue and communication to discuss alternative perspectives of mathematics to reach a valid and practicable description of mathematics (Dossey, 1992). Mathematics researchers, scholars, philosophers, and educators continue to challenge mathematics philosophies that differ from their own point of view. Their point of view may be in conflict when establishing a mathematics philosophy for young children, whose ages range from birth through eight years of age.

In 1631, Jan Amos Comenius published his book, *School of Infancy*, on the education of the child's first six years of life. His curriculum consisted of simple lessons using real objects. Comenius' influence continued throughout the nineteenth century with the Pestallozzian system of education, which emphasized education through observing and manipulating objects. This stimulated the creation of programs for young children which included mathematics, or at least arithmetic, that would be taught through the use of manipulative materials.

A group with a different point of view in early childhood mathematics consisted of the social theorists whose perceptions emerged in the early third of the twentieth century. The social theorists, who generated their philosophy based on direct observation, assumed that mathematics instruction for young children in any form was limited and inappropriate. Although in many ways, the social theorists' influence is still in existence, their view was disregarded with the appearance of the public kindergarten.

MATHEMATICS IN AMERICAN EDUCATION

It can be said that early childhood education in the United States began in colonial times with the establishment of the common school in New England. These schools, though not early childhood education specifically, included young children among their students. The schools were designed essentially to teach children to read in order to enable people to read the Bible themselves. In time, especially after the establishment of the United States of America, they became more secular. They were then primarily concerned with teaching individuals the basics necessary to function as citizens in a democratic society as well as to be competent in the simple acts of commerce of the nation. The basic subjects of reading, writing, and arithmetic became the core of the curriculum in the primary school during that time and has remained the basic core ever since.

Primary education remained essentially the same until the twentieth century. Teaching was done through direct instruction and recitation. Mathematics instruction focused solely on arithmetic, including counting words, and the various arithmetic operations such as addition and subtraction.

Education specifically designed for young children surfaced relatively early in the history of the United States of America. Its theoretical rationale derived from the ideas and ideals of several early European scholars (Saracho & Spodek, 2006). These scholars had different educational theories, which influenced young children's educational experiences, including their mathematics experiences. The section below describes the early childhood historical influences and their impact on mathematics. Mathematics oriented approaches were included in the Infant School, the Froebel kindergarten, and the Montessori *Casa die Bambini* (Children's House).

The Infant School

In 1816 Robert Owen, the social reformer, created the Infant School in New Lanark, Scotland. It was designed to serve the children of workers in his cotton mill both to educate them and to keep them out of the workplace. Owen built his curriculum on the ideas of Pestalozzi. It used experiences with nature and with concrete materials as a source of learning. The curriculum included reading, writing, arithmetic, sewing, geography, natural history, modern and ancient history, dance, and music (Spodek, 1973). This constituted a much broader curriculum than was generally offered in schools for young children. The infant school's approach to arithmetic focused on understanding the different arithmetical operations and, like Pestalozzi, Owen advocated using manipulative materials in teaching arithmetic.

By 1825 at least fifty-five infant schools could be found in England, Scotland, and Ireland, along with several infant school societies. In1827 infant schools were established in Hartford, Connecticut, New York City, Philadelphia, Boston, and other American cities. In addition, Robert Owen lectured extensively in the United States about his new concept of society and about his view of education. He purchased the settlement of New Harmony, Indiana, to found a communitarian society and an infant school. After a few years, serious problems emerged in both the school and the community, which lead to the failure of the community, vestiges of which still exist today. However, infant schools flourished in New England and in the middle Atlantic communities for about the next decade. By the middle of the 1830s, the infant school movement in America had disappeared (Spodek & Saracho, 1994). The negative attitudes of the public school establishment toward this form of education, which was considered "radical and heretical" and the movement toward the early education of children in the home by their parents, led to the demise of this form of education (Strickland, 1982).

During the same decade when the infant schools were founded, Goodrich's (1818) *The Children's Arithmetic* and Colburn's (1821) approach to arithmetic, "Mental Arithmetic" also emerged. These educators assumed that simple levels of numerical reasoning were appropriate for young children. Also the pedagogic innovations and the social movement that started in England provided three- to five-year-old children the opportunity to learn how to count and perform simple arithmetic.

Children's Arithmetic

From the 1820s through the 1830s, pedagogic conceptions provided three- to five-year-old children the opportunity to learn how to count and perform simple arithmetic in formal organized settings (Balfanz, 1999). Samuel Goodrich contended that memorizing rules and rote learning would only preclude children from understanding arithmetic. He believed that children would discover rules by manipulating concrete objects like counters and bead-frames. Through this approach children would physically comprehend the process of addition or multiplication (really successive addition) long before they moved on to abstract numbers. He introduced an easier way to learn arithmetic that focused on operations using whole numbers and easy fractions that excluded complex fractions and transformations between conflicting units of measure.

In 1818 Goodrich published *The Children's Arithmetic*, which proposed that young children discover the rules of arithmetic through the manipulation of tangible objects like counters and bead frames. This discovery technique eliminated the view that arithmetic was based on memorization. This was considered revolutionary since during the colonial era, basic arithmetic knowledge was considered to be too difficult for children younger than age twelve and formal arithmetic instruction was deferred until children reached 10 years of age. Goodrich showed that young children were able to learn arithmetic and refined the methodology and curriculum to facilitate their learning (Balfanz, 1999; Cohen, 1999).

Mental Arithmetic

Later, Samuel Goodrich's concept was expanded and developed by Warren Colburn (1821) who referred to his new approach as "mental arithmetic" (Cohen, 1999). Colburn's approach was influenced by Johann Pestalozzi's educational theory (see Gutek [1968] for a comprehensive review of Pestalozzi's theory). Pestalozzi believed that young children needed to participate in the learning process. Pestalozzi's pedagogical philosophy emphasized that teaching should be from the known to the unknown, incorporate the performance of concrete arts and the experience of factual emotional reactions, and be developmentally appropriate. His concepts derived from the same set of beliefs as those of Johann Friedrich Herbart, Maria Montessori, John Dewey, and, more recently, Jean Piaget.

Mental arithmetic infiltrated the field of mathematics education in the early 1820's. The traditional concept that arithmetic was a memory base subject was considered to be inappropriate and was entirely disclaimed. According to Colburn (1826),

> Our general maximum to be observed with pupils of every age, is never to tell them directly how to perform any example. If a pupil is unable to perform an example, it is generally because he does not fully comprehend the object of it. (p. 5)

Colburn's "mental arithmetic" was based on the belief that simple levels of numerical reasoning are appropriate for young children and as their mind develops, they naturally are able to understand more complex levels (Cohen, 1999). Colburn's "mental arithmetic" had two related but different implicit concepts, which we have labeled *intellectual learning* and *inductive reasoning.*

- *Intellectual learning.*   The name "mental arithmetic," focused on computing arithmetic without pencil and paper. Young children would understand the concept of number initially by using tangible items and later making the transition to written symbols. He stated,

  > Our general maximum to be observed with pupils of every age, is never to tell them directly how to perform any example. If a pupil is unable to perform an example, it is generally because he does not fully comprehend the object of it. (Colburn, 1826, p. 5)

- *Inductive reasoning.*   Children would learn the basic rules of arithmetic for themselves by solving carefully selected problems and that the joy of the solutions would instill the essential arithmetic concepts into the children's schema forever. Colburn strongly advocated an inductive approach, which in many ways suggests that he was the first constructivist. He contended that the inductive reasoning provided each child the capacity to become an original mathematical thinker (Bidwell & Classon, 1970). He stated,

  > . . . without telling what to do. He will discover what is to be done, and invent a way to do it. Let him perform several in his own way, and then suggest some method a little different from his, and nearer the common method. If he readily comprehends it, he will be pleased with it,

and adopt it. If he does not, his mind is not yet prepared for it, and should be allowed to continue his own way longer, and then it should be suggested again. (Colburn, 1826, pp. 4–5)

In 1821, Colburn published his work in a book titled, *First Lessons, or Intellectual Arithmetic on the Plan of Pestalozzi* (Colburn, 1821). Since this text was for children ages four and five, it excluded rules and memory work. It also suggested presenting word problems orally, which allowed young children to solve them mentally (Cohen, 1999). The following are some examples from the first 30 problems to be read to young children:

- How many thumbs have you on your right hand? How many on your left? How many on both together?
- If you have two cents in one hand, and two in another, how many have you in both?
- George had three cents, and Joseph has four; how many have they both together?
- David had seven nuts, and gave three to them to George; how many had he left?
- A man owing seventeen dollars paid all but seven dollars; how much did he pay?
- Two and one are how many?
- Two and two are how many?
- Three and two are how many? (Cited in Bidwell & Classon, 1970, pp. 21–22).

In a later edition of his book, Colburn (1822) stated,

The fondness which children usually manifest for these exercises, and the facility with which they perform them, seem to indicate that the science of numbers to a certain extend, should be among the first lessons taught to them....

To success in this, however it is necessary rather to furnish occasions for them to exercises their own skill performing examples, than to give them rules. They should be allowed to pursue their own method first, and then they should be made to observe and explain it, and if it was not the best, some improvements should be suggested. By following the mode, and making the examples gradually increase in difficulty, experience proves, that, at any early age, children may be taught a great variety of the most useful combinations of numbers. (Bidwell & Classon, 1970, pp. 15–16)

Educators and curriculum writers continuously implemented Colburn's approach. Observations of young children showed that they were able to participate in serious intellectual arithmetic in a playful mode when young children were permitted to explore and discover mathematical concepts in an appropriate mathematical environment. Later Colburn published (1) a second edition of *First Lessons*, or *Intellectual Arithmetic on the Plan of Pestalozzi* (Colburn, 1822) and (2) a sequel titled, *Arithmetic upon the Inductive Method of Instruction* (Colburn, 1826); and (3) an algebra text founded on the same principles. Reports surfaced in the first part of the year 1826 from schools in New England and New York concerning the overwhelming success of Colburn's approach (Cohen, 1999). During this time, Colburn's "mental arithmetic" was receiving wide recognition. In 1822, the *North American Review* wrote,

> These difficulties, with others, arising from the manner in which the study is pursued, and the want of capacity in the instructors, render arithmetic, instead of a most simple and practical thing, one of the most irksome and unintelligible that can be presented to the young mind. Mr. Colburn's books is liable to none of these objections. A child sees, at once, from the examples, that arithmetic is something which he can understand, and which will be of use to him.....

> In another respect, the book is likely to do a great deal of good. It contains excellent instruction for teachers. Directions are often as much required for them as for their pupils. The discipline of the infant mind is almost the only thing for direction which apprenticeship, no experience, and very little information are in his country, at least, supposed to be required. A man is often deemed capable of teaching, for the very reason that he has shown himself incapable of anything else. The only part of us, which is immortal is abandoned to the care of such as are unable to do aught for the body; and he who has not memory, nor taste, nor power of reasoning himself, is to communicate them, or develop and show the best means of improving them, in another. (pp. 382–383)

Colburn's mental process was originally quite popular, though its popularity declined after a while leading him to make revisions in his approach. The many editions and revisions of this book became the most popular arithmetic text ever published. In 1913, *First Lessons* had continued to sell thousands of texts each year (Bidwell & Classon, 1970).

The Arithmetic Movement versus Infant Schools

While it is difficult to assess the generalizability of Goodrich's *The Children's Arithmetic* or Colburn's *Mental Arithmetic*, it was obvious that young children were able to count and do arithmetic in these schools. In her study of numeracy in early and middle American history, Patricia Cohen (1999) refers to the *American Journal of Education* (1828) and the *Connecticut Common Journal* (1839) and states:

Several "infant schools" with pupils in ages from eighteen months to six years, reported success in teaching their charges to enumerate to the millions as well as to add, subtract, multiply and divide to a "considerable extent." (Cohen, 1999, p. 138)

The *American Journal of Education* promoted the infant schools, but later withdrew its support, one of the influences which led the schools to lose their financial sponsors (mainly from wealthy women). Thus, by 1850 both the infant schools and the "children's arithmetic" vanished (Beatty, 1995; Vinovskis, 1995). After the demonization of the infant school movement, during the second quarter of the century, the Froebelian kindergarten was instituted in the United States.

Froebel's Kindergarten and Mathematics

Freidrich Froebel founded the first kindergarten in Germany in 1837. Froebel's kindergarten differed in its philosophy of education and purpose from the infant school. Its curriculum was based on a religious philosophy concerning the unity of nature, God, and humanity. His curriculum had a series of materials and activities for children ages three to six years to assist them in understanding the relationship between nature, God, and humanity. Such activities and materials symbolized these relationships. The program used the *Gifts*, the *Occupations*, and the *Mother's Songs and Plays* to assist children in studying nature (Spodek & Saracho, 1994, 1999; Saracho & Spodek, 2006).

The *Gifts* consisted of small manipulative materials for children to use in prescribed ways. The first set was composed of a series of six yarn balls, each a different color. The single surface of the ball, which was a sphere, represented the unity and wholeness of the universe. The next set included a wooden sphere, a cylinder, and a cube to represent unity, diversity, and the mediation of the opposites, which consisted of the sphere and the cube. Other *Gifts* included cubes of wood divided into smaller parts, succeeded by square and triangular tablets. These were presented to children in a prescribed sequence requiring children to build precise forms, each representing some profounder meaning. During the manipulations, limited consideration was given to the physical properties of the objects, for perception and knowledge of the real world were not considered important.

The O*ccupations* consisted of paper weaving, paper folding, paper cutting, sewing, drawing, painting, and clay modeling, which reflected the occupations of primitive people. The *Mother Songs and Games* were derived from the play of peasant women with their young children (Spodek &

Saracho, 1994). The *gifts* and *occupations* provided young children with the opportunity to create and build using the activities to analyze and synthesize various geometric forms. While the purpose of the children's activities in the Froebelian kindergarten was not to learn mathematics, it is possible that the children learned about mathematics incidentally.

The first kindergarten in America was established n 1856 in Watertown, Wisconsin. The kindergarten movement spread slowly as German kindergarten teachers migrated to the United States and American kindergarten teachers were trained here. Kindergartens followed Froebel's philosophy and methods. They were primarily private institutions, which served children of affluent parents as well as children from poor families.

In addition, many children who were not enrolled in kindergarten experienced Froebel's gifts and benefitted from them. Milton Bradley, for example, sold the Froebel gifts in their toy industry, creating a large home market for Froebel's materials (Brosterman, 1997). According to Brosterman (1997), Froebel's gifts,

> provided opportunities for instruction in...pattern, balance, symmetry, and construction; language—in function, storytelling, planning and conceptual exchange; science—in gravity, weight, trial and error and inductive thinking, and mathematics—geometry, number, measure, classification, fractions and more. (p. 50)

The Froebelian kindergarten made children aware of numerical and geometric relationships with such features as simple counting, measuring, and adding as well as the use of the geometric gifts. This process helped younger children to incidentally learn arithmetic and geometric concepts, while the older children gained knowledge of mathematical relations. Sometimes, the hand work required children to divide the material into halves, quarters, and the like, or some material had to be measured and cut to fit. These experiences helped young children to develop a working knowledge of division and measuring. In addition, young children learned about geometric solids when they built with them. The same occurred when young children cut paper into squares, circles, and triangles. The games in which children were grouped may have required them to use counting. It seems apparent that kindergarten children obtained considerable knowledge, which may be termed mathematical. This knowledge was acquired incidentally and unconsciously through play (Bidwell & Classon, 1970; International Commission on the Teaching of Mathematics, 1911).

Many (e.g., Dewey, 1916; Harris, 1899, Thorndike, 1903) challenged Froebel's kindergarten curriculum. They believed that the Froebel kindergarten curriculum was too artificial and unrelated to the day-to-day experiences children had. Thorndike (1903), for example, was critical of Froebel's symbolic education. He stated that a toothbrush should be substituted for Froebel's first gift of six colored balls (Brosterman, 1997; Thorndike, 1903). John Dewey (1916) referred to the typical kindergarten activities as mindless copying and manipulation of artificial objects (Beatty, 1995). Beatty (1995) also quotes William Torrey Harris from his 1899 article in the *Kindergarten Review.* Although he was a major advocate of public kindergartens, he was concerned that if Froebel's approached proceeded,

> . . . kindergarten children might become "haunted with symmetry" and thus fixated "on a lower stage of art." And spending so much time on Froebel's complex geometric forms might focus the child's mind on "analyzing all physical forms and their parts to such a degree that the analysis gets in his way of thinking about casual relationships." (Beatty, 1995, p. 92)

Many years after the introduction of the Froebelian kindergarten, a split developed within the kindergarten movement. Traditional kindergarten educators believed that Froebel had conceived the important components for the young children's education that related to all children for all times. By the beginning of the twentieth century there was enough concern in the kindergarten community regarding the appropriateness of Froebel's curriculum and methods that the International Kindergarten Union, created a special committee to review his program as well as alternative options. Not being able to reach a consensus, the Committee of Nineteen, as it was called issued three reports, one supporting the Froebel approach, another supporting a child centered approach and a third which suggested a compromise. The report, written by Patty Smith Hill, saw the kindergarten as a place that would have a flexible program based as much on children's interests and purposes as by the teachers' goals. It would build on the children's natural experiences (International Kindergarten Union, 1913).

This report articulated the progressive kindergarten approach that reformed kindergarten education and moved it away from the Froebel model. Children's play became a legitimate part of the program and the children's activities were supported in a holistic way. There was a lack of concern for direct instruction in mathematics. Rather, children would develop a readiness for formal mathematics, and especially arithmetic, learning through activities. Building on the work of Kilpatrick (1914), projects became an important part of the program. Children, for example, might raise chickens, counting the eggs collected each day and each week as well as measuring the feed eaten by the chickens. Or children would build a wooden construction, planning it, and measuring and cutting the wooden planks needed. Additionally, the kindergarten made the transition from the use of small wooden blocks that were part of the Froebel gifts, to larger blocks. Some, like those designed by Patty Smith Hill, were long, with grooved corner posts that allowed children to build large structures to play in. Others, designed by Carolyn Pratt, were based on a single unit of measure with some blocks being twice or four times the length; while others might be half or a quarter of the length. Having the blocks built on a standard set of measurements and constructed of sturdy wood allowed the children to build structures that would stand on their own and allow them to reconstruct their view of their surroundings (Hirsch, 1984).

Child-Centered Education and Mathematics

In the 1890s the child study movement appeared as a result of the development of the new field of psychology. The insights about children, the development of a progressive education philosophy inspired by the work of John Dewey, and a national disapproval of the formal methods of instruction that were used in all school subjects—particularly in elementary arithmetic—were among the influences that led to child-centered education.

Child-centered education had its roots in the work of Jean-Jacques Rousseau, an eighteenth century philosopher. Rousseau believed that a child's development was a natural process and that curiosity led the child to explore his surroundings, learning, and adapting to it. Rousseau expanded his ideas in a book title *Emile* (Rousseau, 1762/1979), describing the child being brought up in the countryside and avoiding the deleterious effects of modern civilization. Rousseau's ideal served as a bellwether for many reformers of education as it continues to do so today.

The main proponent of child study at this time was G. Stanley Hall. When Hall was at Clark University, he established the child study movement in the United States, which was a precursor to the field of child development. The concept that education should be developmentally appropriate—or that education should follow development—was introduced with the work of G. Stanley Hall at the beginning of the twentieth century: Hall urged that all formal teaching of arithmetic be delayed until later in the children's school program. He believed that the earliest school years should be directed to the aggregation of concrete experiences. Thus, readiness for later learning could be established in the early years. Hall's work became an argument for teaching only immediate practical mathematics (Hall, 1907).

Hall's perspectives on mathematics education influenced other scholars. Unfortunately, for various decades attempts to delay formal instruction in arithmetic became heavily dominated by two other developments in American education that became integrated into the scientific movement:

the (1) testing movement and (2) restriction of school curriculum to subjects incorporating social use (Kilpatrick, 1992).

During this era, an anti-intellectual movement in mathematics menaced the inclusion of mathematics as a regular school subject (Kilpatrick, 1992). This diminution of mathematics prompted the creation of the National Council of Teachers of Mathematics (NCTM) in 1920 (Willoughby, 1967). Although research and theory construction concerning the constructivist perspective of intellectual development were initiated in an earlier era, it was not until the 1960s that these thoughts influenced American child development and education by such theorists as Jean Piaget (Spodek & Saracho, 1994).

During the first quarter of the twentieth century, two other approaches to early childhood education were introduced into the United States. One was the nursery school, which originated in England; while the other was the Montessori method, which came from Italy.

The Nursery School

The nursery school was first established by Margaret Macmillan in England in 1911. Its goal was to support the physical and mental development of low income young children. The curriculum of the nursery school focused on play and educating children's imagination. Dramatic play and play with building bricks as blocks were called there, were included, as well as gardening, caring for pets, and a variety of movement activities. As the children grew older they were also provided with lessons in reading, writing, and arithmetic as well as science. No special approach to teaching these content areas were prescribed (Spodek, 1973).

The nursery school came to the United States around the time of World War I. It was expanded during the depression of the 1930s to provide employment for unemployed teachers and developed as a service primarily for children of middle class families. The nursery school, or as it is typically called the preschool, included a program that was based primarily on children's play, without a concern for academic subjects that would be taught to children later in their lives.

Montessori Education

At the beginning of the twentieth century, Maria Montessori, a medical doctor, designed an educational program for mentally challenged children in the Orthophrenic School in Italy. Her program consisted of caring for their physical needs and their intellectual development. Several philosophers and educators (e.g., Rousseau, Pestalozzi, Froebel, Itard, Sequin) influenced Montessori's approach to education. She tried out Sequin's educational strategies and materials, but she made modifications to make them appropriate for handicapped children (Kramer, 1988).

Montessori left the Orthophrenic School to develop her own *Casa Dei Bambini* (Children's House) for poor children in Rome. Using the senses as a basis for learning, she redesigned her educational method to be appropriate for normal children. Montessori's method advanced sensorimotor, intellectual, language, and moral development. In addition to sensory education, she included exercises in practical life, basic academic skills, language, and muscular development. She believed that children needed (1) to know about their environment; (2) to function independently; and (3) to succeed in traditional schools (Montessori, 1964, 1965).

Maria Montessori created her educational method, based on the work of Edouard Sequin, an educator who worked with mentally challenged children, and Freidrich Froebel. She was not influenced by the theories of psychological development that were evolving at that time, but by the work of anthropologists (Spodek, 1973). She believed that children gained information about the world through their senses. Thus, training the senses would make children more intelligent. She developed a series of materials, each focused on a single attribute of human sensation to help the children gain additional knowledge from the outside world. She also provided children with exercises in practical life to enable the children to function in a more self sufficient manner. Montessori helped the children gain knowledge of the basic academic skills through individual work with the manipulative materials she designed.

The first step in learning to write, for example, was by outlining geometric figures or insets. Children learned about shape as they learned to write. She also introduced arithmetic to children through sensory materials, which allowed the children to make comparisons of size and quantity. She introduced numbers using red and blue rods, based upon a unit of the decimal system. They could compare sizes and find multiples of smaller sizes. The units were then given the number names and children learned to trace sand paper numerals before writing them.

She also developed a set of Golden Beads for more elaborate mathematical operations. The beads were strung on wires, which were organized into units to ten, then rows of ten, squares of hundreds, and cubes of thousands. Children worked with these materials, solving problems, and writing the solutions on their own. The materials were considered self-correcting so her system of education was considered self-education, with teachers making suggestions about particular activities, but the children made the choice of what to do, when to do it and how long to do it, as long as the activity was done in the prescribed manner (Spodek, 1973).

Montessori's method was considered to be deeply mathematical in nature. Most of her sensory activities required comparisons, explorations, and identification of patterns, variables, sameness, and differences. Like Froebel, Montessori also believed in teaching young children complex geometric shapes. At an early age, young children explored the properties of the circle, square, triangle, ellipse, rhombus, and pentagon (Balfanz, 1999). Both Montessori and Froebel viewed the development of young children as a process of unfolding. Their work also reflected that education was a self-activity as well as the concepts of self-discipline, independence, and self-direction. A major difference in their philosophy was Montessori's focus on sensory education, which was less important to Froebel than symbolic education, and the designation of sensitive periods of instruction in the children's development (Saracho & Spodek, 2006).

The Curriculum Reform Movement

The 1960s saw a convergence of two trends that reshaped mathematics education for young children. One was the influence of Jean Piaget, whose work was appearing in English translations and made available in the United States. The second influence was the realization that the United States was losing the battle for ascendancy in science and mathematics. As a result of the Cold War, the United States was in a competition with the Soviet Union in all areas, militarily, economically, and scientifically. When the Soviet Union launched a space satellite at a time when the United States was not prepared to do so, there seemed to be an emergency that would only be dealt with by preparing more scientists and mathematicians. As a result, there was a need to reform the school curriculum, from the kindergarten through high school. While the immediate focus was in science and mathematics, the reform spread to include other areas, such as the social studies and even the English curriculum.

Prior to the 1960s the conventional view of the kindergarten was as a vestibule to the elementary school. Children were to be socialized in the kindergarten, which at that time represented the first experience of most young children in any kind of school. They learned the role of the student and how to obey the rules of the school. They were also provided with learning activities that would build readiness, preparing them for the serious learning that would take place once they entered the primary grades.

This notion of kindergarten as readiness was undergirded by the prevailing view of child development at that time, which reflected a maturation notion of development. That is, that children's intellectual development, along with other areas of development, were determined by the individual's genetic makeup. The process of development for the individual was seen as a process of unfolding with inherent qualities in the individual unfolding as the child matured. As a result, learning should follow development and respond to the needs of the children. It was believed that no serious learning occurred before the children were about six years of age. Thus, learning to read as well as learning arithmetic was started at the first grade.

The period of the 1960s saw a convergence of influences that changed educators' views of mathematics instruction at the elementary level. One influence was the availability of research on intellectual development in children. The other was the realization that school mathematics, mostly limited to arithmetic, was out of phase with the scholarly work being done in mathematics. The "New Mathematics" was one result of this new educational thinking.

Piaget was the major influence in this area. His work (Piaget, 1941/ 1952) showed that the concept of number develops out of the child's activity. Piaget strived to integrate the construction of the number concept in the development of logical thinking instead of the operation of counting. He believed that number was a result of reflecting on one's actions. Piaget contended that there was a correspondence between the basic structures of modern mathematics and the mental structures developed by what he referred to as *reflective abstraction*. However, mathematicians challenged several of his interpretations (Freudental, 1973; Kilpatrick, 1992; Rotman, 1977).

Piaget's ideas suggested that learning occurs at all levels, though each level responds to a particular kind of learning. Following Piaget, children were provided with learning activities that, while using concrete materials, allowed children to engage in mature mathematical processes, although not in an abstract manner. In a sense this legitimized Montessori's approach to education and a variety of programs using concrete materials to help children engage in mathematical processes as well as a range of new manipulative materials for teaching mathematics were developed. It was this movement that, over time, led to the kinds of position papers relating to young children learning mathematics that were discussed at the beginning of the chapter.

Currently we are seeing again a call for the reform of mathematics education for children at all levels, including the early childhood level. Among the factors that have led to this call are changes in technology availability in our society. They have changed how mathematics is done and what mathematics need to be known to our citizens. These changes in technology also require knowledge of mathematics for all (e.g., young children, elementary children, secondary school students, adults). Additionally, we are realizing that how we have been teaching mathematics to children is flawed. Finally, there is the realization that traditional approaches to teaching mathematics have not adequately allowed for the construction of mathematics instruction (Baroody, 1993).

The world today is different from what it was in the middle of the twentieth century, let alone the middle of the nineteenth century. Mathematics education for young children also needs to be different.

CONCLUSION

After reviewing the history of early childhood education, it becomes evident that some form of mathematics education was provided in each early childhood curriculum. Sometimes it was limited to teaching numbers and number names along with simple arithmetic operations. Sometimes it included learning about various shapes as well as patterns. Some of the programs taught arithmetic directly, while other programs taught it peripherally or allowed children to pick it up incidentally.

Baroody (2006) identified a continuum of approaches to teaching. These include direct instruction, guided discovery learning, flexible guided discovery learning, and unguided discovery learning. The direct instruction approach has been used most often in our schools. It does not engage the children nor is it the most effective approach. An unguided discovery learning approach will engage learning. It many ways it reflects child-centered education. It is a rather hit-or-miss approach and it is not certain that children will achieve all that they can this way. What seems to be the most effective and the most engaging approach is the guided discovery ones. These characterize progressive education at its best as well as the "open education" movement of the 1970s. While we know that in the past none of the models of early childhood education were practiced by all schools, it needs to be seen what approach to teaching mathematics will be reflected in the schools for young children of the future.

REFERENCES

American Journal of Education. (1828). *American Journal of Education, 3,* 693.

Balfanz, R. (1999). Why do we teach young children so little mathematics? Some historical considerations. In J. V. Copley (Ed.), *Mathematics in the early years.* Reston, VA: National Council of Teachers of Mathematics and Washington, DC: National Association for the Education of Young Children.

Baroody, A. J. (1993). Fostering the mathematical learning of young children. In B. Spodek (Ed.), *Handbook of research on the education of young children* (pp. 151–175). New York: Macmillan.

Baroody, A. J. (2006).The development of young children's early number and operation sense and its implications of early childhood education. In B. Spodek &

O. N. Saracho (Eds.), *Handbook of research on the education of young children* (2nd ed., pp. 187–221). Mahwah, NJ: Erlbaum.

Beatty, F. (1995). *Preschool education in America: The culture of young children from the colonial era to the present.* New Haven, CT: Yale University Press.

Bidwell, J. K., & Classon, R. G. (Eds.). (1970). *Readings in the history of mathematics education.* Washington, DC: National Council of Teachers of Mathematics.

Brosterman, N. (1997). *Inventing kindergarten.* New York: Harry N. Abrams.

Brouwer, L.E.J. (1975). *Collected works 1. Philosophy and foundations of mathematics.* A. Heyting (Ed.). Amsterdam: North-Holland.

Cohen, P. C. (1999). *A calculating people: The spread of numeracy in early America.* New York: Routledge

Colburn, W. (1821). *First lessons, or, intellectual arithmetic on the plan of Pestalozzi.* Boston: Cummings, Hillard, & Co.

Colburn, W. (1822). *First lessons, or intellectual arithmetic on the plan of Pestalozzi, with some improvements* (2nd ed.). Boston: Cummings, Hillard, & Co.

Colburn, W. (1826). *Arithmetic upon the inductive method of instruction.* Boston: Cummings, Hillard, & Co.

Connecticut Common Journal. (1839). *Connecticut Common Journal, 2,* 31.

Dewey, J. (1916). *Democracy and education: An introduction to the philosophy of education.* New York: Macmillan. [For an electronic version, see http://manybooks.net/authors/deweyjoh.html]

Dossey, J. A. (1992). The nature of mathematics: Its role and influence. In D. A. Grouws (Ed.), *Handbook of research on mathematics teaching and learning* (pp. 39–48). New York: Macmillan.

Freudental, H. (1973). *Mathematics as an educational task.* Dordrecht, The Netherlands: Reidel.

Goodrich, S. (1818). *The children's arithmetic.* Hartford, CT: Samuel G. Goodrich.

Gutek, G. L. (1968). *Pestalozzi and education.* New York: Random House.

Harris, W. T. (1899). Two kinds of kindergarten. *Kindergarten Review, 9,* 603–605.

Hall, G.S. (1907). *Aspects of child life and education.* Boston: Ginn.

Hilbert, D., & Ackermann, W. (1928). *Grundzüge der theoretischen Logik* (Principles of Theoretical Logic). New York: Springer-Verlag.

Hirsch, E.S. (1984). *The block book.* Washington, DC: National Association for the Education of Young Children.

International Commission on the Teaching of Mathematics. (1911/1970). Mathematics in the elementary schools. In J. K. Bidwell & R. G. Classon (Eds.), *Readings in the history of mathematics education* (pp. 280–360). Washington, DC: National Council of Teachers of Mathematics.

International Kindergarten Union. (1913). *Reports of the Committee of Nineteen on the theory and practice of the kindergaten.* Boston: Houghton Mifflin.

Kilpatrick, J. (1992). A history of research in mathematics education. In D. A. Grouws (Ed.), *Handbook of research on mathematics teaching and learning* (pp. 3–38). New York: Macmillan.

Kilpatrick, W. (1914). *The Montessori system examined.* Boston: Houghton Mifflin.

Kramer, R. (1988). *Maria Montessori: A biography.* Reading, MA: Addison-Wesley.

Mancosu, P. (Ed.). (1998). *From Brouwer to Hilbert. The debate on the foundations of mathematics in the 1920s* (pp. 123–42). Oxford: Oxford University Press.

Montessori, M. (1964). *The advanced Montessori method.* Cambridge, MA: R. Bentley.

Montessori, M. (1965). *Dr. Montessori's own handbook.* New York: Schocken.

North American Review. (1822). Colburn's arithmetic. *North American Review, 14*(35), 381–384.

Piaget, J. (1941/1952). *The child's concept of number.* New York: Routledge. (originally published in 1941)

Ptolemy. (1952). The almagest. In R. M. Hutchins (Ed.), *Great books of the western world, Vol. 16 Ptolemy: Copernicus & Kepler* (pp. 1–478). Chicago: Encyclopedia Britannica.

Rousseau, J. J. (1762/1979). *Emile: or, On education* (1762/1979). [trans. with an introd. by Allan Bloom]. New York: Basic Books.

Rotman, B. (1977). *Jean Piaget: Psychologist of the real.* Ithaca, NY: Cornell University Press.

Saracho, O. N., & Spodek, B. (2006). Roots of early childhood education in America. In M. Takeuchi & R. Scott (Eds.), *New directions for early childhood education and care in the 21st century: International perspectives* (pp. 252–277). Waterloo, IA: G & R Publishing.

Spodek, B. (1973). *Early childhood education.* Englewood Cliffs, NJ: Prentice-Hall.

Spodek, B., & Saracho, O. N. (1994). *Right from the start: Teaching children ages three to eight.* Boston: Allyn & Bacon.

Spodek, B., & Saracho, O. N. (1999). The relationship between theories of child development and the early childhood curriculum. *Early Child Development and Care, 152*, 1–15.

Strickland, C.E. (1982). Paths not taken: Seminal models of early childhood education. In B. Spodek (Ed.), *Handbook of research in early childhood education* (pp. 321–340). New York: Free Press.

Thorndike, E. L. (1903). Notes on psychology for kindergarteners. *Teachers College Record, 4*, 45–76.

van Atten, M. (2004). *On Brouwer.* Belmont, CA: Wadsworth.

van Atten, M. (2005). *Luitzen Egbertus Jan Brouwer.* Retrieved from http://plato.stanford.edu/entries/brouwer/#Bri on December 9, 2006.

Vinovskis, M. A. (1995). A ray of millennial light: Early education and social reform in the infant school movement in Massachusetts, 1826–1840. In M. A. Vinovskis (Ed.), *Education, society, and economic opportunity: A historical perspective on persistent issues.* New Haven, CT: Yale University Press.

Weyl, H. (1925). Die heutige Erkenntnislage in der Mathematik. *Symposion, 1*,1–23. [English translation in Mancosu (1998)]

Willoughby, S. S. (1967). *Contemporary teaching of secondary school mathematics.* New York: Wiley.

Zach, R. (2003). *Hilbert's program.* Retrieved from http://plato.stanford.edu/archives/fall2006/entries/hilbert-program/#Rel on December 9, 2006.

CHAPTER 2

RETHINKING THE STARTING POINT FOR MATHEMATICS LEARNING

Catherine Sophian

The assumption that counting is at the very core of mathematical development, or at least of the development of numerical knowledge, is so pervasive as to go almost unquestioned. Neuroscientists such as Dehaene (1997) and Butterworth (1999) have posited that the brain has built-in mechanisms for precisely enumerating small collections, and also for obtaining approximate numerical information about large ones. A number of developmental psychologists, similarly, have posited a preverbal form of counting that is already operational in the first year of life and that has important isomorphisms with verbal counting (Gelman, 1991, 1998; Wynn, 1992; Xu, 2003). Mathematics curricula for early childhood have always targeted counting and related numerical skills as key instructional foci (although the standards formulated by the National Council of Teachers of Mathematics, 2003, are much broader than that), and that emphasis is also reflected in the content of standardized tests of young children's mathematics abilities (e.g., Ginsburg & Baroody, 2003).

In this chapter I consider the theoretical and empirical justification for, and the developmental and instructional ramifications of, a very different view: that mathematical thinking begins with comparisons of quantities, which are the foundation for basic mathematical ideas that are essential to

Contemporary Perspectives on Mathematics in Early Childhood Education, pages 21–44
Copyright © 2008 by Information Age Publishing

an understanding of number. This alternative perspective has at its core the recognition that children's knowledge about numbers does not stand alone but is intimately intertwined with their understanding of very general properties of quantities (continuous as well as discrete). Piaget's analysis of the development of number concepts (e.g., Piaget, 1952), which holds that children cannot attain a meaningful understanding of numbers until they have acquired more general quantitative concepts such as conservation, seriation, and class inclusion, reflects this idea, as does the work of the influential Russian psychologist and educator, V. V. Davydov (e.g., Davydov, 1975a).

Following a brief summary of the two points of view, I consider three pertinent lines of developmental research: research on infants' ability to discriminate between different numerical quantities; research on preschool children's reasoning about numerical relations between quantities; and research on children's reasoning about continuous quantities, particularly lengths. I then turn to a discussion of the developmental and instructional ramifications of the comparison-of-quantities position.

TWO VIEWS AS TO THE DEVELOPMENTAL ORIGINS OF MATHEMATICAL KNOWLEDGE

In order to make the contrast between the counting-first and the comparison-of-quantities positions clear, it is important to differentiate the concept of "number" from that of "quantity." In the senses most pertinent to the present discussion, *Webster's New World Dictionary* (Neufeldt & Guralnik, 1994) defines a number as "a symbol or word, or a group of either of these, showing how many or which one in a series," and quantity as "an amount" or, more informatively, "that property of anything which can be determined by measurement." A critical point of contrast in these definitions is ontological: numbers exist only as symbols whereas quantities are properties of things that exist in the physical world. Thus, in counting, we start with a physical quantity, normally a discrete one, and we assign a series of numbers to its elements to arrive at a number that represents the quantity in its entirety. What makes the distinction between numbers (symbolic entities) and quantities (physical entities) difficult is that we often use the label "number" for the physical stuff that we measure by counting; thus we say a bouquet consists of a number of flowers. More technically, however, the numerical properties of collections are termed "numerosities," and distinguishing that term from "number" in its symbolic sense will help to keep the relation between numbers and quantities clear. In brief, quantities are physical properties of things that we can measure, and numbers are symbols that we often use to represent the measured values of quantities. Note, though, that measurement does not have to involve the use of number: it can be as simple as inserting a stick into two holes in succession in order to decide which one is deeper (Bryant & Kopytynska, 1976). Therefore, while counting (other than "rote counting," or the recitation of counting words without relating them to objects) presupposes a quantity (specifically, a numerosity) that will be represented by the number obtained by counting, quantity comparison does not presuppose number.

The Position That Counting is Foundational

An influential developmental thesis is that a preverbal form of counting is already operational in infancy and serves as the foundation for developing an understanding of number (Gelman, 1991, 1998; Wynn, 1992). The most well articulated version of this type of theory posits that an accumulator mechanism in the brain serves as a sort of template for learning to count verbally. The accumulator mechanism consists of an impulse generator, which emits impulses at regular intervals; a gate, which opens briefly to allow impulses to pass through it each time the organism encounters an item to be counted; and an accumulator, which stores the impulses that have passed through the gate. As more items are counted, more impulses reach the accumulator, so that the final state of the accumulator is indicative of how many to-be-counted items were encountered. Because the number of impulses that reach the accumulator each time the gate opens is variable, the end states of the accumulator are somewhat imprecise representations of numerosity, but they are ordered because the contents of the accumulator always increase as more items are counted.

The developmental significance of the accumulator mechanism, according to the counting-first theories, stems from the fact that it embodies important principles that any counting procedure must honor—and to which children's verbal counting in particular must conform—if it is to provide valid numerical information. For instance, the gate opens just once for each item being counted, and the states of the accumulator occur in a fixed order (from less full to more full) each time a series of items is counted. The accumulator thus embodies implicit knowledge about how counting works, knowledge that is thought to guide children in learning to count verbally by directing their attention to important characteristics of verbal counting such as the use of a stable list of counting terms and the mapping of those terms in a one-to-one manner onto the items being counted. Further, it has been hypothesized that knowledge that is initially only implicit in the counting procedure (whether nonverbal or verbal) eventually becomes more explicit, so that, for example, children   can   use   the   relation   between   number   and   one-to-one correspondence that is embodied in counting to reason about number conservation (Gelman, 1982).

Although the theoretical claim that infants are born with an innate counting mechanism is the strongest form of the counting-first position, that position is also consistent with theoretical accounts that do not make such strong innatist claims. For instance, some theories (e.g., Cooper, 1984; Klahr & Wallace, 1976), instead of positing an innate counting mechanism, attribute an important developmental role to subitizing—a perceptual process by which small numerosities (up to about three) are apprehended holistically and concurrently. Even a very limited subitizing process provides a basis for working out the relations among different small numerosities (e.g., that two is less than three) because it gives children a means of observing that when an object is removed from a collection with a numerosity of three, that numerosity changes to two, and conversely that when an object is added to a collection with a numerosity of two, that numerosity changes to three (Cooper, 1984). In addition, by counting or constructing correspondences between sets whose numerosities they can discern by subitizing, children gain an appreciation of the numerical significance of these other processes, which they can then use to extend their numerical processing beyond the limits of subitizing (Klahr & Wallace, 1976). Although subitizing-based theories diverge from innate-counting theories in their claims as to how numerical quantities are initially enumerated, both kinds of theories share the fundamental (and largely unexamined) assumption that the apprehension of numerical information is the starting point for mathematical development.

The Comparison-of-Quantities Position

Notwithstanding the intuitive appeal of the idea that numbers, in particular counting numbers, are the foundation for mathematical thinking, Davydov (1975a) presented a persuasive argument that it is not correct. Working from the assumption that mathematics instruction should begin with the concepts that are most fundamental to mathematics, Davydov critically examined the idea that number is fundamental. He pointed out that numerical systems are defined on the basis of a chain of other concepts, among them the concepts of set and equivalence, and so he argued that those concepts are more fundamental than number. Sets are not merely physical collections, just as a piece of string is not in itself a "length." A collection of objects becomes a set, just as the string becomes a length, only when it is considered as a numerical quantity to be evaluated in relation to other numerical quantities via the concepts of equivalence, greater than, and less than. When we assign a numerical value to a set, we establish that

that set is a member of an equivalence class that contains all sets that have that particular numerosity, and that it stands in a greater-than or less-than relation to sets that differ from it in numerosity.

The numerosity of a collection, moreover, like the numerical measure of a continuous quantity, is not a function of its physical composition alone. In counting a collection of items, just as in measuring a continuous quantity, we must first decide what counts as "one" and then iterate that unit across the collection (Drabkina, 1962; cited in Davydov, 1975a). Thus, the same collection of, say, shoes might be quantified as four PAIRS OF SHOES or as eight INDIVIDUAL SHOES. Different numerical values are obtained when different units are used in counting a collection of discrete items, in exactly the same way that different measurements are obtained for a length of string depending on whether inches or centimeters are adopted as the unit of measure. Thus, the concept of unit is another conceptual prerequisite for an understanding of number.

In children's earliest counting, discrete objects characteristically function as the counting unit (Shipley & Shepperson, 1990; Sophian & Kailihiwa, 1998). However, Gal'perin and Georgiev (1969) argued that equating units with objects is profoundly inadequate conceptually. In order to understand units of measurement, and particularly how variations in unit size affect numerical outcomes, children need to differentiate the mathematical concept of unit from the everyday notion of an object.

While the observations made by Davydov (1975a) and his colleagues about the dependence of the concept of number on more fundamental concepts, such as set, equivalence, and unit, are mathematical rather than cognitive in character, they have profound cognitive-developmental ramifications. They suggest that the origins of children's mathematical thinking may lie neither in the activity of counting nor in the perceptual apprehension of numerical information through subitizing, but rather in the quantitative comparisons on which an understanding of numbers depends. The importance of quantitative comparisons is particularly clear with respect to the formation of the concept of unit, which is comparative in two fundamental ways. First, as Gal'perin and Georgiev (1969) noted, a fundamental aspect of the notion of unit is the idea of equivalence between units. Second, the observation that different units can be applied to the same quantities leads to the recognition that numerical values are essentially representations of the relation between the quantity they represent and a chosen unit.

EVIDENCE FROM DEVELOPMENTAL RESEARCH

Issues concerning the origins of numerical knowledge have attracted increasing research interest in the field of developmental psychology in recent years, stimulated in large part by striking findings concerning the ability of young infants to make numerical discriminations. Because demonstrations of infant numerical discriminations have been taken as important evidence in support of the existence of an innate nonverbal counting mechanism, it is important to ask how the research findings fit with the contrasting comparison-of-quantities position. Following a brief discussion of that issue, two other lines of research that bear on the alternative accounts of early mathematical development are considered. The first of these is research on preschool children's reasoning about numerical relations between sets. The second is research on young children's reasoning about relations between nonnumerical quantities, particularly lengths.

Studies of Infants' Numerical Discriminations

Most research on infants' numerical knowledge has relied on a phenomenon called habituation: a decrease in looking when the same stimulus is presented repeatedly, followed by increased looking or dishabituation when a different stimulus is presented. To test for numerical discrimination using habituation, researchers present a series of slides that all depict, say, three items. Factors such as the size of items and their spatial arrangement are varied from trial to trial within the habituation sequence in order to ensure that numerosity is the only property that all of the habituation arrays have in common. Once looking time to those arrays has declined, indicating that the infant has habituated, the researcher presents several test slides depicting either the same numerosity shown during habituation (e.g., three) or another numerosity (e.g., two or four). Longer looking at the new numerosity than at the one to which the infant was habituated constitutes evidence that the infant discriminates between the two numerosities. Findings of this kind (e.g., Starkey & Cooper, 1980; Strauss & Curtis, 1981) were accepted for many years as evidence that infants discriminate small numerosities—up to three or four—from each other.

Recently, however, it has been suggested that notwithstanding the efforts to control for nonnumerical factors in these studies, infants' looking patterns may in fact have been based on nonnumerical properties of the arrays that generally covary with number: contour length (Clearfield & Mix, 1999) or surface area (Clearfield & Mix, 2001). Contour length refers to the total length of the edges of the items in an array, summed across all the items. Thus, an array of three 1-inch squares would have a contour length of 12 inches (four 1-inch sides per square × three squares). Varying the size of the items across habituation displays would, of course, result in varying contour lengths. Nevertheless, unless the stimuli were carefully constructed to prevent it, on average the contour length across the habituation trials would be more like that of a same-numerosity test display than like that of a different-numerosity test display.

To determine whether this might in fact be the basis for what appears to be numerical discriminations, Clearfield and Mix (1999) used habituation displays that held constant both item size and numerosity, so that contour length as well as number was constant across the habituation trials. After the habituation trials, they presented infants with arrays that corresponded to the habituation arrays in either numerosity or contour length, but not both. The dissociation of numerosity and contour length on these test trials was accomplished by changing the size of the items. For example, by increasing item size, a 2-item test array could be made to match the contour length of 3-item habituation arrays, and by decreasing item size, a 3-item test array could be made to differ in contour length from the 3-item arrays used for habituation. Clearfield and Mix found that infants increased their looking time to test arrays that differed from the habituation arrays in contour length but not in numerosity, but their looking time remained low to arrays that matched the habituation arrays in contour length while differing from them in numerosity. A parallel result was obtained in a subsequent experiment in which surface area was pitted against numerosity (Clearfield & Mix, 2001). Test arrays that differed from the habituation arrays in surface area but not in numerosity elicited increased looking, whereas test arrays that differed in numerosity and not in surface area did not. Thus, the results of this line of research support the idea that infants respond to changes in contour length (or a closely related continuous property of the displays, surface area) rather than to changes in numerosity.

These findings accord nicely with the thesis that comparisons between unenumerated quantities may be developmentally prior to any form of numerical representation. However, it should be noted that some recent studies that have controlled for continuous variables (contour length and/or surface area) have obtained evidence of specifically numerical discriminations. Surprisingly, several studies have obtained this kind of evidence for pairs of relatively large (but widely differing) numerosities, such as 8 versus 16, but not for 2 versus 4 (Lipton & Spelke, 2004; Wood & Spelke, 2005; Xu, 2003). A couple of studies, however, have succeeded—even with strict controls for contour length and/or surface area—in obtaining evidence of infant discrimination between 1- versus 2-item arrays (Feigenson, 2005) and between 2- versus 4-item arrays (Wynn, Bloom, & Chiang, 2002).

Given the inconsistencies across studies, it is not possible at this time to draw firm conclusions about infants' abilities to make numerical discriminations. However, it appears that at least some findings from infancy research are not compatible with the strong conclusion that infants initially respond solely to continuous quantitative properties of stimuli and not to numerical ones. At the same time, the findings as a whole are consistent with the suggestion that continuous quantitative properties may be at least as central as numerical ones to the ways infants perceive events and make quantitative comparisons. Further, even when infants do respond to changes in numerosity, it is not necessarily the case that they are representing the numerical values of the quantities they are comparing. Alternatively, they might be detecting correspondence relations between the quantities without determining the numerical value of either one. Just as we might, from watching a carousel on which only some of the horses were occupied (and there was never more than one child to a horse), conclude that there were more horses than children without knowing how many of either there were, infant numerical discriminations may be based on some kind of matching process that does not entail arriving at numerical values (precise or imprecise) for the sets. While it is not clear at present how such a matching process might work, especially for large-number comparisons, the hypothesis that infant numerosity discriminations are based on the detection of correspondence relations is as consistent with the available data as is the postulation of an innate counting mechanism. We only have evidence that infants detect numerical relations between sets, not that they assign numerical values to those sets.

More important, the units that infants use to make numerical comparisons (whether on the basis of numerical values generated through a counting-like process or on the basis of correspondence relations) are likely to be perceptually defined entities, items that are segmented one from another on the basis of spatial or temporal discontinuities such as gaps between the edges of items in a spatial array or marked changes in rate, magnitude, and/or direction of motion. Certainly, there is no evidence that infants can arrive at different numerical conclusions about a given quantity as a result of adopting different counting units (analogous to counting individual shoes versus pairs of shoes). Thus, in infants' numerical reasoning, units are conflated with everyday objects in exactly the manner which Gal'perin and Georgiev (1969) discussed. Their analysis of the mathematical inadequacy of this way of thinking about units thus suggests that infant numerical discriminations do not constitute evidence for a conceptual understanding of number.

Research on Preschoolers' Reasoning about Numerical Relations

Gelman and Gallistel's (1978) analysis of counting recognized that sound counting presupposes the establishment of a one-to-one correspondence between the items being counted and the terms of a count sequence. It would thus appear that counting presupposes an understanding of one-to-one correspondence. However, Gelman (1982) asserted that knowledge about one-to-one correspondence is initially embedded in children's counting procedures and remains inaccessible in other contexts for some time. On this interpretation of the counting-first position, young children should be able to compare sets on the basis of numerical values obtained by counting before they are able to do so on the basis of correspondence relations between the elements. In contrast, from the comparison-of-quantities perspective, one might expect children to be able to compare sets via correspondence relations before they are able to do so by counting them.

Some data pertinent to this issue comes from a study (Sophian, 1987, Experiment 1), in which 3-year-old children saw arrays composed of two types of objects and were asked whether each of one type of item could be paired with an item of the other type (e.g., "Are there enough trucks for every man?"). When the items were presented in pairs—a man beside each truck, with an extra man on some trials—children almost never counted and yet were correct on a substantial majority of trials, indicating that they used the pairwise presentation to evaluate the relation between the two sets. Presenting the items in a spatially separated manner—a group of men and a group of trucks—led to poorer performance than the paired presentation, and only a modest increase in counting. Thus, when correspondence-based comparisons were precluded, the 3-year-olds rarely counted the sets as a means of comparing them.

In a second experiment (Sophian, 1987, Experiment 2), children were asked to create a second set that was equal in number to the first (e.g., to put out just enough balloons so that every clown could get one), under conditions that either permitted or precluded pairing each new object with one of the items comprising the original set. (In the latter case, the experimenter required that the new items be placed in a separate tray, which was shaped differently than the original array so that children could not reproduce the spatial configuration of those items.) When allowed to pair the items, 3-year-old children generally did so and thereby achieved predominantly correct performance even though they rarely counted the items. When pairing was prevented, however, counting increased only slightly and performance dropped markedly. Even 4- and 4-1/2-year-olds did better on problems where the items could be spatially paired than on ones where that was precluded, notwithstanding substantial age-related increases in the use of counting on the latter problems.

These results suggest that very young children are more facile with comparing sets on the basis of one-to-one correspondence relations between their elements than with comparing them via counting, although counting skills develop rapidly over the latter part of the preschool period. A further study in which reasoning based on one-to-one correspondences was directly contrasted with reasoning based on numerical values corroborates this developmental pattern. Sophian, Harley, and Martin (1995, Experiment 1) presented children with a matching-to-sample task in which they were to identify the pictures that best matched brief stories about two complementary types of things. The story presented information either about the numerical value of one set (e.g., "Here are four clowns") or about the numerical relation between two sets (e.g., "Every clown wants its own umbrella, and there is an umbrella for each clown"), or both. Of particular interest was performance on conflict problems, on which children had to choose among three pictures: one that matched the numerical value in the story, one that matched the relational information in the story, and one that did not match the story in either respect. Children received a block of these problems at the start of the experiment and then another after a series of no-conflict trials on which they received feedback about numerical and relational matches (in counterbalanced order).

Groups of 3-, 4- and 5-year-old children all performed above chance on the no-conflict feedback trials. However, only the 4- and 5-year-olds were above chance in identifying both numerical and relational matches on the conflict trials (choosing each type of matching picture more often than the non-matching picture). The 3-year-olds were at chance on the initial block of conflict trials, and after the training they chose the relational match but not the numerical match significantly more often than the non-matching picture. Thus, the results suggest that children pay more attention to correspondence relations between sets than to specific numerical values in the early part of the preschool period, but the impact of numerical information on children's reasoning increases as they get older.

Young Children's Reasoning about Length Comparisons

The comparison-of-quantities position calls attention to the fact that numerosity is just one among a number of dimensions along which quantities can be compared. Others are length, area, volume, and mass. If it is true that knowledge about number builds on more basic ways of making comparisons between quantities, then one might expect young children to show more facility in making judgments about relations between continuous quantities than about relations between numerical ones.

The extensive data showing that young children have difficulty reasoning about continuous quantities on Piagetian tasks like length seriation (Inhelder & Piaget, 1964) and conservation (Piaget, Inhelder, & Szeminska, 1960) may appear inconsistent with this expectation. However, Piaget's concrete-operational tasks were deliberately constructed so as to require children not just to make a single comparison between quantities but to coordinate that comparison either with another comparison or with some other information (such as information about how an array was modified in a conservation problem). Thus, in length seriation studies, the ability to compare the lengths of two sticks is presupposed: the problem of interest arises when children must determine the proper placement for additional sticks, which are not as long as the longer of the original sticks but longer than the shorter one. What is difficult for the children is to coordinate the two relations: to think of a given stick as simultaneously shorter than one comparison stick and longer than another. If anything, the presupposition in this work that children are able to identify the longer of two sticks is consistent with the idea that young children are facile in comparing two lengths that are spatially aligned with each other.

In length conservation studies, similarly, children's ability to discern the initial equivalence of two lengths is presupposed; the focus is on children's interpretation of transformations that introduce bends in one of the lengths so that the endpoints no longer match. Here the challenge is to recognize that the initial relation between the lengths still holds even after the appearance of the array has been changed. Characteristically, very young children conclude that two lengths that were initially equal are no longer the same after bends have been introduced in one of them (Inhelder, Sinclair, & Bovet, 1974; Light, Buckingham, & Robbins, 1979, Experiment 1; Neilson, Dockrell, & Mckechnie, 1983; Piaget et al., 1960). What is noteworthy about this response is that, although it is incorrect in that total length has not changed, it is consistent with another quantitative property of the stimuli, the distance between endpoints, which does decrease when a bend is introduced. Thus, it may be that non-conservation responses stem from a lack of clear differentiation between different quantitative dimensions, specifically in length conservation problems between the total length of a path versus the as-the-crow-flies distance between its endpoints, rather than from a lack of understanding of how the transformation affects the specific dimension about which the children are queried.

This interpretation of young children's conservation errors fits nicely with the results of an experiment that compared children's responses to two different types of length questions (Miller & Baillargeon, 1990, Study 1). In this study, 3- to 6-year-old children were asked to make judgments about the distance between two blocks before and after a screen was interposed between them (without changing their positions). In the Piagetian version of the task, the post-transformation question was whether the blocks were "now nearer together, farther apart, or still the same distance apart" (p. 106). An alternate version of the task asked children to choose a stick that would just fit between the two blocks so as to form a bridge. Here the post-transformation question was simply, "Now which stick will just fit between the blocks?" (p. 106). Children's performance on the bridge-building task reached 100% correct by 5 years of age and was significantly, and substantially, better than their performance on the parallel Piagetian task at each age level. Although children were not above chance in choosing the correct stick before the transformation, they believed the same stick would fit after the screen was introduced as before. The difference between this result and the tendency of children to judge that the blocks were no longer the same distance apart in the Piagetian version of the task appears to reflect the disambiguating effect of posing the question in terms of the functional goal of spanning the end blocks to form a bridge. The need to actually span the distance between the blocks makes it clear that what is at issue is the total distance and not the empty space or the appearance of the array.

Another finding consistent with the idea that young children do not differentiate clearly between different quantitative dimensions comes from length comparison problems in which the lengths to be compared are made up of different numbers of distinct segments. Inhelder et al. (1974) reported that when shown two straight roads with matching endpoints, one made up of 5 7-cm matchsticks and the other of 7 5-cm matchsticks, some children indicated that the row comprising a greater number of matchsticks would be "longer to walk," a response that appears to reflect reliance on number rather than length in making their judgments. Inhelder et al. found that children were especially likely to respond in this way when the "roads" they were comparing were oriented differently so that their endpoints could not be compared, but in some cases numerical comparisons even took precedence over comparisons between endpoints.

At the same time, in number conservation studies, which also pit the dimensions of number and length against each other, young children often base their judgments on row length (a continuous dimension) rather than number (e.g., Bryant, 1972; Siegler, 1995). Thus, if an array consisting of two rows that are initially equal in length is rearranged (without changing the number of items in each row) so that one row becomes longer than the other, young children tend to judge that the longer row now contains more items. Apparently, number is not necessarily a more salient quantititative dimension than length, but young children have difficulty determining which dimension is the appropriate one to consider in a given problem situation.

DEVELOPMENTAL IMPLICATIONS: CONCEPTUAL
TRANSITIONS IN MATHEMATICAL THINKING

Developmentally, an important difference between the counting-first and comparison-of-quantities positions is that they give rise to very different accounts of the conceptual transitions that occur in the development of mathematical thinking across early and middle childhood. Because the counting-first position holds that preverbal counting provides the conceptual framework for learning to count verbally, it suggests that the acquisition of verbal counting does not entail substantial conceptual change.[1] However, as a consequence of its claim that children's understanding of number derives from counting, the counting-first position suggests that the acquisition of knowledge about fractions does pose a major conceptual hurdle, because fractions do not fit well with the principles of counting. Conversely, the comparison-of-quantities position suggests that the introduction of number involves a profound conceptual transition from earlier nonnumerical reasoning about quantities, because of the dependence of number on the concept of unit, but that, once that transition has been made, the transition from whole numbers to fractions does not involve substantial conceptual change. The interpretation of numbers as representations of the relation between a unit and a quantity applies equally to whole numbers and to fractions.

These alternative developmental accounts are not easy to distinguish empirically. While they differ as to the kinds of new knowledge that are thought to require substantial conceptual change, on both accounts the acquisition of the new knowledge occurs only slowly, and so strong predictions cannot be made about when the critical conceptual changes will be reflected in children's reasoning.

From the counting-first perspective, the crucial new knowledge that must be incorporated in children's mathematical thinking is knowledge about fractions. In particular, in order to understand fractions children need to realize that they are not linked by "next" relations, as counting numbers are, because there are always other fractions between any two fractions. However, the available evidence suggests that, while even preschool children have some knowledge about fractions (Hunting & Davis, 1991), their density is not fully understood even at 15 years of age (Vamvakoussi & Vosniadou, 2004).

From the comparison-of-quantities perspective, the crucial new knowledge that children must incorporate in their thinking is that numerical representations of quantities are relative to the unit that is used. However, while children have already begun to use number words in the first half of their second year of life (Durkin, Shire, Riem, Crowther, & Rutter, 1986), their understanding of the role of units in the numerical representation of quantities is still very shaky several years later (e.g., Sophian & Kaili-hiwa, 1998).

Advocates of the counting-first position find support for their views in the widespread observation that children have a great deal of difficulty with fraction instruction (e.g., Gelman, 1991). However, that phenomenon in itself does not constitute a strong basis for distinguishing between alternative theoretical accounts. Since counting is clearly an activity with which children have had extensive experience before they learn about fractions, difficulties stemming from the differences between fractions and counting numbers are to be expected on almost any account of mathematical development.

The counting-first and comparison-of-quantities positions do differ in the particular kinds of differences between fractions and counting numbers that they emphasize. From the counting-first perspective, a particularly important contrast is that between the density of fractions and the successor ("next") relations among counting numbers. The comparison-of-quantities position, in contrast, emphasizes differences in the way in which units are used in the two kinds of numbers that have particular significance for understanding the ordinal relations between fractions that have the same numerator but different denominators. Because fractions are based on units formed by partitioning a whole into equal parts, and the number of those parts is specified by the denominator, an increase in the denominator corresponds to a decrease in the size of each part and correspondingly to a decrease in the magnitude of the fraction. Insofar as students fail to grasp the logic of fractional units, then, they are likely to have difficulty understanding why, for example, the fraction 3/8 is smaller, rather than larger, than the fraction 3/7. This difficulty is often attributed to the overgeneralization of whole-number knowledge, an account that is consistent with the counting-first position (cf., Ni & Zhou, 2005). However, the comparison-of-quantities position suggests that the more fundamental problem is a lack of the understanding of fractional units that would be needed to appreciate why the ordering of fractions with different denominators (but the same numerator) is the reverse of the ordering of whole numbers.

There is, in fact, considerable evidence that students have difficulty understanding the inverse relation between the denominator of a fraction and the magnitude of the fraction as a whole. Given two fractions with equal numerators, elementary school students often expect the fraction with the larger denominator to be greater rather than smaller in value (Behr, Wachsmuth, Post, & Lesh 1984). This misconception generally declines by the end of elementary school, but it persists among some students even in high school (Stafylidou & Vosnidou, 2004).

Direct evidence that students have difficulty understanding the consequences of partitioning a quantity into different numbers of equal parts comes from a study of young children's understanding of sharing. Sophian, Garyantes, and Chang (1997) asked children to judge what the effect of sharing a given quantity equally among different numbers of recipients would be on the size of each share. Initially, children ranging from 5 to 7 years of age judged that a character would get more to eat by sharing with more rather than fewer other recipients. It was only after they were given the opportunity to observe what happened when equal total quantities were shared among different numbers of recipients that they came to understand that partitioning a given quantity into more parts resulted in smaller parts than partitioning the same quantity into fewer parts. Although children as young as 5 years of age were able to acquire this knowledge quickly when given appropriate training, Sophian et al. pointed out that the lack of developmental differences between untrained 5- and 7-year-olds suggests that children seldom get appropriate learning experiences outside of the experimental context.

The counting-first position predicts confusion about the density of fractions, that is, limitations on students' understanding of the fact that there are always more fractions between any two fractions, no matter how close together they are. Vamvakoussi and Vosniadou (2004) obtained evidence consistent with the idea that students think of fractions as occurring in series, in which the fractions are linked to each other by successor relations, rather than being separated by an indefinite number of other fractions. Specifically, they found that just over half ($9/16$) of a sample of ninth graders expressed the view that fractions form a series (or perhaps multiple such series) within which successive fractions do not have any other fractions between them. These students, for example, asserted that there is only one fraction between $3/8$ and $5/8$, the fraction $4/8$. Similarly, they asserted that there are no other fractions between the two decimals .005 and .006 but that there are eight of them between .01 and .001, because .01 is the same as .010, and so, starting with .001 one could generate intermediate decimal fractions by incrementing the last decimal place to .002, .003, and so on through .009. Vamvakoussi and Vosniadou argued that conceptual reorganization is needed for students to progress from this way of thinking, which reflects children's knowledge about counting, to an appreciation of the density of fractions. Several students in their sample ($4/16$) did recognize that there are infinitely many fractions between some pairs of given fractions but denied it in other cases. Only one student consistently asserted, across five different pairs of decimal and/or common fractions, that there were infinitely many fractions in between the given ones. These results are particularly striking because the ninth graders who participated in the study had already received considerable instruction in fractions. The incorrect notion that fractions form a series with a specific successor to each member of the series and no fractions in between the successive fractions persisted in spite of instruction in common fractions, decimal fractions, and real numbers, including explicit instruction in how to find fractions that are intermediate between two given fractions!

However, a study which examined students' understanding of the density of fractions from a somewhat different perspective (Smith, Solomon, & Carey, 2005) yielded contrasting results, indicating that even elementary school children do have some understanding of the density of rational numbers. Smith et al. focused on children's grasp of the idea that numbers are infinitely divisible. Thirty percent of the third- through sixth-grade children in their sample (15/50) responded to an initial question as to how many numbers there are between zero and one by saying that the number was infinite, or that the numbers went on forever; and another 22% (11/50), although they did not refer to infinity, did say that there are a great many numbers between zero and one (e.g., "lots," "hundreds," or "millions"). Most of the latter students (N = 8) went on, in response to a subsequent question, to endorse the idea that the fractions are in fact infinite by stating that one could divide in half forever (beginning with one) without ever getting to zero.

Two alternative explanations for the divergence between these results and the evidence of a much more limited understanding of fraction density among the ninth-grade students in Vamvakoussi and Vosniadou's (2004) study seem plausible. One is that students fail to generalize the insights into the infinity of fractions between zero and one that they expressed in Smith et al.'s (2005) study to other intervals between numbers. Alternatively, it may be that characteristics of the questions posed in the two studies led students to respond in different ways. Smith et al. probed students who initially responded that there are no numbers between zero and one by asking them about the number 1/2, whereas it appears that Vamvakoussi and Vosniadou accepted students' initial responses without any probing. Thus, it may be that the presentation of pairs of numbers that could easily be construed as members of a systematic series led students to presuppose that the investigator wanted them to consider only other numbers in that series rather than all possible numbers. In contrast, in Smith et al.'s study, when students initially assumed that the investigator wanted them to consider only whole numbers, the investigator's follow-up query as to whether or not 1/2 was a number between zero and one helped to clarify that fractions as well as whole numbers were to be considered. Although these alternative interpretations of the divergence between the two studies suggest substantially different conclusions about the scope of children's understanding of fraction density, neither account is consistent with the view that children's knowledge of the discreteness of counting numbers dominates their thinking about fractions to such an extent that they have no conception of the density of fractions.

INSTRUCTIONAL RAMIFICATIONS OF THE
ALTERNATIVE POSITIONS

An implication of the theory that children's acquisition of knowledge about whole-number arithmetic is guided by innate counting structures is that formal instruction is not necessary for the development of that knowledge. Indeed, it might well be thought that since an understanding of the conceptual principles underlying whole-number arithmetic is assured, the primary objective of instruction in whole-number arithmetic in children's first years of schooling is just to familiarize children with conventional symbol systems and computational procedures. From the same perspective, instruction is crucial for acquiring knowledge about rational numbers, which do not fit well with the ideas about numbers that children are likely to derive from innate counting structures and so are bound to be difficult. However, the conceptual discontinuity between counting numbers and fractions implies that early instruction in whole-number arithmetic can do little to facilitate later fraction learning. Instead, instructional recommendations derived from the counting-first perspective have either focused on the need for extensive practice (e.g., Geary, 1995) or called attention to early nonnumerical ideas about covariation between quantities that may provide a foundation for understanding ratios and proportions (Resnick & Singer, 1993).

While Resnick and Singer's (1993) emphasis on the importance of children's ideas about relations among physical quantities is consistent with the comparison-of-quantities perspective, in general the instructional implications of the comparison-of-quantities perspective are very different from those of the counting-first perspective, and the differences are particularly significant for early childhood mathematics education. First, the comparison-of-quantities perspective suggests that insofar as instruction is important for developing an understanding of units, instruction is as crucial for the learning of basic whole-number arithmetic as it is for rational number concepts, since the critical concept of unit arises as soon as any numerical representations of quantities are introduced. Second, and relatedly, the comparison-of-quantities perspective underscores the interdependence between children's early learning about whole numbers and their later learning about rational numbers, since both involve understanding how units are used to generate and interpret numerical representations.

Teaching Children about Units

From the comparison-of-quantities perspective, the concept of unit arises originates as a tool for comparing quantities. Through the use of units, we can go beyond distinguishing inequality from equality relations to distinguish among different degrees of inequality. We do so by using units to obtain numerical representations for the quantities. In additive reasoning, we apply the same unit to both quantities and thereby create representations that we can compare to obtain a numerical value indicating how much greater one quantity is than another. This value, however, is relative to the unit used, since the choice of a smaller or larger unit would alter both the numerical values obtained for each quantity and the difference between them. In multiplicative reasoning, we use one quantity as a unit with which to measure the other and thereby obtain a numerical value that indicates how many times greater one is than another.

The most basic objective in a curriculum that gives an understanding of units a central place is to foster the understanding that any numerical representation is relative to the unit used. Experience representing the same quantity using different units can help even very young children to recognize not only that the numerical value depends on the unit used but that the relation is an inverse one. In the experimental curriculum that Sophian (2004) developed for Head Start children (predominantly 3- and 4-year-olds), instructional activities using related geometric shapes, such as an equilateral triangle and a rhombus equivalent in area to two adjoining triangles, were used to give children the opportunity to explore the relation between unit size and number. For example, children filled in geometric patterns with different shapes and observed how the number of pieces needed to complete the pattern varied with the size of those pieces.

Similarly, both the curriculum developed by Davydov and his colleagues in Russia (cf., e.g., 1975b) and the related Measure Up curriculum (Dougherty, 2003; Dougherty, Okazaki, Zenigama, & Venenciano, 2005) use measurement activities to help first-grade children recognize the importance of the unit used in assigning a numerical value to a quantity. Children learn to assign numerical values to line segments drawn on graph paper by determining the number of times a specified unit, which may be the length of a single square on the graph paper or of several squares, must be iterated to span the whole line segment, and they learn to represent the relation between the unit and the line segment with a notation that explicitly identifies the unit as well as the numerical relation between it and the line segment. Specifically, both the unit and the total quantity are labeled with letters (e.g., A and B—the labels are arbitrary). An arrow is then used to connect the two, marked with a numeral indicating the number of iterations of the unit in the quantity, for example:

$$A \xrightarrow{6} B$$

Children learn likewise to enumerate collections of discrete objects in relation to a unit, which may consist of several separate objects rather than a single one. For instance, if the unit is considered to be "+ +" then the array

$$+ + + + + +$$

consists of three units; but if the unit is "+ + +" then the same array consists of just two units. Children instructed in this way quickly learn to ask, "What is the unit?" when asked a question about numerical values.

Abstraction as an Instructional Goal Across Grade Levels

In advancing the concept of unit as a key focus of mathematics instruction from the first years of elementary school, the comparison-of-quantities perspective diverges from the commonly-held view that instruction should begin with concrete skills and only later endeavor to convey to children the abstract concepts that underlie them. Davydov (1975a) explicitly criticized the practice of avoiding abstraction in the early grades in an argument based upon the principle that long-term instructional goals should inform the design of early instruction.

Beginning with the observation that abstraction is a fundamental characteristic of mathematical thought, Davydov (1975a) argued that the relationship between the particular and abstract knowledge is not unidirectional: "The general not only follows from the particular...but also changes and restructures the whole appearance and arrangement of the particular knowledge which has given rise to it" (p. 98). The implication of this idea is that early instruction that focuses on particulars and eschews abstraction may result in ways of thinking about the particulars that are not congenial to the abstractions to be studied later. Accordingly, Davydov held that children should be shown the abstractness of mathematical material from the beginning of instruction, and that they should be taught in a way that will develop their capacity for abstraction.

The curriculum that Davydov and his colleagues developed (cf., e.g., 1975b) reflects this thinking in that it begins with instruction in basic quantitative relations rather than in numerical skills. Through the first half-year of first grade, children are encouraged to identify and represent the relations of "equal," "less than," and "greater than" as they characterize pairs of continuous quantities of various kinds (lengths, areas, masses, and volumes) as well as pairs of numerosities. The emphasis on presenting mathematical concepts in their most general form is maintained throughout the curriculum, which extends through the 8th grade. For example, instruction in place value in the second grade incorporates a consideration of a variety of base systems, not just base ten.

Although the idea that young children do not think abstractly featured prominently in Piaget's theory (e.g., Piaget, 1969), more recent lines of research have indicated that even preschool children form a number of abstract concepts, among them the concept of essences and the concept of mental states (Gelman & Wellman, 1991; Wellman & Phillips, 2001). Even so, it seems unlikely that young children will be able to grasp instruction in abstract mathematical concepts unless it is grounded in ideas and relations that are meaningful to them. The comparison-of-quantities perspective suggests both that concepts of quantity and relative amount are likely to be meaningful even to very young children and also that they provide a rich foundation for the exploration and development of general mathematical ideas. What is being proposed is not that abstract concepts should replace concrete activities and observations but rather that they should be developed out of those activities and observations. The starting point for any general mathematical statement is the observation of relationships in a concrete context, or across a number of such contexts. The path from those observations to mathematical abstraction is simply inquiry into the generality of the observed relationships: Is that always true? How can we be sure?

The Importance of a Long-Term Perspective

The comparison-of-quantities perspective underscores the need for a long-term perspective in the formulation of instructional objectives because it highlights ways in which the difficulties students experience with relatively advanced topics such as fractions may derive from an inadequate grasp of much more basic concepts. Other topics that depend fundamentally on an understanding of units include place value, which introduces the idea of composite units, and of course measurement.

Because these and other topics require conceptual knowledge about units that may or may not be established in the course of teaching whole number arithmetic, it is clear that the design of early childhood mathematics instruction cannot be informed solely by a consideration of the specific topics designated for the beginning school years. Early instruction must also consider what sort of conceptual foundation needs to be established in teaching early topics, so that students will be well prepared to make sense of the mathematical material they will encounter later on. Thus, early instruction must be designed with a mindfulness of the relationships between the material being taught to young children and the mathematics that students will encounter in later years. Only by identifying the conceptual interrelations among the mathematical material students will encounter across the entire elementary and middle school curriculum can we ensure that the conceptual content of early instruction supports later conceptual objectives.

A Fresh Look at Mathematics Instruction

One reason it is difficult to change the way mathematics is taught is because the expectations of parents and teachers alike are strongly shaped by cultural norms that dictate what children of a particular age should know. These norms create a sense of consensus that may disguise the fact that they are based more on social conventions than on any principled analysis of instructional objectives and how they can best be met.

In today's climate of concern with empirical outcomes, it is important to remember that the informativeness of outcome data is limited not only by the outcomes we choose to measure but also by the range of instructional approaches we include in our comparisons. Just as a scientist cannot evaluate an hypothesis she or he has never formulated, research on instructional outcomes cannot determine how existing approaches compare with possible ones that have not yet been developed. Therefore, unless we are confident that we have sampled the full range of potentially effective approaches, it is premature to conclude that the most successful within the approaches that have been tried is the best, or even a satisfactory approximation to the best, approach that can be developed.

An important contribution of the comparison-of-quantities perspective, therefore, is that it illuminates just how limited the range of instructional approaches that have been evaluated to date is. This is especially true for beginning mathematics instruction, whether because it has been considered relatively unproblematic or simply because expectations about what students should be learning in the early grades are so strong and so widely shared. But, given the long-term ramifications of early instructional choice, the limited range of innovation in early instructional programs means that we also do not know a great deal as yet about the possible merits of alternative approaches to mathematics education as a whole.

NOTE

1. An exception to this generalization is Wynn's (1992) discussion of the developmental significance of the conjecture that preverbal representations of number are magnitude-based whereas verbal ones are only arbitrarily linked to the numerical magnitudes they represent.

REFERENCES

Behr, M. L., Wachsmuth, I., Post, T. R., & Lesh, R. (1984). Order and equivalence of rational numbers: A clinical teaching experiment. *Journal for Research in Mathematics Education, 15*, 323–341.

Bryant, P. E. (1972). The understanding of invariance by very young children. *Canadian Journal of Psychology, 26*, 78–96.

Bryant, P. E., & Kopytynska, H. (1976). Spontaneous measurement by young children. *Nature, 260*, 773.

Butterworth, B. (1999). *The mathematical brain.* New York: Macmillan.

Clearfield, M. W., & Mix, K. S. (1999). Number versus contour length in infants' discrimination of small visual sets. *Psychological Science, 10*, 408–411.

Clearfield, M. W., & Mix, K. S. (2001). Amount versus number: Infants' use of area and contour length to discriminate small sets. *Journal of Cognition and Development, 2*, 243–260.

Cooper, R.G., Jr. (1984). Early number development: Discovering number space with addition and subtraction. In C. Sophian (Ed.), *Origins of cognitive skills* (pp. 157–192). Hillsdale, NJ: Erlbaum.

Davydov, V.V. (1975a). Logical and psychological problems of elementary mathematics as an academic subject. In L. P. Steffe (Ed.), *Children's capacity for learning mathematics. Soviet studies in the psychology of learning and teaching mathematics* (Vol. VII, pp. 55–107). Chicago: University of Chicago Press.

Davydov, V.V. (1975b). The psychological characteristics of the "prenumerical" period of mathematics instruction. In L. P. Steffe (Ed.), *Children's capacity for learning mathematics. Soviet studies in the psychology of learning and teaching mathematics* (Vol. VII, pp. 109–205). Chicago: University of Chicago.

Dehaene, S. (1997). *The number sense: How the mind creates mathematics.* Oxford: Oxford University Press.

Dougherty, B. (2003, July). *Measure up.* Plenary address at the meetings of the International Group for the Psychology of Mathematics Education, Honolulu.

Dougherty, B., Okazaki, C., Zenigami, F., & Venenciano, L. (2005). *Measure up grade 1, 4th draft. Teacher notes & masters and student materials.* Honolulu, HI: Curriculum Research and Development Group.

Durkin, K., Shire, B., Riem, R., Crowther, R. D., & Rutter, D. R. (1986). The social and linguistic context of early number word use. *British Journal of Developmental Psychology, 4*, 269–288.

Feigenson, L (2005). A double-dissociation in infants' representations of object arrays. *Cognition, 95*, B37-B48.

Gal'perin, P., & Georgiev, L. S. (1969). The formation of elementary mathematical notions. In J. Kilpatrick & I. Wirszup (Eds.), *Soviet studies in the psychology of learning and teaching mathematics: Vol. 1. The learning of mathematical concepts* (pp. 189–216). Chicago: University of Chicago Press.

Geary, D. C. (1995). Reflections of evolution and culture in children's cognition: Implications for mathematical development and instruction. *American Psychologist, 50*, 24–37.

Gelman, R. (1982). Accessing one-to-one correspondence: Still another paper about conservation. *British Journal of Psychology, 73*, 209–220.

Gelman, R. (1991). Epigenetic foundations of knowledge structures: Initial and transcendent constructions. In S. Carey, & R. Gelman (Ed.), *The epigenesis of mind: Essays on biology and cognition* (pp. 293–322). Hillsdale, NJ: Erlbaum.

Gelman, R. (1998). Domain specificity in cognitive development: Universals and nonuniversals. In M. Sabourin, F. Craik, & M. Robert (Eds.), *Advances in psychological science, Vol. 2: Biological and cognitive aspects* (pp. 557–579). East Sussex, UK: Psychology Press.

Gelman, R., & Gallistel, C. R. (1978). *The child's understanding of number.* Cambridge, MA: Harvard University Press.

Gelman, S. A., & Wellman, H. M. (1991). Insides and essences: Early understandings of the non-obvious. *Cognition, 38,* 213–244.

Ginsburg, H. P., & Baroody, A. J. (2003). *The test of early mathematics ability* (3rd edition). Austin, TX: Pro Ed.

Hunting, R. P., & Davis, G. E. (Eds.). (1991). *Early fraction learning.* New York: Springer-Verlag.

Inhelder, B., & Piaget, J. (1964). *The early growth of logic in the child: Classification and seriation.* New York: Harper & Row.

Inhelder, B., Sinclair, H., & Bovet, M. (1974). *Learning and the development of cognition.* Cambridge, MA: Harvard University Press.

Klahr, D., & Wallace, J. G. (1976). *Cognitive development: An information-processing view.* Hillsdale, NJ: Erlbaum.

Light, P. H., Buckingham, N., & Robbins, A. H. (1979). The conservation task as an interactional setting. *British Journal of Educational Psychology, 49,* 304–310.

Lipton, J. S., & Spelke, E. S. (2004). Discrimination of large and small numerosities by human infants. *Infancy, 5,* 271–290.

Miller, K. F., & Baillargeon, R. (1990). Length and distance: Do preschoolers think that occlusion brings things together? *Developmental Psychology, 26,* 103–114.

National Council of Teachers of Mathematics. (2000). *Principles and standards for school mathematics.* http://standards.nctm.org/document/

Neilson, I., Dockrell, J., & McKechnie, J. (1983). Does repetition of the question influence children's performance in conservation tasks? *British Journal of Developmental Psychology, 1,* 163–174.

Neufeldt, V., & Guralnik, D. B., Eds. (1994). *Webster's new world dictionary* (3rd college edition). New York: Simon & Schuster.

Ni, Y., & Zhou, Y.-D. (2005). Teaching and learning fraction and rational numbers: The origins and implications of whole number bias. *Educational Psychologist, 40,* 27–52.

Piaget, J. (1952). *The child's conception of number.* New York: Norton.

Piaget, J. (1969). *The psychology of the child.* New York: Basic Books.

Piaget, J., Inhelder, B., & Szeminska, A. (1960). *The child's conception of geometry.* New York: Harper.

Resnick, L.B., & Singer, J.A. (1993). Protoquantitative origins of ratio reasoning. In: T. Carpenter, E. Fennema, & T. Romberg (Eds.), *Rational numbers: An integration of research* (pp. 107–130). Hillsdale, NJ: Erlbaum.

Shipley, E. F., & Shepperson, B. (1990). Countable entities: Developmental changes. *Cognition, 34,* 109–136.

Siegler, R. S. (1995). How does change occur: A microgenetic study of number conservation. *Cognitive Psychology, 28,* 225–273.

Smith, C. L., Solomon, G. E. A., & Carey, S. (2005). Never getting to zero: Elementary school students' understanding of the infinite divisibility of number and matter. *Cognitive Psychology., 51,* 101–140.

Sophian, C. (1987). Early developments in children's use of counting to solve quantitative problems. *Cognition and Instruction, 4,* 61–90.

Sophian, C., Harley, H., & Martin, C. S. (1995). Relational and representational aspects of early number development. *Cognition and Instruction, 13,* 253–268.

Sophian, C., Garyantes, D., & Chang, C. (1997). When three is less than two: Early developments in children's understanding of fractional quantities. *Developmental Psychology, 33,* 731–744.

Sophian, C., & Kailihiwa, C. (1998). Units of counting: Developmental changes. *Cognitive Development, 13,* 561–585.

Stafylidou, S., & Vosniadou, S. (2004). The development of students' understanding of the numerical value of fractions. *Learning and Instruction, 14,* 503–518.

Starkey, P., & Cooper, R. G., Jr. (1980). Perception of numbers by human infants. *Science, 210,* 1033–1035.

Strauss, M., S., & Curtis, L. E. (1981). Infant perception of numerosity. *Child Development, 52,* 1146–1152.

Vamvakoussi, X., & Vosniadou, S. (2004). Understanding the structure of rational numbers: A conceptual change approach. *Learning and Instruction, 14,* 453–467.

Wellman, H. M., & Phillips, A. T. (2001). Developing intentional understandings. In B. Malle, L. Moses, & D. Baldwin (Eds.), *Intentions and intentionality: Foundations of social cognition* (pp. 125–148). Cambridge, MA: MIT Press.

Wood, J. N., & Spelke, E. S. (2005). Infants' enumeration of actions: Numerical discrimination and its signature limits. *Developmental Science, 8,* 173–181.

Wynn, K. (1992). Evidence against empiricist accounts of the origins of numerical knowledge. *Mind & Language, 7,* 315–332.

Wynn, K., Bloom, P., & Chiang, W.-C. (2002). Enumeration of collective entities by 5-month-old infants. *Cognition, 83,* B55–B62.

Xu, F. (2003). Numerosity discrimination in infants: Evidence for two systems of representation. *Cognition, 89,* B15–B25.

CHAPTER 3

KNOWING THE MATHEMATICS IN EARLY CHILDHOOD MATHEMATICS

Herbert P. Ginsburg and Barbrina Ertle

In recent years, early childhood professionals have been rethinking their approach to mathematics education (Clements, Sarama, & DiBiase, 2004). It has become increasingly evident that free play is not sufficient to promote solid mathematics learning in many children, particularly the poor, who have the greatest need (Bowman, Donovan, & Burns, 2001). As a result, the current view, echoing a position influential in earlier periods of our history (Balfanz, 1999), proposes that intentional teaching of mathematics to young children is both appropriate and desirable. In a joint position statement, the two leading professional organizations in the area (National Association for the Education of Young Children and National Council of Teachers of Mathematics, 2002) assert that, "...high-quality, challenging, and accessible mathematics education for 3- to 6-year-old children are a vital foundation for future mathematics learning" (p. 1).

According to the position statement, mathematics education at this age level should take at least two forms, one of which is familiar to and comfortable for many early childhood educators: teachers should use teachable moments arising in children's everyday play (like building towers of different heights) and in other activities (like lining up or distributing snacks) to introduce or expand upon mathematical ideas, as is intended to be done

Contemporary Perspectives on Mathematics in Early Childhood Education, pages 45–66
Copyright © 2008 by Information Age Publishing

45

in programs like Creative Curriculum (Dodge, Colker, & Heroman, 2002). The second form is controversial: early childhood educators should employ an intentional *curriculum* that deliberately sequences the teaching of mathematical ideas in what is thought to be a coherent and developmentally appropriate manner. "… [E]arly childhood curriculum needs to go beyond sporadic, hit-or-miss mathematics… [and should provide] carefully planned experiences that focus children's attention on a particular mathematical idea or set of related ideas" (National Association for the Education of Young Children and National Council of Teachers of Mathematics, 2002, principle 9).

One justification for the new position favoring mathematics instruction is pragmatic: we need to prepare children, especially low-income children, for schooling. Like it or not, their parents insist on this and so do many politicians. Another rationale offers more intellectual substance: intentional teaching can satisfy children's intellectual needs at the present time and also liberate their growth. "Guidance is not external imposition. *It is freeing the life-process for its own most adequate fulfillment*" (Dewey, 1976, p. 281).

Implementing the recommended approach to early mathematics education presents many challenges. After all, in recent years, mathematics has seldom been taught at the preschool level (Balfanz, 1999) and few teachers have been trained to do so. Organized and rigorous mathematics curricula is a rarity in early childhood education. Many preschool educators are simply unfamiliar (and no doubt uncomfortable) with teaching early mathematics.

Fortunately, research on the teaching of mathematics at the elementary school level and beyond can offer guidance to early childhood educators. One major theme emerging from elementary level research is that effective teaching requires deep understanding of the mathematical content to be taught (Lampert, 2001; Shulman, 1987). Teachers require a "profound understanding of fundamental mathematics" (Ma, 1999) that involves appreciation of the connectedness among mathematical ideas, understanding basic concepts, and taking a longitudinal perspective that illuminates how some concepts must be learned before others and how some concepts set the stage for learning new ones. Clearly teachers need to understand the basic ideas to explain and teach them.

Teachers also need content knowledge to interpret student thinking and to help them take the next step. "Subject matter understanding is essential in listening flexibly to others and hearing what they are saying or where they might be heading. Knowing content is also crucial to being inventive in creating worthwhile opportunities for learning that take learner's experiences, interests, and needs into account" (Ball & Bass,

2000, p. 86). Moreover, teacher knowledge is significantly correlated with student achievement in grades 1 and 3 (Hill, Rowan, & Ball, 2005).

Current research also reveals a major problem: U.S. elementary school teachers often lack the knowledge necessary for solid mathematics teaching. Their understanding of ideas like ratio is limited (Post, Harel, Behr, & Lesh, 1991). Their knowledge of fractions compares poorly with that of Chinese teachers (Zhou, Peverly, & Xin, in press). And in general, "...the knowledge of the Chinese teachers seemed clearly coherent while that of the U. S. teachers was clearly fragmented" (Ma, 1999, p. 107).

This paper explores the role of mathematical knowledge in early education. First we examine the content of preschool mathematics itself. We show that early mathematics, even at the preschool level, entails broad and deep mathematical ideas that need to be understood by teacher and student alike.

Second, we examine the everyday thinking children use to assimilate what is taught. Contrary to the views of many, young children's mathematical thinking is not limited to the concrete and the mechanical; it is often complex and abstract. Since this is the case, understanding the mathematics in children's thinking requires deep subject matter knowledge.

Third, we examine preschool curriculum materials from the *Big Math for Little Kids* program (Balfanz, Ginsburg, & Greenes, 2003; Ginsburg, Greenes, & Balfanz, 2003). We show that they incorporate deep mathematical ideas and are not limited to simple skills or memorized material.

Fourth, we draw upon our observations to show that implementing a complex preschool curriculum like *Big Math for Little Kids* requires the teacher to make many decisions that should be based upon deep knowledge of content and of children's thinking. Implementing a mathematics curriculum cannot be done in a rigid, scripted fashion; it requires flexibility, which in turn must be informed both by knowledge of content and of children.

Fifth, we show that exploiting teachable moments on the fly also requires deep mathematical knowledge, as well as a significant dose of creativity. Preschool teachers often do not put themselves in the position of observing teachable moments at times like free play. Further, even if teachers recognize these moments, capitalizing on them is extraordinarily difficult. Doing so requires a degree of inventiveness that is probably beyond the abilities of all but the most talented teachers.

Sixth, we raise questions about the depth of mathematical knowledge that early childhood educators possess. We have reasons to believe that it is not substantial.

Finally, we discuss the implications of our analysis for teacher education and in-service professional development: more training in mathematics and in mathematics education is required. Implementing this training for teachers will be as difficult as teaching mathematics to preschoolers.

THE MATHEMATICS IN EARLY MATHEMATICS EDUCATION

Early mathematics comprises far more than is implied by that dreadful word "numeracy." Early mathematics is both broad and deep. True mathematics involves *broad* strands of "big ideas," such as number, geometry, measurement, and "algebra," especially pattern (National Association for the Education of Young Children and National Council of Teachers of Mathematics, 2002; National Council of Teachers of Mathematics, 2000). Each of these, in turn, entails interesting subtopics. For example, number covers such matters as the counting words ("one, two, three..."), the ordinal positions ("first, second, third..."), the idea of cardinal value (how many are there?), and the various operations on number like addition and subtraction. Shape includes not only plane figures like circles and triangles, but also hexagons and octagons, as well as solids (like cubes and cylinders) and symmetries in two and three dimensions. The topic of spatial relations includes ideas like position (in front of, behind), navigation ("first go three steps to the left") and mapping (for example, creating a schematic representing the location of objects in the classroom). Mathematics is broad in scope.

Early mathematics is also *deep*. Consider three topics that virtually all preschool educators would consider appropriate for preschoolers to learn: counting words, enumeration (determining how many), and pattern.

The Counting Words

Suppose that we encounter a group of objects, a haphazard arrangement including a red block, a small stuffed dog, and a penny. We want to know "how many" are in the group. To answer the question, we first need to know the counting words (in English, "one, two, three...") and then we need to be able to use them to figure out a set's numerical value.

In most languages, the first ten number words are completely arbitrary. English uses "one, two, three..." but Spanish offers "uno, dos, tres..." In Chinese the words are "yi, er, san." At the same time, the *order* of the number words is not arbitrary. "Two" must follow "one" and not precede it; "eight" must come after "seven," not before it. Learning the first ten number words must involve rote memory. The child has to memorize the first ten or so numbers, in a fixed order. Memorizing the words themselves is not particularly difficult: young children memorize words all the time, for example the names of all the children in their classroom. But the idea of an order is another thing entirely. The child knows that the names of the children in the classroom do not need to be said in a particular order. But for some reason they do not yet understand, the number words apparently must not violate their assigned order. (Later the child will learn key exceptions, like counting by twos.)

It appears, then, as though learning to count is trivial, a mere act of memorization. Not so. Although the first ten words are essentially nonsense syllables (there is no reason why they cannot be "bix, mur, lim . . .") arranged in an arbitrary order (which could just as easily have been "three, eight, two . . ."), most languages use a base ten system to organize number words after ten. The number "fifty," for example, refers to five tens, "sixty" to six tens, and so on. We begin counting by ones, but when we reach "ten," we go on to count by tens and ones. In this system, the set of 53 things is seen as five groups of ten things along with three individual things. The first big idea then is imminent in the very act of counting: we need to organize things in groups of tens and ones.

The second big idea is that the number words embody several patterns. One is that the names for the groups of tens are derived from the words for the numbers of units. "Sixty" refers to six groups of tens, and "eighty" to eight groups of tens. A second pattern is that once the group of tens has been identified, the unit words are appended to it in order. Thus, once we know that there are seven groups of ten or "seventy," we simply add on "one, two, three . . ." as appropriate. A third pattern is that once we reach a decade number plus nine (like "thirty-nine") we switch to the next decade number in the series.

We see then that after the first 10 nonsense-syllable-numbers the sequence of counting words is an important and elegant pattern deriving from the base ten system. Our written numbers exhibit the pattern to perfection. After the first arbitrary 9 numerals (1, 2, 3 . . . 9), 10 designates a single group of ten with zero ones, 11 designates one group of ten plus one more, 12 designates one group of ten and two more, and so on, all the way to 99 (nine tens and nine ones). Unfortunately, the English language botches the job, distorting the pattern and making it difficult to learn. In English, after learning "one" to "ten," a child is next faced with the 'teens', which present their own weird challenge. Instead of speaking the 'tens' and then the 'ones', a child first encounters "eleven." This word (like "twelve") has no apparent relation to the idea of a group of ten and one more, or to the written numeral "11." So memorization is once more necessary, as it is for "twelve." But then the situation becomes even more confused. The child must learn to say, "thirteen, fourteen . . . nineteen." In these numbers, the "ones" value precedes the tens value. By contrast, after "twenty," the reverse is true: we say "twenty-three," not "three-twenty," the analogue of "thirteen."

Look at it this way: The base ten number system is elegant. Its written form is transparent. But in English, we must memorize the first ten or so numbers; learn the next several numbers "backwards" ("thirteen" instead of "ten-three"); and then finally figure out that the rule learned for the numbers from "thirteen" to "nineteen" (ones first, then tens) does not apply to numbers above 20. Another way of saying this is that we force children first to memorize (an unavoidable task), then to learn nonsense, and finally to learn the most orderly (and in this sense simplest) task. There is some justification in the claim that it is easier to count using the larger numbers than the smaller ones.

The spoken number system does not have to be as bizarre or difficult as the English version. The Chinese counting system (and other East Asian languages deriving from it) is perfectly regular (Miller & Parades, 1996). Chinese speakers say arbitrary sounds to indicate the numbers from one to ten, but thereafter say the equivalent of "ten-one, ten-two . . . ten-nine," and then "two-ten, two-ten-one, two-ten-two . . . nine-ten-nine." The Chinese number word system is completely orderly and rule-governed, and clearly related to the base-ten, place value system of written numbers. Indeed, the base-ten logic that is so transparent in the Chinese number word system may facilitate the learning of early arithmetic (Fuson & Kwon, 1992; Miura et al., 1993).

How Many?

We began with a situation in which there was a desire to determine the number of a set of elements. We showed that the counting words are necessary to doing so, and that the counting words depend on memory of a few key elements but then incorporate principles of base ten groupings and exhibit important patterns. But now it is time to count those objects, a haphazard arrangement including a red block, a small stuffed dog, and a penny. The mathematical ideas underlying *enumeration*—determining a set's numerical value—are complex, and among them are the following: One is that any kind of elements in a set can be counted. You can count nickels and cats, big things and small things. You can count one group of apples and another group of oranges. You can count a group containing both apples and oranges. You can even count fantastical ideas like red unicorns existing only in your (one) head. Counting is an enormously powerful tool that can be applied to any discrete real or imagined object.

A second idea is that each number word, "one, two, three . . ." must be associated once and only once with each of the objects in the set. You point at the red block and say "one," the dog and say "two," and the penny and say "three." You can't say both "one" and "two" when referring to the red block, even though you describe it with two words, "red" and "block." You cannot skip an object in the set. Each counting word must be in one-to-one correspondence with each element of the set.

A third idea is that the final number in the sequence, "three," does not refer to the penny alone. You first pointed to the block and said "one." It's true: there is one block. Then you pointed to the dog and said "two." But it's not true that there are two dogs. The two indicates that you have already counted two items, not that the second item, the dog, is itself two. Similarly, even though you say "three" while pointing to the penny, the number word describes not that individual object but instead the whole group of objects—how many there are all together. You could have started your count with the penny, in which case it would have been "one," not "three." Indeed, *any* of the objects in the group could have been "one," "two," or "three," but the group as a whole has three objects whatever the order in which they are counted. The final count word indicates the number of objects in the set as a whole—the total quantity, the cardinal value.

Notice that enumeration entails a very strange and distinctive use of language. In ordinary speech, we call an object a block or a dog or a penny because that is its name. You cannot legitimately call a penny a red block. But when we enumerate, the number name we assign to the objects does not refer to the individual object but to a very abstract property of the set as a whole. When, finishing the enumeration, we point to the penny and say "three," we do not mean that "three" is the name for the penny but that it is a property of all the things we have enumerated as a collection.

And that is just the beginning of the depth of the idea of cardinality. Suppose now you also count the idea of Homer, a mental image of a pink unicorn, and an apartment building. Again there are three altogether, and that three is the same three as the number of the set comprising the red block, small stuffed dog, and penny. Three is three regardless of whom or what belongs to the club.

Pattern

As mentioned earlier, mathematics involves far more than number. One key topic in mathematics is pattern, a notion notoriously difficult to define. Pattern refers to an underlying rule or concept; pattern describes a regularity that determines, explains or predicts observed phenomena. We see a collection of 10 blocks arranged in a line. We see that the first is red, the second yellow, the third red, the next yellow, and so on. We believe that we have detected a pattern, namely an alternation of red and yellow. Knowledge of the underlying pattern allows us to predict, without seeing it, that the eleventh block will be red and so will the one hundred and first in the series. It allows us to fill in the gaps as well: if a block is missing at any point in the line (say between two reds), we know what its color must be (in this case, yellow).

There are several important points to make about pattern. First, patterns may involve many different kinds of phenomena—letters, shapes, numbers, sounds, words (and Freud would say, dreams). Second, patterns are of many types—alternating patterns (RGRG...), alternating patterns with repetition (1, 1, 2, 1, 1, 2...) growing patterns (1, 2, 3...), power patterns (1, 4, 9, 16, 25...). Third, there usually is the possibility of new elements appearing indefinitely: the pattern goes on and on. Fourth, often it is difficult to detect a pattern without encountering a goodly number of examples. For example, it is hard to tell whether a pattern underlies A, B, O, A, B unless we see more letters.

And then there are two things that are not a pattern. The phenomena themselves are not a pattern. Blocks are blocks; pattern is an idea about the blocks (or, in other language, a perception of the structure underlying the blocks). Second, a design is not necessarily a pattern. A design may be a pleasing sight, but it is not a pattern unless some kind of regularity is involved. Thus, ABBA may be aesthetically pleasant but it is not in itself a pattern. On the other hand, ABBAABBAABBAABBA...is a pattern (take AB as the first unit, reverse it for the second, and keep repeating indefinitely).

Why is pattern so important in mathematics (and in other areas too)? One reason is that it involves the search for abstractions that underlie the observed. Knowing the pattern—the abstract concept—enables prediction and generalization. Understanding the pattern gives insight into how things work. It explains what occurs on the surface: these numbers behave as they do because they are governed by a linear function comprised by a regular increase of two units. Some authorities even define mathematics as the search for pattern: "...mathematics is not just about number and shape but about pattern and order of all sorts.... Active mathematicians seek patterns wherever they arise" (Steen, 1990, p. 2).

The Depth of "Basic" Mathematics

We have reviewed a very few mathematical topics that are often taught to preschoolers: counting words, cardinality, and pattern. We have seen that underlying these topics are some very deep concepts. Counting words are an expression of base ten ideas; cardinality refers to abstract ideas of number; and pattern involves the search for underlying regularities. This is not the mathematics of mere memory, mere recognition of a few shapes, or mere execution of the kind of mechanical skills that are so prevalent in the later learning of topics such as long division or even algebra. The topics that preschoolers study may be basic, but they are deep.

THE SPLENDID LITTLE MATHEMATICIAN

Piaget's most fundamental insight, shared by many cognitive psychologists (Bransford, Brown, & Cocking, 1998), was perhaps to "consider assimilation the fundamental fact of psychic development" (Piaget, 1952b, p. 42). By this he meant that all learners incorporate (or interpret) what is taught in terms of what they already know. Teachers should not assume that children are ignorant about the subject of instruction. Children have their own ideas about mathematics and assimilate into them what is taught. Vygotsky concurs: "... children's learning begins long before they attend school.... Consequently, children have their own preschool arithmetic, which only myopic psychologists could ignore" (Vygotsky, 1978, p. 84). And we would add that Vygotsky was wrong only insofar as he attributed myopia only to psychologists. Teachers are in danger of the affliction as well and need to understand the mathematics in children's thinking (Ginsburg & Seo, 1999).

A large body of research (Ginsburg et al., 2006) has shown that young children develop a relatively powerful "everyday" or "informal" mathematics that has several important characteristics. One is that young children have a spontaneous and sometimes explicit *interest* in mathematical ideas. Naturalistic observation has shown, for example, that in their ordinary environments, young children spontaneously count (Saxe, Guberman, & Gearhart, 1987; Walkerdine, 1988) and develop key counting principles (Wagner & Walters, 1982). Indeed, children at this age enjoy counting up to relatively large numbers, like 100 (Irwin & Burgham, 1992) and are even concerned to know what is the "largest number" (Gelman, 1980). Also, mathematical ideas permeate children's play: in the block area, for example, young children spend a good deal of time determining which tower is higher than another, creating and extending interesting patterns with blocks, exploring shapes, creating symmetries, and the like (Seo & Ginsburg, 2004). Much of this activity is spontaneous, occurring without adult guidance. Indeed, adults are often unaware that the children are doing these things. "We can think of young children as self-monitoring learning machines who are inclined to learn on the fly, even when they are not in school and regardless of whether they are with adults" (Gelman, 2000, p. 26).

The second point is that young children are more *competent* in key aspects of early mathematics than Piaget's theory might lead one to believe. From an early age, they seem to understand basic ideas of addition and subtraction (Brush, 1978), ratios (Hunting, 1999) and spatial relations (Clements, 1999). They can spontaneously develop (Groen & Resnick, 1977) various methods of calculation, like counting on from the larger number (Baroody & Wilkins, 1999).

Indeed, simple mathematical "skills" are far more conceptual than we often realize. Consider the apparently simple act of enumeration. Underlying it are several key ideas (Gelman & Gallistel, 1986). For example, children seem to know the one-to-one principle—one and only one number word should be assigned to each object. Children also seem to know the stable order principle—number words should be said in the same order (correct or incorrect) all the time. Thus children may make the mistake of saying, "one, two, four," but consistently use that order. Other guides to enumeration include the cardinal principle (the last number enumerated indicates the total value of the set); the abstraction principle (anything can be counted from stones to unicorns); and the order irrelevance principle (enumeration may begin with any object in the set so long as each is counted once and only once). Determining that there are three toy animals in a set is far from the elementary activity it may seem to be.

A third point is that young children are capable of learning some rather complex mathematics when they are taught. Thus, children can be taught interesting aspects of symmetry (Zvonkin, 1992) and spatial relations, among other topics (Greenes, 1999).

Furthermore, young children in early childhood settings may even enjoy *playing* with the mathematics they have been taught. For example, one Kindergarten teacher, Luzaria Dunatov, reports the following: Joanna and Nick "... are in front of the 100 chart. I have used the 100 chart in my math lessons and daily during morning meeting. It is a well-known resource in our classroom. Joanna is pointing to the numbers as Nick counts. I see them when they are already at the number 79. She points to the numbers in sequence and Nick keeps up with her pointing as he counts. Joanna says, 'Say it louder!' She starts pointing too fast for Nick to keep up with so he falls behind by one number. When Joanna points to the number 98, Nick is saying 97. Joanna waits and stays at 98 until Nick says 98, then she continues and points to 99 and 100. They walk away to find something else to read" (Ginsburg, 2006, p. 153).

In brief, although their thought is in some respects limited and different from adults', as Piaget (1952a) pointed out, young children deal with mathematical ideas in every day and academic play, are curious about the subject, know something about it, and can learn interesting mathematics when taught. Before the onset of formal schooling, young children do not only memorize (for example, the first ten or so numbers) and they do not only employ mechanical skills (as when they know that numbers are different from words or that a particular sequence exhibits a pattern). They do not operate only on a "concrete" level. Instead, we can say fairly that young children are splendid little mathematicians. They deal spontaneously and sometimes joyfully with mathematical ideas. This is what real mathematicians do. It is not what typically happens in school. Early in life, little children often engage in mathematical activity more genuine than that taught in school. We need to prevent early childhood education and later schooling from strangling children's enthusiasm and thinking.

To understand her students' mathematical thinking and then build on it in a way that encourages continued enjoyment of mathematics, the teacher must therefore understand the mathematics it involves.

MATHEMATICAL KNOWLEDGE IN CURRICULUM MATERIALS

Authors carefully construct curriculum materials to convey important mathematical ideas. To teach the curriculum effectively, teachers need to understand the ideas in it. In the case of early childhood mathematics, the task is harder than it might appear. Unlike many textbooks, curriculum materials do not take the form of explicit mathematical statements. Instead, the curriculum typically involves various activities and games in which the mathematics is embedded, sometimes in subtle and non-obvious ways.

Consider two examples, both from the *Big Math for Little Kids* (BMLK) program (Balfanz et al., 2003; Ginsburg et al., 2003). In BMLK, a three-part process is used to help children learn the counting numbers. First, children learn to memorize the first ten or so numbers. They do this by imitating the teacher as she introduces the number words along with various chants or body movements. Thus, the teacher might have the class jump up and down as they say, "One, two … ten," performing each jump in one-to-one correspondence with each number word, eventually reaching 19. This method draws heavily on rote memory, because, as described above, that process is necessary for learning the first ten numbers in almost all languages, and is about the only way to cope with the strange (backwards) numbers that English uses from 13 to 19. But after 19 is reached, the content of the program changes. When children reach 19, they are told to pause and think about what number comes next. The idea is that the decade numbers exhibit a pattern, a rule; they are very much like the units ("forty" is like "four" with the "ty" at the end indicating tens; and "forty" comes after the last of the "threes," namely "thirty-nine," has had its turn). So the teacher indicates that "twenty" comes after "nineteen"; "thirty" after "twenty-nine," and so on. The teacher does not directly *tell* the children these things; she models the ideas, partly through her actions. Thus, she may start a new movement and sound sequence at each new decade. She can do the hopping twenties, the roaring thirties; the whispering forties; the bouncing fifties, and so on. These are the "curriculum materials" for the first two parts in the process of learning to count, and the children engage in these activities every day, gradually expanding the upper limit to which they can count, and hopefully learning something about the rules underlying the counting sequence. Teachers need to understand why the curriculum materials are constructed as they are, and thus appreciate the importance of various elements of the activities, such as: pausing the motions or sounds at the end of a decade, and treating the numbers from n (10), n (10) + 1 ... n (10) + 9 as a meaningful sequence, a chunk of relevant material. Without this understanding, the teacher may not implement the activity as intended, and thus fail to promote key aspects of mathematical learning. But with understanding of the mathematics, teachers can flexibly implement and adapt the activity to the diverse and changing needs of her classroom.

For the third part in the process, BMLK introduces a written number chart to reinforce its view of what counting is all about. As the children count, for example, from 20 to 29, the teacher lays out on the floor or on a vertical surface a distinctive kind of number chart. Unlike the standard number chart, the left-most number in each row is the decades number, 20, 30, and the like. The teacher, or a designated child, places in each space the correct number in the sequence. Thus, as the children say "twenty-one," the written number 21 is placed to the right of the 20, and so on until the 29 is put in its position on the extreme right of the row. The big mathematical idea underlying this activity—whether the children learn it as intended is of course an empirical question—is that the written numbers reveal the underlying base ten structure of the number sequence. The written numbers make vivid the rule for forming the new sequence, namely that the unit values are added to the decade in order, from 1 to 9, and that the sequence stops when one reaches the decades number plus 9, whereupon one proceeds to the next decade.

It is easy enough to jump around and make different sounds. It is not so easy to see why the rows are constructed as they are and how the written and spoken numbers are related. But teachers sometimes do not understand how the BMLK number chart is different from the standard one, or, more important, the reasons for the difference. Yet understanding the rationale for the BMLK number chart is essential for the teacher's successful implementation of the activity (Figure 3.1).

1	2	3	4	5	6	7	8	9	10
11	12	13	14	15	16	17	18	19	20
21	22	23	24	25	26	27	28	29	30
31	32	33	34	35	36	37	38	39	40
41	42	43	44	45	46	47	48	49	50

	1	2	3	4	5	6	7	8	9
10	11	12	13	14	15	16	17	18	19
20	21	22	23	24	25	26	27	28	29
30	31	32	33	34	35	36	37	38	39
40	41	42	43	44	45	46	47	48	49
50									

Standard Number Chart   **BMLK Number Chart**

Figure 3.1.

Consider another example. This excerpt (Figure 3.2) from the teacher manual describes an activity designed to teach cardinality, "Bag It!"

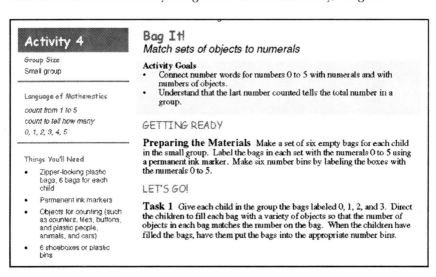

Activity 4

Group Size
Small group

Language of Mathematics
count from 1 to 5
count to tell how many
0, 1, 2, 3, 4, 5

Things You'll Need
- Zipper-locking plastic bags, 6 bags for each child
- Permanent ink markers
- Objects for counting (such as counters, tiles, buttons, and plastic people, animals, and cars)
- 6 shoeboxes or plastic bins

Bag It!
Match sets of objects to numerals

Activity Goals
- Connect number words for numbers 0 to 5 with numerals and with numbers of objects.
- Understand that the last number counted tells the total number in a group.

GETTING READY

Preparing the Materials Make a set of six empty bags for each child in the small group. Label the bags in each set with the numerals 0 to 5 using a permanent ink marker. Make six number bins by labeling the boxes with the numerals 0 to 5.

LET'S GO!

Task 1 Give each child in the group the bags labeled 0, 1, 2, and 3. Direct the children to fill each bag with a variety of objects so that the number of objects in each bag matches the number on the bag. When the children have filled the bags, have them put the bags into the appropriate number bins.

Figure 3.2.

Upon first reading, these directions may seem perfectly clear as to what materials are needed and how the activity is to transpire. The basic idea is that the numeral on a bag indicates to children how many objects to put into it. The children have to enumerate the objects (which may be identical or may differ from one another), probably by counting them one by one, and associate the cardinal number, the last number counted, with the numeral. They have to learn the special case of 0, which indicates that nothing goes in the bag. After inserting the proper number of objects into a bag, children then are instructed to put the bag into a larger bin, along with other bags, often containing other objects, but equivalent in number. Thus, the ideas underlying the task are enumeration, cardinal number, the relation between written number and cardinal number, and the equivalence of sets characterized by the same cardinal number but differing in the objects comprising them. Later, of course, two bags can be combined to obtain another cardinal number or can be compared to learn about "more," "less," or the "same." A good deal of arithmetic can be taught with these little bags—*if and only if* the teacher understands the mathematics behind their use.

In Bag It!, the mathematics is in a sense imminent in the bags and their uses, just as it was imminent in the jumping, shouting and number chart of the counting word activities. Both curriculum activities incorporate deep mathematical ideas; the teacher needs to understand them and how they are contained in the materials.

IMPLEMENTING A CURRICULUM

For the past several years, we have observed teachers implementing the BMLK program in a variety of preschool and Kindergarten settings. As was evident in the illustrated guide for Bag It!, BMLK does not insist that teachers follow a rigid script in doing an activity. Sometimes the program does suggest wording that the teacher may use, but the basic assumption is that implementing a mathematics curriculum cannot be done in a rigid manner; it requires flexibility, which in turn must be informed by knowledge of both content and children. Many teachers do an excellent job of implementing the activities in their own way; other teachers struggle. First we describe how mathematical knowledge and insight into the children inform a successful implementation of Bag It!

> Ms. B was working with a small group of children. She pointed to the one child's 2 bag that contained only a single button. She asked, "How many buttons do you see?" The children in the group responded, "one." Ms. B then pointed to the number on the bag, "What number do you see?" "2." Ms. B then guided the children through the addition of another button, had them count the buttons again, identify the number on the bag, and asked whether they matched. She then repeated this process for a 1 bag, then went to the 3 bag. In each case, when Ms. B would ask how many buttons there were in the bag, she would cover the numeral with her hand so they weren't looking at it, but were instead focused on the number of buttons contained in the bag.

This was exemplary work. Although the teacher's manual did not recommend the activity, Ms. B was able to help the children distinguish between the objects to be counted and the numeral that indicated the number of objects. This subtle teaching maneuver was based both on mathematical knowledge concerning the distinction between the numeral and the number counted, and on the psychological insight that children might have difficulty making the distinction. Both mathematical knowledge and psychological insight are essential for effective implementation of a curriculum.

Other teachers have struggled with ideas underlying Bag It! When doing the activity, some teachers insisted on counting the objects from left to right. Perhaps the intention was to model behavior useful for reading (at least in English). But this practice may promote the incorrect idea that order matters in counting. Indeed, we have encountered some children who are convinced that counting must be done from left to right. Could this have resulted from the way they were taught? Sometimes well-intentioned teachers also place a written number next to each object counted. Thus, the first object is labeled "1," the second, "2," and so on. This may have the undesirable effect of promoting the idea that each object in the collection is a particular number. In the figure (Figure 3.3), the first block on the left may be interpreted as 1; the second, as 2; and so on. In this view, the final number represents an individual object, not the number of the collection as a whole. The teacher probably did not *intend* to convey this idea, but the method of implementation may suggest it.

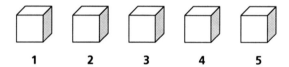

Figure 3.3.

In brief, implementing an apparently straightforward and simple activity like Bag It! entails many complex decisions that are based, at least in part, on the teacher's understanding of both the underlying mathematics and of the children.

THE TEACHABLE MOMENT

One of the central tenets of early childhood education is that teachers should allow children to play in a rich environment, observe the spontaneous activities in which they engage, and then use these activities as a basis for effective teaching. The basic idea is to seize on the teachable moment. This requires several abilities. One is to observe carefully what the child is doing; a second is to understand the mathematics underlying the behavior; and a third is to design an activity to foster the child's further development. In this way, education can be directed at and made responsible to the needs of the individual.

In Shakespeare's words, "'tis a consummation devoutly to be wished." But can the teacher pull it off? The first requirement is to observe carefully the child's behavior, particularly during free play in places like the block area. In our experience, many teachers seldom do this. They are too engaged in behavior management or other activities to be able to spend time carefully observing children. Even if they do observe behavior, the second requirement is that they interpret it accurately. This requires knowledge of both mathematics and children. As Dewey put it many years ago, "Really to interpret the child's present crude impulses in counting, measuring, and arranging things in rhythmic series, involves mathematical scholarship—a knowledge of the mathematical formulae and relations which have, in the history of the race, grown out of such crude beginnings" (Dewey, 1976, p. 282). Can teachers do this accurately? It's a very hard task! And then the third step is to invent—on the fly—new activities that can further the child's learning. This is even a harder task.

We have been able to locate little research touching directly on teachers' abilities to seize on the teachable moment. One study suggests that during free play, teachers tend to act as "stage manager," attempting to get children involved in play, or as "play enhancer/playmate," attempting to facilitate their play. But teachers' "...conversations are not exactly filled with rich, stimulating content" (Kontos, 1999, p. 379). Also, "Unfortunately, the quality of the support they provided appeared to be less than ideal" (p. 380).

Our field notes suggest that teachers seldom exploit the mathematics in children's everyday behavior. Tracy Curran reports the following concerning free play in a preschool:

> One boy began building a tower on top of one of the small bookcases. He placed four rectangular blocks vertically one on top of the other and was standing on his tiptoes trying to place a fifth. Miss Carla, who was standing at least ten feet away warned the boy, "No, no, no, it's gonna fall! Put it on the floor!" The boy complied. I think it would have been much more useful to ask the boy if he could build a structure the same size on the floor (he would have to work on comparing lengths transitively, etc.). I also think that children don't mind too much when their structures fall down—they are simply experimenting with building, balancing, and learning about what happens if blocks are not balanced.

> Later, while Miss Carla was addressing various disputes, a boy was attempting to make a square using four equal-length rectangular blocks. I am quite certain he was attempting to make a square because of the way he kept aligning and realigning the ends of the blocks. At first, the shape was rectangular because, rather than aligning the interior endpoints of the blocks, he aligned the blocks so that the corners were flush (parallel sets of sticks were aligned so that the exterior endpoints of one set were aligned with the interior end-

points of the other set). The boy seemed to be working hard on finding a way to align the endpoints to form a square. He experimented with the structure by moving one side out so that the interior endpoints were aligned. He seemed to be thinking about what to do with the other side when Miss Carla approached him and asked, "Whatcha makin'?" He told her he was building a square. "Oh, nice," she replied. She then said, "You gotta make sure the sides all match." The boy looked away. Miss Carla said, "Look, you're not looking." She pointed to the end points of one side of the structure and said, "Is this the same as here?" (pointing to the opposite side). The boy did not reply. She said, "Look, look, these sides here are all even, but if you look over there, they're not even. What could you do?" At this point the boy said something (unintelligible) to another boy. Miss Carla said, "Would you like some help?" The boy didn't answer. She then aligned the blocks in the same way the boy initially did (a rectangle) (Figure 3.4). She then said, "Now this is a square. All the sides have to be the same to be a square." Just then a dispute over a puzzle erupted at a nearby table (apparently someone caused the puzzle pieces to fight). Miss Carla walked away to bring peace to the puzzle pieces.

The figure on the left is what the boy was working towards (the other one is a rectangle!)

Figure 3.4.

The boy stopped experimenting with making a square after Miss Carla's intervention. Instead, he gathered a bunch of plastic animals to live in the square that was really a rectangle.

During cleanup time, I noticed one girl carefully putting away blocks in the appropriate locations (images corresponding to the shapes of blocks are taped on the shelves indicating where the blocks belong). She seemed quite competent at matching the blocks with the corresponding shape cutouts. However, one block in particular gave her a lot of trouble:

Figure 3.5.

She seemed to have no difficulty understanding that the irregular shape she was holding was the same shape as the corresponding image pasted on the bookshelf. Interestingly, that was not enough for her. For some reason, she wanted to align the irregularly shaped block so that it was in the same position as its image. I watched her rotate the block again and again without success (in order to align the shapes she would have had to rotate it and flip it over). She was working diligently, but seemed to be a bit frustrated. A boy scooted up next to her and said, "It doesn't go like that, it goes like that," as he grabbed the block from her. However, like the girl, the boy rotated the block, but did not flip it over. The girl grabbed the block back from him and yelled, "Miss Carla—I don't know how to do this!" Miss Carla yelled, "You have to match the pattern, match the shape!" She walked over, took the block from the girl and placed it on the shelf (without flipping it over) and said, "Okay, this piece goes right here." She then left the block area to intervene in a debate between two children about who ran into whom. The girl and boy concerned about the proper alignment of the irregularly shaped block finished putting the blocks away but in a more careless manner than before.

I think it is very difficult for an adult to accept the fact that sometimes very young children know more about things and think more deeply about them than the adult does. The boy in the "square" example and the girl in the "irregular shape" example were clearly thinking deeply about the problems they posed to themselves. Unfortunately, the teacher's thoughtless intervention seemed to quash this thinking.

DO THE TEACHERS KNOW THE MATHEMATICS?

This question is especially pertinent because in recent times early childhood educators have seldom taught mathematics (Balfanz, 1999), so that knowledge of it has not been necessary. We do not know of any evidence directly bearing on the issue. But our experience suggests that preschool teachers have a good deal to learn about the relevant mathematics. One reason has to do with preschool teachers' identity. Many simply do not see themselves as teachers of mathematics: their identity tends toward the emotional caregiver rather than the teacher, especially of something (mistakenly) assumed to be so foreign to young children as mathematics. Indeed, some of our early childhood students—at Teachers College, Columbia University—tell us that they chose the profession *because* they would not have to teach mathematics, do not like mathematics, or are not very good at it.

A second reason is that most early childhood teachers (indeed, elementary school teachers) receive a very limited amount of training in mathematics or mathematics education. A good deal of their course work covers pedagogy, perhaps literacy, and social-emotional development, or even general cognitive development, but not mathematics. How can they then be expected to understand something as complex as early mathematical ideas or children's mathematical thinking?

Third, the situation may be especially dire at many daycare centers where providers have not been trained as teachers at all, and indeed may be relatively poorly educated. Now they are being asked, for the first time in many localities, not only to *teach*, but also to teach *mathematics*. Clearly, the demands are unfair unless the daycare providers are given extensive training and support.

Given the issues of identity, of the lack of training in mathematics education for many prospective teachers, and the often poor education of day care providers, is it any wonder that preschool teachers may not be as solidly grounded in mathematics as they should be?

THE CHALLENGE FOR PROFESSIONAL DEVELOPMENT

We have shown that deep knowledge of mathematics is essential for understanding and implementing curriculum and for seizing on the teachable moment, and that many early childhood teachers probably care little about early mathematics and understand little of it. The challenge for professional development is clear: we need to help prospective and practicing teachers to overcome their fear of mathematics and to understand it. Implementing this training for teachers will be at least as difficult as teaching mathematics to preschoolers.

REFERENCES

Balfanz, R. (1999). Why do we teach children so little mathematics? Some historical considerations. In J. V. Copley (Ed.), *Mathematics in the early years* (pp. 3–10). Reston, VA: National Council of Teachers of Mathematics.

Balfanz, R., Ginsburg, H. P., & Greenes, C. (2003). The big math for little kids early childhood mathematics program. *Teaching Children Mathematics, 9*(5), 264–268.

Ball, D. L., & Bass, H. (2000). Interweaving content and pedagogy in teaching and learning to teach: Knowing and using mathematics. In J. Boaler (Ed.), *Multiple perspectives on the teaching and learning of mathematics* (pp. 83–104). Westport, CT: Ablex.

Baroody, A. J., & Wilkins, J. L. M. (1999). The development of informal counting, number, and arithmetic skills and concepts. In J. V. Copley (Ed.), *Mathematics in the early years* (pp. 48–65). Reston, VA: National Council of Teachers of Mathematics.

Bowman, B. T., Donovan, M. S., & Burns, M. S. (Eds.). (2001). *Eager to learn: Educating our preschoolers.* Washington, DC: National Academy Press.

Bransford, J. D., Brown, A. L., & Cocking, R. R. (Eds.). (1998). *How people learn: Brain, mind, experience, and school.* Washington, D.C: National Academy Press.

Brush, L. R. (1978). Preschool children's knowledge of addition and subtraction. *Journal for Research in Mathematics Education, 9*, 44–54.

Clements, D. H. (1999). Geometric and spatial thinking in young children. In J. V. Copley (Ed.), *Mathematics in the early years* (pp. 66–79). Reston, VA: National Council of Teachers of Mathematics.

Clements, D. H., Sarama, J., & DiBiase, A.-M. (Eds.). (2004). *Engaging young children in mathematics: Standards for early childhood mathematics education.* Mahwah, NJ: Erlbaum.

Dewey, J. (1976). The child and the curriculum. In J. A. Boydston (Ed.), *John Dewey: The middle works, 1899–1924. Volume 2: 1902–1903* (pp. 273–291). Carbondale: Southern Illinois University Press.

Dodge, D. T., Colker, L., & Heroman, C. (2002). *The creative curriculum for preschool* (4th ed.). Washington, DC: Teaching Strategies, Inc.

Fuson, K. C., & Kwon, Y. (1992). Korean children's understanding of multidigit addition and subtraction. *Child Development, 63*, 491–506.

Gelman, R. (1980). What young children know about numbers. *Educational Psychologist, 15*, 54–68.

Gelman, R. (2000). The epigenesis of mathematical thinking. *Journal of Applied Developmental Psychology, 21*(1), 27–37.

Gelman, R., & Gallistel, C. R. (1986). *The child's understanding of number.* Cambridge, MA: Harvard University Press.

Ginsburg, H. P. (2006). Mathematical play and playful mathematics: A guide for early education. In D. Singer, R. M. Golinkoff, & K. Hirsh-Pasek (Eds.), *Play = Learning: How play motivates and enhances children's cognitive and social-emotional growth.* New York: Oxford University Press.

Ginsburg, H. P., Cannon, J., Eisenband, J. G., & Pappas, S. (2006). Mathematical thinking and learning. In K. McCartney & D. Phillips (Eds.), *Handbook of early child development* (pp. 208–229). Oxford: Blackwell.

Ginsburg, H. P., Greenes, C., & Balfanz, R. (2003). *Big math for little kids.* Parsippany, NJ: Dale Seymour Publications.

Ginsburg, H. P., & Seo, K. H. (1999). The mathematics in children's thinking. *Mathematical Thinking and Learning, 1*(2), 113–129.

Greenes, C. (1999). Ready to learn: Developing young children's mathematical powers. In J. Copley (Ed.), *Mathematics in the early years* (pp. 39–47). Reston, VA: National Council of Teachers of Mathematics.

Groen, G., & Resnick, L. B. (1977). Can preschool children invent addition algorithms? *Journal of Educational Psychology, 69*, 645–652.

Hill, H. C., Rowan, B., & Ball, D. L. (2005). Effects of teachers' mathematical knowledge for teaching on student achievement. *American Educational Research Journal, 42*(2), 371–406.

Hunting, R. (1999). Rational number learning in the early years: What is possible? In J. Copley (Ed.), *Mathematics in the early years* (pp. 80–87). Reston, VA: National Council of Teachers of Mathematics.

Irwin, K., & Burgham, D. (1992). Big numbers and small children. *The New Zealand Mathematics Magazine, 29*(1), 9–19.

Kontos, S. (1999). Preschool teachers' talk, roles, and activity settings during free play. *Early Childhood Research Quarterly, 14*(3), 363–382.

Lampert, M. (2001). *Teaching problems and the problems of teaching.* New Haven, CT: Yale University Press.

Ma, L. (1999). *Knowing and teaching elementary mathematics.* Mahwah, NJ: Erlbaum.

Miller, K. F., & Parades, D. R. (1996). On the shoulders of giants: Cultural tools and mathematical development. In R. J. Sternberg & T. Ben-Zeev (Eds.), *The nature of mathematical thinking* (pp. 83–117). Mahwah, NJ: Erlbaum

Miura, I. T., Okamoto, Y., Kim, C. C., Steere, M., & Fayol, M. (1993). First graders' cognitive representation of number and understanding of place value: Cross-national comparisons—France, Japan, Korea, Sweden, and the United States. *Journal of Educational Psychology, 85*, 24–30.

National Association for the Education of Young Children and National Council of Teachers of Mathematics. (2002). *Position statement. Early childhood mathematics: Promoting good beginnings,* from http://www.naeyc.org/about/positions/psmath.asp

National Council of Teachers of Mathematics. (2000). *Principles and standards for school mathematics.* Reston, VA: Author.

Piaget, J. (1952a). *The child's conception of number* (C. Gattegno & F. M. Hodgson, Trans.). London: Routledge & Kegan Paul.

Piaget, J. (1952b). *The origins of intelligence in children* (M. Cook, Trans.). New York: International Universities Press.

Post, T. R., Harel, G., Behr, M. J., & Lesh, R. (1991). Intermediate teachers' knowledge of rational number concepts. In E. Fennema, T. P. Carpenter, & S. J. Lamon (Eds.), *Integrating research on teaching and learning mathematics* (pp. 177–198). Albany: SUNY Press.

Saxe, G. B., Guberman, S. R., & Gearhart, M. (1987). Social processes in early number development. *Monographs of the Society for Research in Child Development, 52*(2, Serial No. 216).

Seo, K.-H., & Ginsburg, H. P. (2004). What is developmentally appropriate in early childhood mathematics education? Lessons from new research. In D. H. Clements, J. Sarama,& A.-M. DiBiase (Eds.), *Engaging young children in mathematics: Standards for early childhood mathematics education* (pp. 91–104). Hillsdale, NJ: Erlbaum.

Shulman, L. S. (1987). Knowledge and teaching: Foundations of a new reform. *Harvard Educational Review, 57*(1), 1–22.

Steen, L. A. (1990). Pattern. In S. L. A. (Ed.), *On the shoulders of giants: New approaches to numeracy* (pp. 1–10). Washington, DC: National Academy Press.

Vygotsky, L. S. (1978). *Mind in society: The development of higher psychological processes.* Cambridge, MA: Harvard University Press.

Wagner, S. H., & Walters, J. (1982). A longitudinal analysis of early number concepts: From numbers to number. In G. E. Forman (Ed.), *Action and thought: From sensorimotor schemes to symbolic operations* (pp. 137–161). New York: Academic Press.

Walkerdine, V. (1988). *The mastery of reason: Cognitive development and the production of rationality.* London: Routledge.

Zhou, Z., Peverly, S. T., & Xin, T. (in press). Knowing and teaching fractions: A cross-cultural study of American and Chinese mathematics teachers. *Contemporary Educational Psychology*.

Zvonkin, A. (1992). Mathematics for little ones. *Journal of Mathematical Behavior, 11*(2), 207–219.

CHAPTER 4

MATHEMATICS IN EARLY CHILDHOOD[1]

Julie Sarama and Douglas H. Clements

For over a century, views of young children's mathematics have differed widely. The recent turn of the century has seen a dramatic increase in attention to the mathematics education of young children. We begin with a brief consideration of the history of mathematics in early childhood and then turn to the question of what children know before entering school. The remainder of the chapter examines what children can and should learn about the five major mathematical topics: Number and arithmetic, geometry, measurement, patterning and algebraic thinking, and data and graphing.

MATHEMATICS AND YOUNG CHILDREN THROUGH HISTORY

Popular opinion often holds that introducing mathematics before first grade, and especially before kindergarten, is a new phenomenon with some rallying against starting "academics" too early. However, mathematics and conflicts about the type of mathematical experiences that should be provided, have a long history in early education (Balfanz, 1999). Researchers have repeatedly witnessed children enjoying pre-mathematical activities. (There are similar recent results for children from different countries

Contemporary Perspectives on Mathematics in Early Childhood Education, pages 67–94
Copyright © 2008 by Information Age Publishing
All rights of reproduction in any form reserved.

and different SES groups, Ginsburg, Ness, & Seo, 2003.) However, others expressed fears of the inappropriateness of mathematics for young children, although these opinions were based on broad social theories or trends, not observation or study (Balfanz, 1999). Bureaucratic and commercial imperatives emerging from the institutionalization of early childhood education quashed most of the promising mathematical movements.

The pervasiveness of mathematics from the work of the founder of kindergarten (including pre-K age children), Friedrich Froebel, (Brosterman, 1997), was largely forgotten or diluted. For example, Froebel's fundamental gifts were largely manipulatives, moving from solids (spheres, cylinders, cubes) to surfaces, lines, and points, then the reverse. His mathematically-oriented occupations with such materials included explorations (e.g., spinning the solids in different orientations, showing how, for example, the spun cube can appear as a cylinder), puzzles, paper folding, and constructions. Edward Thorndike, who wished to emphasize health, replaced the first gift (small spheres) with a toothbrush and the first occupation with "sleep" (Brosterman, 1997).

YOUNG CHILDREN'S KNOWLEDGE OF MATHEMATICS

Children of all ages have some knowledge of mathematics. For example, infants can discriminate between a group of 2 objects and a single object (Clements & Sarama, in press-a). Older children often know more than curriculum developers or teachers give them credit. About 2/3 of low-income children entering preschool can verbally count to 5, and almost half can count to 10 (Clements, Sarama, & Gerber, 2005). About 40% can count small groups of objects (2 to 7) and almost 80% of the children could identify prototypical examples of squares, triangles, and rectangles. Examples of children a year later are similar. For example, 58% of entering kindergartners can count higher than many traditional curriculum materials have as their goal for the end of the kindergarten year (NCES, 2000). They can make patterns, read numerals, recognize shapes, and use nonstandard units of measurement. Almost all, about 94%, can count to 10. Such findings indicate that foundational mathematical knowledge begins during infancy and undergoes extensive development over the early childhood years.

Further, children have an interest in situations and activities that are rich with potential for mathematics. For example, adult observers can classify such free play activities as involving—at least implicitly—ideas such as classification (e.g., putting away blocks in categories), magnitude (e.g., "This isn't big enough to cover the table"), enumeration (e.g., a boy says, "Look! I got one hundred!" and he and a friend count to check that estimate), dynamics (e.g., a girl makes a flat circular shape out of dough), pattern and shape (e.g., a boy puts a double unit block on the rug, two unit blocks on the double block, and continues to build a symmetrical structure), and spatial relations (telling a location or direction) (Seo & Ginsburg, 2004). Play does not guarantee mathematical development, but it offers rich possibilities.

Unfortunately, children's potential for learning mathematics is not well realized for many in the U.S. We know because, even before starting kindergarten, *most* children in the U.S. know substantially less about math than children from other countries. Further, children from low resource communities in the U.S. have the least knowledge of any group studied. This is probably due to the lack of everyday opportunities they have to learn math in their home and school environments (Guberman, 2004). For these children especially, the long-term success of their learning and development requires quality experience during their early "years of promise" (Carnegie Corporation, 1998). Better mathematics education can and should begin early. High-quality education results in learning benefits into elementary school, including in mathematics (Fuson, Smith, & Lo Cicero, 1997; Griffin, 2004).

MATHEMATICS FOR YOUNG CHILDREN

The National Council of Teachers of Mathematics' *Principles and Standards for School Mathematics* (PSSM, NCTM, 2000) organizes content into five areas: number and operations, geometry, measurement, algebra and patterns, and data analysis and probability. A national conference of experts in early childhood, mathematics, mathematics education, psychology, and other fields (Clements, Sarama, & DiBiase, 2004) accepted those five areas and elaborated the critical ideas and emphases for these areas (see Figure 4.1). Both documents emphasized that instruction for young children should focus on number and geometry. Experiences in the other mathematical areas should also be provided, usually in the context of supporting number or geometry understandings and skills. As Figure 4.1 shows, fully integrated are the mathematical processes of communicating, connecting, representing, reasoning, and problem solving. In the following sections we will discuss research in each of the five content areas, with proportionately more attention given to the more important areas.

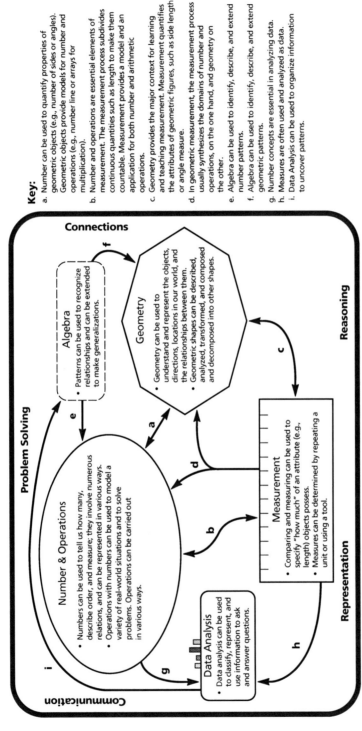

Key:

a. Number can be used to quantify properties of geometric objects (e.g., number of sides or angles). Geometric objects provide models for number and operations (e.g., number line or arrays for multiplication).

b. Number and operations are essential elements of measurement. The measurement process subdivides continuous quantities such as length to make them countable. Measurement provides a model and an application for both number and arithmetic operations.

c. Geometry provides the major context for learning and teaching measurement. Measurement quantifies the attributes of geometric figures, such as side length or angle measure.

d. In geometric measurement, the measurement process usually synthesizes the domains of number and operations, on the one hand, and geometry on the other.

e. Algebra can be used to identify, describe, and extend number patterns.

f. Algebra can be used to identify, describe, and extend geometric patterns.

g. Number concepts are essential in analyzing data.

h. Measures are often used and analyzed as data.

i. Data Analysis can be used to organize information to uncover patterns.

Connections

Problem Solving

Algebra

• Patterns can be used to recognize relationships and can be extended to make generalizations.

Geometry

• Geometry can be used to understand and represent the objects, directions, locations in our world, and the relationships between them.

• Geometric shapes can be described, analyzed, transformed, and composed and decomposed into other shapes.

Number & Operations

• Numbers can be used to tell us how many, describe order, and measure; they involve numerous relations, and can be represented in various ways.

• Operations with numbers can be used to model a variety of real-world situations and to solve problems. Operations can be carried out in various ways.

Measurement

• Comparing and measuring can be used to specify "how much" of an attribute (e.g., length) objects possess.

• Measures can be determined by repeating a unit or using a tool.

Data Analysis

• Data analysis can be used to classify, represent, and use information to ask and answer questions.

Communication

Representation

Reasoning

Figure 4.1. Main mathematics topics for early mathematics (adapted from Clements & Conference Working Group, 2004).

Number and Arithmetic

Number, including beginning arithmetic, is arguably the most important topic. To build a strong number sense, children must develop and link competencies in several areas, especially counting, recognition of the numerosity of small groups, comparing and ordering, and arithmetic.

Counting and Subitizing

Two core numeric competencies are counting objects, and subitizing, or "just seeing" how many objects there are in a group. Evidence for subitizing is found in babies' discrimination of one object from two, and two objects from three (Antell & Keating, 1983; Starkey, Spelke, & Gelman, 1990). This was determined via a *habituation* paradigm in which infants "lose interest" in a series of displays that differ in some ways, but have the same number of objects. For example, if infants are shown a sequence of pictures that contain a small set of objects, differences between pictures, such as different colors or arrangements, initially keep infants' attention. Eventually, however, they *habituate* to the displays; for example, they begin to look at the screen less, and their eyes wander. When they are shown a collection of three circular regions that are similar in attributes to those they had previously seen, their eyes focus intently on this new collection. Such renewed interest when shown a display with a different number of objects provides evidence that they are sensitive to number (Wynn, Bloom, & Chiang, 2002). Thus, infants can discriminate among and match small configurations (1–3) of objects. The experiments also indicate that children's discrimination is limited to such small numbers. Children do not discriminate four objects from five or six until the age of 3 or 4 years (Starkey & Cooper, 1980).

We should not assume children recognize *number* explicitly. Cultural, number-word-based sense of number develops in interaction with, but does not replace (indeed, may always be based on, Gallistel & Gelman, 2005), early intuitive sense of number. That is, the facility with language probably plays a central role in linking relations between different representations and thus making early pre-mathematical cognition numeric (Wiese, 2003).

Of course, number words are even more important to counting. Learning the list of number words to ten requires learning an arbitrary list with no patterns. To count objects, children learn to coordinate this list of words with pointing or moving objects that ties each word said in time to an object to be counted (Baroody, 2004; Fuson, 2004; Steffe, 2004). Children must concentrate and try hard to achieve continuous coordination throughout the whole counting effort. The capstone of this learning, and the necessary building block for all further work with number and operations, is connecting the counting of objects in a collection to the number of objects in that collection. Initially, children may not know how many objects there are in a collection after counting them. If asked how many are there, they typically count again, as if the "how many?" question is a directive to count rather than a request for how many items are in the collection.

In summary, early numerical knowledge has four interrelated aspects: instantly recognizing and naming how many items of a small configuration ("subitizing"; e.g., "That's two fish."), learning the list of number words to at ten and beyond, enumerating objects (i.e., saying number word in correspondence with objects), and understanding that the last number word said when counting refers to how many items have been counted (Clements, Sarama, & DiBiase, 2004). Children gradually connect these four aspects through different kinds of experiences. Each of the four aspects begins with the smallest numbers and gradually includes larger numbers.

Subitizing ability begins simply, but importantly, with naming small collections. From the earliest years, children who are well prepared in number talk with adults and others about "*two* apples" not just "apples" (Hannula, 2005). One particularly rich activity to develop subitizing—which is performed faster—is "Snapshots." The teacher shows a card with a small number of dots to children for 2 seconds (or a small group of objects is revealed and then hidden again under a cloth). Children hold up the number of fingers to show they number they saw. There are many worthwhile variations on this activity. Of course, number and arrangements of dots can change, including arrangements as on dice or dominoes. Finally, have children play snapshots on a computer, which provides exact timing, immediate feedback, and individualization of difficulty level (see Figure 4.2).

Turning to counting, children from ages 2 to 5 years learn more of the system of number words ("one, two, three,...") due to a desire to count larger collections and a curiosity about the number word system itself

(a)   (b)   (c)

Figure 4.2.   An early level of the activity "Snapshots" from *Building Blocks*. (a) Children are shown an arrangement of dots for 2 seconds. (b) They are then asked to click on the corresponding numeral. They can "peek" for 2 more seconds if necessary. (c) They are given feedback verbally and by seeing the dots again.

(Baroody, 2004; Fuson, 1988, 2004; Griffin, 2004; Steffe, 2004). They learn the verbal number words to ten as they do general language or the ABCs. So, effective teachers develop counting skills with rhythms, songs, and other daily activities, such as counting stairs.

Counting objects accurately and meaningfully takes considerable amount of experience. Thus, large group activities such Simon Says (e.g., "Simon says jump up 10 times") can be an effective and efficient use of instructional time. Such games are a fertile ground for the growth of mathematical reasoning, especially strategic reasoning, and autonomy, or independence, as well as number ideas.

Games such as Memory ("Concentration") can be used to match sets, or sets to numerals, as they simultaneously encourage children to use memory strategies and to gain experience with rows and columns. Computer versions can be motivating and played alone or in pairs. "Race" or "path" board games usually include generating a number with dice or a spinner, and moving the number of spaces indicated. This provides a different, complementary way of making sense of numbers, closely connected to measurement (Clements & Sarama, in press-b; Griffin, 2004).

A variety of real (counting for attendance) and fanciful (make-believe setting for word problems) settings can be used to encourage meaningful counting. As necessary, have children touch objects as they count and have them counting objects organized into a row at first. Rhythms are often helpful as well. As they gain competence, children should *use* the results of their counting; for example, in voting, or getting the right number of scissors for the children at a table.

In summary, subitizing and counting are related but distinct methods of quantification. In both, mathematical knowledge develops not just as increasing skill, but qualitatively. For example, children's ability to *"see small collections"* grows from perceptual, to imagined, to numerical patterns (Steffe, 1992). Perceptual patterns are those the child can, and must, immediately see or hear, such as domino patterns, finger patterns, or auditory patterns (e.g., three beats). Later, children develop the ability to visualize, or imagine, such patterns. Finally, children develop numerical patterns, which they can operate on, as when they can mentally decompose a five pattern into two and three and then put them back together to make five again. These types of patterns may "look the same" on the surface, but are qualitatively different. All can support mathematical growth and thinking, but numerical patterns are the most powerful. Kathy Richardson (2004) tells that for years she thought her children understood number patterns on dice. However, when she finally asked them to reproduce the patterns, she was amazed that they did not use the same number of counters, matching a dice five with an "X" arrangement that did not have five dots. Thus, without appropriate tasks and close observation, she did not see that her children did not even accurately imagine patterns, and their patterns were not numerical. Such insights are critical in understanding and promoting children's mathematical thinking.

Comparing and Ordering

Human beings naturally make perceptual judgments of relative quantities. Infants begin to construct equivalence relations between sets by establishing correspondences (spatial, temporal, or numerical) as early as 10 months and at most by 24 months of age (Langer, Rivera, Schlesinger, & Wakeley, 2003). At 3 years of age, children can identify as equivalent or nonequivalent static (simultaneously presented) collections consisting of a few (1 to about 4) highly similar items (e.g., Huttenlocher, Jordan, & Levine, 1994; Mix, 1999). For instance, they can identify ▯▯▯ and ▯�[▯]▯ as equal and different from ▯▯ or [▯]▯ (the researchers describe this as a non-verbal competence, but children may have subitized the arrays). At 3.5 years, they can match different homogeneous visual sets and match sequential and static sets that contain highly similar items. At 4.5, they can nonverbally match equivalent collections of random objects and dots—a heterogeneous collection and a collection of dissimilar items.

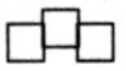

Children need to build on these early intuitive abilities and learn the cultural methods of matching and counting to find out more dependably which quantity is more.

Children should develop counting words into a kind of "mental number line" by the age of 5 or 6. They can then count each of two collections and use their mental number line to determine which number comes later and thus which collection is larger. This is surprisingly challenging for some children, who may count the sets, recognize the number is the same, but still maintain that one set has more (Piaget & Szeminska, 1952). Indeed, children from 4 to 5 years of age do compare set sizes on the basis of misleading length cues, even when the situation is set up to encourage counting (Fuson, 1988).

Research has identified some aspects of effective educational interventions for comparing numbers. One main implication is that young children need to learn about the significance of the results of counting. To help them generalize, teachers should provide a variety of meaningful tasks and situations in which counting is a relevant strategy and inferences must be made. Prompting children to count in these situations, such as when comparing sets or producing equivalent sets, is often helpful (Fuson, 1988). Children have to learn that the same number implies the same numerosity and that different numbers imply (and necessitate) different numerosities (Cowan, 1987). That is, many children up to first grade need to learn about the significance of the results of counting in different situations, such as comparing sets or producing equivalent sets (Nunes & Bryant, 1996). Further, they may not have a concept of space that is sufficiently articulated and unitized to reconcile the perceptual evidence and numerical interpretation of the situation (Becker, 1989).

Finding out *how many more* (or less/fewer) there are in one collection than another is more challenging. Children have to understand that the number of elements in the collection with fewer items is contained in the number of items in the collection with more items. That is, they have to mentally construct a "part" of the larger collection (equivalent to the smaller collection) that is not visually present. They then have to determine the "other part" or the larger collection and find out how many elements are in this "left-over amount."

In instruction, children should be able to use matching or counting to determine if two groups of the same number of objects, or, if not, which has more. As one example, number cards provide experiences with counting and comparison. Card games can be used or adapted for learning mathematics and reasoning, such as "Compare" ("War"), Odd Card ("Old Maid"), and Go Fish (for example, children can "fish" for matching numbers). Games such as that in Figure 4.3 also involve comparison of number.

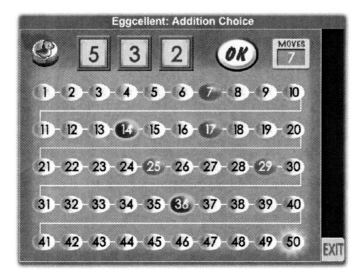

Figure 4.3. A computer version of a race game for learning arithmetic from the *Building Blocks* software package (Clements & Sarama, 2007). Students use strategies to identify which of two sums will enable them to reach the final space on a game board in the fewest number of moves. Often that means the larger of two sums, but sometimes, the smaller will let the player hit a positive or avoid a negative "action space."

The situational language in comparing situations in which children agree to find out how many more in one group that another is complex. Children need considerable experience solving comparing problems and hearing and telling comparing stories. These are arithmetic strategies, to which we turn.

ARITHMETIC: ADDING TO/TAKING AWAY AND COMPOSING AND DECOMPOSING NUMBER

Educational practice, past and present, often takes a skills hierarchy view that arithmetic follows counting and other simple work with number and therefore is beyond children's grasp until about first grade. However, decades ago, researchers illustrated the possibility of arithmetic competence in children before kindergarten (Gelman & Gallistel, 1978; Groen & Resnick, 1977; Hughes, 1981). Young children use two different strategies to solve addition problems, reflecting the difference—and also the relationships—between counting and subitizing.

Adding to and taking away. Even toddlers notice the effects of increasing or decreasing small collections by one item. For example, 5-month-olds gaze longer when an incorrect result is revealed after seeing 1 or 2 dolls hidden behind a screen and a hand place another doll behind the screen (Wynn, 1992). This knowledge grows throughout the early years to the point that children can solve problems such as four and two more by counting. For example, children count objects for the initial collection of six items, count out two more items, and then count the items of the two collections together. These children naturally use such counting methods to solve story situations as long as they understand the language in the story. Children then build on these solution methods. For example, when items are hidden from view, children may put up fingers sequentially while saying, "1, 2, 3, 4, 5, 6" and then continue on, putting up two more fingers, "7, 8. Eight." Children abbreviate these counting methods even further. Rather than putting up fingers sequentially to count the six hidden items, children who can count-on simply say, "S-i-x—7, 8. Eight." Such counting on is a landmark in children's numerical development. It is not a rote step. It requires mentally putting the six inside the total, eight.

Counting on when increasing collections and the corresponding counting-back-from when decreasing collections are powerful numerical strategies for children. However, they are only beginning strategies. In the case where the amount of increase is unknown, children count-up-to to find the unknown amount. If six items are increased so that there are now nine items, children may find the amount of increase by counting, "S-i-x; 7, 8, 9. Three." And if nine items are decreased so that six remain, children may count from nine down to six as follows: "Nine; 8, 7, 6. Three." However, counting backwards, especially more than three counts, is difficult for children (Fuson et al., 1997). When children realize that they can find the amount of decrease by putting the items back with the six and counting from six up to nine, they establish that subtraction is the inversion of addition and from that time on, addition can be used instead of subtraction. Children in many parts of the world learn to count up to the total to solve a subtraction situation because they realize that it is much easier. For example, the story "8 apples on the table. The children ate 5. How many now?" could be solved by thinking, "I took away 5 from those 8, so 6, 7, 8 (raising a finger with each count), that's 3 more left in the 8." This is another landmark in children's numerical development, and it is at this point that children can be encouraged to use strategic reasoning. For example, some children go on to invent recomposing and decomposing methods using doubles (6 + 7 is 6 + 6 = 12. 12 + 1 more = 13).

There are many situations that call for solving word problems with such strategies. Children need to be presented with a range of addition and subtraction types and to be encouraged to invent, adapt, use, discuss, and explain a variety of solution strategies that are meaningful to them. In addition, many games provide practice in addition and subtraction, for example, "War" can be changed into "Double War" in which each child flips over two cards and the highest sum wins. Again, race games—now involving addition—can also be useful in developing arithmetic strategies and mathematical reasoning (see Figure 4.3).

Composing and decomposing numbers. Another way to add or subtract is by combining and separating. They strengthen children's concepts of "parts" and "wholes." For example, children can develop the ability to recognize that the numbers 2 and 3 are "hiding inside" 5, as are the numbers 4 and 1. Kindergartners can learn to separate a group into parts in various ways and then to count to produce all of the number "partners" of a given number; for example, 6 as 5 + 1, 4 + 2, or 3 + 3. They can use such combinations in solving problems.

Children can develop composing and decomposing operations by bringing together two aspects of their early numerical knowledge: "seeing numbers" (visualizing little numbers inside bigger numbers, including seeing 3 as 1 and 1 and 1) and counting. Children can come to see all of the different number "partners" for a given number by working with objects (e.g., 6 objects). Within a story context (e.g., animals in 2 different pens), children can separate the 6 objects into different partners that make 6 (5 and 1; 4 and 2; 3 and 3 are all 6-partners). Two kinds of special patterns are especially powerful and easy for children to see: doubles (3 + 3), which eventually allow access to combinations such as 3 + 4 (one more than 3 + 3), and fives (6 made as 5 + 1, 7 as 5 + 2, etc.), which allow for decomposition into fives and tens. Such strategies develop number sense but also meet another major goal in early childhood mathematics—strategic reasoning. Snapshot activities, presenting two groups of dots, can be helpful in developing these abilities.

Integrating counting and composing. Children can develop sophisticated composing and decomposing operations by bringing together two aspects of their early numerical knowledge: "seeing numbers" (visualizing little numbers inside bigger numbers, including seeing 3 as 1 and 1 and 1) and counting. Children can come to see all of the different number "partners" for a given number by working with objects (e.g., 6 objects). Within a story context (e.g., animals in 2 different pens), children can separate the 6 objects into different partners that make 6 (5 and 1; 4 and 2; 3 and 3 are all 6-partners). Two kinds of special patterns are especially powerful and easy for children to see: doubles (3 + 3, 7 + 7), which allow access to combinations such as 7 + 8, and fives (6 made as 5 + 1, 7 as 5 + 2, etc.), which allow for decomposition into fives and tens. These number patterns and the number ten can later in Grade 1 or 2 become the basis for adding and subtracting numbers by recomposing. Recomposing around ten is a powerful and general method taught in many parts of the world (e.g., 8 + 6 = 8 + 2 + 4 = 10 + 4 = 14. These methods are especially useful in multidigit addition and subtraction, which work with tens in each position. These recomposing methods use the embedded numbers children learned earlier. In addition, the arithmetic principles of commutativity (5 + 2 = 2 + 5) and associativity ((5 + 2) + 8 = 5 + (2 + 8)) can be developed and discussed in such problem-solving sessions.

Such strategies develop number sense but also meet another major goal in early childhood mathematics—strategic reasoning. If children interpret 15 − 8 as finding how many numbers from 8 up to and including 15, they can reason strategically: 8 and 2 more are 10, and 10 and 5 more are 15, so adding 5 and 2 gives the difference. Strategic reasoning empowers children and adds enormously to their sense of numerical competence.

Children are fascinated with "big numbers," and elaborating their counting strategies to find sums and differences of two-digit numbers enhances this fascination. For example, to find the sum of 28 and 16, children might to count, "Twenty-eight; thirty-eight, 39, 40, 41, 42, 43, 44." And, to find the difference of eighty-one and thirty-five, children might count, "81; 71, 61, 51; 50, 49, 48, 47, 46." Some children also count from thirty-five up to eighty-one by tens and ones; others find many other strategies. Counting by tens and ones to find sums and differences of two-digit numbers is not meant to replace computational algorithms. Instead, these counting strategies are meant to enhance the children's sense of numerical competence.

Strategies involving counting by tens and ones can be altered along with children's developing understanding of numeration and place value. In fact, altering these sophisticated counting strategies is a natural site for developing children's understanding of numeration and place value. Rather than count by tens and ones to find the sum of 38 and 47, children could decompose 38 into its tens and ones and 47 into its tens and ones. This encourages the children to reason with ten as a unit like the unit of one and compose the tens together into 7 tens, or 70. After composing the ones together into 15 ones, they have transformed the sum into the sum of 70 and 15. To find this sum, the children take a 10 from the 15 and give it to the 70, so the sum is 80 and 5 more, or 85. Strategies like this are modifications of counting strategies involving ten and one just like strategies for finding the sum of 8 and 7 (children who know that 8 and 2 are 10 take 2 from 7 and give it to 8. So, 10 and 5. 15) are modifications of counting strategies involving only one.

GEOMETRY

Geometry and spatial reasoning are inherently important because they involve "grasping...that space in which the child lives, breathes and moves...that space that the child must learn to know, explore, conquer, in order to live, breathe and move better in it" (Freudenthal, in NCTM, 1989, p. 48).

Shape

Through their everyday activity, children build both intuitive and explicit knowledge of geometric shapes. We asked children from 4 to 6 years of age to identify shapes in collections of shapes on paper (Clements et al., 1999); replication studies have been conducted in Singapore (Yin, 2003) and Turkey (Aslan, 2004). Children were very accurate identifying circles and non-circles, scoring about 92%, 96%, and 99% for 4-, 5-, and 6-year-olds, respectively on the paper measures. They scored about 82%, 86%, and 91% on squares, about 57%, 58% and 61% on triangles, and about 51%, 51%, and 59% on rectangles. Children tended to accept triangular forms with curved sides and reject triangles that were too "long," "bent over," or "point not at the top. " Children tended to accept "long" parallelograms or right trapezoids as rectangles.

In follow-up study, we asked children to identify manipulable shapes cut from wood (Hannibal & Clements, 2000). The shapes were in different orientations and contexts. For example, sometimes we had the children handle the shapes, and other times we asked them to identify shapes in either a "fixed rectangular frame" or a round hoop. Children responded differently to different tasks. First, when we placed the wood shapes into a hoop, children were less likely to notice or care about whether they were "long"; that is, not having a rectangular frame of reference seemed to affect what shapes they accepted. Second, when we included obvious non-examples, such as circles, in with a group of triangular shapes, children accepted more types of triangles and more "pointy" forms that were *not* triangles. Similarly, children accepted more ovals as circles when shapes were drawn inside each other. Third, children often changed their decisions when asked to justify their choices and, usually, more of their decisions were correct. For example, one five-year-old increased her score by 26 percentage points when asked to explain her choices.

Children sometimes can name attributes that they do not fully understand. For example, a teacher asked children to stand on a triangle (there were several taped outlines of shapes on the floor). One child immediately stood on the triangle and explained, "It has 3 sides and 3 angles." When asked what she meant by three angles she said, "I don't know."

Of course, they have a lot they can learn, but most curricula do not teach them much in the preschool and primary grades (Clements, 2004; Lehrer et al., 1993). For example, most children can recognize and name some familiar 2-D shapes at 4 years of age, but they do not add to this knowledge much through elementary school. One study found that kindergarten children had a great deal of knowledge about shapes and matching shapes before instruction began. Their teacher tended to elicit and verify this prior knowledge but did not add content or develop new knowledge. That is, about two-thirds of the interactions had children repeat what they already knew in a repetitious format as in the following exchange (Thomas, 1982). The teacher asked, "Could you tell us what type of shape that is?" Children responded, "A square." The teacher responded only, "OK. It's a square," and immediately moved on. Most teachers did not add new content. When they did, however, some were incorrect, such as saying that "all diamonds are squares." Others were, at best, unfortunate, such as telling a child that "two triangles put together always make a square" and "a square cut in half always gives two triangles."

Instead, teachers are more effective if they guide children to build new knowledge about the parts and properties of shapes. The parts include sides and angles. Children can observe and check if a four-sided shape's sides are all the same length—if so, it is a rhombus. They can then check if the shape's angles are all equal and all right angles—if so, it is a square. In general, children will learn richer concepts about shape if their educational environment includes four features: varied examples and nonexamples, discussions about shapes and their characteristics, a wider variety of shape classes, and interesting tasks. Quality curricula and teaching ensure that children experience many different examples of a type of shape, so that they do not form narrow ideas about any class of shapes. Showing nonexamples and comparing them to similar examples help focus children's attention on the critical attributes of shapes and prompts discussion. For example, they might compare a chevron (△) or kite (△) to a triangle (△). These discussions should encourage children's descriptions while encouraging the development of language. Children can learn to explain why a shape belongs to a certain category—"It has three straight sides" or does not belong (⟍ "The sides aren't straight!"). Eventually, they can internalize such arguments; for example, saying (about ____), "It is a weird, long, triangle, but it has three straight sides!"

Curricula and teachers should include a wide variety of shape classes. Early childhood curricula traditionally introduce shapes in four basic level categories: circle, square, triangle, and rectangle. The unfortunate notion that a square is not a rectangle is rooted by age 5. Instead, children should encounter many examples of squares and rectangles, varying orientation, size, and so forth, including squares as examples of rectangles. As an example of how computer might facilitate such thinking, 5-year-old Chris is making shapes with a computer (Clements, Battista, & Sarama, 2001). He has been typing "R" (for rectangle) and then two numbers for the side lengths. This time he chooses 9 and 9. He sees a square and laughs.

> **Adult**: Now, what do the two 9s mean for the rectangle?
> **Chris**: I don't know, now! Maybe I'll name this a square rectangle!

Chris uses his invented terminology repeatedly on succeeding days. In a similar vein, children should experiment with and describe a wider variety of shapes, including but not limited to semicircles, quadrilaterals, trapezoids (◁▷), rhombi (▱, informally called diamonds), and hexagons.

This brings us to our fourth feature of a high-quality, early childhood geometry environment—interesting tasks. Activities that promote reflection and discussion include building models of shapes from components. Children might explore a shape secretly put into a "feely box." At first, they would match it to one of a visible collection of shapes. Later, they could name it, and still later, describe it so that *others* could name it.

As another example, one teacher had challenged her kindergartners to make various shapes with their bodies (Sarama, Clements, & Vukelic, 1996). Two boys tried to do the rhombus. They sat down facing each other and stretched their legs apart. With their feet touching each other, they made a very good rhombus. One of the children in the circle suggested "if they put another child in the middle, they would make two triangles." Immediately the children called Ray into service, because he was the smallest, and they asked him to scrunch in the middle. Later, they tried the hexagon. After a brief discussion, the boy who suggested making a hexagon called on five more children. Under his direction, the children began to lie down on the floor. They all freely used the terms "horizontal," "vertical," and "diagonal" to tell each other how they should be lying on the floor. They created a good representation of a regular hexagon.

Putting Together Shapes

The ability to describe, use, and visualize the effects of putting together and taking apart shapes is important because the creating, composing, and decomposing *units* and *higher-order* units are fundamental mathematics (Clements et al., 1997; Reynolds & Wheatley, 1996; Steffe & Cobb, 1988). Further, there is transfer: Composition of shapes supports children's ability to compose and decompose numbers (Clements et al., 1996).

Young children move through levels in the composition and decomposition of 2-D figures. From lack of competence in composing geometric shapes, they gain abilities to combine shapes into pictures, then synthesize combinations of shapes into new shapes (composite shapes), eventually anticipating making larger shapes out of smaller shapes and combining those composite shapes, which they then think of as new units, or shapes. The middle column in Figure 4.4 describes these levels.

Age	Developmental Progression	Instructional Tasks	
0–3	**Pre-Composer.** Manipulates shapes as individuals, but is unable to combine them to compose a larger shape.	These levels are not instructional goal levels. However, several preparatory activities may orient 3–4-year-old children to the task, and move them toward the next levels that do represent (some) competence In "Shape Pictures," children play with pattern blocks and Shape Sets, often making simple pictures.	
	Make a picture	In the "Mystery Toys" series of software activities, the stage is set for this learning trajectory. Children only match or identify shapes, but the *result* of their work is a pictured made up of other shapes—a demonstration of composition.	
4	**Piece Assembler.** Makes pictures in which each shape represents a unique role (e.g., one shape for each body part) and shapes touch. Fills simple "Pattern Block Puzzles" using trial and error.	In the first "Pattern Block Puzzles" tasks, each shape is not only outlined, but touches other shapes only at a point, making the matching as easy as possible. Children merely match pattern blocks to the outlines.	
	Make a picture	Then, the puzzles moved to those that combine shapes by matching their sides, but still mainly serve separate roles.	

Figure 4.4.   A developmental sequence for putting together shapes, including instructional tasks (from Clements, Wilson, & Sarama, 2004).

Age	Developmental Progression	Instructional Tasks
5	**Picture Maker.** Puts several shapes together to make one part of a picture (e.g., two shapes for one arm). Uses trial and error and does not anticipate creation of new geometric shape. Chooses shapes using "general shape" or side length. Fills "easy" "Pattern Block Puzzles" that suggest the placement of each shape (but note below that they child is trying to put a square in the puzzle where its right angles will not fit). *Make a picture*	These levels are not instructional goal levels. However, several preparatory activities may orient 3–4-year-old children to the task, and move them toward the next levels that do represent (some) competence In "Shape Pictures," children play with pattern blocks and Shape Sets, often making simple pictures. The "Pattern Block Puzzles" at this level start with those where several shapes are combined to make one "part," but internal lines are still available. Later puzzles in the sequence require combining shapes to fill one or more regions, without the guidance of internal line segments. "Piece Puzzler 3" is a similar computer activity. In the first tasks, children must concatenate shapes, but are helped with internal line segments in most cases; these internal segments are faded in subsequent puzzles.
	Shape Composer. Composes shapes with anticipation ("I know what will fit!"). Chooses shapes using angles as well as side lengths. Rotation and flipping are used intentionally to select and place shapes. In the "Pattern Block Puzzles" below, all angles are correct, and patterning is evident. *Make a picture*	The "Pattern Block Puzzles" and "Piece Puzzler" activities have no internal guidelines and larger areas; therefore, children must compose shapes accurately.
6–8	**Substitution Composer.** Makes new shapes out of smaller shapes and uses trial and error to substitute groups of shapes for other shapes to create new shapes in different ways. *Make a picture with intentional substitutions*	At this level, children solve "Pattern Block Puzzles" in which they must substitute shapes to fill an outline in different ways. "Piece Puzzler" tasks are similar; the new task here is to solve the same puzzle in several different ways.

Figure 4.4. (continued)   A developmental sequence for putting together shapes, including instructional tasks (from Clements, Wilson, & Sarama, 2004)

Instructionally, free play with various shape sets, from building blocks to tangrams to pattern blocks, is helpful. A more targeted activity that helps young children develop these abilities is solving pattern block or tangram puzzles. The last column in Figure 4.4 shows example puzzles that would be appropriate to use at different levels of competence.

As with 2-D figures, children need more and richer experiences with identifying, describing, and putting together 3-D figures. Manipulation and play with solids should lead to discussions of their overall shape ("it's like an ice-cream cone") and attributes ("all these are round and roll"). Construction activities involving nets (foldout shapes of solids) help children learn to discriminate between 2-D and 3-D figures.

Building with blocks, of course, provides rich potential for learning about 3-D figures. Children may adjust two cylinders so that the distance between them just equaled the length of a long block. They estimated how many more blocks they needed to finish a surface. They estimated that they needed eight blocks if each of four sizes of a square were covered with two blocks (Seo & Ginsburg, 2004). In addition, block building provides a view at children's initial abilities to *compose* 3-D objects (as well as their formation of a system of logic, cf. Forman, 1982). As they do with 2-D shapes, children initially build structures from simple components and later explicitly synthesize 3-D shapes into higher-order 3-D shapes. Children either engage in little systematic organization of objects or show little interest in stacking in their first year (Forman, 1982; Kamii, Miyakawa, & Kato, 2004; Stiles & Stern, 2001). Stacking begins at 1 year, thus showing use of the spatial relationship of "on" (Kamii et al., 2004). The next-to relation develops at about 1.5 years (Stiles-Davis, 1988). At 2 years, children place each successive block congruently on or next to the one previously placed (Stiles-Davis, 1988), appearing to recognize that blocks stacked vertically do not fall. At this point, children begin to reflect (think back) and anticipate (Kamii et al., 2004). At 3 to 4 years of age, children regularly build vertical and horizontal components within a building (Stiles & Stern, 2001). At 4 years, they use multiple spatial relations, extending in multiple directions and with multiple points of contact among components, showing flexibility in how they generate and integrate parts of the structure. Some children begin to build towers with all blocks; for example, by composing the triangular blocks, making subparts to coordinate with the whole (Kamii et al., 2004).

TRANSFORMATIONS AND SYMMETRY

Before the primary years, children may be limited in their ability to mentally transform shapes, but they can do so in solving simple problems, at least by the age of 5 or 6 years. Further, they can learn to slide, turn, and flip objects (physical or virtual), and a curriculum rich with such experiences, including physical manipulatives and computer tools, help them develop their mental imagery. They can flip shapes to determine whether they are symmetric.

Infants as young as four months dishabituate more quickly to symmetric figures than asymmetric figures, at least for vertical symmetry (Bornstein, Ferdinandsen, & Gross, 1981; Bornstein & Krinsky, 1985; Ferguson, Aminoff, & Gentner, 1998; Fisher, Ferdinandsen, & Bornstein, 1981; Humphrey & Humphrey, 1995). A preference for vertical symmetry seems to develop between 4 and 12 months of age and vertical bilateral symmetry remains easier for children than horizontal symmetry, which in turn is easier than diagonal symmetries (Genkins, 1975; Palmer, 1985; Palmer & Hemenway, 1978). Explicitly recognizing and constructing symmetric figures is well within the reach of primary grade children. Indeed, children often prefer to create designs with both line () and rotational () symmetry with manipulatives and in other art media. They can learn to draw the other half of a geometric figure to create a symmetric figure and identify lines of symmetry. Computer environments can be particularly helpful in learning symmetry and especially transformations (Clements et al., 2001). Directing the computer to creation of symmetric figures, testing symmetry by flipping figures via commands, and discussing these actions apparently encouraged children to build richer and more general images of symmetric relations. Children had to abstract and externally represent their actions in a more explicit and precise fashion in computer activities than, say, in forehand drawing of symmetric figures.

In summary, for people of all ages, symmetric shapes are detected faster, discriminated more accurately, and often remembered better than asymmetrical ones (Bornstein et al., 1981). However, many explicit concepts of symmetry are not firmly established before 12 years of age (Genkins, 1975).

Locations and Directions

Along with small shapes or numbers, children have considerable intuitive knowledge of the shape of their environments. With guidance, they can learn to mathematize the informal knowledge about getting around their school or other area. They can learn beginning ideas about direction, perspective, distance, symbolization, and location. Even young children can use and create simple maps. Children as young as 2 years of age can connect oblique and eye-level views of the same space, finding their mother behind a barrier after observing the situation from above (Rieser et al., 1982). In another study, 2.5-year-olds could locate a toy shown a picture of the space (DeLoache, 1987; DeLoache & Burns, 1994).

Some studies have identified 5 to 6 years of age as a good time to provide informal experiences, especially those that emphasize building imagery from physical movement, and to introduce learning of simple maps (Clements & Sarama, in press-a). For example, they might use blocks to make a model of the classroom. Alternatively, they could use blocks and toys to make simple maps of routes around the school or playground. Primary grade child can make drawings and start to add measures, a topic to which we now turn.

MEASUREMENT

Young children naturally encounter and discuss quantities, such as comparing clay "snakes" to see whose is longer (Seo & Ginsburg, 2004). They compare two objects directly and recognize equality or inequality. At this point, they are ready to learn to measure, connecting number to the quantity.

Many curricula lead through a sequence of comparing objects directly, then measuring with nonstandard units such as paper clips, then with standard units. Recent research suggests that following this sequence rigidly may not be best. Children benefit from using objects such as centimeter cubes and rulers to measure as their ideas and skills develop (Clements, 1999). Not only do children prefer using rulers, but also they can use them meaningfully and in combination with manipulable units to develop understanding of length measurement. Even if they do not understand rulers fully or use them accurately, they can use rulers *along with* manipulable units such as centimeter cubes and arbitrary units to develop their measurement skills. This is not to say that we should return to simple goals of "using a conventional ruler accurately." Rather, we use many materials flexibly to develop conceptual building blocks of measurement.

Children should learn to measure with meaning. Very young children naturally encounter and discuss quantities in their play (Ginsburg, Inoue, & Seo, 1999). They first learn to use words that represent quantity or magnitude of a certain attribute. Facilitating this language is important not only to develop communication abilities, but for the development of mathematical concepts. Simply using labels such as "Daddy/Mommy/Baby" and "big/little/tiny" helped children as young as 3 years to represent and order items by length, even in the face of distracting visual factors. Language provides an invitation to form comparisons and an aid to memory (Rattermann & Gentner, 1998).

Informal activities should establish the attribute of length and develop concepts such as "longer," "shorter," and "equal in length" and strategies such as comparison. Children should make such comparisons for a purpose, as in comparing the lengths of two objects. For example, you might ask whether a doorway is wide enough for a table to go through. This involves an indirect comparison (and transitive reasoning) and therefore emphases problem solving and thinking rather than rote procedures.

Children might develop increasingly accurate measuring procedures by repeating a unit in many similar situations. For example, they lay down manipulatives such as popsicle sticks without leaving spaces to measure the lengths of tables. As long as the tasks and interactions with teachers and peers emphasize meaningful use, rulers can also be used (Clements, 1999). Teachers can help children begin to develop concepts and procedures such as starting at zero and focusing on the lengths of the units rather than only the numbers on the ruler.

PATTERNING AND ALGEBRAIC THINKING

Algebra begins with a search for patterns. Identifying patterns helps bring order and predictability to seemingly unorganized situations and allows us to generalize beyond the information we have. Although all preschoolers engage in pattern-related activities and recognize patterns in their everyday environment, research has revealed that an abstract understanding of patterns develops gradually during the early childhood years (Clarke, Clarke, & Cheeseman, in press).

By the age of 4 or 5, children can learn to extend and create simple linear patterns. They can learn to recognize the relationship between patterns with nonidentical objects or between different representations of the same pattern (e.g., between visual patterns and movement patterns). This helps children generalize and reveal common underlying structures. Beginning in kindergarten, children must learn to identify the core unit (e.g., AB) that either repeats (ABABAB) or "grows" (ABAABAAAB), and then use it to generate both these types of patterns.

Preschoolers also engage in rhythmic and musical patterns. They can add more complicated, deliberate patterns, such as "clap, clap, slap; clap, clap slap..." to their repertoires. They can talk about these patterns, representing the pattern with words. Kindergartners enjoy making up new motions to fit the same pattern, so clap, clap slap...is transformed to jump, jump, fall down; jump, jump, fall down...and soon symbolized as an AABAAB pattern. Extending into the primary grades, children can describe such patterns with numbers (two of something, then one of something else"). Two central themes of primary grade work are making generalizations and using symbols to represent mathematical ideas and to represent and solve problems (Carpenter et al., 1999). For example, children might generalize that when you add zero to a number the sum is always that number or when you add three numbers it does not matter which two you add first (Carpenter et al., 1999). Thus, students in the primary grades can learn to formulate, represent, and reason about generalizations and conjectures, although their justifications do not always adequately validate the conjectures they create. These are the first clear links among patterns, number, and algebra.

DATA ANALYSIS: CLASSIFICATION AND GRAPHING

Data analysis contains one big idea: Classifying, organizing, representing, and using information to ask and answer questions. The developmental continuum for data analysis includes growth in classifying and counting and in data representations. Children initially learn to sort objects and quantify their groups.

After gathering data to answer questions, children's initial representations often do not use categories. Their interest in data is on the particulars (Russell, 1991). For example, they might simply list each child in their class and each child's response to a question. They can learn to classify these responses and represent data according to categories.

To develop classifying and graphing abilities, teachers might ask children to sort a collection of buttons into those with one to four holes and count to find out how many they have in each of the four groups. To do this, they focus on and describe the attributes of objects, classifying according to those attributes, and quantify the resulting categories. Children eventually became capable of simultaneously classifying and counting; for example, counting the number of colors in a group of objects, as described previously.

To move children from graphing particular to classify and graph responses, children should use physical objects to make graphs (objects such as shoes or sneakers, then manipulatives such as connecting cubes), then picture graphs, and, finally, bar graphs that include grid lines to facilitate reading frequencies (Friel, Curcio, & Bright, 2001). They can compare parts of the data, make statements about the data as a whole, and generally determine whether the graphs answer the questions posed initially. By second grade, most children should be able to organize and display data through both simple numerical summaries such as counts, tables, and tallies, and graphical displays, including picture graphs, line plots, and bar graphs (Russell, 1991). They can compare parts of the data, make statements about the data as a whole, and generally determine whether the graphs answer the questions posed initially.

CONCLUSIONS

Our world can be better understood with mathematics. Early childhood is a good time for children to become interested in counting, sorting, building shapes, patterning, measuring, and estimating. Quality preschool mathematics is not elementary arithmetic pushed down onto younger children. Instead, it invites children to experience mathematics as they play in, describe, and think about their world.

NOTE

1.   This chapter was based upon work supported in part by the National Science Foundation under Grant No. ESI-9730804 to D. H. Clements and J. Sarama "Building Blocks—Foundations for Mathematical Thinking, Pre-Kindergarten to Grade 2: Research-based Materials Development" and in part by the Institute of Educational Sciences (U.S. Department of Education, under the Interagency Educational Research Initiative, or IERI, a collaboration of the IES, NSF, and NICHHD) under Grant No. R305K05157 to D. H. Clements, J. Sarama, and J. Lee, "Scaling Up TRIAD: Teaching Early Mathematics for Understanding with Trajectories and Technologies.

REFERENCES

Antell, S. E., & Keating, D. P. (1983). Perception of numerical invariance in neonates. *Child Development, 54*, 695–701.

Aslan, D. (2004). *The investigation of 3 to 6 year-olds preschool children's recognition of basic geometric shapes and the criteria they employ in distinguishing one shape group from the other (Anaokuluna devam eden 3–6 yas grubu çocuklarina temel geometrik sekilleri tanimalari ve sekilleri ayirtetmede kullandiklari kriterlerin incelenmesi).* Unpublished Masters, Cukurova University, Adana, Turkey.

Balfanz, R. (1999). Why do we teach young children so little mathematics? Some historical considerations. In J. V. Copley (Ed.), *Mathematics in the early years* (pp. 3–10). Reston, VA: National Council of Teachers of Mathematics.

Baroody, A. J. (2004). The developmental bases for early childhood number and operations standards. In D. H. Clements, J. Sarama, & A.-M. DiBiase (Eds.), *Engaging young children in mathematics: Standards for early childhood mathematics education* (pp. 173–219). Mahwah, NJ: Erlbaum.

Becker, J. (1989). Preschoolers' use of number words to denote one-to-one correspondence. *Child Development, 60*, 1147–1157.

Bornstein, M. H., Ferdinandsen, K., & Gross, C. G. (1981). Perception of symmetry in infancy. *Developmental Psychology, 17*, 82–86.

Bornstein, M. H., & Krinsky, S. J. (1985). Perception of symmetry in infancy: The salience of vertical symmetry and the perception of pattern wholes. *Journal of Experimental Child Psychology, 39*, 1–19.

Brosterman, N. (1997). *Inventing kindergarten.* New York: Harry N. Abrams.

Carnegie Corporation. (1998, June 13). *Years of promise: A comprehensive learning strategy for America's children.* from http://www.carnegie.org/execsum.html

Carpenter, T. P., Fennema, E. H., Franke, M. L., Levi, L., & Empson, S. B. (1999). *Children's mathematics: Cognitively guided instruction.* Portsmouth, NH: Heinemann.

Clarke, B. A., Clarke, D. M., & Cheeseman, J. (in press). The mathematical knowledge and understanding young children bring to school. *Mathematics Education Research Journal.*

Clements, D. H. (1999). Teaching length measurement: Research challenges. *School Science and Mathematics, 99*(1), 5–11.

Clements, D. H. (2004). Geometric and spatial thinking in early childhood education. In D. H. Clements, J. Sarama, & A.-M. DiBiase (Eds.), *Engaging young children in mathematics: Standards for early childhood mathematics education* (pp. 267–297). Mahwah, NJ: Erlbaum.

Clements, D. H., Battista, M. T., & Sarama, J. (2001). Logo and geometry. *Journal for Research in Mathematics Education Monograph Series, 10.*

Clements, D. H., Battista, M. T., Sarama, J., & Swaminathan, S. (1997). Development of students' spatial thinking in a unit on geometric motions and area. *The Elementary School Journal, 98*, 171–186.

Clements, D. H., & Conference Working Group. (2004). Part one: Major themes and recommendations. In D. H. Clements, J. Sarama, & A.-M. DiBiase (Eds.), *Engaging young children in mathematics: Standards for early childhood mathematics education* (pp. 1–72). Mahwah, NJ: Erlbaum.

Clements, D. H., & Sarama, J. (2007). *Building blocks* [Computer software]. Columbus, OH: SRA/McGraw-Hill.

Clements, D. H., & Sarama, J. (in press-a). Early childhood mathematics learning. In F. K. Lester, Jr. (Ed.), *Second handbook of research on mathematics teaching and learning.* Charlotte, NC: Information Age Publishing.

Clements, D. H., & Sarama, J. (in press-b). Effects of a preschool mathematics curriculum: Summary research on the *Building blocks* project. *Journal for Research in Mathematics Education.*

Clements, D. H., Sarama, J., Battista, M. T., & Swaminathan, S. (1996). Development of students' spatial thinking in a curriculum unit on geometric motions and area. In E. Jakubowski, D. Watkins, & H. Biske (Eds.), *Proceedings of the 18th annual meeting of the North America Chapter of the International Group for the Psychology of Mathematics Education* (Vol. 1, pp. 217–222). Columbus, OH: ERIC Clearinghouse for Science, Mathematics, and Environmental Education.

Clements, D. H., Sarama, J., & DiBiase, A.-M. (2004). *Engaging young children in mathematics: Standards for early childhood mathematics education.* Mahwah, NJ: Erlbaum.

Clements, D. H., Sarama, J., & Gerber, S. (2005). *Mathematics knowledge of low-income entering preschoolers.* Manuscript submitted for publication.

Clements, D. H., Swaminathan, S., Hannibal, M. A. Z., & Sarama, J. (1999). Young children's concepts of shape. *Journal for Research in Mathematics Education, 30,* 192–212.

Clements, D. H., Wilson, D. C., & Sarama, J. (2004). Young children's composition of geometric figures: A learning trajectory. *Mathematical Thinking and Learning, 6,* 163–184.

Cowan, R. (1987). When do children trust counting as a basis for relative number judgments? *Journal of Experimental Child Psychology, 43,* 328–345.

DeLoache, J. S. (1987). Rapid change in the symbolic functioning of young children. *Science, 238,* 1556–1557.

DeLoache, J. S., & Burns, N. M. (1994). Early understanding of the representational function of pictures. *Cognition, 52,* 83–110.

Ferguson, R. W., Aminoff, A., & Gentner, D. (1998). *Early detection of qualitative symmetry.* Submitted for publication.

Fisher, C. B., Ferdinandsen, K., & Bornstein, M. H. (1981). The role of symmetry in infant form discrimination. *Child Development, 52,* 457–462.

Forman, G. E. (1982). A search for the origins of equivalence concepts through a microanalysis of block play. In G. E. Forman (Ed.), *Action and thought* (pp. 97–135). New York: Academic Press.

Friel, S. N., Curcio, F. R., & Bright, G. W. (2001). Making sense of graphs: Critical factors influencing comprehension and instructional implications. *Journal for Research in Mathematics Education, 32,* 124–158.

Fuson, K. C. (1988). *Children's counting and concepts of number.* New York: Springer-Verlag.

Fuson, K. C. (2004). Pre-K to grade 2 goals and standards: Achieving 21st century mastery for all. In D. H. Clements, J. Sarama, & A.-M. DiBiase (Eds.), *Engaging young children in mathematics: Standards for early childhood mathematics education* (pp. 105–148). Mahwah, NJ: Erlbaum.

Fuson, K. C., Smith, S. T., & Lo Cicero, A. (1997). Supporting Latino first graders' ten-structured thinking in urban classrooms. *Journal for Research in Mathematics Education, 28,* 738–760.

Gallistel, C. R., & Gelman, R. (2005). Mathematical cognition. In K. Holyoak, & R. Morrison (Eds.), *Cambridge handbook of thinking and reasoning* (pp. 559–588). Cambridge: Cambridge University Press.

Gelman, R., & Gallistel, C. R. (1978). *The child's understanding of number.* Cambridge, MA: Harvard University Press.

Genkins, E. F. (1975). The concept of bilateral symmetry in young children. In M. F. Rosskopf (Ed.), *Children's mathematical concepts: Six Piagetian studies in mathematics education* (pp. 5–43). New York: Teaching College Press.

Ginsburg, H. P., Inoue, N., & Seo, K.-H. (1999). Young children doing mathematics: Observations of everyday activities. In J. V. Copley (Ed.), *Mathematics in the early years* (pp. 88–99). Reston, VA: National Council of Teachers of Mathematics.

Ginsburg, H. P., Ness, D., & Seo, K.-H. (2003). Young American and Chinese children's everyday mathematical activity. *Mathematical Thinking and Learning, 5,* 235–258.

Griffin, S. (2004). Number Worlds: A research-based mathematics program for young children. In D. H. Clements, J. Sarama, & A.-M. DiBiase (Eds.), *Engaging young children in mathematics: Standards for early childhood mathematics education* (pp. 325–342). Mahwah, NJ: Erlbaum.

Groen, G., & Resnick, L. B. (1977). Can preschool children invent addition algorithms? *Journal of Educational Psychology, 69*, 645–652.

Guberman, S. R. (2004). A comparative study of children's out-of-school activities and arithmetical achievement. *Journal for Research in Mathematics Education, 35*, 117–150.

Hannibal, M. A. Z., & Clements, D. H. (2000). *Young children's understanding of basic geometric shapes.* Manuscript submitted for publication.

Hannula, M. M. (2005). *Spontaneous focusing on numerosity in the development of early mathematical skills.* Turku, Finland: University of Turku.

Hughes, M. (1981). Can preschool children add and subtract? *Educational Psychology, 1*, 207–219.

Humphrey, G. K., & Humphrey, G. K. (1995). The role of structure in infant visual pattern perception. *Canadian Journal of Psychology, 43*(2), 165–182.

Huttenlocher, J., Jordan, N. C., & Levine, S. C. (1994). A mental model for early arithmetic. *Journal of Experimental Psychology: General, 123*, 284–296.

Kamii, C., Miyakawa, Y., & Kato, Y. (2004). The development of logico-mathematical knowledge in a block-building activity at ages 1–4. *Journal of Research in Childhood Education, 19*, 13–26.

Langer, J., Rivera, S. M., Schlesinger, M., & Wakeley, A. (2003). Early cognitive development: Ontogeny and phylogeny. In J. Valsiner, & K. J. Connolly (Eds.), *Handbook of developmental psychology* (pp. 141–171). London: Sage.

Lehrer, R., Osana, H., Jacobson, C., & Jenkins, M. (1993). *Children's conceptions of geometry in the primary grades.* Paper presented at the Annual Meeting of the American Educational Research Association, Atlanta, GA.

Mix, K. S. (1999). Preschoolers' recognition of numerical equivalence: Sequential sets. *Journal of Experimental Child Psychology, 74*, 309–332.

NCES. (2000). *America's kindergartners (NCES 2000070).* Washington, DC: National Center for Education Statistics, U.S. Government Printing Office.

NCTM. (1989). *Curriculum and evaluation standards for school mathematics.* Reston, VA: National Council of Teachers of Mathematics.

NCTM. (2000). *Principles and standards for school mathematics.* Reston, VA: National Council of Teachers of Mathematics.

Nunes, T., & Bryant, P. (1996). *Children doing mathematics.* Cambridge, MA: Balckwell.

Palmer, S. E. (1985). The role of symmetry in shape perception. *Acta Psychologica, 59*(1), 67–90.

Palmer, S. E., & Hemenway, K. (1978). Orientation and symmetry: Effects of multiple, rotational, and near symmetries. *Journal of Experimental Psychology, 4*, 691–702.

Piaget, J., & Szeminska, A. (1952). *The child's conception of number.* London: Routledge and Kegan Paul.

Rattermann, M. J., & Gentner, D. (1998). The effect of language on similarity: The use of relational labels improves young children's performance in a mapping task. In K. Holyoak, D. Gentner, & B. Kokinov (Eds.), *Advances in analogy research: Integration of theory & data from the cognitive, computational, and neural sciences* (pp. 274–282). Sophia: New Bulgarian University.

Reynolds, A., & Wheatley, G. H. (1996). Elementary students' construction and coordination of units in an area setting. *Journal for Research in Mathematics Education, 27*(5), 564–581.

Richardson, K. (2004). Making sense. In D. H. Clements, J. Sarama, & A.-M. DiBiase (Eds.), *Engaging young children in mathematics: Standards for early childhood mathematics education* (pp. 321–324). Mahwah, NJ: Erlbaum.

Rieser, J. J., Doxsey, P. A., McCarrell, N. S., & Brooks, P. H. (1982). Wayfinding and toddlers' use of information from an aerial view. *Developmental Psychology, 18,* 714–720.

Russell, S. J. (1991). Counting noses and scary things: Children construct their ideas about data. In D. Vere-Jones (Ed.), *Proceedings of the Third International Conference on Teaching Statistics.* Voorburg, The Netherlands: International Statistical Institute.

Sarama, J., Clements, D. H., & Vukelic, E. B. (1996). The role of a computer manipulative in fostering specific psychological/mathematical processes. In E. Jakubowski, D. Watkins, & H. Biske (Eds.), *Proceedings of the 18th annual meeting of the North America Chapter of the International Group for the Psychology of Mathematics Education* (Vol. 2, pp. 567–572). Columbus, OH: ERIC Clearinghouse for Science, Mathematics, and Environmental Education.

Seo, K.-H., & Ginsburg, H. P. (2004). What is developmentally appropriate in early childhood mathematics education? In D. H. Clements, J. Sarama, & A.-M. DiBiase (Eds.), *Engaging young children in mathematics: Standards for early childhood mathematics education* (pp. 91–104). Mahwah, NJ: Erlbaum.

Starkey, P., & Cooper, R. G., Jr. (1980). Perception of numbers by human infants. *Science, 210,* 1033–1035.

Starkey, P., Spelke, E. S., & Gelman, R. (1990). Numerical abstraction by human infants. *Cognition, 36,* 97–128.

Steffe, L. P. (1992). Children's construction of meaning for arithmetical words: A curriculum problem. In D. Tirosh (Ed.), *Implicit and explicit knowledge: An educational approach* (pp. 131–168). Norwood, NJ: Ablex g.

Steffe, L. P. (2004). *PSSM* From a constructivist perspective. In D. H. Clements, J. Sarama, & A.-M. DiBiase (Eds.), *Engaging young children in mathematics: Standards for early childhood mathematics education* (pp. 221–251). Mahwah, NJ: Erlbaum.

Steffe, L. P., & Cobb, P. (1988). *Construction of arithmetical meanings and strategies.* New York: Springer-Verlag.

Stiles, J., & Stern, C. (2001). Developmental change in spatial cognitive processing: Complexity effects and block construction performance in preschool children. *Journal of Cognition and Development, 2,* 157–187.

Stiles-Davis, J. (1988). Developmental change in young children's spatial grouping ability. *Developmental Psychology, 24,* 522–531.

Thomas, B. (1982). *An abstract of kindergarten teachers' elicitation and utilization of children's prior knowledge in the teaching of shape concepts.* Unpublished manuscript,

School of Education, Health, Nursing, and Arts Professions, New York University.

Wiese, H. (2003). Iconic and non-iconic stages in number development: The role of language. *Trends in Cognitive Sciences, 7*, 385–390.

Wynn, K. (1992). Addition and subtraction by human infants. *Nature, 358*, 749–750.

Wynn, K., Bloom, P., & Chiang, W.-C. (2002). Enumeration of collective entities by 5-month-old infants. *Cognition, 83*, B55-B62.

Yin, H. S. (2003). Young children's concept of shape: van Hiele visualization level of geometric thinking. *The Mathematics Educator, 7*(2), 71–85.

CHAPTER 5

MATHEMATICS LEARNING AND TEACHING IN THE EARLY YEARS

Ann Anderson, Jim Anderson, and Carolyn Thauberger

In this chapter, we examine research conducted over the past 10 years focusing on mathematics learning and teaching in the early years (birth to 8 years). We begin with a brief history of early childhood mathematics and the major theories (i.e., Piaget and Vygotsky) that inform much of the work we review. We then review research studies in young children's mathematics organized as: infants and mathematics, preschool children's development and knowledge, preschoolers experiences at home and at childcare centers; students' mathematical knowledge and development; intervention studies and primary children's knowledge, and international comparisons of children's mathematics learning. Then we review research on teachers knowledge and practice and curriculum and instruction issues. We conclude by highlighting the major findings of the review and offer suggestions for research strands.

HISTORY AND THEORY

While there continues to be a great deal of interest in young children's mathematical development, this field has had a relatively long history. Ginsburg, Klein and Prentice (1998) point out that educators, philoso-

Contemporary Perspectives on Mathematics in Early Childhood Education, pages 95–132
Copyright © 2008 by Information Age Publishing

phers and psychologists have been interested in this area for more than 100 years. They credit the educator and philosopher, John Dewey, with postulating similar theories of children's mathematical development that were later popularized by Jean Piaget and are still very influential. And while contemporaries of Dewey such as the psychologists Buswell and Judd also began to examine young children's mathematical thinking from developmental or cognitive perspectives, interest waned as educators came under the influence of Thorndike and his behavioral theories of learning. These theories emphasized drill and practice of sub-skills until they were "over learned," and thus automatic. Ginsburg et al. put it simply: "Dewey lost and Thorndike won." It was not until the emergence of Piaget's work in the middle of the twentieth century that cognitive perspectives of children's mathematical learning came to the forefront.

Much of the current thinking about young children's mathematical learning and understanding can be traced to the constructivist philosophy articulated by Piaget (1972). Central to Piaget's theory was the notion that young children "construct" knowledge by interacting with their environment. As Nunes, (1999) states,

> Piaget's central thesis was that the basic meanings of mathematical concepts stem from children's schemas of action—that is generalizable and structured actions which can be applied to a variety of objects and which center on the relations between objects and transformations rather than the objects per se (p. 34).

According to Piaget's theory, children are able to integrate information that fits within their current schemata by a process called "assimilation." However, when children encounter information that does not fit their schemata, they rethink their hypotheses about the particular concept through a process called "accommodation." Thus, cognitive disequilibrium that results when new information conflicts with current understanding is important in children's conceptual development. While some educators have questioned what they see as Piaget's rigid formulation of developmental stages (sensory motor, concrete operational, etc.), there is little doubt that his influence on what he called children's logico-mathematical understanding still pervades.

However, we see the work of Vygotsky (1978) and other sociocultural theorists as increasingly influential in the work in early mathematics development. Central to this theory is the notion that learning is social with more competent others supporting learning in culturally specific ways. Classroom-based research and research in children's homes, (appropriately, we think), reflect this perspective as researchers and educators try to understand *how* children learn mathematics.

RESEARCH IN YOUNG CHILDREN'S MATHEMATICS

Infants and Mathematics

Research in early childhood mathematics education spans a broad age range including studies with infants. Indeed, some contemporary theories of numerical development assume that infants engage in some form of counting. Wynn (1998), for example, examined the numerical competence of children, ages 5 to 8 months. In particular, her study investigated infants' ability to enumerate physical actions, a puppet jumping 2 or 3 times, and she concluded "infants are able to identify individual jumps and enumerate them" (p. 9). In two later refinements of her initial experiment, she found that these very young children discriminated the number of actions of the puppet. As with most work in this area, the method involved habituating infants to a specific number of objects, actions, or sounds and then timing how long they looked at sets of a different number compared to that with which they were habituated. In addition, Wynn (1998) reviewed studies that have shown that representing and reasoning about number is not unique to humans but has also been found in animals.

But, as Sophian (1998) cautioned,

> it is not possible to decide whether infants in fact do use a nonverbal counting process or a more limited subitizing mechanism. What we do know is that infants are able to detect the kinds of properties of events to which older children and adults might attach numerical representation (p. 33).

However, some researchers interpret this line of research differently. Mix, Huttenlocher, and Levine (2002), while acknowledging that there is "evidence that infants are sensitive to quantitative information in their environment" contend that the research does not "prove that infants have a sophisticated sense of number" (p. 20). Infants have the ability to discriminate between different sizes of sets of objects but Mix et al. conclude, "there is no solid evidence that infants can recognize any kind of numerical relation before 10 months of age and only scant evidence that they can do so for certain relations in their later infancy" (p. 21). Overall, then, research on infants' mathematics continues to be inconclusive regarding the nature of the infants' number abilities, although researchers concur that from a very young age, children can distinguish quantitatively different sets from each other.

Preschool Children's Development and Knowledge

In addition to the work with preverbal infants, researchers for some time have been interested in the mathematical development and understanding of preschoolers. For instance, Pepper and Hunting (1998) investigated how counting and sharing might be related by examining the strategies preschool children used to subdivide items. Twenty-five preschool children (age 4–10 to 6–2) participated in two interviews where they completed a set of counting tasks and then a set of sharing tasks. Children were then classified into three groups: poor, developing, or good counters, and poor, intermediate, or good sharers. The results showed no significant relationship between counting and sharing competence. Rather, the children demonstrated systematic dealing (one for you, one for you) procedures, involving no apparent use of counting or measuring skills, in order to successfully partition groups of discrete items equally. Thus, dealing or sharing competence did not relate directly to counting skill. Pepper and Hunting (1998) suggested that teachers should be able to involve young children in problems of sharing even if those children have not yet become rational counters. They argued that dealing tasks might assist children's developing counting skills through opportunities to check or verify the sizes of shares.

In a more recent study, Hunting (2003) examined the mathematics behavior of young children in part-whole settings in which a small set of items was partitioned such that one subset was hidden. Fourteen 3 and 4-year-old children attending a university preschool were interviewed 4 times over 6 weeks. Since 12 children were successful with at least three steps, Hunting argued that these young children conceived of number with cardinal properties. He observed that children used finger sets as physical representation for unavailable sets, which provided both kinesthetic and visual feedback. He concluded that a major cognitive tool for these children was an ability to visualize sequences of actions when outcomes of such actions were hidden.

Muldoon, Lewis, and Freeman (2003) investigated children's conception of counting by focusing on their ability (1) to recognize when counting goes wrong and (2) to reason about miscounting in terms of consequences for numerical judgments. In the first experiment, 23 children (ages 42–57 months) were selected from nursery classes in two schools serving predominantly white, urban, blue-collar populations. Each child was given 6 tests (e.g., deceptive box, procedural counting, count miscount discrimination, wrong cardinal, set creation, and set comparison) in fixed order with appropriate breaks (Muldoon et al., 2003, p. 702). More than 60% of the children understood that in the set-creation task, the cardinal value for the number of frogs could be extended to the number of boats needed for the frogs. Interestingly, five of the 17 children with mastery of procedural counting failed this set-creation task. On the other hand, all 9 children, who were able to discriminate correct counts and miscounts, passed the set-creation task. Children who knew how to use counting to create equivalent sets, were likely to know how counting could be used to check two sets for equivalence. In a second experiment, 30 children (age 47–57 months) who had not participated in Experiment 1 were selected. No significant difference was found between the prompt and no-prompt conditions that were introduced in Experiment 2. Children's ability to detect a puppet's violation of the cardinality principle was the best predictor of whether they would use counting to create equivalent sets. The researchers concluded that young children have the capacity to realize that miscounting has consequences and that this recognition is associated with their flexibility in the use of counting.

In a naturalistic study in a preschool classroom, Zur and Gelman (2004) identified activities in which four-year-old children had an opportunity to use their knowledge of counting in a number-relevant reasoning task. Based on a Donut Song Game carried out in class, the researchers designed similar problems wherein (1) children counted an array of items, (2) the experimenter changed the number of items in the array by adding or subtracting some items, (3) the children were asked to predict how many items there are after the change, and (4) the children checked their predictions. Then, three different groups of children—the four-year-olds who had experienced the in-class set up, four-year-old children from a different class and a group of three-year-old children—participated in video taped interviews. Findings revealed that when making a prediction, children typically replied immediately with a cardinal value whereas during the checking phase, all the children counted.

Rittle-Johnson and Siegler (1998) reviewed research on preschool and school aged children's number development in order to clarify, what develops first, procedural or conceptual knowledge. As they indicated, educators often describe preschoolers as having sophisticated conceptual understanding that guides their generation of procedures while consistently lamenting that school aged children have impoverished conceptual understanding that leads to their generating flawed and illogical procedures. Based on recent research where children count skilfully before they understand the underlying principles, Rittle-Johnson and Siegler stated that knowledge of the procedure for counting precedes understanding of the underlying concepts. In contrast, most 5-year-olds understand the concepts underlying single digit addition before they generate the count-on procedure. With respect to operating on multi-digit numbers, Rittle-Johnson and Siegler (1998) reported that most children show conceptual understanding of multi-digit numbers prior to, or concurrent with, using a correct procedure. When they examined research on operations on fractions, the trajectory varied in that when children added fractions, conceptual knowledge emerged first, but when they multiplied fractions, correct procedures were seen first. Thus, the order in which conceptual and procedural knowledge develops seems to depend on the mathematical topic(s) under consideration.

Other researchers such as Singer, Kohn, and Resnick (1997) investigated preschool children's knowledge of concepts that are not quantitative in nature. For instance, proto-quantitative schemas enable children to reason without the benefit of, or interference from, numerical quantification. Indeed, the evidence that Singer et al. (1997) described makes it clear that intuitive bases for ratio, proportion and functional reasoning are available to young children. When they are not forced to quantify, children are able to make good judgments about intensives such as ratio and density (p. 130).

Munn (1998) also chose not to focus on counting but instead reviewed research regarding young children's progression in symbolic function from resemblance-based number symbols (tallies, pictograms) to conventional symbolization (numerals). Munn (1998) proposed that,

> children will build their cognitive models around the social context of their teaching/learning, and not around abstract logical structures. This means that models with similar logical structures (numeral system and Dienes' blocks) will not necessarily be linked. For most children, one cognitive model of number will be created around a verbal number system, another around objects used in counting and calculating and yet another around number symbols (p. 57).

Munn (1998) drew heavily on a longitudinal study of preschool literacy and numeracy conducted in the mid-90s. Fifty-six preschoolers (average age 46 months) were interviewed during 4 visits spread over their final year of nursery school and first term of primary school. Based on their responses to Munn's modified labeling task, two groups of children emerged: non-functional children who did not use labels at all and guessed which tin had an extra block, and functional children who incorporated labels into the problem and said "this one cause it [the label] says 2 and it's three" (Munn, 1998, p. 63). Interestingly, over time, more children acquired the tendency to involve their written record in their numerical goal.

Miyakawa, Kamii, and Nagahiro (2005) investigated 1- to 4-year-old children's logico-mathematical development by having them work with a cylindrical object and an inclined plane. Fifty middle class children attending a child care center in Okayama, Japan were randomly selected with 10 children in each age range (1;0 to 1;5, 1;6 to 1;11,...3;0 to 3;5). The researchers observed and videotaped individual children as they played with the objects. After modeling the construction of the inclined plane and rolling the cylinder, the researchers asked the child to imitate their actions. Analysis revealed that all children older than fifteen months were able to imitate the interviewer in rolling the cylinder. Younger children responded in a number of ways, including incorrect ways whereas older children always responded correctly. In other words, "when children made spatial relationships between roundness and rolling, they were always successful" (p. 297). However, children demonstrated four distinct developmental levels when constructing the inclined plane. Miyakawa et al. (2005) suggested that educators should focus on children's development of logico-mathematical knowledge as a network of interrelated mental relationships rather than discrete tasks and objectives.

Yuzawa et al. (2005) sought to clarify what strategies and knowledge three to six year olds use for comparing sizes of two geometric figures and to determine how those strategies relate to children's judgement and ages. They focused on a placement strategy "one on another" and the adjustment strategy "general shape." They recruited sixty-nine 3–6 year olds from middle class families who attended nursery school in a mid-size city in Japan. Experimenters recorded children's responses to three tasks—Size Comparison, Superimposition and Choice—that were videotaped. Results indicated that some children used both the "one on another" and "general shape" strategies, but many others used only "general shape" or another strategy entirely to compare sizes successfully. In addition, children were successful in the Superimposition task but did not apply the knowledge exhibited there when comparing the sizes of the figures. Yuzawa et al. (2005) concluded that educators should pay attention first to children learning a "general shape" adjustment strategy and knowledge of the relative sizes of areas of figures placed on each other. If children learn that a figure that includes another has a larger area, they become sensitive to the directions of 2 figures and adjust them so that one fits (will include) the other.

Wolfgang, Stannard, and Jones (2001) investigated the impact of block play with preschool age children. A cohort of 37 preschoolers (age 4) attending a play-oriented pre-school was tested (Lunzer 5-Point Play Scale [1955]) to obtain block performance measures. After this group had completed high school, records (including standardized test scores, teacher based grades, number of advanced courses) were obtained for their third, fifth, seventh grades and high school mathematics. Findings indicated that although there were no significant correlations in the elementary grades, children's measure of block play at age 4 reliably predicted mathematical achievement at seventh grade and beyond. Wolfgang et al. (2001) speculated that block building helped children develop basic underlying cognitive structures that enhanced achievement in higher level, abstract mathematics which is usually not tested until grade seven onward.

Benson and Baroody (2002) reported the first author's naturalistic observations of her son Blake, (18 through 36 months) at home and when attending Kumon sessions. The researchers also administered nonverbal matching and production tasks to Blake at 26 and 30 months. Initially,

Blake used isolated number words in a nonfunctional manner, then later used number words more effectively to identify partially visible and non-visible collections. During the study period, Blake was unable to recognize the numerosity of sound sequences. The researchers also shared instances where the child's performance in Kumon was inconsistent with his performance in everyday situations. For instance, at 32 months when Blake counted things (e.g., stairs) spontaneously, he did not count with one-to-one correspondence but continued to 10 even when items were exhausted. If there were more items than words, he repeated the numbers. When completing Kumon worksheets, however, he stopped counting after his last touch. The researchers speculated that either the mother gave clues or that the structure at Kumon may have assisted Blake.

Overall then, research into preschool children's knowledge points to young children's strong capacity to deal with number prior to school, thus diminishing the value of the conventional practice that pre-number activities are more appropriate for this age group upon school entry. In addition, much of this recent research involving preschool children's knowledge provides insights into the relationships these young children establish between particular mathematical concepts or processes, such as addition and subtraction, counting and sharing, and so on. It was noteworthy that our search of current literature did not uncover more studies into preschool children's knowledge of other areas of mathematics such as geometry, patterning, and so forth.

PRESCHOOL CHILDREN'S MATHEMATICS EXPERIENCES AT HOME AND CHILD CARE CENTERS

Interest in the home and childcare experiences of preschool children is a relatively recent development in early childhood mathematics research. Fuson, Grandau, and Sugiyama, (2001) argued that young children aged 3 to 7 can learn a great deal about numbers as they experience daily routines, in a home or day care environment. They emphasized that informal teaching activities in these settings need to be encouraged and modeled by adults or more advanced children (p. 522).

Ginsburg, Inoue and Seo (1999) contended that much of the research in early mathematics development has been constrained in that the studies are designed by psychologists who tend to engage children in activities and tasks that reflect a limited range of mathematical ideas. They observed and videotaped 30 young African American and Latino preschoolers from low-SES homes as they engaged in free play at day care. Ginsburg et al. found that 44% of the free play involved mathematical activity (p. 95). The mathematical engagement was as follows: Patterns and shapes (36%); dynamics-exploration of the processes of change or transformation (22%); relations-magnitude evaluation or comparison (18%); classification-sorting grouping or categorizing (13%); and enumeration-quantification or numerical judgment (11%) (pp. 95–96). They concluded that these young low-income African-American and Latino children "seem to possess the intellectual abilities to engage in interesting and relatively advanced mathematical explorations and activities in general to succeed in school" (p. 96). Based on their findings, Ginsburg and his colleagues argued for a more varied and conceptually rich curriculum for preschools.

The primary goal of Tudge and Doucet's (2004) study was to assess the extent to which young children engaged in mathematics and literacy in the course of their everyday activities and to examine any variation due to ethnicity or social class. Families of thirty-nine preschoolers (11 White middle class, 9 Black middle class, 9 White working class, 10 Black working class) were asked to maintain daily routines as much as possible during the observation period. Each child was observed, for 20 hours over the course of one week, and the final two hours were videotaped. Tudge and Doucet chose to time sample the activities and code only what they termed "academic lessons" and "play with academic objects." Findings revealed that the children did not engage in many (informal) math lessons and mathematics-related play was also infrequent. Few literacy activities were observed, although there was more evidence of children engaging with books and writing than mathematics. There was a great deal of individual variation in the extent to which these children engaged with mathematics, with standard deviations typically as large as or larger than the means. Tudge and Doucet admit that they might have underestimated the extent to which children were engaging in mathematics because of their focus on explicitly stated mathematics.

As Benigno and Ellis (2004) point out, much of the work on parents mediation of learning has "focused almost entirely on one-on-one adult-child interaction" (p. 18). Their study was designed to test the effect of having a young sibling also engage in an activity alongside a parent and a young child. They videotaped 19 dyads and 16 triads as they played *The Picnic*, a 20" by 20" board game similar to Monopoly. The participants were mainly middle class and Caucasian. Begigno and Ellis concluded that the board game was indeed a context in which parents engaged in counting and so forth, but the parents' responsiveness declined when a second child was involved. As they pointed out, notions of mediated learning and scaffolding that follow from Vygotsky's (1978) foundational work imbue early childhood curriculum. But as they also point out, much of the empirical study of mediation has not involved a significant other and two or more children, a much more realistic situation that children are likely to find themselves in at home or at preschool. Furthermore, much learning is an artefact of an activity where the goal is not children's cognitive or intellectual development.

Over the last decade, we (first and second authors) have been engaged in research into parent mediation of preschool mathematics learning (e.g., Anderson & Anderson, 1995; Anderson, Anderson, & Shapiro, 2005). For example, Anderson and Anderson (1995), in a longitudinal case study of their daughter, identified how mathematics played an important role in constructing meaning as they shared books with the preschooler. Interestingly, much of the mathematical discourse was initiated by the child and involved both the illustrations and the storyline in books that are not commonly thought of as having mathematical foci.

Anderson (1997) investigated the ways in which parents and their 4-year-old children engaged in mathematics as they shared four sets of materials (blocks, worksheets, drawing materials, story book) in 15 minute sessions at home over two days. A variety of mathematics concepts were discussed within and across families and block play and shared book reading were identified as two contexts in which these families mediated mathematics frequently.

Shapiro, Anderson, and Anderson (1997) videotaped 12 parent-child dyads as they shared two children's books (*Mr. McMouse* and *Swimmy* by Leo Lionni) at home or at preschool according to the preference of the parents. Interestingly, "size" was the most frequent mathematical concept that arose, although there were also examples of "counting," "shape," and so forth.

Working with four parent-child dyads, Anderson, Anderson and Shapiro (2004) investigated the mathematical discourse in the shared reading of *One Snowy Night* (Butterworth, 1989). As was the case in the Shapiro et al. study, there was considerable variation in the ways in which the families shared the books and the ways in which they attended to and talked about mathematics. One family, for example, focused exclusively on "size" whereas in two of the families, counting, subitizing and problem solving occurred. In two of the dyads, the mothers initiated all of the mathematical discourse whereas in another family, the child did.

In a follow-up to the Shapiro et al. study, Anderson et al. (2005) videotaped 39 parents and their four-year-old children from a culturally diverse metropolitan area as they shared *Mr. McMouse* and *Swimmy*. Again, there was considerable variation in terms of the mathematical discourse and the ways in which mathematics was shared across families. Interestingly though, all but one of the families engaged in mathematical talk. "Size" was the most frequent concept that arose, while different aspects of number were next in frequency. Thus, as Anderson et al. (2005) indicated, "shared book reading holds considerable potential for parents [and teachers] to draw attention to mathematical vocabulary and concepts" (p. 5).

In addition to shedding light on parent's mediation of children's mathematics in the home, this body of research also links children's literature to mathematics learning in these homes. This coincides then with the use of children's literature to support the teaching and learning of mathematics (e.g., Evans, Leija, & Falkner, 2001; Griffiths & Clyne, 1991) in school. Indeed, the National Council of Teachers of Mathematics (2000) has endorsed this perspective and a plethora of suggestions for teachers on how to use children's books as *springboards* for mathematical activities is available. Yet, there is very little research as to how mathematics is embedded in the actual shared reading of children's books. Our research on preschool children's experiences with shared book reading in the home attempts to fill this research gap.

Overall, then, this body of observational research expands on earlier studies (e.g., Saxe, Guberman, & Gearhart, 1987) that relied on parents' reports of the types of experiences in which they engaged their children in mathematics prior to school. However, what stands out in this research is the variation in the amount and types of mathematics found in these settings and the ways in which caregivers engage with, or are aware of, the children's mathematical learning. Despite a prevailing view that the ways in which children come to think about mathematics is heavily dependent on mathematical experiences they have had prior to school (Tudge & Doucet, 2004, p. 25), we have only begun to explore young children's everyday experiences with mathematics. Researchers need to continue to document children's early mathematical development through their participation in everyday experiences and events.

Students' Mathematical Knowledge and Development (Ages 5–8 Years)

Much of the research into young children's mathematical thinking has involved students enrolled in grades K–3. Somewhat like the studies in preschool, an emphasis on number and number operations is pervasive. For instance, Kamii, Lewis, and Booker (1998) investigated whether formal instruction of missing addends is needed, if children's numerical reasoning is strong. One hundred and ten children, from classrooms in which their constructivist teachers did not formally teach missing addends, were tested in classroom groups, using a six-question missing addends paper and pencil test late in the year. Ninety-two percent of the children received perfect papers or had only one error. Kamii et al. (1998) argued that card games and life-related problems that were a focus in the curriculum keep children focused on numerical reasoning rather than counting and writing, and that any difficulty the study children had with missing addends was in understanding the written form of the problem, rather than with the numerical reasoning.

Kamii, Lewis, and Kirkland (2001) conducted two studies on children's fluency with addition and subtraction. In one study, 33 kindergarten children, enrolled in two classes of a constructivist "school within a school" located in an upper-middle class suburb, were given a one-to-one correspondence task. Twenty-six children answered the "addition" question correctly but only 16 answered the "subtraction" questions correctly. In the second study, 21 first-graders from one class and 38 fourth graders from two classes were individually interviewed in the same constructivist "school within a school" as a part of the routine assessment conducted at the beginning and end of the school year. The assessment contained 70, one-, two-, and three-digit computational problems involving all four operations (Kamii et al., 2001, p. 37). Nineteen of the 21 first graders immediately produced sums, but only 10 of them produced differences. It was also found that addition was always easier than subtraction for the fourth graders. Interestingly, Kamii et al. (2001) also noted that children deduced differences from their knowledge of sums rather than retrieving independent subtraction facts that they had internalized.

In their 3-year longitudinal study, Carpenter, Franke, Jacobs, Fennema, and Empson (1998) investigated the development of children's understanding of multi-digit number concepts and operations. Eighty-two children were selected from 27 Grades 1–3 classes. Students were given an opportunity to solve problems using a variety of strategies and alternative strategies were discussed with the entire class or in small groups. Regular algorithm instruction proceeded according to the curriculum. Students were individually interviewed 5 times (spring and fall) on a variety of tasks involving base-ten number concepts and addition and subtraction problems. About 90% of the students used invented strategies, with 27 of them doing so, well before they encountered algorithms. These 27 students demonstrated better knowledge of base-ten number concepts and were more successful in extending their knowledge to new situations than were the 18 students who learned standard algorithms first. These findings pointed to a relationship between the development of base-ten number concepts and the ability to use invented strategies, but do not provide evidence of which came first.

In Dowker's (1998) study into children's arithmetical abilities, each of 213 students (ages from 5 to 9 years) drawn from three state schools was tested individually. According to their performance on a mental calculation task, the children were divided into five levels. They were then given an arithmetical reasoning test, which entailed giving the children the answer to a problem and asking them to solve another problem that could be solved quickly using the provided answer, together with the principle under consideration. The results showed strong associations between calculation and estimation, calculation and derived fact strategy use, and most of all, between estimation and derived fact strategy use. Dowker concluded that (1) individual differences in arithmetic are marked; (2) arithmetic is not unitary and it is relatively easy to find children with marked discrepancies between different components; and (3) in particular, it is risky to assume that a child "does not understand math" because he or she performs poorly in some calculation tasks (Dowker, 1998, p. 300).

Gonzalez and Espinel (2002) investigated whether strategies, used by children with low achievement in arithmetic and high IQ differed from those used by children with low achievement and low IQ when solving arithmetic word problems. One hundred and forty-eight Spanish children (ages 7 to 9 years) from average SES backgrounds attending urban state schools were grouped according to an arithmetic standard score and an IQ score to form three groups: arithmetic learning disabled (ALD), garden-variety poor performer (G-V) and typical achiever. Children received 40 word problems in 3 individual sessions of 20 minutes each with the order of problems counterbalanced. Findings showed that strategies used by ALD children and G-V poor performers were not qualitatively different as the same cognitive processes underlie their performance. Specifically, these children depended on strategies that are less memory based (i.e., counting and modeling) than typically achieving children.

To understand how knowledge of addition might facilitate the learning of subtraction combinations, Baroody (1999) undertook two studies. Forty children (25 Kindergarteners, 15 first graders, ages 4 to 7 years) enrolled in a university-affiliated primary school with a gifted program comprised the sample of the first study. Three preliminary tasks ensured participants had prerequisite knowledge to comprehend the "complement" task and checked children's developmental level in subtraction. A complement task entailed asking children whether an addition equation was helpful in completing a subtraction expression when both were presented together. Also, the measure of complementary knowledge in study 1 involved a reaction time (RT) criterion to minimize including correct answers determined by computation. The results indicated that although children typically indicated that an equation had helped them answer expressions with pairs involving an identity or communtativity, few consistently found addition equations helpful in completing subtraction and almost half never appeared to find the complement principle helpful (Baroody, 1999, p. 8). In the second study, a research assistant provided instruction in the complementary relation, the number before rule, and the difference of 1 rule, and a post-test checked for children's transfer to non-practiced examples of each of these three. Twenty-one first graders (from a small farming community) who had no arithmetic instruction in Kindergarten were given a pre-test at the beginning of year, a Complement task 10 days later, and a subtraction timed test over the course of several weeks. They were then assigned randomly to two training conditions and trained in groups of two, three times a week for 9 weeks with each session lasting about 30 minutes.

There was little evidence in the pre-test that children recognized a general complementary relation, and post-test results on the complement task were only somewhat more positive. Baroody (1999a) therefore concluded that the association between addition and subtraction is not obvious to children and it is not easily taught to them, at least not when a take-away meaning of subtraction is used (p. 18).

Research by Fuson, Carroll, and Landis (1996) examined relations between two major linguistic forms of matching problems (compare and equalize), two phrasings of relational statements (positive, negative) and three quantities in the situation that can be unknown (big, small, extra). Beginning of the year participants were 6 classes of first graders and 5 classes of second graders from two schools which were racially and economically heterogeneous; their midyear participants were 93 first and 119 second graders from 12 classes in a school serving families from middle/ upper-middle class backgrounds. All participants had little or no experience with the word problems used in the study. In the second week of school, a 24-problem test was given over 4 days to all beginning of the year children. In January, midyear children were given 9 problems on each of two days. Children were not given blocks or counting objects. Both correct answers and correct strategies were evaluated. Findings showed that "equalize" problems had about 20% higher correct solutions than "compare" problems but only for beginning of year first graders on unknown extra and consistent problems. For the most advanced children, (second grade, midyear) in the most difficult problems, "equalize inconsistent problems" were easier than "compare inconsistent," which was the opposite of what was predicted. Based on their results, Fuson et al. (1996) speculated that if children had a preference for beginning solutions with an unknown, "inconsistent problems" would be easier to solve.

Baroody (1999b) examined children's mental multiplication in the earliest phase of development and over time. Thirty-six third graders were randomly assigned to two groups, which practiced different subsets of multiplication combinations for 15 minutes three times a week for 8 weeks. Each group was then tested on the subset of facts they had practiced, the commuted versions of those facts, and the other group's test. The results showed that children devised increasingly flexible and accurate estimation strategies and used relational knowledge such as the commutative principle to master combinations.

To investigate the initial stages of children's understanding of intensive quantities, Nunes, Desli, and Bell (2003) conducted two studies with primary aged children. In study 1, they investigated whether the type of intensive quantity—those where variables combine to form one whole and those where variables remain separate - had an effect on children's performance on non-conceptual tasks. Individual participants (105 children, ages 6 to 8 years) were presented 8 "taste" and 8 "cost" problems with the help of drawings. Children were not required to carry out any computations, only to consider relations between the extensive and intensive quantities involved. The findings revealed that all children at all ages performed above chance on the direct questions; in contrast, only about 10% of the 6 year olds, 26% of the 7 year olds and 60% of the 8 year olds performed above chance on the inverse questions. Thus, Nunes et al. concluded that the difficulty with intensive quantities is due to the need to consider inverse relations. To test that hypothesis, a second study was designed and one hundred thirteen 7 to 9 year olds from three different primary schools worked individually during a whole class presentation of the problems. Since the ANOVA showed significant effect of type of quantity and type of relation (but no significant effect of school year), the difficulty of reasoning about inverse proportional relations did not account for children's difficulty with understanding intensive quantities. Rather, different intensive quantities posed different types of challenges.

Squire and Bryant (2002) investigated 5 to 8-year-old children's ability to solve partitive division problems when presented with a concrete model of a problem about sharing sweets between dolls. With each problem, children were given one of 2 types of concrete models (group by divisor, group by quotient). In experiment 1, 87 children were seen individually outside class in a single 15-minute testing session. In the baseline trial, the appropriate number of sweets to be shared was placed in a pile in front of the children and dolls placed in a line on a table. The child was told how many sweets and how many dolls and was asked how many sweets he or she thought each doll would get. The child was not allowed to move sweets and was not given feedback. Instead the experimenter proceeded to group sweets for the experimental trial. In the "grouping by divisor" condition, the experimenter placed sweets for a particular doll in a vertical line in front of the doll and placed a box over the sweets. In "grouping by quotient" condition, the experimenter took the same number of sweets as there were dolls from the pile of sweets and shared them, saying "one for her," "one for her." These sweets were placed in a horizontal line in front of a row of dolls and the experimenter placed a box over the sweets. Each child was then asked how many boxes were used, how many sweets were in each box, and how they figured it out. Results indicated that five and six year olds achieved significantly lower on baseline problems. However, there was very little difference between age groups in the mean scores obtained in the "grouping by divisor" condition, and the mean score in "grouping by divisor" was significantly higher than "grouping by quotient." Also, there was a steady increase in the mean score with age for "grouping by quotient." In experiment 2, the spatial arrangement was improved by elongating the boxes placed horizontally so they were the same length as the row of dolls and sharing was the same way for each condition. In addition, in experiment 2 cumulative tasks were included in which children were asked questions about the number of boxes/sweets each time the experimenter set up groups of sweets. Since the 89 different children chosen for experiment 2 posted similar results as those in experiment 1, it was concluded that spatial factors or differences of method of sharing sweets did not cause the difference between "grouping by quotient" and "grouping by divisor" conditions (Squire & Bryant, 2002, p. 22). The third experiment investigated the effect of making the spatial arrangements of groups identical by aligning boxes in one long column in both conditions. In addition, the 91 different children in Experiment 3 were presented with pictures of dolls and boxes rather than actual dolls and boxes. Interestingly, the all-vertical spatial arrangement was more difficult than the original spatial arrangement. Squire and Bryant (2002) concluded that the "studies provide consistent empirical evidence that young children find partitive division problems much easier to solve when the size of the portions coincides with the quotient (grouping by divisor) than when it coincides with the divisor (grouping by quotient)" (p. 35).

Heirdsfield and Cooper (2002) selected two children Clare and Mandy from their sample of 16 children who attended a year 3 (7 years old) class in an inner city Brisbane school. In an interview that probed the children's mental computation, Clare was found to be accurate and flexible (used more than one strategy) while Mandy was seen as accurate and inflexible (used a single strategy). Both participated in a further set of "in depth interviews involving tasks for number fact knowledge, mental computation, computational estimation, numeration, effect of operation on number" and "questions regarding attribution, self-efficacy, beliefs and metacognition" (p. 60). Clare's mental computation strategies, including a separation strategy in both directions and a holistic strategy, revealed her numeration understanding, knowledge of the effect of an operation on number, estimation, and facility with facts. Indeed, Clare provided quick accurate answers both by recall and a derived fact strategy. Mandy, on the other hand, was accurate in mental computation but consistently employed the same strategy, a mental image of the pen and paper algorithm. Mandy was fast and accurate with number facts but when unsure, she resorted to counting. Interestingly, these two cases also shed light on the load mental computation places on working memory. As expected, Clare's use of "efficient" strategies placed little load on her working memory. Somewhat surprisingly, Mandy's familiarity and perception of her "inefficient" mental image paper and pencil algorithm resulted in less load on her working memory than expected.

In her case study, Wright (2001) explored the role that direct kinesthetic experience plays in supporting a third grader's (Karen) learning of mathematics of motion. Karen was not academically confident and was not regarded as a strong student academically. Drawing from two interviews with Karen and observations of her classroom participation, the researcher analyzed the role that physical enactment played in mathematics. In the first example, Karen used her body to predict the outcome of a two-person race. In a second example, Karen used her hands in lieu of dropped objects described in the problem to compare speed patterns. In a third example, Wright described how Karen's enactment of trips and understanding of motion enabled her to make sense of a data table. The researcher concluded that Karen's physical enactments of the trips contributed to her learning.

Baroody (1995) examined the development of children's proficiency with n+1, 1+n combinations and the evolution of counting-on strategies. Data from a case study of a mentally challenged 11 year old boy, Steve, were combined with data for 9 other "mentally handicapped" cases and five Kindergarteners' with normal IQ. Of the 13 participants in a year long training experiment with intellectually challenged children, Steve was the only one who invented a counting-on strategy and used it consistently. Baroody (1995) detailed Steve's development from concrete strategies to "count-on-from-first" (COF) and finally "count-on-from-larger" (COL) strategies and how they related to Steve's discovery of the number-after rule and commutativity. Baroody (1995) concluded that "... children can discover a number after rule for n+1 combinations or at least a generic proto-rule before inventing a counting-on strategy" (p. 206). A year long study of Kindergarteners provided an opportunity to check the hypothesis generated by Steve's case and confirmed that n+1 combinations developed before a count-on strategy and played a role in discovering the "disregard for order" rule.

Researchers have also explored children's developing knowledge of measurement. For instance, Outhred and Mitchelmore (2000) described the strategies young children used to solve rectangular covering tasks before they had been taught area measurement. A sample of 115 children randomly selected from grades 1 to 4 were observed while they solved various array-based tasks, and their drawings were collected and analyzed. The interviewer inferred children's strategies from a combination of observation and careful questioning as they worked through tasks. Children's solution strategies were classified into 5 developmental levels: Level 0— incomplete covering the area by drawing units, Level 1—Primitive covering, Level 2—Array covering, constructed from the unit, Level 3—Array covering, constructed by measurement, and Level 4—Array implied, solution by calculation. The authors argued that children learned 4 principles underlying rectangular covering as they proceeded up these levels.

In another study of measurement, Magina and Hoyles (1997) examined how children of different ages negotiated meaning within different settings that involved conceptions of angles, from a dynamic context (hands on a watch). Fifty-four students across grades 1 to 8 in middle class private schools in Brazil participated. Various sizes of circular and oval cardboard watches, with and without face numbers, were used to present prediction activities (e.g., Where will the minute hand be in half an hour?), and comparison activities (e.g., Which of six watch times show who has worked the longest?). Although age and schooling effects could not be distinguished, the prediction activities proved to be differentiated by age. The youngest students (age 6/7) had considerable difficulty with all of the tasks while the oldest students (age 14) had almost errorless performance. Comparison activities were also differentiated by age. The youngest students were influenced more by the figure formed by the hands of the watch (close together/far apart) than by time elapsed.

With respect to children's measurement of length, Kamii (1997) examined the role of transitivity and unit iteration. Three hundred eighty-three children in grades 1–5 attending public schools that served low-to-middle-income populations were interviewed individually in the middle of the school year. Children were presented a sheet of paper with an inverted T, a strip of tag board 12 inches long and 5 small plastic blocks and were asked, "Can you use this to prove (or show) that this line is longer than that line?". Seventy-two percent of the children were able to construct transitive reasoning by grade two and 76% of them were able to construct unit iteration by grade 4. These findings confirmed Piaget's view that two mental abilities are necessary to compare two lengths that cannot be compared directly. Yet, as Kamii pointed out, typical instruction treats measurement as an empirical procedure rather than as a procedure requiring reasoning.

More recently, Long and Kamii (2001) investigated children's construction of transitivity, unit iteration and conservation of speed. One hundred twenty students (30 students each at grade levels K, 2, 4, 6) from two schools serving a middle class population were interviewed at the end of the school year. Transitivity was demonstrated by about half the children in second grade. Children did not demonstrate unit iteration or conservation of speed until sixth grade.

Reece and Kamii (2001) also sought to determine the grade level at which a majority of children demonstrate transitivity and unit iteration when measuring volume. Two hundred fifty-seven children (grades 2–5), who attended two elementary schools serving a middle to upper-middle class suburban population, were interviewed individually. Only 33% of the second graders and 51% of the third graders demonstrated transitivity. Similarly, 15% of the children in second grade, 47% in third grade and 56% by grade 4 demonstrated unit iteration.

The purpose of Clements, Wilson, and Sarama's (2004) study was to chart mathematical actions-on-objects young children use to compose geometric shapes. They posited that children move through several distinct levels of thinking and competence in the domain of composition and decomposition of geometric figures. In the context of a software/print curriculum development project, *Building Blocks*, they observed children using the shapes software and generated their shape composition learning trajectory. Seven levels, (e.g., Precomposer; Piece Assembler; Picture Maker; Shape Composer; Substitution Composer; Shape Composite Iterater [Clements, et al., 2004, p. 168]) constituted the developmental progression and items representing each were randomly placed in the assessment instrument. Once items stabilized, both researchers and teachers interviewed 5–10 children and wrote case studies of each (56 children in all) and these initial analyses validated the developmental progression (at least, the first 4 levels). Eighteen children from each grade level, preK–2 across 6 classrooms (72 children) were randomly selected for a summative study. All of the children were interviewed by a graduate research assistant. Findings indicated that levels of thinking could be reliably differentiated and children were reliably assigned to a level. In closing, Clements et al.'s (2004) called for further research where free form composition tasks are used, since most research to date uses puzzles.

The final review in this section focuses on a relatively new curriculum topic, probability. To investigate whether children are able to make probability judgments on the basis of part-part relations, Spinillo (2002) interviewed 40 middle class children attending grades 1 and 2 (ages 7 and 8) in Brazil. In a single session, each child was presented with 12 trials, each consisting of three sets of blue and pink marbles. They were asked to order the sets according to the degree of chance of getting a blue marble. Spinillo found that children correctly estimated and ordered different sets according to the probability of drawing a given element by representing the task in part-part terms (favorable vs. unfavorable cases) rather than in part-whole terms (favorable vs. possibilities). The main age difference was that the 7-year-old tended to relate the quantities in absolute terms, by attending to the favorable cases or the unfavorable cases without integrating them. Moreover, these children had difficulties in taking into account the three sets of marbles at the same time. Based on his findings, Spinillo recommended that children's intuitions be *invited* into classroom instruction since they play a crucial role in the development of mathematical reasoning (Spinillo, 2002, p. 368).

Overall then, research into primary age children's mathematics thinking involves large scale interviewing techniques which attempt to explicate children's understanding of relationships among concepts or skills, rather than specific topics in isolation. Some of the studies included only a single grade but most looked at children across the early years (K–3) and some-times beyond (grades K–6). Although in our search we uncovered only one article on probability and one on geometry, we acknowledge the recent interest to infuse topics traditionally seen as secondary school topics into the early years and the need for research in these areas specific to young children's learning. Also noteworthy is the range of specific mathematical topics examined across the studies reviewed. Regardless, whether research-ers studied multi-digit operations or measurement, the children's inven-tiveness was highlighted. Whether in partitive division or intensive quantities, young children's responses assisted researchers in coming to better understand the nature and difficulty of the tasks at hand.

Intervention Studies and Primary Children's Knowledge (Ages 5–8 Years)

Research into school age children's mathematics knowledge, at times incorporates a teaching component aimed at supporting or improving children's learning. For instance, Shayer and Adhami (2003) described an intervention program designed to enhance the cognitive development of 5 to 7 year olds. The intervention was delivered partly through the context of mathematics and partly through an existing Year 1 intervention focused on Piaget's concrete operations stage. The intervention schools were in a lower SES area and had a distribution of cognitive development that was below the national average while the average in the control school was somewhat above the national average. Detailed descriptions were made of each lesson, what the teacher did and said, and what problems were observed. Results indicated that the portion of 7-year-old children with "mature concrete ability" was increased to be equal to or higher than that of the control schools.

Young-Loveridge (2004) examined the effectiveness of a program designed to improve the numeracy of young children that used number books and board games with pairs of children (p. 84). The one hundred and fifty-one 5-year-old children (86 boys, 65 girls) involved in the program attended 6 low socioeconomic schools in New Zealand and scored on the lower two thirds measures of numeracy. The children were ethnically diverse (48% European; 44% Maori; 4% Pacific Islander; and 4% other ethnicity). Significant program effects were found between comparison of pre and post measures but diminished over time as the following effect sizes reveal: 1.99 end of intervention; 1.12 six months after intervention; .50 fifteen months after intervention. Young-Loveridge suggested this washout might be because the teachers were "still committed to" a waiting for readiness philosophy, they did not capitalize on the enhanced numeracy learning of their pupils, even though the researcher had shown them what the children were capable of by the end of the program" (p. 89). Furthermore, the design of the study did not allow her to tease out the effect of the literature versus the games.

Theorizing that many of the difficulties that children experience in school are caused by an inadequate conceptual understanding of units, Sophian (2004) developed a program for 3 and 4 year olds in Head Start programs in the United States. The curriculum reflected what she termed a *prospective* developmental approach and focused on "familiarizing children with the concept of unit." The curriculum had a heavy "measurement" orientation but also included work in geometry. Forty-six children (25 boys, 21 girls) participated in two instructional segments that ran from September–December and February–May. Pre- and post-test scores using the relevant components of the Developing Skills Checklist and an instrument designed for the study were obtained for the participants and for a comparative group. Although significant program effects were found, the effect sizes (.08 and .09) were quite modest, especially considering the possible washout effects experienced by other interventions.

Fuson, Smith, and Cicero (1997) reported on a year long classroom teaching experiment in two Latino Low SES urban first grade classrooms (one English speaking, one Spanish) where teacher-researchers sought to support thinking of 2-digit quantities as tens and ones. The instruction was based on a constructivist view of learning and a Vygotskian view of teaching and learning where assistance included using activities that enabled children to construct knowledge. The teacher-researcher's role was to set problem activities, enable discussion of solutions, monitor and assess progress, initially model or lead knowledge building, and gradually withdraw support. Data consisted of notes about learning and samples of errors made on homework and class work and end-of-year interviews. Results indicated that there were many different learning paths to children's understanding of place value and multi-digit addition and subtraction, rather than a unitary linear progression. Children learned mathematics with the support provided much better than they ordinarily would have without this kind of support. Children's achievement in these two grade 1 classrooms was equal to that of East Asians who typically outperform their North American peers. In fact, these students were performing at a level equal to the grade 3 students in the United States, when results were compared with the results of large-scale assessment.

Informed by the perspective that mathematical development has its roots in children's action schemas, Kamii, Rummelsburg, and Kari (2005) hypothesized that giving physical knowledge games to low-performing, low SES first graders would enhance their logico-mathematical understanding of number as described by Piaget. Twenty-six students engaged in physical-knowledge activities and games such as "pick up sticks" during the math hour instead of typical math instruction. During the second half of the school year, when they showed "readiness" for arithmetic, the children were given arithmetic games and word problems that stimulated the exchange of viewpoints. At the end of the year, the children in the experimental group were compared with a similar group of 20 first graders who received traditional exercises focusing narrowly on number (e.g., counting objects, making one-to-one correspondences, and answering questions like 2 + 2). While both groups scored essentially the same on a Houghton Mifflin oral group readiness test at the beginning of the year, at the end of the year, the experimental group was significantly superior both in mental arithmetic and in logical reasoning.

Using a similar quasi-experimental intervention method, Park and Nunes (2001) sought to assess two hypotheses about the origin of multiplication in children's reasoning: (1) that the concept of multiplication is grounded in the understanding of repeated addition, and (2) that repeated addition is only a calculation procedure and that the understanding of multiplication has its roots in the schema of correspondence. Pupils from two English primary schools (mean age 6 years 7 months) who had not been taught about multiplication in school were pre-tested in additive and multiplicative reasoning. They were then randomly assigned to one of two treatment conditions: teaching multiplication (1) through repeated addition or (2) through correspondence. The intervention consisted of 16 problems delivered in an hour of instruction across two days. Results showed that both groups made significant progress from pre-test to post test. The group taught by correspondence made significantly more progress in multiplicative reasoning than in additive reasoning. The group taught by repeated addition made similar progress in both types of problems. At post-test, the correspondence group performed significantly better that the repeated addition group in multiplicative reasoning problems even after controlling for differences in the level of performance at pretest. Thus, this study supported the hypothesis that the origin of the concept of multiplication is in the schema of correspondence, rather than in the idea of repeated addition.

In a study designed to examine the relationships between children's early mathematics knowledge and later achievement, Aubrey, Dahl, and Godfrey (2006) administered three forms of the Utrecht Early Mathematical Competency Test to 300 children in 21 schools. They later correlated these results with scores on the SAT, a national standardized measure. They found that the scores on the early mathematics test predicted later achievement scores. They concluded, "Without active intervention, it seems likely that children with little mathematical knowledge at the beginning of formal schooling will remain low achievers throughout their primary years and probably, beyond" (p. 44).

Overall then the intervention studies reviewed here were successful in enhancing the children's learning experiences to varying degrees. Of course, the long term impact of such interventions is, for the most part, unknown.

International Comparisons of Children's Mathematics Learning

It is generally acknowledged that Asian students outperform North American students in mathematics and this difference begins to be manifested early in children's development (e.g., Ginsburg et al., 1997). For example, Ho and Fuson (1998) report that "Asian students perform better than Western students" in "abstract counting to 100, in representing place values of numbers with ten-structured blocks early in first grade and in mental addition in kindergarten" (p. 536). One theory attempting to explain these differences is the regularity in the numbers 10 to 100 associated with Asian languages such as Chinese, Japanese and Korean and the irregularity of these numbers in English. To test the theory, Ho and Fuson (1998) administered a counting sequence task and a hidden object task to three groups of four-year-olds from middle class backgrounds comprised thus: (1) 36 children who lived in Hong Kong and spoke only Chinese; (2) 36 children who spoke Chinese English; and (3) 12 children who spoke American English. They found that the Chinese children outperformed their English-speaking peers "in rote counting, in place value numeration, in embedded-ten cardinal understanding and in applying the knowledge to solving simple problems" (p. 543). However, Ho and Fuson cautioned that the differences in learning might be the result of factors other than the differences in linguistic regularity of the languages. For example, Chinese caregivers perceive it appropriate for young children to develop understanding of what Ho and Fuson term "embedded ten cardinality" whereas American caregivers tend not to encourage children to develop this understanding but instead encourage children to count by ones. As they elaborated, the differences in children's understanding is probably also attributable to the cultural differences in the mediation caregivers provide young children through activities at school and at home.

In their essay, Towse and Saxton (1998) examined various cultural and linguistic perspectives as to differences in developing competency in numeracy. They highlighted a number of factors, especially in terms of why Asian students outperform students from western countries. First, countries such as Japan have an extensive and elaborate system of early childhood education. Secondly, Asian teachers tend to ask conceptual questions of their students early on whereas American teachers, for example, tend to ask computational questions that are vague (p. 137). Towse and Saxton also argued that Japanese textbooks are superior to those used in western countries in that they offer more examples and use accompanying illustrations that better support the concept being learned and taught. Furthermore, they contended, American textbooks tend to underestimate children's abilities and present material that is not challenging (pp. 137–138). Moreover, parents and children in Taiwan and Japan associate children's success with hard work; American parents and children attribute performance in mathematics to innate ability and poor teaching.

Ginsburg et al. (1997) hypothesized that Asian children entered school with more fully developed informal mathematical abilities (e.g., counting, mental addition) than children from other countries as a result of the cultural mediation practices that encourage such development early. Ginsburg et al. drew a trans-national sample of preschool children from China, Colombia, Japan, Korea and the United States representing different SES strata. They had children pretend to attend a birthday party and had them engage in 10 tasks—count by ones, comparison of number, concrete addition, concrete subtraction, digit span memory, finger displays of number, informal addition, informal subtraction, perception of more and production from 10. Results showed that the Chinese, Korean, Japanese children scored significantly higher than those from the United States and Colombia (pp. 176–177). As well, Asian students tended to be more accurate and consistent than the other children. Furthermore, the Chinese children outperformed all others, which Ginsburg et al. attributed to the Chinese emphasis on academics. Interestingly, there was very little difference between the performance of African American and Caucasian American students, although as a group, African American children tend to perform much more poorly than their white counterparts later in school. Ginsburg et al. contended that this later finding challenges the fairly common notion that African American children come to school with intellectual deficits; clearly this was not the case here as these children were performing at par with their mainstream counterparts.

In an attempt to understand the role of cultural practices and mathematics achievement, Guberman (2004) examined relationships between ethnicity, out-of-school activities, and arithmetical performance. Forty-nine Latin American and Korean American children in grades 1, 2, and 3 in one Los Angeles working class district school were involved in the study. Data collection included (a) parents' educational attitudes and beliefs, (b) parents' reports of children's everyday activities (frequency and arithmetic complexity of activity) that provided opportunity to use money and arithmetic, and (c) children's performance on arithmetic tasks consisting of (1) problems that required summing monetary denominations and (2) the same problems solved using cardboard denominational chips. With both problem sets, children had to identify denominations, distinguish between absolute value and relative value (3 nickels = 15 cents), and combine various denominations. The test scores of children with high and with low involvement with money were compared. Few differences emerged in parents' attitudes about education. Results indicated that there were differences in out-of-school activities, with Latin American children more often engaged in instrumental activities with money, and Korean American children more often engaged in activities with a more academic focus intended to support their learning. Performance in arithmetic mirrored these activities. Latin American children solved correctly more tasks with money than chips. Korean American children solved correctly more tasks with chips than money. Korean children correctly solved more problems of both types. Thus the effect on children's arithmetical achievements varied by their involvement in the different activity types and that involvement was related to cultural practice differences based in ethnicity.

To summarize then, a number of factors appear to influence young children's mathematical competence. These include linguistic regularity, parental and teacher mediation styles, different cultural expectations, and how mathematics is practiced within different cultural groups, both in and out of school.

TEACHERS' KNOWLEDGE AND PRACTICE

While individual children's mathematical thinking has received considerable attention from researchers, educators have also examined teaching practice and how pedagogy affects children's mathematical development. For example, as part of a larger study investigating mathematics teaching, Aubrey (1995) attempted to document how mathematical knowledge was presented and how teachers and children understood that knowledge. She analyzed discourse as three teachers worked with children in reception classes during mathematics lessons from September to May. Underlying the study was the theory that learning "math is a process of being supported by an adult into a particular form of discourse which embodies its own sequence of development, moving from a grounding in practical and social contexts toward a more symbolic and abstract system" (p. 3). Aubrey found considerable variation in what she termed the "richness" of the quality of experiences in terms of the degree to which the individual teachers were able to link new knowledge with children's prior knowledge. The amount of time in which children were able to engage in mathematics also varied, as did the number of children that teachers worked with during the lesson. For example, whereas one teacher tended to begin with whole class instruction that was followed by group work, others tended to work with small groups with no whole class instruction. Aubrey suggested the pedagogical stances ranged from didactic, direct instruction to indirect, discovery oriented teaching.

A fairly systematic and prolonged reform effort in mathematics learning and teaching undertaken in Australia is the Early Numeracy Research Project (ENRP) that has been underway since 1999 (e.g., Clarke et al., 2001). The project has a three pronged approach: (1) helping develop teacher's understanding of young children's mathematical development; (2) having teachers conduct individual interviews with children and using mathematical tasks; and (3) ongoing professional development aimed at furthering teachers' understandings of children's mathematical thinking as a result of the interviews and the implications for instruction. Based on a sample of nearly 12,000 students, Clarke et al. (2001) reported enhanced mathematical performance of Year (grade) 1 and Year (grade) 2 children in the trial schools compared to children in the reference schools. Using different data collection techniques such as questionnaires, focus group sessions, and teacher journals, Clarke et al. analyzed the impact of the project on teaching practice. They found that ENRP teachers: focused more on the growth points of children; used more open ended questions; provided children more time to explore topics and concepts; offered children more opportunities to share strategies they used in problem solving; provided greater challenges because of higher expectations based on knowledge garnered from the individual interviews as to children's mathematical capabilities; emphasized links between mathematical ideas and classroom and out-of-school or real life math; and placed less emphasis on having children record algorithms (pp. 12–13). Furthermore, teachers reported that children were better at explaining their reasoning, they expected to be challenged in mathematics and demonstrated greater persistence, they engaged meta-cognitively about their learning, and enjoyed greater success in early mathematics.

Working with pre-service teachers, McDonough, Clarke, and Clarke (2002), had them conduct individual interviews with 5 and 6-year-old children involving different mathematical tasks. This work was also associated with the Early Numeracy Research Projects (ERNP) undertaken in Australia and described earlier. Using a combination of interviews, questionnaires, and focus group sessions, McDonough et al. attempted to determine the effects of the individual interviews with the children on instruction. Overall, the pre-service teachers reported positively on their experiences, reporting that the interviews provided insights into children's mathematical thinking. Indeed, they tended to have enhanced views of children's mathematical abilities. Interestingly, the pre-service teachers did not perceive the one-on-one work as providing opportunities to inform their planning for instruction. The researchers noted that less experienced teachers (and pre-service teachers) tended to focus on the individual students with whom they worked and tended not to generalize what they had learned to teaching young children mathematics in general. Interestingly, the pre-service teachers noted the different strategies employed by children, children's varying degrees of confidence and the ability to articulate mathematical understanding and processes, and differences in the ways that children responded to tasks. McDonough et al. concluded that having teachers/student teachers work with individual children is indeed an effective way to help them understand young children's mathematical thinking and hence to inform curriculum and pedagogy. Indeed, the ENRP project has "taken hold" internationally and is being adapted and adopted in schools in British Columbia, Canada, for example.

Another well known and well-regarded attempt at reforming the teaching and leaning of mathematics is Cognitively Guided Instruction or CGI (Carpenter, Fennema, & Franke, 1996). In CGI, the focus is on having teachers examine and understand students' mathematical thinking and through this framework, teachers' own mathematical knowledge is advanced (Carpenter et al., 1996, p. 4). As they explained, "understanding children's strategies forces teachers to confront their own understanding of these properties" (p. 15). Carpenter et al. reported that their studies demonstrate that teachers trained in CGI are much better at determining the problems their students are capable of solving and the strategies they use to solve them. Furthermore, as Franke (2001) explained, "Teachers expectations of their students' mathematical understanding changed dramatically. First grade teachers saw that their students could solve word problems often omitted from the curriculum until third grade" (p. 4). In CGI, the knowledge that students bring to mathematical problems is recognized as very important with the teachers' role being that of helping children connect that knowledge with the problem at hand and to guide them to solving it. Carpenter et al. summarized the impact of CGI training on teachers thus: "Recognizing students have knowledge worth listening to and building on, teachers evaluate their general philosophies about their role as dispenser of knowledge, nature of class interactions, use of different forms of grouping, etc." (p. 16). While CGI originally focused on grade one children and teachers, Franke (2001) described how the project expanded to involve teachers from kindergarten to grade 5 with similar results in terms of children's enhanced mathematical learning and more responsive and appropriate teaching based on children's abilities and needs.

While results from the CGI and ENRP studies revealed considerable positive change in teachers' practice as a result of their having carefully and systematically examined children's mathematical thinking, the results of a study by Warfield, Wood, and Lehman (2005) were more guarded.

They worked with 7 beginning teachers who taught first, second or third grade in three different schools in one school district. None of the teachers used commercial texts but instead utilized "project materials" developed in a previous study (p. 443). In the summer prior to commencing their first year of teaching, the participants attended a one-week workshop in which they learned about children's mathematical thinking and the ways that materials can influence that thinking. Teachers videotaped their math lessons over two years, once a month during the initial year and twice monthly in year two. The videotape of the initial lesson in year one served as a baseline from which to compare the teaching across the length of the project. The analysis over 2 years revealed distinct differences in development of teachers' practices. One group engaged in teaching that was consistent with the reform agenda of the instruction being led by an examination of children's thinking; the other group of teachers maintained the same (and more traditional) teaching evidenced in their initial teaching (Warfield et al., 2005, pp. 446–448). The more conventional teachers tended not to question children in ways that enabled them to explicate their thinking and in some cases actually curtailed children's thinking (p. 448). Teachers in the second group though, developed more complex teaching practices that reflected an "inquiry classroom culture" in which strategy reporting was encouraged and featured their asking clarification questions to extend children's explanation (p. 448). Interestingly, teachers in the first group tended to speak of "high/low" kids whereas the teachers in the second group tended not to differentiate children in this way.

In addition to the contributions these projects have made to our understanding of children's mathematical knowledge, they have evolved to the point that recent reports are shedding important light on teacher development and knowledge. Thus, research that examines teachers' knowledge and children's mathematical learning, such as that reported here, strongly promotes teachers' knowledge of student thinking as a very promising avenue that supports change in classroom practice. As teachers come to understand and recognize the strengths children bring to the mathematics classroom and ways to assess children's knowledge, the more able they are to provide environments which elicit and extend that knowledge.

CURRICULUM AND INSTRUCTION ISSUES IN EARLY CHILDHOOD MATHEMATICS

Informed by current research, mathematics educators and researchers are working together to create learning conditions that begin with children's experiences and then support the use of their reasoning capacities to build conceptual knowledge (Clements, Sarama, & DiBiase, 2004). Engaging children in play provides informal experiences from which mathematics learning can emerge. Fuson et al. (1997) reported that certain games encourage the development of flexible thinking about mathematics. During play, children learn comparison, estimation, patterns, symmetry, and spatial relations (Ginsburg et al., 1999). Kamii (2003) demonstrated how a common children's board game was adapted to foster kindergarteners' logico-mathematical thinking including classification, seriation, and spatial and temporal relationships. Teachers have an active role in realizing the mathematical thinking possibilities of the use of games (Seo, 2003) and in using games as an opportunity to gather additional information about their student's learning (Kamii, 2003).

Another commonly used vehicle for presenting experiences from which children may learn mathematics is to pose problems and then assist children in discovering strategies to solve them. Fuson et al. (1997) reported on four different projects that used a problem solving approach to develop children's concepts and methods for addition and subtraction of multi-digit numbers. The teacher's role was to provide sustained opportunities for children to construct the triad of conceptual structures that relate ten-structured quantities, number words, and written 3-digit numerals. The children then used these conceptual triads in solving problems. The categories of methods children devised for solving multi-digit addition and subtraction problems followed a developmental pattern. Children first learned to construct the problems with physical objects, then developed count-on strategies, and finally reached a third level where they could combine and separate quantities in flexible ways. Children gradually learned more and more number combinations as memorized facts. By the time they got to three and four -digit numbers, the children needed to use written records of their calculating as a memory support, and to provide a record to support discussion and reflection.

Social interaction as found in play or in group-problem-solving approaches may offer a pathway to enhancing mathematics learning in several ways. Yackel, Cobb, and Wood (1999) studied a Grade 2 classroom that followed an inquiry mathematics tradition. Students and teacher constituted mathematical truths as they engaged in explaining and justifying activity in order to get others to agree that their solutions were legitimate. The students developed increasingly sophisticated concepts of ten as they attempted to partition numbers in many different ways.

Cicero, De La Cruz, and Fuson (1999), reporting on the two central activities in the Children's Math Worlds program, suggested linking mathematical activities in classrooms to children's mathematical experiences outside of school. They postulated that using the narratives that children bring to school can support the creation of a rich and sustained environment for learning to write, solve, and explain ways of solving word problems. Classroom conversation may be co-constructed as children and teachers listen, put their stories in a mathematical context, use children's labeled mathematical drawings and number drawings, and elicit explanations from each other about how they solved the problems. The use of outside school experiences also offers teachers a window into differences among children's mathematics thinking that relate to differences among the students' cultural and experiential backgrounds.

A teacher's use of mathematical language can be important for developing mathematical concepts. In discussing how understanding of the term "difference" might be better developed in Australian early primary school, Clarke (2003) found that many children had little exposure to that term, had no idea or incorrect notions of what "difference" meant, and had difficulty with tasks involving the notion of difference. This finding suggests that teachers should talk explicitly about mathematical concepts using a variety of the words that relate to that concept so as to help children develop a mathematics vocabulary and to insure as much as possible that children understand what is being discussed.

According to Nunes (1999), mathematics is a cultural practice, situated in time and space and defined by the community of mathematicians. She elaborates that, "To learn mathematics is to become socialized into its particular ways of knowing," (p. 33). However, when children first start to learn mathematics in school, they bring to the mathematics classroom meanings that they will assign to the systems of mathematical signs that they are taught. According to Nunes, Piaget's (1972) central thesis was that the basic meanings of mathematical concepts stem from children's schemas of action, that is, from generalizable and structured actions which can be applied to a variety of objects and which center on the relations between objects and transformations, rather than the objects themselves. Carefully designed curricula and pedagogy capitalize on children's existing schemata that have been developed prior to formal instruction. They also support children in utilizing the mathematical practices from their homes and communities as they learn the more formalized mathematics of school.

Baroody (2000) addresses the question of how best to provide mathematics experiences for young children. Following his review of some recent research on young children's number and arithmetic concepts and skills, he argues for an investigative approach wherein instruction begins with a worthwhile task through which teachers help children build on what children already know. In particular, he provides suggestions for "making math experiences for young children purposeful, meaningful and inquiry based by using everyday situations, children's questions, games and children's literature" p. 65 Although Baroody (2000) acknowledges that learning is more likely to occur if wiser adults or older children mediate younger children's experiences, he urges teachers to encourage children to discover and do as much for themselves as possible.

Several attempts at developing such curricula are evident in the literature. For example, *Big Math for Little Kids* is a joyful, comprehensive, research-based program for pre-kindergarten children (Greenes, Ginsburg & Balfanz, 2004, p. 159). The program aims to:

1. build on children's knowledge and interests;
2. integrate mathematics into routine class activities;
3. introduce and enrich ideas in a playful way;
4. develop complex mathematical ideas;
5. promote language and reflection;
6. encourage thinking like a mathematician;
7. provide repetition (pp. 160–161).

Observational evidence obtained during implementation suggests the children were able to engage in thinking abstractly in ways "not usually thought to be characteristic of young children" (p. 164). Greenes et al. suggest that the program contributes to language development as well, noting that young speakers of languages other than (or in addition to) English might especially benefit from the program as they are not at a disadvantage to native speakers who are also learning the mathematical language.

Sarama and Clements (2004) described their curriculum project, *Building Blocks*. It includes specification of mathematical ideas (computer objects or manipulatives) and processes/skills (software tools or actions) which have been extensively field tested from first inception through to a large summative evaluation. They indicate that like other researchers, they too have found that children are more competent than most programs assume. However, they have also uncovered profound variability and suggest we need research that identifies effective ways of combining group work with individual assessment and teaching. They have found that teachers who understand the learning trajectories of mathematical strands (such as the ones they have developed) were more effective at teaching small groups. Indeed, a key feature of *Building Blocks* is "a management system that guides children through fine grained research based learning trajectories. These activities on and off the computer connect children's informal knowledge to more formal school math" (Sarama, & Clements, 2004, p. 188).

Casey, Kersh, and Young (2004) developed a series of supplementary math books for early childhood classrooms (preK–2), called *Round the Rug Math: Adventures in Problem Solving*. A key feature of this series is the incorporation of story telling as a medium for teaching math. They explained, "The stories are intended to be delivered in a traditional storytelling manner, rather than simply read out loud from a book. This allows the storyteller to establish a deeper connection with the audience through eye contact, personal expression and interaction" (Casey et al., 2004, p 188). In addition, the sagas or long epic adventures allow math concepts to be taught in a systematic, hierarchical progression. Stories interwoven with mathematics extend over 6–8 lessons, with each lesson presented in the form of a new problem students must help characters solve in order for a story to progress. Other important features include the role puppets play as the narrators and the strong visualization/spatial-reasoning component.

CONCLUSION

When we consider the research literature reviewed in this chapter, it becomes apparent that the Piagetian influence has been enormous in the area of early mathematics development. This is manifested by the fact that much of the research is framed within Piagetian notions of development and that a bulk of the research focuses on individual children's knowledge construction. Piaget (1970) once asserted, "Each time that one prematurely teaches a child something he could have discovered for himself, that child is kept from inventing it and consequently from understanding it completely" (p. 715). We conjecture that few contemporary educators and researchers would support such an individualistic view of learning or development.

In that regard, research based on Vygotskian notions of mediation and mathematics as situated learning is beginning to emerge. However, we uncovered no research on collaborative learning for children in the age group focused on in this review. Another trend in this research is the emphasis placed on school aged children's mathematical knowledge, with only a smattering of studies of 3 and 4 year olds. In addition, we see that the age band from 10 months to 36 months is relatively absent from the literature. This may be due to limited accessibility (although children of this age group do attend childcare facilities) or the need to devise ways in which to study their mathematical development without relying on written and oral communication. In addition to the prominence of one-on-one interviews in this literature, research has also begun to observe young children in various learning settings, although school-like contexts are more prevalent.

Perhaps most striking about the findings of research in early childhood mathematics is the overall competence children demonstrate. Indeed, young children demonstrate knowledge and understanding of mathematics concepts and skills that typically we associate with older children. This review of research strongly supports the premise that we currently underestimate what young children can do. We believe that curricula that continue to emphasize pre-number activity and keep number and number operations out of the pre-K and kindergarten classrooms, for instance, are doing children a disservice. As researchers reiterate time and again, children construct a substantial amount of mathematical knowledge prior to school and we need to recognize and build on their prior knowledge in our classrooms. It is encouraging that many of the reform efforts are attempting to do so. Noteworthy also is the fact that research is beginning to emerge on the role of significant others, such as parents, siblings or teachers, in supporting and extending young children's mathematics learning. In early childhood mathematics, we are only just beginning to look at the role of language, culture, ethnicity, and social class in meaningful ways, beyond their role as independent variables in experimental research. Interestingly, our review uncovered no research on young children's beliefs about, perceptions of, or attitudes toward, mathematics and in this regard, young children's voices are silent. In the past 10 years, we have clearly begun to broaden our lens beyond the individual and what mathematics he or she knows, but much remains to be done if we are to better understand the ways in which young children experience mathematics in the early years, especially from a mathematics as social practice perspective.

REFERENCES

Anderson, A. (1997). Families and mathematics: A study of parent-child interactions. *Journal for Research in Mathematics Education, 28,* 484–511.

Anderson, A., Anderson, J., & Shapiro, J. (2005). Supporting multiple literacies: Parents' and children's mathematical talk within storybook reading. *Mathematics Education Research Journal, 16,* 5–26.

Anderson, A., Anderson, J., & Shapiro, J. (2004). Mathematical discourse in shared storybook reading. *Journal for Research in Mathematics Education, 35,* 5–33.

Anderson, A., & Anderson, J. (1995). Learning mathematics through children's literature: A case study. *Canadian Journal of Research in Early Childhood Education, 4,* 1–9.

Aubrey, C., Dahl, S., & Godfrey, R. (2006). Early mathematical development and later achievement: Further evidence. *Mathematics Education Research Journal, 18,* 27–46.

Aubrey, C. (1995). Teacher and pupil interactions and the processes of mathematical instruction in four reception classrooms over children's first year in school. *British Educational Research Journal, 21*(1), 31–49.

Baroody, A. J., (2000, July). Does mathematics instruction for three- to five-year-olds really make sense? *Young Children,*, 61–67.

Baroody, A. (1999a). Children's relational knowledge of addition and subtraction. *Cognition and Instruction, 17*(2), 137–176.

Baroody, A. (1999b). The roles of estimation and the commutativity principle in the development of third graders mental multiplication. *Journal of Experimental Child Psychology, 74,* 157–193.

Baroody, A. (1995). The role of the number-after rule in the invention of computational shortcuts. *Cognition and Instruction, 13*(2), 189–219.

Benigno, J., & Ellis, S. (2004). Two is greater than three: Effects of older siblings on parental support of preschoolers' counting in middle income families. *Early Childhood Research Quarterly, 19,* 4–20.

Benson, A., & Baroody, A. (2002, April). *The case of Blake: Number-word and number development.* Paper presented at American Educational Research Association, New Orleans.

Butterworth, N. (1989). *One snowy night.* London: HarperCollins.

Carpenter, T., Fennema, E. & Franke, M. (1996). Cognitively Guided Instruction: A knowledge base for reform in primary mathematics instruction. *Elementary School Journal, 97*(1),3–20.

Carpenter, T. P., Franke, M. L., Jacobs, V. R., Fennema, E., & Empson, S. (1998). A longitudinal study of invention and understanding in children's multidigit addition and subtraction. *Journal for Research in Mathematics Education, 29*(1), 3–20.

Casey, B., Kersh, J., & Young, J. (2004). Storytelling sagas: An effective medium for teaching early childhood mathematics. *Early Childhood Research Quarterly, 19,* 167–172.

Clements, D., Sarama, J., & DiBiase, A. (2004). *Engaging young children in mathematics: Standards for early childhood mathematics education.* Mahwah, NJ: Erlbaum.

Clements, D., Wilson, D., & Sarama, J. (2004). Young children's composition of geometric figures: a learning trajectory. *Mathematical Thinking and Learning, 6,* 163–184.

Cicero, A., De La Cruz, Y., & Fuson, K. (1999). Teaching and learning creatively: Using children's narratives. *Teaching Children Mathematics, 5,* 544–547.

Clarke, D. (2003), An issue in teaching and learning subtraction: What's the difference? *Australian Primary Mathematics Classroom, 8*(3), 4–11.

Clarke, D., Cheeseman, J., Clarke, B., Gervasoni, A., Gronn,D., Horne, M., McDonough, A., Montgomery, P., Rowley, G., & Sullivan, P. (2001, July). *Understanding, assessing, and developing young children's mathematical thinking: Research as a powerful tool for professional growth.* Keynote paper presented at the annual conference of Mathematics Education Research Group of Australasia, Sydney, Australia.

Correa, J., Nunes, T., & Bryant, P. (1998). Young children's understanding of division: The relationship between division terms in a non-computational task. *Journal of Educational Psychology, 90,* 321–329.

Dowker, A. (1998). Individual differences in normal mathematical development. In C. Donlan (Ed.), *The development of mathematical skills* (pp. 275–302). Hove, UK: Psychology Press Limited.

Evans, C., Leija, A., & Falkner, T. (2001). *Math links: Teaching the NTCM Standards through children's literature.* Englewood, CO: Teacher Idea Press.

Franke, M. (2001). Learning to teach mathematics: Focus on student thinking. *Theory into Practice, 40*(2), 102–110.

Fuson, K., Carroll, W., & Landis, J. (1996). Levels in conceptualizing and solving addition and subtraction compare word problems. *Cognition and Instruction, 14*, 345–371.

Fuson, K., Grandau, L., & Sugiyama, P. (2001). Achievable numerical understanding for all children. *Teaching Children Mathematics, 7*, 522–526.

Fuson, K., Smith, S., Cicero, A., (1997). Supporting Latino first graders' ten-structured thinking in urban classrooms. *Journal for Research in Mathematics Education 28*(6), 738–766.

Fuson, K., Weare, D., Hiebert, J., Murry, G., Human, P. G., Olivier, A. I., Carpenter, T. P., & Fennema, E. (1997). Children's conceptual structures for multidigit numbers and methods of multidigit addition and subtraction. *Journal for Research in Mathematics Education, 28*, 130–162.

Ginsburg, H., Choi, E., Lopez, L., Netley, R., & Chao-Yuan, C. (1997). Happy Birthday to you: Early mathematical thinking of Asian, South American and US children. In T. Nunes & P. Bryant (Eds.), *Learning and teaching mathematics: An international perspective* (pp. 163–201). London: Psychology Press.

Ginsburg, H., Inoue, N., & Seo, K. H. (1999). Young children doing mathematics: Observations of everyday activities. In J.V. Copley (Ed.). *Mathematics in the early years* (pp. 88–99). Reston, VA: National Council of Teachers of Mathematics.

Ginsburg, H., Klein, A., & Prentice, S. (1998). The development of children's mathematical thinking: Connecting research and practice. In I. Sigel & K. Renninger (Eds.), *Handbook of child psychology, Vol. 4, Child psychology in practice* (5th ed., pp. 401–476). New York: Wiley.

Greenes, C., Ginsburg, H., & Balfanz, R. (2004). Big math for little kids. *Early Childhood Research Quarterly, 19*, 159–166.

Griffiths, R., & Clyne, M. (1991). Once upon a time. *Australian Mathematics Teacher, 47*, 10–13.

Gonzalez, J., & Espinel, A. (2002). Strategy choice in solving arithmetic word problems: Are there differences between students with learning disabilities, G-V poor performance and typical achievement students? *Learning Disability Quarterly, 25*, 113–122.

Guberman, S. (2004). A comparative study of children's out of school activities and arithmetical achievements. *Journal for Research in Mathematics Education, 35*, 117–150.

Heirdsfield, A., & Cooper, T. (2002). Flexibility and inflexibility in accurate mental addition and subtraction: Two case studies. *Journal of Mathematical Behavior, 21*, 57–74.

Ho, C., & Fuson, K. (1998). Children's knowledge of teen quantities as tens and ones: Comparisons of Chinese, British and American kindergartens. *Journal of Educational Psychology, 90*, 536–544.

Hunting, R. (2003). Part-whole number knowledge in preschool children, *Journal of Mathematical Behavior, 22*, 217–235.

Kamii, C. (2003, September). Modifying a board game to foster kindergarteners' logico-mathematical thinking. *Young Children*, 20–26.

Kamii, C (1997). Measurement of length: The need for a better approach to teaching. *School Science and Mathematics, 97,* 116–122.

Kamii, C., Lewis, B., & Booker, B. (1998). Instead of teaching missing addends. *Teaching Children Mathematics, 4,* 458–41.

Kamii, C., Lewis, B., & Kirkland, L. (2001). Fluency in subtraction compared with addition. *Journal of Mathematical Behavior, 20,* 33–42.

Kamii, C., Rummelsburg, J., & Kari, A. (2005). Teaching arithmetic to low-performing, low-SES first graders. *Journal of Mathematical Behavior, 24,* 39–50.

Lionni, L. (1992). *Mr. McMouse.* New York: Knopf.

Lionni, L. (1963). *Swimmy.* New York: Pantheon.

Long, K., & Kamii, C. (2001). The measurement of time: Children's construction of transitivity, unit iteration and conservation of speed. *School Science and Mathematics, 101,* 125–133.

Magina, S., & Hoyles, C. (1997). Children's understanding of turn and angle. In T. Nunes & P. Bryant (Eds.) *Learning and teaching mathematics: An international perspective.* Hove, UK: Psychology Press.

McDonough, A., Clarke, B., & Clarke, D. (2002). Understanding, assessing and developing children's mathematical thinking: The power of a one-to-one interview for preservice teachers in providing insights into appropriate pedagogical practices. *International Journal of Educational Research, 37,* 211–226.

Miyakawa, Y., Kamii, C., & Nagahiro, M. (2005). The development of logico-mathematical thinking at ages 1–3 in play with blocks and an incline. *Journal of Research in Childhood Education, 29,* 292–301.

Mix, K., Huttenlocher, J., & Levine, S. (2002). *Quantitative development in infancy and early childhood.* Oxford: Oxford University Press.

Muldoon, K., Lewis, C., & Freeman, N. (2003). Putting counting to work: preschoolers' understanding of cardinal extension. *International Journal of Educational Research, 39,* 695–718.

Munn, P. (1998). Symbolic function in pre-schoolers. In C. Donlan (Ed.), *The development of mathematical skills* (pp. 47–71). London: Psychology Press.

National Council of Teachers of Mathematics. (2000). *Principles and standards for school mathematics.* Reston, VA: Author.

Nunes, T. (1999). Mathematics learning as a socialization of the mind. *Culture and Activity, 6,* 33–53.

Nunes, T., Desli, D., & Bell, D. (2003). The development of children's understanding of intensive quantities. *International Journal of Educational Research, 39,* 651–675.

Outhred, L., & Mitchelmore, M. (2000). Young children's intuitive understanding of rectangular area measurement. *Journal for Research in Mathematics Education 31,* 144–167.

Park, J,, & Nunes, T. (2001). The development of the concept of multiplication. *Cognitive Development, 16,* 763–773.

Pepper, K., & Hunting, R. (1998). Preschoolers' counting and sharing. *Journal for Research in Mathematics Education, 29,* 164–183.

Piaget, J. (1972). *The psychology of intelligence* (M. Perry & D. E. Berltyne, Trans.) Totowa, NJ: Littlefield, Adams, & Co. (Original work published in 1947).

Piaget, J. (1970). Piaget's theory. In P. H. Mussen (Ed.), *Carmichael's manual of child psychology* (Vol. I, pp. 703–732). New York: Wiley.

Reece, C., & Kamii, C. (2001). The measurement of volume: Why do young children measure inaccurately? *School Science and Mathematics, 101,* 356–362.

Rittle-Johnson, B., & Siegler, R. (1998). The relation between conceptual and procedural knowledge in learning mathematics: A review. In C. Donlan (Ed.), *The development of mathematical skills* (pp. 75–109). Hove, UK: Psychology Press.

Sarama, J., & Clements, D. (2004). Building blocks for early childhood mathematics. *Early Childhood Research Quarterly, 19,* 181–189.

Saxe, G., Guberman, S., & Gearhart, S. (1987). Social processes in early number development. *Monographs of the Society for Research in Child Development, 52* (2, Serial No. 216).

Seo, K-H. (2003). What children's play tells us about teaching mathematics. *Young Children, 61*(1), 28–34.

Shapiro, J., Anderson, J., & Anderson, A. (1997). Diversity in parental storybook reading. *Early Child Development and Care, 127–128,* 47–59.

Shayer, M., & Adhami, M. (2003). Realizing the cognitive potential of children 5–7 with a mathematics focus. *International Journal of Educational Research, 39,* 743–775.

Singer, J., Kohn, A., & Resnick, L. (1997). Knowing about proportions in different contexts. In T. Nunes & P. Bryant (Eds.), *Learning and teaching mathematics: An international perspective* (pp. 115–132). Hove, UK: Psychology Press.

Sophian, C. (2004). Mathematics for the future: Developing a Head Start curriculum to support mathematics learning. *Early Childhood Research Quarterly, 19,* 59–81.

Sophian, C. (1998). A developmental perspective on children's counting. In C. Donlan (Ed.), *The development of mathematical skills* (pp. 27–46). Hove, UK: Psychology Press.

Spinillo, A. (2002). Children's use of part-part comparison to estimate probability. *Journal of Mathematical Behavior, 21,* 357–369.

Squire, S., & Bryant, P. (2002). The influence of sharing on children's initial concept of division. *Journal of Experimental Child Psychology, 81,* 1- 43.

Towse, J., & Saxton, M. (1998). Mathematics across national boundaries: Cultural and linguistic perspectives on numerical competence. In C. Donlan (Ed.), *The development of mathematical skills* (pp. 129–150). Hove, UK: Psychology Press.

Tudge, J., & Doucet, F. (2004). Early mathematical experiences: observing young Black and White children's everyday activities. *Early Childhood Research Quarterly, 19,* 21–39.

Vygotsky, L. (1978). Interaction between learning and development. In M. Cole, V, John-Steiner, S. Scribner & E. Souberman (Eds.), *Mind in society: The development of higher psychological processes* (pp. 79–91). Cambridge, MA: Harvard University Press.

Warfield, J., Wood, T., & Lehman, J. (2005). Autonomy, beliefs and the learning of elementary mathematics teachers. *Teaching and Teacher Education, 21,* 439–456.

Wolfgang, C., Stannard, L., & Jones, J. (2001). Block play performance among preschoolers as a prediction of later school achievement in mathematics. *Journal of Research in Childhood Education, 15,* 173–180.

Wright, T. (2001). Karen in motion: The role of physical enactment in developing an understanding of distance, time, and speed. *Journal of Mathematical Behavior, 20*, 145–162.

Wynn, K. (1998). Numerical competence in infants. In C. Donlan (Ed.), *The development of mathematical skills* (pp. 3–25). London: Psychology Press.

Yackel, E., Cobb, P., & Wood, T. (1999). The interactive constitution of mathematical meaning in one second grade classroom: An illustrative example. *Journal of Mathematical Behavior 17*, 469–488.

Young-Loveridge, J. (2004). Effects on early numeracy of a program using number books and board games. *Early Childhood Research Quarterly, 19*, 82–98.

Yuzawa, M., Bart, W., Yuzawa, H., & Junko, I. (2005). Young children's knowledge and strategies for comparing sizes. *Early Childhood Research Quarterly, 20*, 239–253.

Zur, O., & Gelman, R. (2004). Young children can add and subtract by predicting and checking. *Early Childhood Research Quarterly, 19*, 121–137.

CHAPTER 6

DEVELOPMENT OF CHILDREN'S MATHEMATICAL THINKING IN EARLY SCHOOL YEARS

Jennifer M. Young-Loveridge

INTRODUCTION

In the last decade or so, the teaching of mathematics has undergone major reform worldwide. A major catalyst for these reforms was the publication in the 1990s of results from the Third International Mathematics and Science Study [TIMSS] (Garden, 1996, 1997; National Center for Educational Statistics, n.d.). International comparisons of mathematics achievement showed that students from many western countries performed poorly relative to those from Asia (i.e., Korea, Singapore, Japan, & Hong Kong). For example, Scotland, England, and New Zealand were substantially below the international average at Years 4 and 5 (Grades 3 and 4), and performance at Years 8 and 9 (Grades 7 and 8) was little better. The positioning of Australia, Canada and the United States at or below the international average was disappointing for those nations also.

The TIMSS results raised concerns about the quality of mathematics teaching and prompted many education systems to develop a radically dif-

Contemporary Perspectives on Mathematics in Early Childhood Education, pages 133–156
Copyright © 2008 by Information Age Publishing
All rights of reproduction in any form reserved.

ferent approach to teaching mathematics (British Columbia Ministry of Education, 2003; Commonwealth of Australia, 2000; Department for Education and Employment, 1999; Ministry of Education, 2001; National Council of Teachers of Mathematics, 2000). Several education systems, including New Zealand and various states/provinces of Australia and Canada, began work on initiatives that focused initially on the early years of school (Bobis et al., 2005). These initiatives share several common features, including professional development programs for teachers to improve the teaching of mathematics, the construction of developmental frameworks to describe progressions in the learning of mathematics, individual task-based interviews to assess the mathematics learning of students, a strong emphasis on students' mathematical thinking and reasoning, and a constructivist/socioconstructivist view of mathematics teaching and learning. The following sections describe each aspect in more detail.

COMMON FEATURES OF NUMERACY INITIATIVES

Programs to Enhance the Professional Practice of Teachers

A major focus of many of the numeracy initiatives has been on improving the professional capability of teachers through ongoing reflective professional development (PD). Teachers have been helped to make sense of research information about the mathematical thinking of their students, reflect on it with their colleagues, and make adjustments to their planning for individual students, and groups (Bobis et al., 2005). This process continued over several months or even years—a very different kind of professional development from the "one-shot" PD programs of earlier times. As part of the PD program, teachers have been given a series of tools with which to work more effectively with their students to enhance their mathematics learning. Learning frameworks have provided teachers with a structure reflecting developmental progressions in number understanding. Individual diagnostic interviews have helped teachers assess their students' understanding of mathematical concepts and processes and make decisions about where on the learning framework their students were positioned. Workshops and in-class modeling by mathematics facilitators/consultants enabled the introduction of new ways of working with children to support their mathematics learning.

An important aspect of these initiatives has been the involvement of the whole school (i.e., all staff at the relevant grade levels), rather than just selected teachers. In New Zealand, where the numeracy initiative covers all years of compulsory schooling, a school wanting the PD program for teachers working with its early years students, must make a commitment to involve *all* its teachers, including those working with older elementary students. Further efforts to maintain the continuity of the initiative for students can be seen in the introduction of the initiative to teachers working in the middle/intermediate years and the early secondary levels (Ministry of Education, 2001).

The PD programs associated with the various numeracy initiatives are consistent with much of the current literature on effective teaching that stresses the importance of finding out what students are ready for and need to learn, then choosing appropriate tasks and activities in order to build on students' understanding (e.g., Fuson, Kalchman, & Bransford, 2005; Horowitz, Darling-Hammond, & Bransford, 2005). Programs have been premised on the idea that teachers need to have good knowledge of mathematics and the ways that they can help students to develop better mathematical knowledge and understanding (pedagogical content knowledge).

The initiatives are aimed not just at improving teachers' knowledge of children's learning in mathematics and the quality of their teaching, but also at increasing their confidence in teaching mathematics. Evaluations of the initiatives confirm that many teachers have experienced a substantial boost to their confidence as a result of participating in one of the initiatives (Bobis et al., 2005; Thomas & Ward, 2001, 2002).

A distinctive aspect of the New Zealand numeracy initiative has been the development of a separate PD program for teachers working in Maori-medium settings (Te Poutama Tau; TPT). Because many of these teachers are second-language learners of Maori rather than native speakers, an added challenge has been the need to improve their fluency in Te Reo Maori (the Maori language), as well as work on their subject knowledge and pedagogical content knowledge of mathematics. The development of tools such as the developmental framework and the diagnostic interview in Te Reo Maori has raised some interesting linguistic issues (see Christensen, 2003). Because there are no established patterns of discourse about many of the ideas being introduced in the numeracy initiative, there has been a need to develop specialized vocabulary. The transparent (decade-based) structure of the Maori counting system (unlike the English counting system) has meant that the answers to some of the questions in the diagnostic interview are so obvious that they may "trick" children into thinking that the answer must be something different from the question. For example, "Eighty" in Maori is *waru tekau* (meaning *eight tens*) and "fourteen" in Maori is *tekau ma wha* (meaning *ten and four*), so the answer to the question: "How many tens in eight tens?" is "eight," while the answer to the question: "What are ten and four?" is "ten and four." This can be extremely confusing for young children.

Although other countries such as Australia and Canada have set up initiatives to improve the mathematics learning of their indigenous students, the lack of a common indigenous language has prevented them from utilizing indigenous language and culture to strengthen mathematics learning.

Developmental Frameworks

At the core of many of the numeracy initiatives are the learning frameworks, consisting of progressions of increasingly sophisticated strategies in particular mathematical domains (Bobis et al., 2005). Many of the initiatives include a sequence of stages outlining progressions in number, reflecting the perceived importance of number in the curriculum, and the comprehensive foundation of research that is available to support this (Kilpatrick, Swafford, & Findell, 2001). The work of Steffe has been extremely influential in the development of progressions in the domain of number (Steffe, 1992). Frameworks for other domains of mathematics in addition to number have been developed by some education systems (Bobis et al., 2005).

Individual Task-Based Assessment Interviews

Another key aspect of many of the numeracy initiatives is the individual diagnostic assessment interview that is aligned with the relevant learning framework, and designed to provide teachers with valuable information about their students' knowledge and mental strategies (Bobis, et al., 2005). Although these assessments take considerably longer than pencil-and-paper tests, the benefits in terms of improved validity and reliability support their continued use. Unlike written mathematics tests, which yield information about the number of correct answers given by a student using any method, an individual interview provides a teacher with a comprehensive picture of a student's thinking and reasoning for different types of mathematical problems.

Evidence to support the use of individual interviews rather than written tests come from the analysis of effect sizes for ethnicity differences. The effect sizes for ethnicity differences are substantially smaller for individual interviews (in New Zealand's Numeracy Development Project [NDP]) than for written tests, such as used for TIMSS (0.2 & 0.7 for European vs. Maori on NDP & TIMSS, respectively; 0.3 & 1.0 for European vs. Pacific Islands, on NDP & TIMSS, respectively; see Young- Loveridge, 2006a). These findings suggest that students from minority groups may be disadvantaged by the use of written tests, perhaps because literacy difficulties prevent some students from engaging with the mathematics itself. Interviews have obvious advantages for early years students with limited literacy skills, and provide a fairer means of assessing students' mathematical thinking.

The focus of diagnostic interviews is typically on the nature of the student's mathematical thinking and its level of sophistication relative to a learning framework. Information gathered from the diagnostic interview is expected to be used by teachers to inform their planning for individuals and groups. Teachers participating in the New Zealand numeracy initiative are expected to use the diagnostic interview to assess their students at the beginning of the project (after the PD workshop on diagnostic interviews), and at the end (after 15–20 weeks of PD) (see Book 2: Ministry of Education, n.d.).

Emphasis on Mathematics Thinking and Reasoning

A key message coming through in the PD programs with teachers has been the importance of focusing on students' mathematical thinking and reasoning, not just within the assessment process, but also as part of classroom instruction. One of the earliest programs to do this was Cognitively Guided Instruction (CGI), a program developed in the United States that helped teachers to identify key aspects of students' thinking, which could then be used in planning classroom mathematics instruction (Carpenter et al., 1999; Carpenter, Franke, & Levi, 2003). *Understanding* mathematics (instead of the mindless application of rote procedures) has been a key aspect of most numeracy initiatives. Often there is an explicit statement urging teachers not to teach standard written methods (i.e., vertical written algorithms) until their students have a good understanding of part-whole relationships and can use mental calculation strategies (Book 1: Ministry of Education, n.d.; Department for Education & Employment, 1999).

The emphasis in most numeracy initiatives on students' thinking and reasoning is consistent with literature on the importance of mathematical reasoning for mathematics learning (e.g., National Council of Teachers of Mathematics, 2000; Russell, 1999; Tang & Ginsburg, 1999). According to Russell, mathematical reasoning is about developing, justifying, and using mathematical generalizations. It leads to interconnections between aspects of mathematical knowledge, and this web of mathematical understanding is the foundation that provides insight into mathematical problems. By emphasizing mathematical reasoning in the classroom, teachers can capitalize on flawed or incorrect reasoning as a means of assisting students toward a deeper understanding of mathematics.

Theoretical Orientation to the Teaching and Learning of Mathematics

The constructivist/socioconstructivist approach has been an important influence on the development of numeracy reforms (Hufferd-Ackles, Fuson, & Sherin, 2004; Mulligan & Vergnaud, 2006). Such an approach views students as actively constructing their knowledge and understanding. The developmental perspective evident in the number frameworks used by many education systems reflects a view that there are general patterns of progression in the ways that new understanding builds on prior competencies and understanding, reminiscent of Piaget's theory of cognitive development. Other writers such as Von Glasersfeld, Cobb, and Steffe have taken a more "radical" view to learning than Piaget, and have been referred to as "radical constructivists" (Mulligan & Vergnaud, 2006).

A socioconstructivist approach to mathematics learning, according to Hufferd-Ackles et al. (2004), combines radical constructivism (learning as self-organization) and sociocultural perspectives. A key aspect of the sociocultural approach is the recognition that an individual's learning is affected by participation in the wider culture, including the classroom, the family, and the outside world (Forman, 2003; Lampert & Cobb, 2003; Sfard, 2003; Yackel & Cobb, 1996). Discourse is also important to the sociocultural perspective, because "taken-as-shared mathematical meanings are constructed through a process of interacting in a community" (Hufferd-Ackles et al., 2004, p. 83). Sfard (1998) argues that both "acquisitionist" (individualistic) and "participationist" (social) metaphors of learning offer valuable perspectives, and hence it is dangerous to "choose just one" of these. Many writers have discussed the value to students' mathematics learning of working collaboratively with peers, and the importance of productive discourse, argumentation, and justification of solution strategies (e.g., White, 2003; Wood, 1999). Related to the sociocultural approach is Yackel and Cobb's (1996) distinction between "sociomathematical norms" which to refer normative understandings of what is acceptable or valuable with respect to mathematics (e.g., what is mathematically sophisticated, or what is an acceptable mathematical explanation), and more general "social norms" which refer to what is acceptable or valuable, whatever the subject (e.g., challenging others' thinking, or justifying one's own interpretation). Both general classroom social norms and sociomathematical norms are important components of a classroom's culture and have enormous implications for students' mathematics learning. The socioconstructivist approach (Hufferd-Ackles et al., 2004) includes aspects of both sociocultural and radical constructivist views, and can be seen in the materials provided for teachers who participate in a numeracy initiative (e.g., Book 3: Ministry of Education, n.d.).

NEW ZEALAND'S NUMERACY INITIATIVE

Overview of the Initiative

New Zealand's numeracy initiative involves a series of approximately five workshops for teachers, combined with in-class visits by numeracy facilitators/consultants who model high quality teaching and assessment practices to teachers using a teacher's own students in his/her own classroom, and observation of teachers' newly acquired practices within their own classrooms. The workshops, which bring teachers together as a group, are spaced out evenly over the school year to enable teachers to read the project materials, develop new mathematics resources for their classrooms, try out different teaching methods with their students, share ideas with their colleagues who are also participating in the project, and consolidate their learning before the next workshop. Each teacher gets approximately 16 hours of a facilitator's time, but this does not include additional telephone, email, or face-to-face contact, if and when the need arises. Each facilitator has responsibility for approximately 60–90 teachers each year.

New Zealand's number framework focuses exclusively on number learning and shares many of the features of number frameworks used by other education systems (see Book 1: Ministry of Education, n.d.). The framework consists of a sequence of global strategy stages describing the mental processes students use to solve problems with numbers (*Strategies*), as well as the key pieces of knowledge that students need in order to be able to use strategies effectively (*Knowledge*). Operational strategies include three domains: addition and subtraction, multiplication and division, and proportion and ratios. Number Knowledge consists of six domains: forwards and backwards number-word sequences, numeral identification, knowledge of fractional numbers and of basic facts, and understanding of place value. The global strategy stages consist of two different kinds of strategies: counting strategies and part-whole strategies (see Figure 6.1). The first five stages consist of increasingly sophisticated counting strategies that can be used to solve problems. Although Stage 1 marks the beginning of counting, students at this stage are not yet able to use their counting skills to solve problems involving the joining or separating of two collections. Stage 2 marks the beginning of counting for the purpose of finding out "how many" when collections are joined or separated, and the counting depends on having materials available to count, starting from one. This is referred to in other number frameworks as "perceptual counting" (see Bobis et al., 2005), or "direct modeling" (Carpenter, Fennema, Franke, Levi, & Empson, 1999). Stage 3 is marked by a shift to counting mentally, starting from one (referred to other number frameworks as "figurative counting"; see Bobis et al., 2005). Stage 4 is the highest counting stage, and is character-

Stage	Description
0	*Emergent* Cannot count
1	*One-to-One Counting* Can count a small collection up to 10, but cannot use counting to add or subtract collections.
2	*Counting from One on Materials* Can add two collections by counting, but counts all the objects in both collections
3	*Counting from One by Imaging* Adds two collections by counting all, but counts mentally by imaging objects
4	*Advanced Counting* Recognises that the last number in a counting sequence stands for all the objects in the collection, so counts on for the second collection
5	*Early Additive Part-Whole Strategies* Recognises that numbers are abstract units that can be partitioned (broken up) & recombined (part-whole thinking). Uses known number facts to derive answers
6	*Advanced Additive Part-Whole Strategies* Chooses from a range of different part-whole strategies to find answers to addition and subtraction problems
7	*Advanced Multiplicative Part-Whole Strategies* Chooses from a range of different part-whole strategies to find answers to multiplication and division problems
8	*Advanced Proportional Part-Whole Strategies* Chooses from a range of different part-whole strategies to find answers to problems involving fractions, proportions, and ratios

Figure 6.1.   New Zealand's Number Framework.

ized by the ability to count on (or back) from one of the collections. Most number frameworks identify counting on as a distinct stage in the development of strategies (Bobis et al., 2005; Carpenter et al., 1999; Department for Education & Employment, 1999). Stage 5 is an important landmark for children because it marks the replacement of counting strategies by the use of number properties and relationships to solve problems. Children at Stage 5 are able to break numbers apart and recombine them in ways that make a problem easier to solve, or can find answers to new problems by deriving them from known answers to related problems (derived number facts). These so-called "part-whole" strategies are also referred to as "thinking strategies" (Lampert & Cobb, 2003) or "derived-fact strategies" (Carpenter et al., 1999). Stage 6 involves elaboration and consolidation of part-whole strategies in a range of addition and subtraction contexts. Stage 7 marks the replacement of additive thinking with multiplicative reasoning for multiplication and division problems. Stage 8 marks the replacement of multiplicative thinking with proportional reasoning for problems involving proportion and ratio.

New Zealand's number framework has been informed by research showing that there are identifiable progressions in how children develop number concepts (e.g., Carpenter et al., 1999; Cobb et al., 1997; Young-Loveridge & Wright, 2002). Although the number framework focuses on number and arithmetic, as students move through the framework stages, they learn how to reason algebraically as they acquire methods for manipulating numbers. There is now recognition that early algebraic reasoning within the context of arithmetic provides an important foundation for later algebra (Carraher et al., 2006; Department for Education & Employment, 1999; Perry & Dockett, 2002). Evidence shows that the focus on manipulation of numbers that students experience as part of the New Zealand numeracy initiative leads to greater success with algebra (Irwin & Britt, 2005).

New Zealand's numeracy initiative was first implemented in 2000, and at the time of writing, approximately 500,000 students and close to 15,000 teachers in approximately 2000 schools having participated in the project. It is intended that by 2007, virtually every teacher of Year 1 to 6 students, and most teachers of Year 7 and 8 students, will have had the opportunity to participate in the project. Teachers at the early secondary level (Years 9 & 10) have also recently begun involvement in the project. The implementation of mathematics education reform on such a large scale has been termed "going to scale" (e.g., Coburn, 2003).

The impact of New Zealand's numeracy initiative has, like other numeracy initiatives, been closely monitored through tightly focused evaluations (Bobis et al., 2005). The outcomes include quantitative data on students' achievement, and qualitative data on teacher capability and the perspectives of facilitators/consultants, principals, teachers, and their students.

The Impact of the Numeracy Initiative on Teachers

The PD program has been positively received by participating teachers, principals and facilitators. Teachers have reported developments in their professional knowledge as a result of their involvement in the project (in particular their pedagogical content knowledge), and have noted changes in their classroom practices to accommodate their new knowledge and understandings (Thomas & Ward, 2001, 2002). Teachers made comments such as:

"I am much more aware now of how students reach their conclusions. I am taking more notice of their use of strategy" "There are many ways to a correct answer and as a class we have explored that more thoroughly than before."

Teachers also noted increases in confidence and enthusiasm for mathematics teaching (Thomas & Ward, 2001, 2002). One teacher commented that:

> "This project has been the most worthwhile [professional] development I have been involved in ... far more effective than a two-day course."

Another commented on how she or he was *"amazed at how students could be extended."*

No matter how positive teachers are about their experiences of the numeracy initiative, ultimately the measure of its success lies with improvements in students' mathematics learning.

The Impact of the Numeracy Initiative on Students' Mathematics Learning

In the New Zealand numeracy project, data from diagnostic interviews with students at the beginning and end of the project is sent by teachers to a secure web-site where it can be later analyzed. This extensive data set provides valuable information, not just about what constitutes reasonable expectations for student achievement and progress at particular year levels, but also about how the initiative impacts on students, and the extent to which this varies as function of their age, gender, ethnicity, SES, or some combination of these variables (see Young-Loveridge, 2005a, 2006a). Table 6.1 provides an example of one kind of analysis, presenting the percentages of Year 0 to 3 students (110,000 in total) at each stage on the strategy

TABLE 6.1
Percentages of Students at Each Stage on the Number Framework as a Function of Project Status (Initial or Final) and Year Level 2002–2005

Year Level	0–1		2		3	
Number of students	32,737		38,680		42,143	
Project Status	Initial	Final	Initial	Final	Initial	Final
0 Emergent	18.5	3.3	4.1	1.0	1.7	0.4
1 One-to-one Counting	29.7	10.6	13.3	2.7	5.0	1.0
2 Counting All with materials	41.4	43.9	42.6	20.0	19.9	6.3
3 Counting All with imaging	7.4	22.2	17.0	19.0	12.6	8.1
4 Counting On	2.8	18.0	20.4	43.6	46.1	44.0
5 Early Additive Part-Whole	0.1	2.0	2.5	13.1	13.8	35.6
6 Advanced Additive Part-Whole	0.0	0.0	0.1	0.7	0.8	4.6

section of the number framework, at the initial and final interviews. A comparison of the initial and final data for each year level shows substantial improvement. For example, the percentage of Year 2 students at the advanced counting stage (counting on) or higher increased from 23% to 57%. The percentage of Year 3 students at the early additive part-whole stage or higher increased from 15% to 40%.

Other findings related to the student achievement data include:

- All students benefitted from participation in the NDP, regardless of ethnicity, gender, or socioeconomic status.
- Asian and European students began the project at higher stages on the Number Framework, and benefitted more from participation in the project, than did students of Maori or Pacific Islands descent.
- Gender differences were small, with slightly more boys progressing to higher framework stages than girls.
- Students at schools in high socioeconomic areas started the project at higher framework stages, and made larger gains over the course of the project, than did students at schools in low and medium socioeconomic areas.
- Analysis of the patterns of progress showed that even when starting point was taken into account, progress varied as a function of ethnicity, and the patterns of differential progress varied according to whether the starting point was high or low on the framework (Young-Loveridge, 2005a, 2006a). At middle and higher framework stages, European and Asian students made greater progress on the Number Framework over the course of the project than did Maori or Pacific Islands students. At lower framework stages, the pattern was reversed, with Pacific Islands students tending to outperform other groups in terms of progress. Overall, the "achievement gap" was not narrowed appreciably by the project.

The Magnitude of Effects

It was not immediately obvious from the analysis of their performance whether students in the New Zealand numeracy initiative made progress because they had been part of the project, or simply as a result of "normal" aging. In a traditional experimental design, comparisons are made of the progress (as measured by the difference between pre-test and post-test scores) of the group that received the "treatment" with that of a "control" group that did not. An important dimension of New Zealand's numeracy initiative is that students are assessed by their own teachers, as part of the PD program that comprises the "treatment." As this is an essential component of the intervention process itself, it is not possible to have a control group in the traditional sense. However, one way around the lack of a control group is to use data from the students at the beginning of the program as a comparison with data gathered at the end of the program. Young-Loveridge (2005a, 2006b) used adjacent age groups to explore the differences between *younger* students *after* the project and *older* students *before* the project (e.g., 5-year-olds *after* the project with 6-year-olds *before* the project, 6-year-olds *after* the project with 7-year-olds *before* the project, and so on). Because the PD program took place over about nine months of the school year, by the end of the program, the younger students were, on average, still about a quarter of a year younger than the older students had been at the beginning of the program when they were initially assessed. This meant that the younger students at the end of the program were at a slight disadvantage developmentally, compared with their (one-year) older peers at the beginning of the program. Hence this younger-older comparison provides a fairly conservative measure of progress, so any statistically significant differences in favour of younger students at the end of the program reflect the sizeable benefits to these students of participating in the project. Analysis of initial framework stages for adjacent age groups was done to ascertain the pattern of "normal" development before intervention, and this showed that adjacent age groups differed by between half and three-quarters of a standard deviation in terms of framework stage (Young-Loveridge, 2005a). All comparisons of *younger* children *after* the program with *older* children *before* the program were statistically significant at or beyond the 0.001 level. Effect sizes (based on the standardized mean difference between groups) were calculated for adjacent ages and the median effect worked out for each of the three domains (see Table 6.2). The average (across three domains in 2003 and 2004) of the median effect sizes for children in the first four years of school was 0.41, close to the value considered to be "medium" in magnitude (Fan, 2001), and substantially greater than the 0.18 effect size reported for the National Numeracy Strategy in England (Brown et al., 2003).

Students' Perspectives on their Mathematics Learning

Data on children's perspectives can provide an alternative window into classrooms, reflecting shifts in teachers' beliefs and practices as a result of involvement in a numeracy initiative. A study of children's perspectives on their mathematics learning found that children's view varied considerably from school to school, and these differences were not clearly associated with participation in a numeracy initiative (Young-Loveridge, Taylor, & Hawera, 2005). The responses of children from a school that had

TABLE 6.2
Summary of Effect Sizes for Comparisons between Framework Stages of Younger Children *After* the Project with Those of Older Children *Before* the Project of Children in Adjacent Age Groups

2003			2004		
Age groups compared	Number of younger children	Effect size	Age groups compared	Number of younger children	Effect size
Addition/Subtraction					
4 & 5	3,562	0.45	4 & 5	2,614	0.34
5 & 6	14,009	0.24	5 & 6	8,008	0.06
6 & 7	18,324	0.10	6 & 7	8,211	0.05
7 & 8	17,849	0.11	7 & 8	9,033	0.18
8 & 9	16,976	0.17	8 & 9	9,863	0.27
Median		*0.17*	Median		*0.18*
Multiplication/Division					
5 & 6	471	0.60	5 & 6	389	0.75
6 & 7	3,473	0.62	6 & 7	2,317	0.48
7 & 8	8,276	0.49	7 & 8	5,938	0.35
8 & 9	12,178	0.39	8 & 9	8,449	0.36
Median		*0.55*	Median		*0.42*
Proportion/Ratio					
5 & 6	472	0.73	5 & 6	380	0.83
6 & 7	3,412	0.68	6 & 7	2,303	0.56
7 & 8	8,164	0.58	7 & 8	5,901	0.41
8 & 9	12,082	0.46	8 & 9	8,376	0.41
Median		*0.63*	Median		*0.49*

embraced the reforms enthusiastically showed a high level of awareness about the value of communicating mathematical ideas with peers. However, other children responded in ways that indicated that key aspects of the reform process such as communicating mathematical strategies with peers were not happening in their classrooms.

This study of students' perspectives on mathematics learning showed that many students whose teachers had participated in the numeracy initiative felt strongly that it was *not* important to know how other people work out their answers. The following comments from students in Years 2–4 illustrate this view:

"No, because then that is cheating, because of you knowing how they do it, and then you do what they do, and then you might look at their's to see if they're still doing it the same way, and then you'll get the answer. That's what could happen." (7-year-old girl)

"No, it's just their own business." (7-year-old girl)

"No, because you should find out how to do it by yourself." (7-year-old girl)

"No, because I've got one way and other people have got another way." (8-year-old girl)

A few children recognized the benefits of learning from others, as this comment shows:

"Sometimes, 'cause they might know something different that I don't, and they can teach me it." (8-year-old boy)

On the other hand, more children agreed that explaining their strategy to other people was valuable, as evident in the following comments:

"Yes, because they could have done it a different way, and next time you could try that way, and they could try it your way." (7-year-old boy)

"Yes, so they can know another way." (8-year-old girl).

"Yes, I want other people to be smart like me." (8-year-old boy).

However, there were still some children who felt that explaining their way of working out the answer should not be shared with others, as the following comment shows:

"No, because they can find out their selves." (7-year-old girl)

The pattern of responses of these children from years 2–4 were similar to those of older (Yr 5 & 6) students who felt it was important to be able to communicate their mathematical thinking and explain their strategies to others, but were less inclined to agree that knowing about the strategies used by other students might be helpful to their own learning (Young-Loveridge et al., 2005). However, compared to students who had not yet participated in the numeracy initiative, students with project involvement were, on average, more likely to appreciate the value of listening to and learning from the strategies of their peers.

Younger students seemed less inclined to want to communicate about solution strategies than older students. It is possible that because relatively few of the younger students are able to use part-whole thinking, their view is limited by whatever their current level of sophistication with counting is. It is only once part-whole thinking is acquired that a variety of different solution strategies become possible. Because New Zealand teachers tend to group students for mathematics according to ability (or framework stage), students are not exposed to the strategies used by others in different ability groups. Alternatively, it could simply have been that the egocentrism typical of children in the early school years made it difficult for them to appreciate that others might have ideas worth listening to.

Although the mathematics reforms have called for mathematics to be a more public activity, with learners communicating openly about their ways of solving problems, the examples given here show that it is not easy to achieve this goal. There were still quite a number of students in numeracy project schools who, despite having experienced the sharing of mathematics strategies as part of the numeracy projects (in particular, in-class modeling by numeracy facilitators/consultants), still seemed to believe that mathematics is a private activity ("no one else's business"), that is carried out by individuals on their own. This finding highlights the difficulties involved in bringing about changes in students' ideas and beliefs about learning mathematics. Similar comments have been made about the challenges of mathematics reform for teachers and students in the United States (Lampert & Cobb, 2003).

CHALLENGES IN IMPLEMENTING
A NUMERACY INITIATIVE

When an education system invests a lot of money on implementing a new initiative, it is important to ensure that the money is being well spent. An ongoing process of evaluation has continued to monitor the impact of the New Zealand numeracy initiative. Although the data on improvements in students' mathematics achievement and teachers' positive responses to the initiative provides strong evidence of its effectiveness, anecdotal evidence from teachers and facilitators/consultants suggests that the project has not been equally effective for all teachers. Now that the implementation process is coming to an end for teachers working at the early years level, the focus for facilitators is shifting to issues of sustainability and the need to provide support for particular groups of teachers (e.g., beginning teachers). Evaluation research continues to explore ways to increase the effectiveness of the initiative by gaining insights into the ways that facilitators and teachers have responded to it.

Time seems to have been an important factor, not just in terms of the amount of time spent participating in the project, but also how early or late in the implementation process teachers participated in the PD program. Numeracy facilitators/consultants have recently commented informally on the ways that their advice and support to teachers have improved substantially over the years since the project began, as they have acquired more experience and a deeper understanding of students' mathematics learning. Hence teachers who participated in the earlier years of the initiative may not have benefitted to the same extent as teachers who participated more recently. Unfortunately many of the schools in the initial years of implementation were those serving low SES communities—schools which needed the most support.

Evidence suggests that while some teachers have embraced the initiative enthusiastically and changed their mathematics teaching substantially in the ways that it was hoped they would, others may have gone back to teaching the way they did previously. Because each year, facilitators are given a new cohort of teachers to advise and support, there is little time to offer ongoing support to the teachers who were involved in previous years. There are questions about whether one year is really sufficient to enable early years teachers to fully appreciate all major aspects of the initiative. The decision to make the PD program for early years teachers one year was an attempt to balance the time needed to understand and implement a different way of teaching mathematics with the need to ensure that all teachers working with students at this level would eventually get the opportunity to be involved in a PD program. It was decided that teachers in the later grades would be given additional time in the PD program, on the grounds that coming to fully understand the complexities of multiplicative and proportional reasoning as well as additive thinking would require more time. Decisions about the length of time for the PD program took no account of the individual learning needs of the teachers, which varied considerably, as one might expect. Informal feedback suggests that some teachers began with quite low levels of pedagogical content knowledge. For example, the idea that numbers could be partitioned in order to make operations easier, was for some teachers a revolutionary idea. It later transpired that some of these teachers had, up until the project, been relying on counting strategies.

Efforts to examine differences in the way that reforms impact on teachers show just how complex the process is. For example, Higgins (2005) identified two very different orientations adopted by New Zealand teachers toward the numeracy initiative. She contrasts a "design adherence orientation" with a "contextually responsive orientation." The design adherence orientation emphasizes material-based activities for children and adherence to program design, as reflected in the handbooks provided to teachers to explain the ways that various materials and activities can be used to strengthen children's mathematical thinking, The "contextually responsive orientation," on the other hand, emphasizes the structural components of the program designed to enable teachers to gain a deeper understanding of these components so that so they can use them flexibly as part of their classroom practice. Whereas the "design adherence orientation" involves the slavish following of the "program," the "contextually responsive orientation" involves using and adapting the tools provided as part of the program in order to extend children's concepts and understanding to a higher level. Higgins provides examples of teachers' comments that reflect each of these two orientations. This area of investigation provides a fruitful direction for exploring individual differences in the ways that the reforms have impacted on teachers, and their students.

The issue of sustainability of the initiative over the longer term is a major concern. Data from diagnostic interviews with students gathered by teachers at the end of the PD program provide information about improvements in framework stages that reflects teachers' very recent exposure to the numeracy initiative. An obvious question that must be asked is what happens once the novelty has worn off, facilitators are no longer providing regular support, and the content of the PD program becomes just a distant memory. In an effort to find out what happens over the longer term, Thomas and Tagg (2005, 2006) collected data from a representative group of schools that had participated in the PD program in previous years (the Longitudinal Study). They found that teachers continued to use tasks from the diagnostic interview to assess their students strategies stages on the number framework. They also found even better performance by students the number framework compared to same-aged students whose teachers had only just completed the PD program. This has been taken as evidence that sustained commitment to the numeracy initiative over several years can produce even greater benefits to students' mathematics learning than are evident at the end of the PD program. However, a possible problem with this approach is that not all of the schools that agreed to send in their data actually did so, so it may be that only schools that were happy with their data sent it in, thus inflating the results for the Longitudinal Study.

It seems likely that some teachers needed more time to work with different approaches to teaching mathematics, and that instead of acquiring a deeper understanding of students' mathematics learning and possible ways they could enhance this, they acquired a rather superficial knowledge of the program that did not empower them to respond more appropriately to the learning needs of their students. The challenge for the future is to find ways to identify those teachers who need additional support in coming to understand ways that they can address the mathematics learning needs of their students. Certain factors have probably exacerbated this problem, including high levels of staff turnover, particularly in schools serving low SES communities. A case study of a school in a medium SES area has provided evidence of what is possible when teachers are fully committed to the reform process and involve the children in decisions about their learning, including the setting of personal learning goals and the responsibility for helping others in their classroom to learn about different ways of solving mathematics problems (Young-Loveridge, 2005b). The children at this school showed strong evidence of their ability and inclination to communicate mathematically with their peers, whereas this was much less evident for the children from lower SES schools (Young-Loveridge, 2005c).

The importance of establishing classroom norms, both social and sociomathematical norms, has been discussed extensively by Yackel and Cobb (1996). However, shifting classroom discourse away from a traditional teaching approach toward a greater focus on students' communicating their mathematical reasoning, justification and argumentation, is no easy matter. Anecdotal evidence suggests that only a small minority of teachers have been able to make such a shift toward establishing a community of mathematical learners who participate in collective problem-solving. Hunter (2006) has documented the experiences of one New Zealand teacher in a low SES school who managed to shift her classroom discourse away from teacher questioning and student explaining, toward building a community of learners who were able to challenge each other and justify their mathematical reasoning. It was a lengthy process for the teacher to change children's expectations about appropriate ways of engaging with mathematical reasoning and debate within the classroom. She had to teach her students how to disagree with each other honestly but respectfully. Hunter's findings are consistent with those of other researchers who have explored argumentation in classrooms (e.g., Hufferd-Ackles et al., 2004; White, 2003; Wood, 1999).

New Zealand's numeracy initiative can, like other similar initiatives, be challenged on the grounds that decisions made about the inclusion of particular features in the initiative reflect a particular view of mathematics and of mathematics learning. Such decisions may have long-reaching implications for students' mathematics learning over an entire generation, or even longer. For example, the definition of numeracy adopted by the initiative, and reflected in the PD program, the materials, and assessment instruments, has been criticized for being too narrow (Walls, 2004). New Zealand's definition of numeracy is "the ability to use mathematics effectively in our lives—at home, at work, and in the community" (Ministry of Education, 2001). Although this definition is almost identical to that of Australia, a major difference is that New Zealand's numeracy initiative has focused almost exclusively on number and algebra, apart from producing one booklet that highlights the connections between number, algebra, geometry, measurement, and statistics (Book 9: Ministry of Education, n.d.). Walls (2004) argues that the view of numeracy adopted by the New Zealand numeracy initiative is not culturally neutral, nor can it be assumed to be a universal good. Instead it constitutes "a restricted and restricting model of mathematical 'knowing' and 'doing'" (2004, p. 27).

Other decisions that are contentious include the particular kinds of materials and activities selected for inclusion in the booklets produced for teachers as part of a numeracy initiative (see Books 4 to 9: Ministry of Education, n.d.). Walls (2004), asserts that "there is little encouragement within the [New Zealand numeracy] project to make use of ... everyday meaningfully contextualised representations of number arrangements and sequences to explore important number skills" (p. 31). She points out that the specialized number equipment, such as ten-frames, Slavonic abacus, "fail to link with children's everyday lives [and] may unintentionally limit their mathematical development" (p. 31) because children may not appreciate the "mathematical significance" of the way that it is structured, a point echoed by Perry and Dockett (2002). Although the materials provided for teachers are intended to be helpful and empowering, there is a danger that they may perpetuate the idea that locating some appealing activities is all that teachers need to do once they have assessed their students.

The decision to adopt a hierarchically organized learning framework to show developmental progressions in mathematics learning is also potentially contentious. Begg (2005) argues that learning progressions assume that learning occurs in a single linear pathway, and may lead to a self-fulfilling prophecy that limits what learners can learn. Walls (2004) takes issue with the way that part-whole thinking strategies are valued more highly than counting strategies because they are quicker. Her concern is that subtle pressure to use part-whole strategies because they are faster may be an unfortunate reminder to many students who have experienced the emphasis on speed as profoundly alienating.

The way that a numeracy initiative conveys its message about what are desirable ways of teaching mathematics is also potentially contentious. It has been argued that the New Zealand's numeracy initiative is "essentially mechanistic and prescriptive" (Wall, 2004). Anecdotal evidence suggests that different teachers and facilitators take quite different approaches to the way they use the program materials. Some follow the guidelines suggested in the materials much more rigidly than others. Furthermore, there seems to be a body of unwritten information about the "proper" way to implement the project that gets passed from one person to another. In the process, messages become distorted from repeated retelling, and this can result in ideas that bear little resemblance to the original messages being conveyed. However, the New Zealand numeracy initiative appears to provide a far more flexible and professionalizing approach for teachers than some other numeracy initiatives. For example, England's National Numeracy Strategy lays out exactly what concepts and skills are to be covered on what days of the teaching year in its *Yearly teaching programmes and planning grids* (see Department for Education & Employment, 1999). In addition, the so-called *Numeracy Hour* specifies exactly what kinds of activities are to be included in each segment of the one-hour period each day. Regular inspections by the Office for Standards in Education (Ofsted) add to the pressure on teachers to follow the guidelines for the National Numeracy Strategy very closely. Although New Zealand schools are reviewed regularly, they do have considerably autonomy, and are responsible for making their own decisions about what programs best meets the learning needs of their students.

The findings presented and the issues raised here are consistent with a huge body of literature on the difficulties of bringing about large-scale reform in education (e.g., Coburn, 2003; Earl et al., 2002; Elmore, 1996; Fullan & Earl, 2002). However, New Zealand has the advantage of being a relatively small country and that has probably made the implementation of the reform process somewhat easier. There have been many benefits to mathematics education, quite apart from improvements in students' mathematics learning. The numeracy initiative has provided the impetus for building and strengthening the mathematics education community. The needs of the PD program have led to the development of an infrastructure to disseminate information out to teachers, schools, and teacher educators. Regular conferences with presentations by well-known international researchers bring the New Zealand mathematics community together and encourage debate and discussion. The evaluation process associated with the initiative has grown and expanded as researchers have been able to pursue some of their own research interests as well as investigating the questions they are required to by the system that provides the funding.

CONCLUSION

The numeracy initiatives that have developed as a consequence of mathematics reforms have played an important part in improving the mathematics learning of students and teachers. However, anecdotal evidence suggests that changes in the teaching of mathematics may have been relatively superficial for some teachers. There is still a great deal of work to be done to help teachers gain a better appreciation of the social dimension of mathematics learning, and the value of involving more-skilled others (peers, older children, and adults) in supporting and facilitating children's mathematics learning. The importance of helping children learn to communicate their thinking and reasoning mathematically cannot be underestimated. More research is needed to monitor the impact of numeracy initiatives on teachers and students, particularly over the longer term. Evidence suggests that the challenges of sustaining the benefits of the numeracy initiatives are many. The reform process is a long and difficult one. It will take time and commitment to bring about the kind of deep and lasting change that mathematics educators envisage for the future.

ACKNOWLEDGMENTS

The Numeracy Development Project was funded by the New Zealand Ministry of Education. The views expressed in this chapter do not necessarily represent the views of the New Zealand Ministry of Education.

REFERENCES

Begg, A. (2005). Curriculum: Time for a change. *New Zealand Mathematics Magazine, 42*(1), 1–13.

Bobis, J., Clarke, B., Clarke, D., Thomas, G., Wright, R., Young-Loveridge, J., & Gould, P. (2005). Supporting teachers in the development of young children's mathematical thinking: Three large scale cases. *Mathematics Education Research Journal, 16*(3), 27–57.

British Columbia Ministry of Education. (2003). *Supporting early numeracy: BC early numeracy project (K–1).* Province of British Columbia: Author.

Brown, M., Askew, M., Millet, A., & Rhodes, V. (2003). The key role of educational research in the development and evaluation of the National Numeracy Strategy. *British Educational Research Journal, 29,* 655–672.

Carpenter, T. P., Fennema, E., Franke, M. L., Levi, L., & Empson, S. B. (1999). *Children's mathematics: Cognitively guided instruction.* Portsmouth, NH: Heinemann.

Carpenter, T. P., Franke, M. L., & Levi, L. (2003). *Thinking mathematically: Integrating arithmetic and algebra in elementary school.* Portsmouth, NH: Heinemann.

Carraher, D. W., Schliemann, A. D., Brizuela, B. M., & Earnest, D. (2006). Arithmetic and algebra in early mathematics education. *Journal for Research in Mathematics Education, 37,* 87–115.

Christensen, I. (2003). *An evaluation of Te Poutama Tau 2002.* Wellington: Ministry of Education.

Cobb, P., Gravemeijer, K., Yackel, E., McClain, K., & Whitnack, J. (1997). Mathematizing and symbolizing: The emergence of chains of signification in one first-grade classroom. In D. Kirshner & J. A. Whitson (Eds.), *Situated cognition theory: Social, semiotic, and neurological perspectives* (pp. 151–233). Mahwah, NJ: Erlbaum.

Coburn, C. E. (2003). Rethinking scale: Moving beyond numbers to deep and lasting change. *Educational Researcher, 32* (6), 3–12.

Commonwealth of Australia. (2000). *Numeracy, a priority for all: Challenges for Australian schools: Commonwealth numeracy policies for Australian schools.* Author.

Department for Education and Employment. (1999). *The National Numeracy Strategy: Framework for teaching mathematics from reception to year 6.* London: Author.

Earl, L., Watson, N., & Torrance, N. (2002). Front row seats: What we've learned from the National Literacy and Numeracy Strategies in England. *Journal of Educational Change, 3,* 35–53.

Elmore, R. F. (1996). Getting to scale with good educational practice. *Harvard Educational Review, 66,* 1–26.

Fan, X. (2001). Statistical significance and an effect size in educational research: Two sides of a coin. *Journal of Educational Research, 94,* 275–282.

Forman, E. A. (2003). A socio-cultural approach to mathematics reform: Speaking, inscribing, and doing mathematics within communities of practice. In J. Kilpatrick, W. G. Martin, D. Schifter (Eds.), *A research companion to Principles and Standards for School Mathematics.* (pp. 333–352). Reston, VA: National Council of Teachers of Mathematics.

Fullan, M., & Earl, L. (2002). United Kingdom National Literacy and Numeracy Strategies: Large scale reform. *Journal of Educational Change, 3,* 1–5.

Fuson, K. C., Kalchman, M., & Bransford, J. D. (2005). Mathematical understanding: An introduction. In M. S. Donovan & J. D. Bransford (Eds.), *How students learn: Mathematics in the classroom* (pp. 217–256). Washington, DC: The National Academies Press.

Garden, R. A. (1996). *Mathematics performance of New Zealand Form 2 and Form 3 students: National results from New Zealand's participation in the Third International Mathematics and Science Study.* Wellington: Ministry of Education.

Garden, R. A. (1997). *Mathematics and science performance in middle primary school: Results from New Zealand's participation in the Third International Mathematics and Science Study.* Wellington: Ministry of Education.

Higgins, J. (2005). Pedagogy of facilitation: How do we best help teachers of mathematics with new practices? In H. L. Chick & J. L. Vincent (Eds.), *Proceedings of the 29th Conference of the International Group for the Psychology of Mathematics Education* (Vol 3, pp. 137–144). Melbourne: PME.

Horowitz, F. D., Darling-Hammond, L., & Bransford, J. (2005). Educating teachers for developmentally appropriate practice. In L. Darling-Hammond & J. Bransford (Ed.), *Preparing teachers for a changing world: What teachers should learn and be able to do.* (pp. 88–125). San Francisco: Jossey-Bass.

Hufferd-Ackles, K., Fuson, K., & Sherin, M.G. (2004). Describing levels and components of a math-talk learning community. *Journal for Research in Mathematics Education, 35,* 81–116.

Hunter, R. (2006). Structuring the talk towards mathematical inquiry. In P. Grootenboer, R. Zevenbergen, & M. Chinnappan (Eds.), *Identities cultures and learning spaces. Vol 1 (Proceedings of the 29th annual conference of the Mathematics Education Research Group of Australasia)* (pp. 309–317). Adelaide, SA: MERGA.

Irwin, K. C., & Britt, M. S. (2005). The algebraic nature of students' numerical manipulation in the New Zealand Numeracy Project. *Educational Studies in Mathematics, 58,* 169–188.

Kilpatrick, J., Swafford, J., & Findell, B. (2001). *Adding it up: Helping children learn mathematics.* Washington: National Academic Press.

Lampert, M., & Cobb, P. (2003). Communication and language. In J. Kilpatrick, W. G. Martin, & D. Schifter (Eds.), *A research companion to Principles and Standards for School Mathematics* (pp. 237–249). Reston, VA: National Council of Teachers of Mathematics.

Ministry of Education. (2001). *Curriculum Update No. 45: The Numeracy Story.* Wellington: Learning Media.

Ministry of Education. (n.d.). New Zealand Numeracy Project material. Retrieved March 1, 2006 from http://www.nzmaths.co.nz/Numeracy/project_material .htm

Mulligan, J., & Vergnaud, G. (2006). Research on children's early mathematical development. In A. Gutierrez & P. Boero (Eds.), *Handbook of research on the psychology of mathematics education: Past, present and future* (pp. 117–146). Rotterdam: Sense.

National Center for Educational Statistics. (n.d.). TIMSS results. Retrieved November 12, 2004, from http://nces.ed.gov/timss/results.asp

National Council of Teachers of Mathematics. (2000). *Principles and standards for school mathematics.* Reston, Va: Author.

Perry, B., & Dockett, S. (2002). Young children's access to powerful mathematical ideas. In L. D. English (Ed.), *Handbook of international research in mathematics education* (pp. 81–111). Mahwah, NJ: Erlbaum.

Russell, S. J. (1999). Mathematical reasoning in the elementary grades. In L. V. Stiff & F. R. Curcio (Eds.), *Developing mathematical reasoning in grades K–12: 1999 yearbook.* (pp. 1–12). Reston, Va: National Council of Teachers of Mathematics.

Sfard, A. (1998). On two metaphors for learning and the dangers of choosing just one. *Educational Researcher, 27*(2), 4–13.

Sfard, A. (2003). Balancing the unbalanceable: The NCTM standards in light of theories of learning mathematics. In J. Kilpatrick, W. G. Martin, & D. Schifter (Eds.), *A research companion to Principles and Standards for School Mathematics* (pp. 352–392). Reston, VA: National Council of Teachers of Mathematics.

Steffe, L. (1992). Learning stages in the construction of the number sequence. In J. Bideaud, C. Meljac, & J. Fisher (Eds.), *Pathways to number: Children's developing numerical abilities* (pp. 83–88). Hillsdale, NJ: Erlbaum.

Tang, E. P., & Ginsburg, H. P. (1999). Young children's mathematical reasoning: A psychological view. In L. V. Stiff & F. R. Curcio (Eds.), *Developing mathematical reasoning in grades K–12: 1999 yearbook.* (pp. 45–61). Reston, Va: National Council of Teachers of Mathematics.

Thomas, G., & Tagg, A. (2005). Evidence for expectations: Findings from the Numeracy Project Longitudinal Study. In J. Higgins, K. C. Irwin, G. Thomas, T. Trinick, & J. Young-Loveridge (Eds.), *Findings from the New Zealand Numeracy Development Project 2004* (pp. 21–34). Wellington: Ministry of Education.

Thomas, G., & Tagg, A. (2006). Numeracy Development Project Longitudinal Study: Patterns of Achievement. In F. Ell, J. Higgins, K. C. Irwin, G. Thomas, T. Trinick, & J. Young-Loveridge (Eds.), *Findings from the New Zealand Numeracy Development Projects 2005* (pp. 22–33). Wellington: Ministry of Education.

Thomas, G., & Ward, J. (2001). *An evaluation of the Count Me In Too pilot project.* Wellington: Ministry of Eduction.

Thomas, G., & Ward, J. (2002). *An evaluation of the Early Numeracy Project 2001.* Wellington: Ministry of Education.

Walls, F. (2004). The New Zealand Numeracy Projects: Redefining mathematics for the 21st century? *New Zealand Mathematics Magazine, 41*(2), 21–43.

White, D. Y. (2003). Promoting productive mathematical classroom discourse with diverse students. *Journal of Mathematical Behavior, 22,* 37–53.

Wood, T. (1999). Creating a context for argument in mathematics class. *Journal for Research in Mathematics Education, 30,* 171–191.

Yackel, E., & Cobb, P. (1996). Sociomathematical norms, argumentation, and autonomy in mathematics. *Journal for Research in Mathematics Education, 27,* 458–477.

Young-Loveridge, J. (2005a). Patterns of performance and progress: Analysis of 2004 data. In J. Higgins, K. C. Irwin, G. Thomas, T. Trinick, & J. Young-Loveridge (Eds.), *Findings from the New Zealand Numeracy Development Project 2004* (pp. 5–20, 115–127). Wellington: Ministry of Education.

Young-Loveridge, J. (2005b). Students' views about mathematics learning: A case study of one school involved in the Great Expectations Project. In J. Higgins, K. C. Irwin, G. Thomas, T. Trinick, & J. Young-Loveridge (Eds.), *Findings from the New Zealand Numeracy Development Project 2004* (pp. 107–114). Wellington: Ministry of Education.

Young-Loveridge, J. (2005c). Students' views about mathematics learning: A case study of one school involved in the Great Expectations Project. In J. Higgins, K. C. Irwin, G. Thomas, T. Trinick, & J. Young-Loveridge (Eds.), *Findings from the New Zealand Numeracy Development Project 2004* (pp. 107–114). Wellington: Ministry of Education.

Young-Loveridge, J. (2006a). Patterns of performance and progress on the Numeracy Development Project: Looking back from 2005. In F. Ell, J. Higgins, K. C. Irwin, G. Thomas, T. Trinick, & J. Young-Loveridge (Eds.), *Findings from the New Zealand Numeracy Development Projects 2005* (pp. 6–21, 137–155). Wellington: Ministry of Education.

Young-Loveridge, J. (2006b). *Using adjacent age groups as "controls" for comparison with the "treatment" to measure the magnitude of impact of a numeracy initiative.* Manuscript in preparation.

Young-Loveridge, J., Taylor, M., & Hawera, N. (2005). Going public: Students' views about the importance of communicating their mathematical thinking and solution strategies, In J. Higgins, K. C. Irwin, G. Thomas, T. Trinick, & J. Young-Loveridge (Eds.), *Findings from the New Zealand Numeracy Development Project 2004* (pp. 97–106, 115–127). Wellington: Ministry of Education.

Young-Loveridge, J. & Wright, V. (2002). Validation of the New Zealand Number Framework. In B. Barton, K. Irwin, M. Pfannkuch, & M. Thomas (Eds.), *Mathematics education in the South Pacific* (Proceedings of the 25th annual conference of the Mathematics Education Research Group of Australasia, Auckland) (pp. 722–729). Sydney: MERGA.

CHAPTER 7

DEVELOPMENT OF MATHEMATICAL REASONING AMONG YOUNG CHILDREN

How Do Children Understand Area and Length?

William M. Bart, Masamichi Yuzawa, and Miki Yuzawa

INTRODUCTION

The primary topic of this chapter is the development of mathematical reasoning among young children. Among the most prominent forms of conceptual development among young children is the development of the concepts of area and length. The development of those two concepts constitutes the special focus of this chapter.

But why should there be any concern for the development of elementary mathematical concepts such as those of area and length? A context for this inquiry will provide the rationale why such inquiry on the development of elementary mathematical concepts among young children is important for the design of educational programs.

Contemporary Perspectives on Mathematics in Early Childhood Education, pages 157–185
Copyright © 2008 by Information Age Publishing
All rights of reproduction in any form reserved.

Societal Considerations

Learning mathematics is arguably second in importance only to learning a national language for a learner. Mathematics permeates practically all sciences and technologies. Without training in mathematics, it is a daunting if not impossible task to master any science or technology.

Mathematics is viewed in the United States as a STEM discipline with STEM referring to science, technology, engineering, and mathematics. Students master STEM disciplines in order to become scientists and engineers. In addition, societies need adequate arrays of scientists and engineers in order to become modern technological societies or to maintain their status as modern technological societies. As a result of those considerations, it is easy to understand why the learning of mathematics is typically a valued educational objective throughout the world and why the development of mathematical reasoning is a popular and central topic among developmental psychologists.

Mathematical Considerations

Mathematics is often termed the "Queen of the Sciences" for good reason considering its centrality to the sciences, engineering, and technology. Without mathematics, it is doubtful as to whether there would be innovation and advances in the sciences, engineering, and technology.

The subject matter of mathematics may be subdivided into the three disciplinary branches of algebra, analysis, and geometry. Algebra is concerned with the study of mathematical structures such as groups and rings that consist of elements, operations, and rules (Karush, 1989). Algebra includes not only the study of elementary school arithmetic, but also more advanced subjects such as the theory of numbers, the theory of groups, and Boolean algebra.

Analysis is another branch of mathematics. It is primarily an outgrowth of the development of the Calculus by Sir Isaac Newton, Leibniz, and other mathematicians (Karush, 1989). Analysis includes not only secondary school analytic geometry, but also more advanced subjects such as the Calculus and real analysis. It typically deals with concepts such as limit and continuity.

Finally, geometry is concerned with the nature of space and properties such as shape and size of spatial figures (Karush, 1989). Geometry includes not only Euclidean plane geometry that is often taught in elementary school or secondary school, but also more advanced subjects such as projective geometry, solid geometry, and topology. It typically deals with forms of space such as typical three-dimensional Euclidean space, entities in space such as spheres and cubes, and spatial transformations such as rotation about an axis.

Each of these three branches of mathematics has concepts and ideas, which groups of learners could learn. Some of the concepts and ideas are appropriate for young learners, others are appropriate for intermediate learners, and others are appropriate for mature advanced learners. Learning elementary concepts and ideas in the three main branches of mathematics well often facilitates the learning of intermediate concepts and ideas in those same branches and that learning if done well often facilitate the learning of advanced mathematical concepts and ideas.

Within the mathematical branches of algebra, analysis, and geometry, certain concepts and ideas are more basic than other concepts and ideas. For example, the Pythagorean theorem is one of the landmark ideas in geometry. Among the landmark ideas that young learners learn are the concepts of unit, area, and length. If young learners learn to understand those concepts well, then those same young learners would likely be in a better position to learn more advanced mathematical concepts and ideas. The development of those concepts among young children is a focus of this chapter and contributes to improvements in mathematical reasoning among learners.

PSYCHOLOGICAL PERSPECTIVES ON MATHEMATICAL REASONING

Gardner's View of Mathematical Reasoning

Mathematical reasoning has a special place in many theories of intelligence (e.g., Mackintosh, 1998). For example, Howard Gardner (1993a) in his famous theory of multiple intelligences posited logical-mathematical intelligence as one of seven types of human intelligence along with linguistic intelligence, musical intelligence, spatial intelligence, bodily-kinesthetic intelligence, and two social intelligences (intrapersonal intelligence and interpersonal intelligence). Gardner (1998) later expanded his list of multiple intelligences to include naturalist intelligence that relates to the ability to discern and classify natural objects.

To Gardner, logical-mathematical intelligence relates to competency with logical/mathematical symbols and expressions and enjoyment at exploring meanings in such logical/mathematical expressions. Skill at mathematical reasoning requires well-developed logical-mathematical intelligence. Examples of individuals with well-developed logical-mathematical intelligence are mathematicians such as Archimedes, theoretical scientists such as Marie Curie, and logicians such as Albert Tarski.

One shortcoming to Gardner's theory of multiple intelligences is the paucity of discussion of how the various types of human intelligence interact productively. For example, one may argue that mathematical reasoning often requires not only logical-mathematical intelligence, but also spatial intelligence as would be the case when solving many problems in solid geometry.

Gardner (1993b) and others (e.g., Fogarty & Bellanca, 1995) have suggested ways to apply this model in the schools so that students can develop the various kinds of intelligence. Although their suggestions are often appealing and even attractive to educators, there is little evidence as to the effectiveness of interventions based on those suggestions in developing and improving kinds of human intelligence, including logical-mathematical intelligence and spatial intelligence that tend to underlie mathematical reasoning.

Piagetian View of Mathematical Reasoning

Without doubt, Jean Piaget and his Genevan colleagues contributed enormously to our understanding of the development of mathematical reasoning. Piaget posited four stages of cognitive development: the stage of sensorimotor operations (birth–2 years), the preoperational stage of thought (2–7 years), the stage of concrete operations (7–12 years), and the stage of formal operations (12 years-adulthood) (e.g., Flavell, 1963; Piaget, 1971).

The stage of sensorimotor operations is marked by the capacity of the infant to act on the world with the use of motoric actions and to assimilate features of the world with the use of sensory schemes. Two major accomplishments of this stage are the capacities of an infant to imitate behaviors of others and to discern that objects remain the same even though they may be hidden from view (object permanence).

The stage of preoperational thought is marked by the capacity of the young child to use language and other symbolic forms to represent thought. One major accomplishment of this stage is the capacity of the young child to learn language. Another major accomplishment is the awareness that objects can stay the same even if their appearance changes.

The stage of concrete operations is marked by the capacity of the child to classify discrete objects and to arrange objects along continuous dimensions such as height and weight. Concrete operational children are able to classify discrete objects into groups (classification), to arrange objects along continuous dimensions (seriation), and to be aware that objects stay the same in fundamental ways even with changes in appearance of the objects (conservation).

The stage of formal operations is marked by the capacity of the adolescent to make valid deductions from hypotheses under consideration (hypothetico- deductive thinking) and the capacity to think abstractly (abstract thinking). Formal operational adolescents can solve mathematical and scientific problems such as density and torque problems requiring understanding of the concepts such as proportionality and probability. They can understand and solve problems involving systems of interacting variables. In other words, they can deal with complexity.

The research of Piaget and his colleagues resulted in many important findings regarding mathematical reasoning. One finding relates to the development of geometric reasoning. Another finding relates to the development of numerical reasoning. A third finding relates to development of cognitive strategies underlying mathematical and scientific reasoning.

Regarding the former finding, Piaget determined that the course of geometric thinking in human development is opposite to the history of geometric thinking (e.g., Beth & Piaget, 1966). Children first are aware of topological features of objects such as inside and outside and open and closed before they are aware of projective features of objects such as the similarity of shapes and projections. In addition, children are aware of projective geometric features of objects before they are aware of Euclidean geometric features of objects such as area and shape congruence. The history of geometry is in the opposite order. The development of Euclidean geometry, a creation of the ancient world in Greece, Rome, and the Levant, preceded the development of projective geometry, a creation of the Renaissance in Italy, which in turn preceded the development of topology centuries later in Europe.

Regarding the second finding, Piaget ascertained that young children are unable to conserve number when faced with perceptual change (e.g., Piaget & Szeminska. 1952). When young children less than 6 years of age view two equally spaced rows of equivalent objects (e.g., blue buttons) with the same numbers of objects in each row (e.g., 5 buttons in each row), they will tend to say that the two rows have unequal numbers of objects if the spaces in one row are increased. The young children will contend that the longer row of objects has more objects in it. This lack of conservation of number is quite common among young children.

Regarding the third finding, Piaget and his colleagues (e.g., Inhelder & Piaget, 1958) identified an array of cognitive strategies that learners use when attempting to solve mathematical and scientific problems. The strategies determine how the learners solve classes of problems with the solutions being correct with certain problems and often incorrect with other problems. The strategies that learners use when solving problems can often change over time until the strategies used by learners are no longer defective ones but are rather correct rules that permit the correct solution of practically all problems in a problem class. That cognitive strategies, defective and correct, underlie mathematical reasoning is pregnant with meaning for early education professionals and educational and developmental psychologists.

One problem with Piaget's formulation of cognitive strategies is that the strategies are not precisely defined. In other words, there is ambiguity as to how learners using certain strategies would solve certain problems.

Approach of Vygotsky to Mathematical Reasoning

Another psychologist who contributed to our understanding of the development of mathematical reasoning as profoundly as Piaget is Vygotsky. For Vygotsky (e.g., 1978), cognitive development is characterized as the acquisition of mediational means of cognition. Mediational means of cognition are cultural tools that include language, various systems for counting, mnemonic techniques, algebraic symbol systems, works of art, writing, diagrams, maps, and so on. The development of mathematical reasoning is regarded as the acquisition of mathematical tools that have been historically used in mathematics. Through interpersonal interactions, children encounter and learn such cultural tools and knowledge.

The incorporation of mediational means into human action does not simply make such action easier or more efficient in a quantitative sense, but leads to a qualitative transformation. For example, in the "forbidden colors game" (Vygotsky, 1978), children were instructed not to use particular color terms or to use any other color terms twice with colored cards provided for use in any way they wish. As a result, older children used the cards as psychological tools to eliminate colors or to remind them of which color terms they had already used, whereas, young children tended not to use the colored cards at all. Vygotsky argued that the use of the colored card changed the task from one of recall to one of thinking.

Moreover, according to Vygotsky, human mental functioning originates in inter-individual activities and only gradually develops into intra-mental process. This suggests that, by participating in social interaction with older children or adults, children appropriate mathematically mediated thinking or problem-solving first for external, social activity. With development, children internalize the thinking or problem-solving for individual cognitive activity.

Siegler's View of Mathematical Reasoning

Siegler (e.g., 1976, 1991) formulated the rule assessment approach to the study of mathematical and scientific reasoning. Within this approach,

Siegler clearly stated precise rules (defective or correct) that learners may use when solving scientific problems such as torque problems. He then provided problems at various levels of difficulty to predict how learners using the various rules would solve them. His predictions of how students in various age intervals would respond to the items were often correct.

With the rule assessment approach, the cognitive diagnosis of errors could likely occur when learners solve selected cognitive tasks, if the responses of learners result from the utilization of rules (defective or correct) that a researcher has clearly and precisely defined. The rule assessment approach to the study of mathematical and scientific reasoning is an extension of Piaget's approach. In addition, it provides a generative setting by which assessment, cognition, and instruction could all be examined in an integrated manner. The cognitive tasks and items used by Siegler can often be used by researchers to infer cognitive strategies used by learners when attempting to solve the cognitive tasks or items and knowing the cognitive strategies used by learners can inform the selection of training and instructional procedures to be used by researchers and practitioners to improve the cognitive strategies used by the learners.

With this information as background, we will direct our attention to the focus of this chapter—the development of the concepts of area and length. Those two concepts are profoundly important and relevant in the lives of children as well as adolescents and adults. In fact, they are among the landmark concepts in mathematical reasoning. We begin our examination of these concepts and how children come to understand them with a realistic event.

ROLES OF THE UNIT CONCEPT AND SUPERIMPOSITION IN THE DEVELOPMENT OF UNDERSTANDING AREA AND LENGTH DURING PRESCHOOL YEARS

Imagine a situation in which a young child has a bar of chocolate that is to be shared equally with a friend. She has to figure out how she can obtain two portions of chocolate that are equal in amount. She might cut a bar of chocolate into many small pieces of equal amount and share the equal numbers of small pieces with her friend. On the other hand, she might cut the bar of chocolate directly into two pieces of equal amount. Either way the necessary procedure in making both her and her friend happy with the obtained chocolate is to make sure that the cut portions are the same irrespective of whether they are two large whole pieces or sets of smaller pieces. How could she achieve this?

A basis for such a procedure is the role of the unit in the conception of length and area of objects. According to Piaget, Inhelder, and Szeminska

(1960), to obtain measures of length and area, one must compare a part belonging to a whole with the remainder by successive superimposition of the part on the whole, which is known as unit iteration. It has been shown that such an operation is difficult for young children (Beilin & Franklin, 1962), and sometimes even for older children. For example, in their longitudinal study of children's conceptions of measurement, Lehrer, Jenkins, and Osana (1998) found that children aged 6–7 years may understand qualities of measure like the inverse relation between counts and size of units, but fail to appreciate the function of identical units or the operation of iteration of unit. The children often imposed on a length different units such as their thumbs, pencil erasers, or other invented units, and counted each without attending to inconsistencies among these units. Even given identical units, some children failed to iterate units of measure spontaneously when they ran out of units.

On the other hand, there is evidence suggesting that young children have rudimentary understanding of unit in quantification of objects (Frydman & Bryant, 1988; Shipley & Shepperson, 1990; Sophian, 2000; Sophian & Kailihiwa, 1998). Frydman and Bryant (1988) asked children from 4 to 6 years of ages to provide chocolate blocks to two recipients, so that each recipient ended up with the same total amount. There were two types of chocolate blocks: one type was a single block, and the other was a double block, which was twice as long as the single block. The children were then told that one of the recipients only accepted double blocks and the other only single blocks. It was found that most of the 4-year-old children gave the recipient, who accepted double blocks, twice as much chocolate in total as the recipient, who accepted singles, because for every single block that they gave one recipient, they handed out a double block to the other. In contrast most of the 5-year-olds performed the task correctly: they gave the double block to one recipient and then immediately two single blocks to the other, and repeated the procedure until all the chocolate was distributed.

Shipley and Shepperson (1990) asked 4- and 5-year-old children to count arrays composed of some intact objects (e.g., forks) and some that had been broken in half. It was found that 4-year-old children were reluctant to count the two halves of an object as a single item, even though they were explicitly asked to count "fork," whereas, 5-year-old children did. Shipley and Shepperson also asked children how many colors or how many kinds of things were present in arrays containing several exemplars of each color or kind. It was found that 4-year-olds again tended to count each individual item separately, whereas, 5-year-olds treated a group of similar objects as a single unit.

These results suggested that, at around 5 years of age, children become able to treat a collection of objects as a single unit and evaluate its properties such as total amount. This ability is considered to be closely related with children's rudimentary number concept called cardinality or the principle of one-to-one correspondence, which means that two or more different sets of objects that have the same number are equal in amount and that, for every member of each set of objects that have the same number, there will be an equivalent member in the other set (Bryant & Nuñes, 2002). In addition, this ability should lay a foundation for children's appreciation of area and length, because, if children construct identical units flexibly across boundaries of objects or in a part of an object, the children can evaluate area and length precisely by recognizing how many units will be included in the area or length.

On the other hand, young children will have to learn how to recognize precisely whether given units of area or length are identical or not, although young children can assess sizes of objects roughly by using different kinds of relative size standards (i.e., normative, perceptual, and functional ones) (Ebeling & Gelman, 1988, 1994; Gelman & Ebeling, 1989). In addition, it is well known that preschoolers tend to judge the sizes of geometric figures by only one dimension or one salient aspect of the stimulus (Bausano & Jeffrey, 1975; Hobbs & Bacharach, 1990; Maratsos, 1973; Piaget et al., 1960; Raven & Gelman, 1984; Russell, 1975; Sena & Smith, 1990) or by an additive combination of the height and width (Anderson & Cuneo, 1978; Cuneo, 1980; Wilkening, 1979), and this tendency prevents young children to perceive area and length precisely.

It was indicated that children start to use the procedure of placing one object on another spontaneously as a tool for judging relative areas at around 5- or 6-years of age (Yuzawa & Bart, 2002; Yuzawa et al., 1999). It was also suggested that placing one object on another plays an important role in young children's correct judgment of length and area (Miller, 1984, 1989; Wolf , 1995; Yuzawa, Bart, & Yuzawa, 2000). For example, Miller (1984) contrasted a perceptual judgment of areas with a judgment based on a functional measurement. He required 3-year-olds to estimate the sizes of rectangles under two conditions. In a functional condition, children figured out how many small square "tiles" would be needed to cover a larger rectangular "floor." In a control condition, children received an area-rating task in which they made a perceptual estimation of sizes of rectangles on a 19-point-scale. As a result, children in the control condition conformed to the Height + Width adding rule as previous research indicated (Anderson & Cuneo, 1978; Cuneo, 1980). Children in the functional condition, however, obeyed a normative Height × Width rule.

Based on the findings reviewed thus far, we propose that young children develop a basis for appreciation of area and length by relating the informal quantity knowledge with the knowledge of numbers (i.e., the concept of unit) and using a cognitive tool (i.e., the procedure of placing one object on another) spontaneously for comparing magnitudes of the quantities. In the following subsections, we will review our studies to support our proposal.

Change in Strategies of Dividing Area and Length Evenly

In this subsection, we will report a study (Yuzawa, Yuzawa, & Watanabe, 2006) that examined how young children divide area and length evenly. In a related study by Miller (1984), children at each of ages 3 and 5 years, and grades 2 and 4 were asked to divide materials evenly. The materials included "candies," strips of clay "spaghetti," clay squares of "fudge," and glasses of "kool-aid," which emphasized number, length, area, and volume respectively. The children's measurement behavior was observed as to the procedures that they employed. It was found that procedures employed in measuring area and length were similar to each other. A dominant strategy in preschoolers was to cut the material into arbitrary pieces and count them to ensure the same number of pieces. Another strategy of preschoolers, which increased with age, was to cut the material directly into fractions of approximately equal size. Use of units of constant size was rare in preschool children.

These results are interesting, because they reveal that young children can adopt systematic procedures to determine equality. However, the results did not provide the data explaining what role the procedure of putting one thing on another plays in early measurement for area. Children did not use the procedure of putting one thing on another, perhaps because the task of children was to divide "fudge" equally (i.e., children would not place some fudge on other fudge to compare the amounts). Therefore, for the materials to be divided, we used sheets of paper that could be easily cut and placed on each other.

There were two tasks in which children were asked to cut a sheet of paper imagined to be chocolate or cookie and divide it evenly between two friends. One was the Area task in which children divided a square sheet into two shares of the same amount. The other was the Length task, in which children divided a long strip sheet into two shares of the same amount.

Each of the tasks was presented to children under four conditions. In the Half line condition, the sheet had a line that divided the sheet exactly in halves. In the Multiple lines condition, the sheet had five or ten lines that divided the sheet into small pieces of the same shape. In the Misleading condition, the sheet had a line that divided the sheet unevenly into two parts. In the No line condition, the sheet had no line. Twenty-four 3-year-olds, twenty 4-year-olds, and forty-one 5-year-olds received the Area and Length tasks under the four conditions.

Children's responses to the tasks were categorized into four types: "Middle" meant that the sheet was divided exactly or nearly into two halves; "Off the Middle" meant that the sheet was divided into two uneven parts; "Multiple Division" meant that the sheet was divided into more than three parts; The responses not categorized as the above three types were categorized into "Others." Table 7.1 shows the percentages of each type of responses in the Area and Length tasks under the four conditions.

Children's strategies as to how they made sure that the two recipients had the same amounts were also categorized into four types: (a) "Superimposition" meant that children folded the sheet in half before cutting, or that children placed a cut half on the other half; (b) "Counting" meant that children counted the cut pieces; (c) "Giving Alternately" meant that children gave one cut piece to one recipient and one to the other successively, and repeated the procedure; and (d) "Giving Pairwise" meant that children gave two cut pieces to the two recipients at the same time, and repeated the procedure. Table 7.2 shows the mean frequencies of usage of each strategy across the four conditions.

The differences in age were apparent in Tables 7.1 and 7.2. First of all, 4-year-olds had a strong tendency to cut the sheet into many different pieces and to divide them into two piles irrespective of whether the sheet had only one line or multiple lines. Although they paid no attention to the sizes of individual pieces, they used the strategies of Giving Alternately and Giving Pairwise to make sure that the number of pieces for each recipient was the same. On the other hand, children from 5 years of age more often cut the sheet directly into two parts even under the Multiple lines condition. This change might be related to the previous finding that, at around 5 years of age, children become able to treat a collection of objects as a single unit, because 5-year-olds were able to regard a half sheet divided by lines into multiple parts as a whole to be given to one recipient. However, 5-year-olds made an uneven division under the Misleading condition, perhaps because they did not use superimposition as a tool for judging the relative amounts. Six-year-old children divided the sheet equally into two halves even under the Misleading condition by using superimposition as a tool for judging the relative amounts.

It was suggested that young children rely on knowledge of numbers in order to divide length and area evenly into two halves, which may make 4-year-old children pay attention only to the number and ignore the sizes of individual pieces. However, the same knowledge may help 5-year-olds pay attention to a half as a whole, because, if they give one half to one recipient and one half to the other, the number of pieces for each recipient was the same. Moreover, it was suggested that children use not only the knowledge

TABLE 7.1
Percentages of Each Type of Responses in the Area and Length Tasks Under the Four Conditions (based on Yuzawa et al., 2006)

Condition	Age	Area Task				Length Task			
		Middle	Off the Middle	Multiple Division	Others	Middle	Off the Middle	Multiple Division	Others
No lines	4-year	.17	.13	.63	.08	.13	.21	.67	.00
	5-year	.70	.00	.30	.00	.55	.10	.35	.00
	6-year	.59	.02	.37	.02	.54	.05	.37	.05
Half line	4-year	.38	.04	.58	.00	.21	.08	.71	.00
	5-year	.75	.05	.20	.00	.65	.00	.35	.00
	6-year	.63	.12	.24	.00	.63	.02	.32	.02
Multiple lines	4-year	.25	.08	.67	.00	.21	.17	.58	.04
	5-year	.40	.20	.40	.00	.40	.15	.45	.00
	6-year	.54	.07	.39	.00	.49	.10	.39	.02
Misleading line	4-year	.00	.42	.54	.04	.04	.25	.67	.04
	5-year	.20	.60	.20	.00	.35	.35	.30	.00
	6-year	.37	.27	.37	.00	.49	.15	.34	.02

TABLE 7.2
Mean Numbers of Use of Each Strategy across the Four Conditions (based on Yuzawa et al., 2006)

Task	Age	Superimposition	Counting	Giving Alternately	Giving Pairwise
Area	4-year	0.00	0.00	0.67	0.88
	5-year	0.30	0.00	0.10	0.20
	6-year	0.90	0.27	0.34	0.32
Length	4-year	0.08	0.13	0.75	0.83
	5-year	0.40	0.10	0.50	0.10
	6-year	1.44	0.41	0.34	0.27

of number but also the cognitive tool of superimposition to make sure that the amounts were the same.

Change in Strategies of Judging Relative Area

In tasks by Yuzawa et al. (2006), one of the challenges for young children was to regard a half as a whole, because they were free to cut the sheet arbitrarily into many parts. What if children were given two separate figures that were compared with each other? Would it be easier for young children to use the cognitive tool of superimposition spontaneously?

One prominent view concerning young children's judgment of relative areas is Piaget's (Piaget et al., 1960), which asserts that the pre-operational thought in children up to perhaps 6 or 7 years of age is centrated, meaning that thought tends to focus on a single salient aspect of a situation to the exclusion of other aspects. In line with Piaget's view, much research indicated that preschoolers judge the areas of geometric figures by only one dimension or one salient aspect of the stimulus (Bausano & Jeffrey, 1975; Hobbs & Bacharach, 1990; Maratsos, 1973; Raven & Gelman, 1984; Russell, 1975; Sena & Smith, 1990). However, some researchers argue that even preschoolers integrate more than one aspect of stimuli, but judge areas by an additive combination of the height and width (Anderson & Cuneo, 1978; Cuneo, 1980; Wilkening, 1979).

The biggest problem in these studies is that they did not allow the children to interact actively with the figures to be compared in the experiments. Previous research was based on the view that the developmental progression in the concept of area consists in the way that perceived information is integrated or logically operated. However, children's active role in the acquisition of knowledge has been recognized recently, and it is found that young children construct informal knowledge of mathematics through interacting with objects at hand in everyday life (e.g., Ginsburg, Klein, & Starkey, 1998; Resnick, 1989). Therefore, in our study (Yuzawa et al., 2005), we observed strategies that young children used actively for comparing the sizes of two given geometric figures to examine how the strategies were related with the children's judgment and ages.

There were three types of tasks: a Size comparison task, a Superimposition task, and a Choice task. In the Size Comparison task, children were asked to compare sizes of geometric figures and their strategies as to how they handled the figures were observed. In the Superimposition task, children were presented with the geometric figures that were placed on each other by an experimenter, and asked to judge the relative sizes of the figures. In the Choice task, children were presented with strategies for comparing sizes and asked to choose the most effective one. Sixty-nine children from the ages 3 to 6 years received the three types of tasks.

Children's strategies for the Size Comparison task were coded in terms of placement and adjustment. Figure 7.1 shows schematic examples of each code of the placement and the adjustment. Placement referred to the arrangement of two figures. Placement strategies were coded as "one on another," "on one side," or "side by side." First, when a child placed one figure on the other, the strategy was coded as "one on another." Second, when a child aligned two figures with the sides touching, the strategy was coded as "on one side." Finally, when a child placed two figures without a side of the figures touching, the strategy was coded as "side by side."

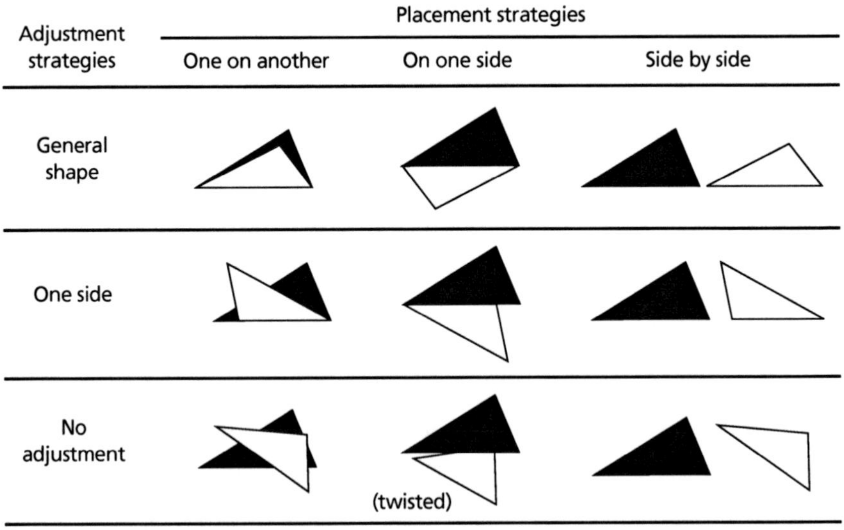

Figure 7.1.   Visual displays of adjustment and placement strategies.

Adjustment referred to the directional manipulation of two figures. Adjustment strategies were coded as "general shape," "one side," or "no adjustment." First, when a child adjusted the figures so that they looked as similar as possible, the strategy was coded as "general shape." Second, when a child adjusted the figures so that they could be compared along the dimension of one side, the strategy was coded as "one side." Finally, when a child did not adjust the figures, the strategy was coded as "no adjustment."

We classified children into several groups based on their patterns of responses including the following four variables: the number of correct responses, and the numbers of uses of the "one on another" placement strategy and the "general shape" adjustment strategy in the Size Comparison task, and the number of correct responses in the Superimposition task. As a result, four meaningful clusters were obtained. Table 7.3 shows mean scores of the variables in children of the four clusters. Table 7.3 also shows mean ages of months, the first quartile (Q1), and the third quartile (Q3) of ages of children of the four clusters. In addition, Table 7.4 shows the frequencies with which children in each cluster selected "one on another" as the best among the three placement strategies on two trials and those with which children in each cluster selected "general shape" as the best strategy among the three adjustment strategies on three trials in the Choice task.

Children in Cluster 1 made few correct judgments about the relative areas of the figures placed on each other in the Superimposition task. However, children in Cluster 1 had a significantly higher score of correct judgments in the Size Comparison task than the expected one that would

TABLE 7.3

Mean Scorres of the Variables in Children of the Four Clusters (based on Yuzawa et al., 2005)

	Cluster 1	Cluster 2	Cluster 3	Cluster 4
N	10	18	23	18
Mean months of age	49	56	59	62
Q1	45	48	55	52
Q3	55	63	63	72
Superimposition task				
Correct response[a]	0.80	2.56	2.83	2.17
Size comparison task				
General shape	0.50	0.39	2.78	2.94
One on another	0.20	0.11	0.13	2.50
Correct response[a]	1.60	1.67	1.78	2.33

[a] Score range: 0–3

TABLE 7.4
Mean Numbers of Selection of "one on another" and "general shape" in the Choice Task among Children of Each Cluster (based on Yuzawa et al., 2005)

	Cluster 1	Cluster 2	Cluster 3	Cluster 4
One on another[a]	0.30	0.44	0.43	0.72
General shape[b]	1.10	1.11	1.48	2.22

[a] Score range: 0–2
[b] Score range: 0–3

be obtained by chance, which suggested that even young children have some intuitive knowledge that helps them judge relative areas correctly.

Children in Cluster 2 made correct judgments about the relative areas of the figures placed on each other in the Superimposition task. The results suggested that children in Cluster 2 should have the knowledge that a figure that includes the other has the larger area. However, these children rarely used the "one on another" placement strategy or the "general shape" adjustment strategy in the Size Comparison task. They did not apply the knowledge actively to the task.

Children in Cluster 3 very often used the "general shape" adjustment strategy, but rarely used the "one on another" placement strategy in the Size Comparison task. The fact that children adjusted the figures in terms of two dimensions suggested that they started to pay attention to the two dimensions of the figures. However, the use of "general shape" did not lead to an increase in correct judgments, which suggested that they did not make judgments based on two dimensions of the figures.

Finally, children in Cluster 4 very often used both the "one on another" placement strategy and the "general shape" adjustment strategy in the Size Comparison task. In addition, they made more correct responses to the Size Comparison task. Only in this group did children apply the knowledge that a figure that includes the other has the larger area, and made correct judgments based on the knowledge. In addition, children in Cluster 4 selected as effective the strategy of adjusting figures based on two dimensions.

Although the mean ages increased gradually from Cluster 1 to Cluster 4, the ranges of ages of the clusters overlapped fairly well with each other. It was indicated that there was considerable variation in the age at which children used new strategies for problems in domains such as arithmetic (e.g., Siegler, 1996). However, some sequential relations between knowledge and strategies that were characteristic of the clusters were evident. First, children who often used the "general shape" adjustment strategy or the "one on another" placement strategy almost always made correct judgments in the Superimposition task, but children who made correct judgments in the Superimposition task did not necessarily use the "general shape" adjustment strategy or the "one on another" placement strategy. These patterns suggested that the knowledge that a figure that includes the other has the larger area should be a basis for spontaneous uses of the strategies of "one on another" and "general shape."

Second, children who often used the "one on another" placement strategy also often used the "general shape" adjustment strategy, but children who often used the "general shape" adjustment strategy did not necessarily use the "one on another" placement strategy. It was suggested that the use of "general shape" should precede the use of "one on another."

Finally, the uses of strategies precede the metacognitive awareness that the strategies are useful, because only children in Cluster 4, who used both the "one on another" placement strategy and the "general shape" adjustment strategy, selected "general shape" as the best strategy, but did not select "one on another" as the best strategy.

Spontaneous Use and Internalization of "One on Another" as a Cognitive Tool for Size Comparison

The study reported in the previous subsection (Yuzawa et al., 2005) suggested that the spontaneous use of the "one on another" placement strategy is a developmental cornerstone for area judgment. However, some questions arise concerning the development of the area concept organized by the procedure of placing one object on another.

First, is it necessary for children to manipulate figures directly in order to tap their knowledge that a figure that includes the other has the larger area? If they internalize the procedure of placing one object on another, children will not have to handle objects directly to compare the sizes. "Internalization" is a popular concept for describing the development of cognitive functioning, since Vygotsky (1978) argued that an operation that initially represents an external activity is reconstructed and begins to occur internally with the development.

Second, could the procedure of placing one object on another facilitate correct judgment of relative sizes of figures even if the figures are not overlaid completely with each other? If the figures that are not overlaid completely are placed on each other, children would have only to pay attention to the areas that are not overlaid, which might help children judge the relative sizes correctly. This judgment should be related with the two-dimensional appreciation of areas, because it requires judgment concerning the compensation of the parts that are not overlapped with each other (i.e., whether the part of one figure that is not overlaid will compensate for the part of the other figure that is not overlaid) like the one required in the Piagetian conservation tasks.

Third, are there individual differences in the ability to manipulate the procedure internally? Yuzawa et al. (2005) suggested that there are individual differences in the patterns of uses of the procedures of placing one object on another and adjusting two figures by two dimensions. If the procedure of placing one object on another plays a central role in the development of young children's area concept, those children who use the procedure spontaneously should have a more developed concept of area, because it is suggested that domain knowledge supports the flexible use of cognitive procedures even in young children (e.g., Bjorklund, Muir-Broaddus, & Schneider, 1990; Brown, 1989; Chi & Koeske, 1983).

To address these questions, we (Yuzawa et al., 2000) gave 45 preschoolers from the ages, 4.25 to 6.17 years, area choice tasks in which children were presented with five target figures and were asked to choose the one that was equal to two standard figures in area. There were two comparison conditions. In the perceptual judgment condition, children compared the standard figures with the target figures just by looking, and in the manipulative judgment condition, they placed the standard figures on the target figures. Moreover, there were two types of target figures: squares and rectangles. One of the five target rectangles could be overlaid completely with the two standard figures, but none of the five target squares could.

The difference between the perceptual and manipulative judgment conditions was whether or not children were allowed to manipulate the figures directly to use the procedure of placing one object on another. The conditions might interact with the types of standard figures, because the procedure of placing one figure on another is beneficial especially for the target rectangles that could be overlaid completely with the standard figures. However, if children internalize the procedure of placing one object on another, not only the manipulative judgment condition but also the perceptual judgment condition would facilitate correct responses for the target rectangles. That is, children would make better comparisons for the target rectangles than for the target squares, irrespective of the conditions. In addition, if the procedure of placing one object on another facilitates correct judgment of relative sizes of figures even if the figures are not overlaid completely with each other, children would make better comparisons in the manipulative judgment condition than in the perceptual judgment condition, irrespective of the types of target figures.

However, those facilitative effects of the target rectangles and the manipulative judgment condition might be limited to those who have a more sophisticated concept of area. In order to examine the individual differences in the development of an area concept, we gave children the Size Comparison task in which children were asked to compare the sizes of geometric figures, and observed their strategies to comparing sizes. We divided children into the group who spontaneously used the procedure of placing one figure on another and the group who did not. The numbers of spontaneous users and nonusers of the procedure of placing one figure on another were 14 and 11 under the perceptual condition, and 8 and 12 under the manipulative condition, respectively.

Figure 7.2 shows the mean numbers of correct responses to each type of targets in spontaneous users and nonusers under the perceptual condition and in spontaneous users and nonusers under the manipulative condition. For spontaneous users, the mean numbers of correct responses to the target rectangles were significantly higher than the mean numbers of correct responses to the target squares both in the perceptual judgment condition and in the manipulative judgment condition. For nonusers, however, the mean number of correct responses to the target squares was significantly higher than that to the target rectangles only in the manipulative judgment condition. In addition, the mean number of correct responses to the target rectangles by spontaneous users was significantly higher than that by nonusers in the perceptual judgment condition. It is suggested that the advantage of rectangles was limited to spontaneous users of "one on another" and that only those children internalized the procedure of placing one object on another and applied the procedure to the target rectangle internally in the perceptual judgment condition.

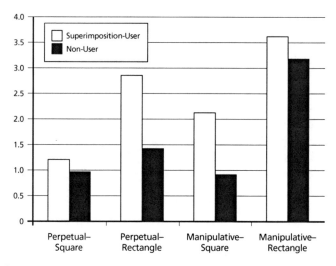

Figure 7.2.   Mean numbers of correct responses of superimposition-users and non-users to target rectangles under two conditions.

As for the effect of condition, the mean number of correct responses to the target rectangles was significantly higher in the manipulative judgment condition than in the perceptual judgment condition only among nonusers, but the mean number of correct responses to the target squares was not significantly higher in the manipulative judgment condition than in the perceptual judgment condition even among spontaneous users. However, the mean number of correct responses to the target squares by spontaneous users was significantly higher than that by nonusers in the manipulative judgment condition. It is suggested that the spontaneous users of "one on another" could benefit more from the procedure of placing one object on another in judging sizes of squares.

As expected, only among those children, who used the procedure spontaneously for size comparison, were the target rectangles advantageous not only in the manipulative condition but also in the perceptual judgment condition, suggesting that the children internalize the procedure of placing one object on another. It was also found that only among those children was the procedure of placing one figure on another advantageous not only for the target rectangles, but also for the target squares that were not overlaid completely with the standard figures. These results suggested that spontaneous use of "one on another" is related to the internalization of the procedure and the two-dimensional appreciation of areas.

SUGGESTIONS FOR FUTURE RESEARCH

In the previous section we reviewed our studies and related research that support our proposal that young children develop a basis for appreciation of area and length by relating the informal quantity knowledge with the knowledge of numbers (i.e., the concept of unit) and using a cognitive tool (i.e., the procedure of placing one object on another) spontaneously for comparing magnitudes of the quantities. In this section, we will discuss some suggestions for future research in children's appreciation of area and length based on our proposal.

First, our proposal is related to Vygotsky's (1978) assertion that the use of tools and signs plays a critical role in higher human intellectual activity. For example, when a person ties a knot in her handkerchief as a reminder, she constructs the process of memorizing by the mediation of an external object, which is fundamentally different from forming a direct relation with the environment. In the same way, young children's thinking about relative sizes of figures is influenced greatly by the procedures they use. For example, the uses of numbers in the appreciation of area and length would provide young children with a tool of expressing the relative amounts, but it would lead the children to a misunderstanding of the relative amounts if the children regard as the same in amount, objects of any sizes that are labeled with numbers (Frydman & Bryant, 1988), as in the cases of 4-year-olds who cut the sheet into many different pieces and divided them into two piles of the same number, irrespective of the sizes of individual pieces (Yuzawa et al., 2006).

In addition, it was indicated that the use of different procedures for identifying relative sizes would lead to a different judgment (Yuzawa et al., 2005). For example, the use of "general shape" preceded the use of "one on another" that is most related to correct judgment. This relation between strategies could be explained as follows: Children could pay attention to the overall shapes of the figures and adjust them by two dimensions without placing one figure on another; whereas, if the figures were placed on each other, children would find it easy to adjust the figures by the overall shapes, because they just have to pay attention to the areas of one figure not covered by another figure.

Therefore, it is suggested that children's spontaneous use of different procedures plays an important role in the development of an area concept. In the similar vein, Miller (1989) argued that children's thinking about quantity is organized in terms of the procedures used to measure amount and the measurable attributes that these procedures quantify. In the case of area, the key procedure could be regarded as overlaying objects with other objects or standard areas. It was suggested that the development of mathematical concepts such as length and area should be explored in terms of the procedure children use spontaneously.

Second, our proposal is also related to Vygotsky's (1978) assertion that an interpersonal process that initially represents an external activity using signs is transformed into an intrapersonal one. In Yuzawa et al. (2005), children under the manipulative judgment condition were, in a sense, helped by examiners to use the procedure of placing one figure on another. Under that condition, even those children at a lower developmental level who did not use the procedure spontaneously could perform at the same level for the target rectangles as those who used the procedure spontaneously. It was under the perceptual judgment condition that a difference between those two groups of children emerged. The children who used the procedure spontaneously performed for the target rectangles at the same level under the perceptual judgment condition as under the manipulative judgment condition. It was suggested that those children reconstructed the procedure to be operated internally without help from an adult.

Moreover, Yuzawa et al. (2005) suggested that the procedure of placing one object on another not only functions as a tool to compare areas, but also helps children appreciate the two-dimensional properties of areas. Only those children who used the procedure spontaneously for judging areas increased correct choices for the target squares under the manipulative judgment condition. Those children could perform better only with a support in the manipulative judgment condition. On other hand, those children who did not use the procedure spontaneously did not benefit from the external help under the manipulative judgment condition. These results suggested that the development of mathematical concepts should be explored in terms of the relationships among children, mediating tools (e.g., the procedure of placing one object on another), and supportive environment (e.g., an adult).

Third, how the use of strategy of placing one object on another is related to the internalization of the strategy and correct judgment for two-dimensional areas should be explored in future research. In Experiment 2 by Yuzawa et al. (2006), we examined whether the use of the strategy of placing one object on another was causally related to the internalization of the strategy and correct judgment for two-dimensional areas. Thirty-nine 4-to 6-year-old children (eighteen children in the experimental condition and twenty-one children in the control condition) were selected who did not reliably use the strategy of placing one object on another in the Size Comparison task at the Pretest participated in the experiment. On the first day, children received Pretests including the Size Comparison task and the Area Choice tasks that were conducted in the perceptual and manipulative judgment conditions in the same way as the ones used in Yuzawa et al. (2000). For the next three days, only children in the experimental condition received Training sessions in which the children were encouraged to use the strategy of placing one object on another in the Size Comparison tasks. On the fifth day, children received a Posttest including the Area Choice task. As a result, only among children in the experimental condition did the numbers of correct responses to the target rectangles increase significantly from Pretest to Posttest in the perceptual judgment condition.

It was suggested that the training for the use of placing one object on another was causally related to the internalization of the procedure, but there was no evidence obtained supporting that the use of the strategy of placing one object on another is related to correct judgment for two-dimensional areas.

SUGGESTIONS FOR EDUCATIONAL PRACTICE
FOR YOUNG CHILDREN

One evident suggestion for educational practice for young children from the information presented thus far in this chapter is that early educational programs should have components that are supportive of the development of mathematical reasoning and spatial reasoning. Schifter (1999) has even suggested that teacher and their writings can be sources of ideas for methods to promote learning of geometry among young learners. The components should form a curriculum that allows young children to play and have fun but that is also structured and sequential. Young children should be allowed to play with shapes and spatial games including Tangrams, origami, Othello, checkers, and chess.

Such curricula that provide children with sequential activities that support the development of spatial reasoning have been proposed for young children (e.g., Clements, Battista, & Sarama, 1998; Lehrer et al., 1998). Measurement and spatial reasoning require understanding the concept of an iterated unit that entails the construction of an organization of unit lengths or areas in a structured array. It is suggested that there are several levels of sophistication in children's structuring of a two-dimensional area (Battista et al., 1998; Outhred, & Mitchelmore, 2000). Therefore, the curriculum for children should take into consideration the level of sophistication of children's structuring of space to assist them to understand principles underlying space structuring.

On the other hand, an instructional curriculum for preschool children should help children to develop a basis for the appreciation of area and length by relating informal quantity knowledge with knowledge of numbers (i.e., the concept of unit) and the procedure of placing one object on another. As an example of such a curriculum, we (Yuzawa et al., in prep.) have recently conducted a project of instructional activities with 12 one-hour-long sessions for 5- and 6-year-olds. The project dealt consistently with "bridges," because bridges are familiar objects even for young children.

Children were provided with opportunities to pay attention to the functions, structures, and forms of bridges. In the first half of the sessions, children examined and discussed various types of bridges. In the latter half of the sessions, children made bridges of clay or wood for four types of rivers that differed in width. When children made bridges, they had to take some measures to establish correspondences among widths of rivers, lengths of bridges, and sizes of pieces of clay or wood. The teachers advised children to make drawings on paper in advance to capture the widths of rivers. As children made drawings for different bridges four successive times, they gradually made more precise correspondences among the widths of rivers, the widths of the drawings, and the lengths and sizes of the bridges made of clay or wood. In order to make precise correspondences, most children placed a ruler on a river, and used the whole ruler as a unit of measurement for length. When the ruler did not reach both sides of the river, they repeatedly placed the ruler and counted the number of successive ruler placements (e.g., twice).

Some children placed on the river the drawing that they made to make sure that the length of the drawing would match that of the river. These examples illustrate the importance of the concept of unit and the procedure of placing one object on another in the spatial reasoning of preschool children, and it was suggested that a series of activities to make bridges helped children to appreciate the importance of the concept and the procedure more deeply.

The following are general points that are relevant in the American preschool educational context. In the United States, there tends to be a preoccupation with reading and early literacy in elementary and secondary schools and colleges of education with much less concern shown to mathematics learning and spatial literacy. A balance needs to be established between educational initiatives oriented toward the development of verbal reasoning and those oriented toward the development of mathematical reasoning and spatial reasoning. In addition, instructional materials that permit young children to play with shapes and figures and to solve area and length problems in an informal manner should be made available to educators in early education.

Curricula and instructional materials oriented toward the development of mathematical and spatial reasoning should have certain properties. First, they should be sequential and cumulative. The instructional booklets containing tasks for young children should form a hierarchical structure so that educators have an idea as to the order of using the booklets. Educators should use the booklets that have easier tasks before they use the booklets that have more difficult tasks.

The widely popular Suzuki approach to music education provides a fine model of how instructional booklets can be arranged in a systematic, sequential manner. Children following the Suzuki method master musical pieces in a set of pieces indicated in a book. The musical task books form a sequence from Book 1 to Book n where n is the last book to be used for musical instruction for an instrument. Students learning an instrument start with Book 1 for the sequence of musical task books for that instrument. After mastering the musical pieces in Book 1, they proceed to Book 2. After they master the musical pieces in Book 2, they proceed to Book 3 and so on to the other books in the instructional programs. Knowing what book a student is attempting to master can clearly indicate what the student can do. This same instructional program design could be fashioned with visual-spatial activities and games such as origami, Tangrams, chess, and Othello.

Second, younger children should receive corrective feedback soon after they engage in the tasks to determine not only whether they were successful with the tasks but also how to correct performance errors and to be more effective and efficient with the tasks. This property relates to the principle of deliberate practice of K. Anders Ericsson (e.g., Ericsson & Smith, 1991). According to that principle, extensive practice with tasks augmented with corrective feedback from the instructor and arranged from easy to difficult is a precondition to the development of expertise in a field.

Third, the instruction should be playful, interactive, and constructive. Young children like to play and they tend to have limited attention spans. The instruction should be fun and involve play in some way. The tasks should permit the young children the opportunity to be interactive and to construct—i.e., to interact with things and to make things.

Fourth, the instructional activities should be moderate in pace, rate, and goals. The instructional activities should be moderate in pace by having the young children learn only a few new skills during any instructional period. The instructional activities should be moderate in rate by expecting the young children to learn only a few new skills during any week of early education. The instructional activities should be moderate in goals by having mathematical and spatial reasoning goals that are developmentally appropriate.

At this point, a cautionary note is in order. One cannot expect young children to be experts in various fields. However, they could improve their performances with spatial and mathematical instructional tasks carefully selected for early education.

If instructional programs with the heretofore-stated properties are formulated that engender cognitive gains in mathematical reasoning and/or spatial reasoning among children, then such programs may be termed "cognitive enhancers." Bart (2004) has introduced the term "cognitive enhancer" and has suggested that origami training and chess training are likely cognitive enhancers for spatial reasoning. Collaborative research between psychologists and educators are needed to see if cognitive enhancement programs can be developed, validated, and implemented for the benefit of young children. Such programs would be a definite contribution to early childhood education.

AUTHOR NOTE

Correspondence regarding this chapter may be sent as an e-mail message to William M. Bart at bartx001@umn.edu. Correspondence regarding this chapter may also be sent by regular mail to William M. Bart, 211 Burton Hall, University of Minnesota, 178 Pillsbury Drive S.E., Minneapolis, MN 55455.

NOTE

Figures 7.1 and 7.2 are reprinted from *Cognitive Development, 15*, Yuzawa, M., Bart, W., and Yuzawa, M. Development of the ability to judge relative areas: Role of the procedure of placing one object on another, 135–152, 2000, with permission from Elsevier.

Tables 7.3 and 7.4 are reprinted in part from *Early Childhood Research Quarterly*, *20*, Young children's knowledge and strategies for comparing sizes, Yuzawa, M., Bart, W., Yuzawa, M., and Junto, I. 239–253, 2005 with permission from Elsevier.

REFERENCES

Anderson, N., & Cuneo, D. (1978). The height + width rule in children's judgments of quantity. *Journal of Experimental Psychology: General, 107*, 335–378.

Bart, W. (2004, May). *Cognitive enhancement: An approach to the development of intelligence.* Paper presented a the American Psychological Society convention. Chicago, IL.

Battista, M. T., Clements, D. H., Arnoff, J., Battista, K., & Borrow, C. (1998). Students' spatial structuring of 2D arrays of squares. *Journal of Research in Mathematics Education, 29*, 503–532.

Bausano, M., & Jeffrey, W. (1975). Dimensional salience and judgments of bigness by three-year-old children. *Child Development, 46*, 988–991.

Beilin, H. & Franklin, I. (1962). Logical operations in area and length measurement: Age and training effects. *Child Development, 33*, 607–618.

Beth, E., & Piaget, J. (1966). *Mathematical epistemology and psychology.* Dordrecht: D. Reidel.

Bjorklund, D., Muir-Broaddus, J., & Schneider, W. (1990). The role of knowledge in the development of strategies. In D. Bjorklund (Ed.), *Children's strategies: Contemporary views of cognitive development* (pp. 93–128). Hillsdale, NJ: Erlbaum.

Brown, A. L. (1989). Analogical learning and transfer: What develops? In S. Vosniadou & A. Ortony (Eds.), *Similarity and analogical reasoning* (pp. 369–412). New York: Cambridge University Press.

Bryant, P., & Nunes, T. (2002). Children's understanding of mathematics. In U. Goswami, (Ed.), *Blackwell handbook of childhood cognitive development* (pp. 412–439). Malden, MA: Blackwell.

Chi, M., & Koeske, R. (1983). Network representation of a child's dinosaur knowledge. *Developmental Psychology, 19*, 29–39.

Clements, D. H., Battista, M. T., & Sarama, J. (1998). Development of geometric and measurement ideas. In R. Lehrer, & D. Chazan, (Eds.), *Designing learning environments for developing understanding of geometry and space* (pp. 201–226). Mahwah, NJ: Erlbaum.

Cuneo, D. (1980). A general strategy for quantity judgments: The height + width rule. *Child Development, 51*, 299–301.

Ebeling, K., & Gelman, S. (1988). Coordination of size standards by young children. *Child Development, 59*, 888–896.

Ebeling, K., & Gelman, S. (1994). Children's use of context in interpreting "big" and "little." *Child Development, 65*, 1178–1192.

Ericsson, K., & Smith, J. (1991). Prospects and limits in the empirical study of expertise: An introduction. In K. A. Ericsson and J. Smith (Eds.). *Toward a general theory of expertise: Prospects and limits* (pp. 1–38). Cambridge: Cambridge University Press.

Flavell, J. (1963). *The developmental psychology of Jean Piaget.* Princeton, NJ: Van Nostrand.

Fogarty, R., & Bellanca, J. (Eds.). (1995). *Multiple intelligences: A collection.* Arlington Heights, IL: Allyn & Bacon.

Frydman, O., & Bryant, P. (1988). Sharing and the understanding of number equivalence by young children. *Cognitive Development, 3,* 323–339.

Gardner, H. (1993a). *Frames of mind* (2nd ed.). New York: Basic Books.

Gardner, H. (1993b). *Multiple intelligences: The theory in practice.* New York: Basic Books.

Gardner, H. (1998). A multiplicity of intelligences. *Scientific American Presents, 9,* 18–23.

Gelman, S., & Ebeling, K. (1989). Children's use of nonegocentric standards in judgments of functional size. *Child Development, 60,* 920–932.

Ginsburg, H., Klein, A., & Starkey, P. (1998). The development of children's mathematical thinking: Connecting research with practice. In W. Damon (Series Ed.), I. Sigel, & K. Renninger (Vol. Eds.), *Handbook of child psychology, Vol. 4: Child psychology in practice* (5th ed., pp. 401–476). New York: Wiley.

Hobbs, M., & Bacharach, V. (1990). Children's understanding of big buildings and big cars. *Child Study Journal, 20,* 1–18.

Inhelder, B., & Piaget, J. (1958). *The growth of logical thinking from childhood to adolescence.* New York: Basic Books.

Karush, W. (1989). *Webster's New World Dictionary of Mathematics.* New York: Webster's New World.

Lehrer, R., Jacobson, C., Thoyre, G., Kemeny, V., Strom, D., Horvath, J., Gance, S., & Koehler, M. (1998). Developing understanding of geomentry and space in the primary grades. In R. Lehrer & D. Chazan (Eds.), *Designing learning environment for developing understanding of geometry and space* (pp. 169–200). Mahwah, NJ: Erlbaum.

Lehrer, R., Jenkins, M., & Osana, H. (1998). Longitudinal study of children's reasoning about space and geometry. In R. Lehrer & D. Chazan (Eds.), *Designing learning environment for developing understanding of geometry and space* (pp. 137–167). Mahwah, NJ: Erlbaum.

Mackintosh, N. (1998). *IQ and human intelligence.* New York: Oxford University Press.

Maratsos, M. (1973). Decrease in the understanding of the word "big" in preschool children. *Child Development, 44,* 747–752.

Miller, K. (1984). Child as the measurer of all things: Measurement procedures and the development of quantitative concepts. In C. Sophian (Ed.), *Origins of cognitive skills: The eighteenth annual Carnegie symposium on cognition* (pp. 193–228). Hillsdale, NJ: L. Erlbaum.

Miller, K. (1989). Measurement as a tool for thought: The role of measuring procedures in children's understanding of quantitative invariance. *Developmental Psychology, 25,* 589–600.

Outhred, L. N., & Mitchelmore, M. C. (2000). Young children's intuitive understanding of rectangular area measurement. *Journal of Research in Mathematics Education, 31,* 144–167.

Piaget, J. (1971). *The construction of reality in the child.* New York: Ballantine Press.

Piaget, J., Inhelder, B., & Szeminska, A. (1960). *The child's conception of geometry.* London: Routledge & Kegan Paul.

Piaget, J., & Szeminska, A. (1952). *The child's conception of number.* New York: Humanities Press.

Raven, K., & Gelman, S. (1984). Rule usage in children's understanding of "big" and "little". *Child Development, 55,* 2141–2150.

Resnick, L. B. (1989). Developing mathematical knowledge. *American Psychologist, 44,* 162–169.

Russell, J. (1975). The interpretation of conservation instructions by five-year-old children. *Journal of Child Psychology and Psychiatry, 16,* 233–244.

Schifter, D. (1999). Learning geometry: Some insights drawn from teachers' writing. *Teaching Children Mathematics, 5,* 360–366.

Sena, R., & Smith, L. (1990). New evidence on the development of the word "big." *Child Development, 61,* 1034–1052.

Shipley, E., & Shepperson, B. (1990). Countable entities: Developmental changes. *Cognition, 34,* 109–136.

Siegler, R. (1976). Three aspects of cognitive development. *Cognitive Psychology, 8,* 481–520.

Siegler, R. (1991). *Children's thinking* (2nd ed.). Englewood Cliffs, NJ: Prentice-Hall.

Siegler, R. (1996). *Emerging minds: The process of change in children's thinking.* New York: Oxford University Press.

Sophian, C. (2000). From objects to quantities: Developments in preschool children's judgments about aggregate amount. *Developmental Psychology, 36,* 724–730.

Sophian, C., & Kailihiwa, C. (1998). Units of counting: Developmental changes. *Cognitive Development, 13,* 561–585.

Vygotsky, L. (1978). *Mind in society: The development of higher psychological processes.* Cambridge, MA: Harvard University Press.

Wilkening, F. (1979). Combining of stimulus dimensions in children's and adults' judgments of area: An information integration analysis. *Developmental Psychology, 15,* 25–33.

Wolf, Y. (1995). Estimation of Euclidian quantity by 5- and 6-year-old children: Facilitating a multiplication rule. *Journal of Experimental Child Psychology, 59,* 49–75.

Yuzawa, M., & Bart, W. (2002). Young children's learning of size comparison strategies: Effect of origami exercises. *The Journal of Genetic Psychology, 163,* 459–478.

Yuzawa, M., Bart, W., Kinne, L., Sukemune, S., & Kataoka, M. (1999). The effect of origami practice on size comparison strategies among Japanese and American children. *Journal of Research in Childhood Education, 13,* 133–143.

Yuzawa, M., Bart, W., & Yuzawa, M. (2000). Development of the ability to judge relative areas: Role of the procedure of placing one object on another. *Cognitive Development, 15,* 135–152.

Yuzawa, M., Bart, W., Yuzawa, M., & Ito, J. (2005). Young children's knowledge and strategies for comparing sizes. *Early Childhood Research Quarterly, 20*, 239–253.

Yuzawa, M., Yuzawa, M., Bart, W., & Maki, R. (in preparation). *When preschool children make a bridge: A mediating role of drawings in the appreciation of the length.* Unpublished manuscript.

Yuzawa, M., Yuzawa, M., & Watanabe, D. (2006). How are the use and internalization of cognitive tools related with conceptual development? Roles of superimposition and number in the development of quantity concept. *The Japanese Journal of Developmental Psychology, 17*, 171–181.

CHAPTER 8

THE IMPACT OF METHOD ON ASSESSING YOUNG CHILDREN'S EVERYDAY MATHEMATICAL EXPERIENCES[1]

Jonathan Tudge, LinLin Li, and Tiffany Kinney Stanley

Many children arrive at school with an impressive understanding of mathematics. As Baroody, Lai, and Mix (2006) pointed out in a recent review of the literature on children's development of a sense of number, "mathematical learning begins early, very early" (p. 196). Although there is still a good deal of debate at precisely when this learning starts (see, for example, Baroody, 2004; Mix, Huttenlocher, & Levine, 2002; Starkey, Spelke, & Gelman, 1990; Wynn, 1998), it is clear that by age 3 or 4 children have had a great deal of mathematical experiences (for reviews, see Baroody et al., 2006; Ginsburg, Cannon, Eisenband, & Pappas, 2006; Ginsburg, Klein, & Starkey, 1998). Ginsburg and his colleagues were thus led to state that we have "a rich understanding of the ways in which children construct an informal knowledge of mathematics in the everyday environment" (1998, pp. 401–402). However, as Hannula (2005) pointed out with regard to number, "nearly all our knowledge of young children's number recognition skills is based on studies that explicitly direct children's attention to the aspect of number" (p. 11). The same is true of the other areas of math-

Contemporary Perspectives on Mathematics in Early Childhood Education, pages 187–214
Copyright © 2008 by Information Age Publishing
All rights of reproduction in any form reserved.

ematics, with a relative dearth of research focusing on how much, and under what conditions, young children play with mathematical shapes, talk about time, estimate distance, and so on in the course of their typically occurring everyday activities. Our focus in this chapter will be on this type of informal mathematics that occurs during the course of preschool-aged children's typically occurring everyday activities, rather than what can be seen in laboratory or other controlled conditions. As we will show, however, the methods used to assess children's involvement in everyday mathematics heavily influence the apparent extent of their involvement.

SOME THEORETICAL PERSPECTIVES ON EVERYDAY MATHEMATICAL EXPERIENCES

There has for several centuries been a strand of ideas about education that have stressed the active role of the developing child coming to gain an early understanding of mathematics. Although these ideas are often portrayed as simply allowing children to develop in as natural a way as possible, the guiding role of adults is still very important. This position can be seen clearly in Rousseau's writings, particularly *Emile* (1762/1969) which begins: "God makes all things good; man meddles with them and they become evil.... Yet things would be worse without this education... Under existing conditions a man left to himself from birth would be more of a monster than the rest" (p. 5). One can trace the development of these early ideas about educating children through the work of Pestalozzi, Froebel, Montessori, Dewey, and others, including the notion that it was possible to help young children to learn mathematics by having adults provide appropriate opportunities for them (Balfanz, 1999; Baroody et al., 2006; Nourot, 2005).

Piaget on Mathematics

There are two misconceptions about Piaget's ideas that are relevant to this chapter. First, there is the widespread notion that Piaget viewed children as developing on their own, "little scientists" actively working alone on the physical and logico-mathematical world as a way of coming to understand it. Second, some authors (see, for example, Baroody & Wilkins, 1999; Hughes, 1986) have attributed to Piaget the view that children's early experiences in counting are irrelevant to their understanding of number.

What seems clear, however, is that Piaget believed that too much attention was being paid to the teaching and formative role of adults by representatives of the contemporary dominant paradigm in psychology—behaviorism. He was not simply critical of behaviorists, however; Piaget

(1935/1970) also felt that Froebel, Montessori, and Dewey encouraged adults to be too directive with young children, and was explicit about the fact that the development of early mathematics cannot be explained simply by teaching.

> It is a great mistake to suppose that a child acquires the notion of number and other mathematical concepts just from teaching. On the contrary, to a remarkable degree he develops them himself, independently and spontaneously. When adults try to impose mathematical concepts on a child prematurely, his learning is merely verbal; true understanding of them comes only with his mental growth. (Piaget, 1953, p. 74)

Notice, however, that Piaget did not say that teachers (or other adults) have no role to play in the acquisition of mathematical understanding, merely that it will be in vain if it is "imposed prematurely." It is also worth noting that the apparently maturationist position that children's understanding appears "only with mental growth" is belied by numerous other of Piaget's books and articles. Elsewhere he stressed that the child's maturation is only one of four interrelated factors that account for development. Maturation is important, but as children mature they increasingly have experiences with the physical and logico-mathematical world, and with the social world (which includes factors of "social transmission, the educative factor in the large sense" Piaget, 1962/1973, p. 28). The fourth, and most important, factor is that of equilibration, the drive to resolve cognitive conflict in an increasingly adaptive way, through successive accommodations that follow periods of assimilation.

What Piaget argued, in fact, was that teachers do indeed have an important role to play in helping children learn mathematics, but that this role should be changed from the provision of "lessons" to that of "someone who organizes situations that will give rise to curiosity and solution-seeking in the child" and who, when the child has problems, needs not "directly to correct him, but to suggest such counterexamples that the child's new exploration will lead him to correct himself" (Piaget, 1973, pp. 85–86). Piaget (1970) devoted an entire book, *Science of education and the psychology of the child*, to this topic, including in it a chapter about how teachers need to be trained to teach in a way most likely to help children learn. Elsewhere he wrote about the need for teachers to provide materials likely to challenge children's logico-mathematical thinking, allowing them to try to learn by discovery in groups as well as individually, and to respond to their questions rather than trying to teach them (Piaget, 1930–1976/1998).

Many scholars have criticized Piaget for underestimating preschool-aged children's understanding of basic mathematical concepts (see, for example, Donaldson, 1978; Hughes, 1986). Baroody and Wilkins (1999) note the common assumption that "little or no mathematical learning occurs before children begin school" (p. 49) and attribute theoretical support for this assumption to both Piaget and Thorndike. Baroody et al. (2006) make the same claim, namely that Piaget has influenced psychologists and teachers to take a highly pessimistic view of what children can do mathematically.

This is clearly a misrepresentation of Piaget's position, which is built on the basis that it is precisely through children's early experiences (with numbers, objects, shapes, space, time, etc.) that they develop conservation of number, length, volume, etc. Much of *The child's conception of number* (Piaget, 1941/1952) and *The child's conception of space* (Piaget & Inhelder, 1948/1967) is devoted to showing this gradual development. Piaget provides innumerable examples of young children who are able to count but who are not yet able to conserve. As Piaget argued: "At the point at which correspondence becomes quantifying, thereby giving rise to the beginnings of equivalence, counting aloud may, no doubt, hasten the process of evolution. Our only contention is that the process is not begun by numerals as such" (1941/1952, p. 64). In other words, counting may well be beneficial, but the ability to count, in and of itself, is no evidence of understanding.

Vygotsky on Mathematics

Vygotsky's cultural-historical theory has been used in some senses as a counterweight to ideas that have been linked, erroneously in our opinion, to Piaget. Nourot (2005), for example, writes that "Vygotsky (1967) adds to [Piaget's] model the importance of the social context for children's learning" (p. 22). However, our reading of Piaget is that such a contrast cannot be so clearly drawn. Nonetheless, it certainly is fair to say that whereas Piaget devoted most of his energy to exploring the ways in which children constructed their views of reality by acting on the physical and logico-mathematical world, Vygotsky was more interested in the connections between children's development and the sociocultural world in which they lived. Although he did not write a great deal about the development of mathematical understanding he described, as he also did for thinking and speech, the relations between the natural and cultural lines of development.

Vygotsky (1931/1997), like Piaget (1941/1952), wrote about the distinction between a perception of number and its concept. He gave examples of young children being able to perceive, directly, the similarity and differences between small numbers (e.g., in a game of dominoes), and of a child who could count the number of fingers on her own hand but was unable to tell how many fingers were on someone else's hand. He described this initial ability as children's natural, or "primitive," ability, and contrasted it with what occurs after children have gone to school, and learned the "cultural" (or schooled) approach to number. Although he described the stages that children go through in their ability to count (Vygotsky, 1929/

1994), his argument was that the natural line does not simply develop into the cultural line, but that there is a "chasm" between children's perception of number and the use of cultural signs.

> There is no straight line in the child's development, [but] a discontinuity, a replacement of one function by another, a displacement and conflict of two systems. How can the child be carried through what is a dangerous point for him?... [I]n no case can we ignore all the features of primitive arithmetic of the preschool child. They are the point of support from which the leap must be made. But neither can we ignore the fact that the child must decisively give up this support. (Vygotsky, 1931/1997, pp. 225–226)

The culturally mediated systems developed over historical time within society thus come to play an enormous role in the subsequent development of children's mathematical understanding.

In the United States, at least, Vygotsky's ideas have been appropriated by those interested in the development of young children as related simply to his concept of the zone of proximal development, which is commonly treated as synonymous with scaffolding, or teachers' need to provide assistance just above the children's current level of understanding (see, e.g., Baroody et al., 2006; Berk & Winsler, 1995). As others (e.g., Sophian, 1995, 1999; Tudge & Scrimsher, 2003b) have made clear, however, Vygotsky's cultural-historical theory necessarily ties activities, such as engaging in mathematics, to the historically derived cultural practices of a group. This position has been well illustrated with regard to the street and school mathematics of children in Brazil (e.g., Nunes, Schliemann, & Carraher, 1993; Saxe, 1991), the approach to counting developed by the Oksapmin of New Guinea (Saxe, 1982; Saxe & Esmonde, 2005), and the everyday mathematical practices of adults (e.g., Lave, 1988; Scribner, 1984).

From the perspective of both Piaget and Vygotsky, then, there is much to be gained from studying the ways in which children engage in mathematics in the course of their everyday lives in the years before they enter school. The remainder of this chapter will be devoted to discussion of the ways in which researchers have examined preschool-aged children's everyday activities, with particular reference to mathematics, as a way of showing that the extent of children's involvement in mathematics depends in large part on the methods used by those researchers.

CHILDREN ENGAGING IN EVERYDAY MATHEMATICS

What do we know about the everyday, or informal, mathematics in which children engage? As we will portray in the next sections of this paper, the answer to that question depends to a large extent on the methods used to collect data. Essentially, four types of methods are used. One involves collecting data by asking parents to report on what their young children do during their regular day, and is related to the diary (or experience sampling) methods that have been used fairly widely with adolescents and adults (see, e.g., Bolger, Davis, & Rafaeli, 2003). The proponents of diary methods (e.g., Hofferth & Sandburg, 2001) argue that the data gained are both valid and reliable, citing research comparing the time parents report watching television with the time they actually spend on that activity. However, it is far easier to remember watching a certain number of TV programs (each of which lasts for a certain period of time) than to remember the time spent in activities that have no such obvious duration. Moreover, a good deal of mathematics might occur unobtrusively as part of another activity, such as a child counting silverware as it is being laid on the table, and thus not be considered by the parent.

The remaining three approaches move away from a reliance on parents to do the reporting, and researchers themselves observe (or listen to) what children actually do in the settings in which they spend their time or, more rarely, train childcare teachers to observe what occurs while children are with them. This approach clearly has advantages over the first method, in that the researcher does not have to rely on parents' memories of what occurred, and can be more assured of observing children's activities even when the parents are not present. However, although live observations may be a good way of assessing the extent to which children are focused on mathematics, they may be a less effective way to provide a detailed account of the nature and type of the mathematics that occurs. One proposed solution is to audiotape, either in conjunction with observations or without the presence of an observer. This method may be a better means to note all details of the mathematical dialog that occurs in the child's presence, but is clearly limited in that it misses all mathematics that occurs nonverbally. The final method that we will discuss is videotaped recording of what children do. It is this approach that is most clearly able to capture the extent to which mathematics occurs frequently and regularly in young children's lives.

Parental and Teacher Reports

One of the first large-scale reports of how young children spend their time was conducted by the University of Michigan Survey Research Center in 1975–1976 and 1981–1982 (Juster & Stafford, 1985). Although the main focus was not on young children, parents were asked to report on the use of time by children as young as three years of age (Timmer, Eccles, & O'Brien, 1985). Parents were asked to provide, by phone, an ordered account of all the activities in which their children were involved during the previous 24 hours. The results suggested that, in their waking hours, three- to five-year-olds spent about three and a half hours a day in play during the weekday, about an hour longer at the weekends, a little over two hours in some type of formal childcare or preschool setting, almost two hours watching TV, and almost an hour and a half eating. These young children were said to spend about seven minutes looking at books or being read to, two minutes a day in other school-relevant activities (including mathematics), and were involved in some type of household work about 15 minutes a day. However, Timmer and his colleagues pointed out the limitations of using the same type of diary for children of all ages and adults. "If we want to know what young children do when they play, or what parents and children do when they are together, it might be better to tailor a diary to these activities, getting detailed reports of time the children spend with their parents or of a child's activities during a typical play period" (Timmer et al., 1985, pp. 356–357).

Hofferth and Sandburg (2001) used part of the 1997 Panel Study of Income Dynamics to get very similar information, collected in the same way as had Timmer et al. (1985) on U.S. children from birth to 12 years of age. Parents were asked to report on the starting and ending times of children's "primary activities" and any activity occurring simultaneously during the previous 24 hours (with data collected during one weekend day and once during the week). The main activities of the three- to five-year-olds in this nationally representative sample look fairly similar to those reported by Timmer and his colleagues. During their waking hours, the preschool-aged children spent, on average, about two and a half hours a day in play, almost two hours a day watching TV, almost one and a half hours eating, and a little over an hour being cared for. Eighty-one percent of these children were involved in some type of household work, for an hour a day, on average, although 20% of the children were never involved in any type of work. The children, on average, spent almost three hours of their time in some type of formal childcare arrangement (with half of the children going to preschool and 25% of them in a childcare center). The children, on average, spent about seven minutes a day in conversation and 12 minutes a day looking at books, but these were activities that between 40% and 50% of the children were reported as never doing. About five minutes a day, on average, were spent in other types of school-related activities (including mathematics), but more than 80% of the children were reported to never be involved in these types of activities.

The type of methods used in these two studies are almost certainly not the most appropriate to get a sense of how much children are involved in mathematics, focusing as they do on broad categories of activities in which children could be involved. More explicit attention on school-relevant activities was found in the time-budget approach used to assess the extent to which English five- to six-year-olds were involved in school-related activities at home (Plewis, Mooney, & Creeser, 1990). Parents of more than 150 children from London were interviewed, by phone, three times over a six-week period and responded to questions about their child's reading, writing, and mathematical activities during the previous day. The average (median) child was reported to have spent two and a half minutes a day reading to a parent, less than two minutes reading to him or herself, one and a half minutes being read to, 13 minutes a day looking at books, no minutes writing, and no minutes a day involved in any type of mathematical activity. Some children (but fewer than 50% of the sample) did engage in writing (and did so, on average, almost five minutes a day), and some (30%) were reported as having done some mathematical activity in the previous 24 hours, but only for about two minutes on average.

Saxe, Guberman, and Gearhart (1987) also found little evidence that children were much involved in mathematics. They recruited almost 80 mother–child dyads, evenly divided by social class and age of the child (two- and four-year-olds). All dyads were of European American background from a borough of New York City. The dyads were seen in the home and also brought to the laboratory, and the children engaged in a series of number assessment tasks, while the mothers were interviewed about their attitudes about their children's preschool experiences and expectations for the future. Most relevant to this chapter, however, they also asked the mothers to respond both to a questionnaire and to an interview about the kinds of number-related activities in which their children engaged at home.

During the interview, the mothers were asked to describe each number activity and indicate how often the children engaged in them. The majority of the children were said to initiate some type of number activity (counting things, reading number books, and using numbers in play) at least three times a week, and most of the mothers reported that their children were involved in various other types of number play more than once a week. Children from middle-class homes were reported as engaging in play that was more complex than was the case for working-class children and, as might be expected, the same was true for the older than the younger children. Interestingly, even though these children were typically reported as doing something mathematical less than once a day, Rogoff (1987) commented on these findings by saying that they showed that the children were "heavily involved" at home in games and activities involving mathematics.

Blevins-Knabe and Musun-Miller (1996) conducted two studies in which they asked parents to estimate how often their kindergarten children had engaged in number-related activities and skills in the previous week. In both studies, one with mothers of 40 European American three- to five-year-olds and the other with mothers and fathers of 49 European American and African American four- to six-year-olds, parents were interviewed by phone, and asked to respond to the extent to which their children had engaged with number either in activities by themselves or with a parent. In both studies, the researchers asked the parents to respond to a specific list of 33 activities, of which 20 involved parent–child interaction. The activities to which parents responded included such items as whether the child had used "more" in a sentence, sung a number song, and put objects in order from smallest to biggest. It is interesting to note, however, that the activities of counting objects, reciting a series of numbers, using the words one, two, or three, and using the words from four to ten were treated as four separate activities. The parents were also able to mention any other type of number-related activity in which their children had participated.

On average, mothers in the first study said that their children had engaged in each of the different activities between two to three times a week, although Blevins-Knabe and Musun-Miller (1996) pointed out that there was a good deal of variability across both items and children. The second study, in which both mothers and fathers were asked to report on their children's engagement in mathematics, revealed an overall average (between two and three times a week) virtually identical to that of the first study, despite a greater diversity of parent gender, race/ethnicity. On the other hand, the children in the second study were older than those recruited for the first study. The results of these two studies reveal, in other words, that when parents are prompted for specific mathematical activities they seem far more likely to say that their children had engaged in them during the previous week than occurs in the relatively open-ended questioning that Saxe and his colleagues (1987) used to ask about children's books and games involving number.

Mathematics, needless to say, does not occur simply in the home, and many children spend a good deal of their time in some type of childcare setting in the years before school. However, we have been only able to find a single study in which childcare educators were specifically asked to report on the extent to which the children engaged in mathematics, focusing specifically on number. Hannula, Mattinen, and Lehtinen (2005), as part of a quasi-experimental longitudinal study to determine whether three-year-old children could be helped to focus more on mathematics, asked teachers from seven different preschools in Turku, Finland, to mark on a specially-designed chart whenever a child spontaneously counted or used numbers in some other way. Although one child of the 34 who participated was noted to focus on number 59 times one week and 65 times the second week, the remaining children focused between zero and 15 times during the two-week period of the study. The average was approximately four times during the first week and a little over five times during the second week. Using a chart prompted the teachers for certain types of mathematical activity, but they were not explicitly asked (unlike in the Blevins-Knabe and Musun-Miller 1996 study) about the extent to which the children engaged in different mathematical activities. Nonetheless, there seems little indication that Finnish children are greatly involved, spontaneously at least, in mathematics in preschool.

In summary, then, it seems clear that when parents (or, occasionally, teachers) are asked to report on children's engagement, informally, in mathematics the results obtained depend, to a certain extent, on whether or not parents are prompted for specific types of mathematical activity. Without such prompting, they are likely to say that children are involved very infrequently in mathematics (once or twice a day) but with such prompting up to 30 different types of mathematical activities several times a week. One interpretation is that prompting reminds parents of a specific type of mathematical activity (they might not otherwise have thought of their child asking for "more milk" as constituting a number-related activity); however, it might also be the case that social desirability could influence the extent to which they "remember" the child engaging in one or more of these activities.

However, parents and preschool teachers may not be the most suitable people to ask about how much their children are involved in mathematics. First, they have other things to do than simply observe their children. Second, their definition (explicit or implicit) of mathematics might be more restrictive (primarily dealing with number, for example) than that used by researchers, although this problem might be avoided by the type of close questioning used by Blevins-Knabe and Musun- Miller (1996). Third, parents, teachers, and the children themselves may not have mathematics as their primary focus during a particular activity but as subservient to their main focus (dividing a cake in order to eat it, building a tower that needs to be higher than the sofa, and so on), and so the parents or teachers do not think about the mathematics that is actually involved in the activity. In this case, it should be possible to see more evidence of mathematics when researchers themselves are doing the observations, rather than asking parents or teachers to report on the extent of children's engagement in mathematics.

Observations of Naturally Occurring Mathematics at Home and at Preschool

One of the first researchers, at least in the United States, to examine the naturally occurring activities and interactions of preschool-aged children was Jean Carew (1980; Carew, Chan, & Halfar, 1976). As she pointed out, she and her colleagues were "interested in the role played in their intellectual and social development by their normal, everyday, encounters with people, places and things rather than in the effects of extraordinary traumatic events or special experiences contrived by social scientists" (1976, p. 5). They observed 24 children from the Boston area at home three to five times during each of four periods from 12 months until 33 months and a further 22 children were observed once a month at their childcare center, with these observations starting either at 18 or 24 months and continuing until the children reached 34 months (Carew, 1980). Both at home and in childcare the children were observed for a 40-minute period, 15 seconds for observation followed by 15 seconds during which the observer quietly recorded her observations into a tape recorder. In addition, the mothers were interviewed at home, and asked to describe the children's activities during the previous 24 hours, although the majority of the discussion of children's experiences is based on the observations.

Carew and her colleagues (1976) provided many vignettes from the lives of eight of the children, and several of them (all taken from when the children were 24 months) are clear examples of mathematical experiences: Sam filling up different sized jars and pouring them carefully from one to the other; Matthew building various towers with four different-sized blocks and then playing a game with his mother involving the naming (and misnaming) of squares and circles; Sonja's mother pointing to the number "4" and counting the objects in the picture and then measuring the tower that Sonja has just built against her own size; and Vicky's mother telling her, while trying to dress her, that she needs to extend one foot and not two. Unfortunately, Carew et al. did not provide any indication of the extent to which mathematical experiences occurred. Carew (1980) went slightly further, noting that "intellectual experiences" (including mathematics) were seen in about 19% of the observations in the home and about 27% of the observations in childcare. These figures, clearly, are far higher than those reported by parents in the use-of-time studies described above.

Munn and Schaffer's (1993) research in 10 nursery schools in Scotland, with two- and three-year-olds from deprived backgrounds, provided a more effective examination of the extent to which the children were involved in mathematics as they observed all activities of six children per school for 40 minutes each, noting all literacy and numeracy "events" that the children were engaged in, regardless of whether they involved language. "Numeracy" was defined as enumeration, classification, seriation, comparison, or one-to-one correspondence. Events were coded during 20-second intervals for five minutes in each of four different contexts (story time, during an adult-led activity, free play, and at mealtime) on two different days. Munn and Schaffer found that such events were far more likely to occur when the children were in the company of an adult than with peers, that numeracy events occurred far less frequently than did those involving literacy, and that numeracy was more likely to occur during the course of literacy (e.g., during the reading of a story such as the *Three Little Pigs*) than alone. Both literacy and numeracy events occurred more frequently during story time and during the adult-led activities than during free play or mealtime. Across all contexts, however, an activity involving numeracy occurred in only 10% of the intervals (7% involving literacy as well and 3% simply as numeracy), whereas literacy occurred in more than 30% of the intervals. Munn and Schaffer noted that despite the abundance of materials relevant to numeracy and/or literacy, "the relatively low proportion of literacy/numeracy intervals without any adult interaction demonstrated the dependence on adults of such young children for literacy and numeracy experiences" (p. 71).

Tudge and Doucet (2004) also gathered observational data on children's everyday mathematics, as part of a larger cross-cultural and longitudinal study (the Cultural Ecology of Young Children, or CEYC project) designed to describe children's participation in all types of everyday activities (Tudge, 2008; Tudge et al., 2006; Tudge, et al., 2000; Tudge et al., 2003). Like Tizard and Hughes, they gathered their data using the same methods in any of the settings in which children spent their time. Their intent, unlike that of Tizard and Hughes, however, was to describe the full range of activities that occurred across the equivalent of a full day in the lives of the children. Tudge and Doucet described the mathematical activities in which 39 American three-year-olds engaged, based on 18 hours of observation of each child. Observations occurred in blocks of two and four hours over six days, with one observation period starting prior to the child waking, another occurring in the hours prior to bedtime, and the other blocks filling up the remaining parts of the day. Observations described what occurred during a 30-second period every six minutes, with the remaining time devoted to coding and writing field notes, leading to approximately 180 observations on each child. The children were evenly divided by race/ethnicity (20 of the children were from European American homes, and the remainder from African American homes) and each group consisted of equal numbers of middle-class and working-class families. Engagement in some type of mathematics was coded either as a "lesson" (trying to teach the child something mathematical or a child asking for information, such as "let's count together how many rabbits are in this picture" or "what is this shape called?") or in the course of children's play, when they were observed playing with objects that were designed with mathematics in mind (playing the card game "Uno," putting together a puzzle based on geometric shapes, or counting for the fun of it [i.e., not as part of any apparent curriculum]).

The results revealed that these children appeared to be very little involved in mathematics; on average the children were involved in less than one lesson and approximately one example of playing with objects that were designed to help children with mathematics. Too much weight should not be placed on these averages, however, as there was a good deal of variability. Between 40% and 70% of the children in each group were never observed in a math lesson, between 20% and 40% of each group only involved in one or two such lessons, and about 10% of each group were involved in three or more lessons. The same was true in the case of playing with math-relevant objects; between 45% and 80% of the children in each group were never observed in such play, between 10% and 45% of the children were observed just once or twice, although in all groups except the Black middle-class children, approximately 10% of the children were observed in math play three or more times.

These very low numbers for engagement in mathematics are somewhat misleading. Although observers gathered data over 18 hours, the time-sampling method used means that data were in fact only gathered for a total of 90 minutes. For children to be observed, on average, having a math lesson once every 90 minutes, with data sampled over a full-waking day, translates to a little over nine lessons a day, assuming that children are awake for 14 hours. Given an average of one lesson and one time playing with some math-related object per 90 minutes, this would translate to children being involved with mathematics 18 times a day, on average. However, as Tudge and Doucet (2004) pointed out, their observational methods were such that the children were only coded as engaging in mathematics when this was their focus of attention. Arranging four sets of silverware on the table may well have helped the children with counting, conservation, classification, and so on, but if their focus were simply on helping a parent they would have been coded as engaging in work; the children would only have been coded as also engaging in mathematics if they had been counting, or showing in some way their focus on mathematics.

In sum, then, we can say that whether from studies involving parental reports or live observation in the home or preschool setting, children do not seem heavily involved in mathematics, which leaves open to question how it is that by the time they arrive in school many of them have developed rather sophisticated mathematical understandings. One possibility is that these methods are simply not sensitive enough to see the extent of young children's mathematical experiences, particularly those that are not occurring deliberately and that are not the focus of the child's attention. It also seems likely that observations in the home or childcare center, as is the case with parental reports, are not able to provide sufficient detail about the type and quality of mathematics that occurs in children's lives. One approach that some scholars have adopted, as a way to get a more detailed examination of children's mathematical experiences, is to audiotape children's dialog, sometimes in conjunction with live observations.

Relying on Audiotape to Assess Young Children's Engagement in Mathematics

Tizard and Hughes (1984) noted the widespread view that early experiences in the home are of critical importance to children's development and, like Carew (1980), expressed surprise that virtually no research had been conducted to examine actually what went on in the home, apart from some intensive observations of very few children. (They also noted a study of children's language development, by Wells, 1984, about which we will have more to say.) Tizard and Hughes declared that "the central interest of our study was to describe the educational contexts of the home" (p. 15). They therefore observed 30 English girls from London who were approaching their fourth birthday, half from middle-class and half from working-class homes, all of whom were attending the same nursery schools in the mornings and at home with their mothers in the afternoons. The children were fitted with a wireless microphone, and all the adult-child conversations were recorded during two afternoons at home and three mornings in the children's schools.

Tizard and Hughes (1984) wrote a good deal about the obvious problems entailed in observing in the home, including changing behaviors because of the observer's presence, difficulties of ensuring that the children would wear the microphone and transmitter, and the amount of work entailed transcribing and then analyzing the corpus of data that would be gathered, even though they decided not to use the data gathered on the first afternoon and the first morning. The opposing point of view was made by Blevins-Knabe and Musun-Miller (1996) who wrote as follows:

> Studying the home environment presents immediate methodological problems. Naturalistic observation of behaviours in the home by an outside observer provides valuable information, but it may not present a complete or accurate picture due to reactivity on the part of family members and limitations on observer time. (p. 36)

Tizard and Hughes, however, made a strong case for the validity of their observational method (see also Hughes et al., 1979).

Tizard and Hughes (1984) noted that some children played card games with their mothers, which involved relatively sophisticated knowledge of number order, and had puzzles that required matching a number symbol with the correct number of objects. Others, apparently completely spontaneously, asked questions about simple addition or joined in as their mothers counted the number of objects in a shopping list. The authors wrote:

> The contexts of the home provided many natural settings for counting. The mothers counted knives as they set the table, counted the items on their

shopping list, asked the children to count the number of people coming to tea, or the number of sausages they had put on each plate. The children obviously enjoyed counting and often initiated it themselves. (p. 94)

Nonetheless, the *Learning at home* about which Tizard and Hughes wrote seemed to involve relatively little mathematics, certainly by comparison with the extent of conversation about the children's play, about controlling the children, the children asking questions or asking for something, and so on. The mathematics that does arise, for the most part, does so embedded in conversations with a very different focus—one child being told that she can have "one more drink of rosehip" so that she does not drink "the whole bottle" (1984, pp. 104–105); another child talking about putting her toys into her toy pushchair and her mother telling her "I don't know if they will all three fit in" (p. 96); a third child, in the course of being helped to write her name, was told that an "m" has "two humps" (p. 64); a fourth child being told that it's not the correct time to collect her cousin from school as she is there "till three o'clock. It's only about half past one now" (p. 165).

On the other hand, some of the mothers, particularly those from working-class backgrounds, also gave explicit lessons in mathematics, mostly dealing with numbers and counting; these mothers seemed concerned that the children were not getting sufficient formal lessons in their nursery schools. They were certainly correct in their supposition that the nursery school teachers viewed their role as providing the types of play materials that would help the children learn, in the course of their play, but as not explicitly teaching these concepts except as a part of drawing the children's attention to concepts that the teachers (but not necessarily the children) felt were relevant. One of the problems of this study is that although we know that children clearly were involved in mathematics we have no information on just how frequently they were involved.

This lacuna is filled, in part, by Aubrey, Bottle, and Godfrey (2003) who conducted an analysis similar to that of Tizard and Hughes (1984), although drawing on the transcript corpus collected originally in Bristol by Gordon Wells (1984), mentioned earlier. As Aubrey and her colleagues noted, the Wells corpus had been examined only from the point of view of children's language, and they examined it for its mathematical content. The original data were gathered from 128 English children from the age of 15 months until they reached five, with 24 30-second recordings done between nine in the morning and six in the evening every three months. Unlike in the case of Tizard and Hughes' research, no observer was present; researchers returned to the home in the evening in order to play back the tape and get information about the context.

Aubrey et al. (2003) examined the transcripts of 10 of the children, across a wide range of social classes, and found that about 2% of the sampled conversations at 30 months contained some reference to mathematics, and that the amount of mathematics increased (approximately 2.3% each month) as the children got older. Approximately 2/3 of the language was related to numbers and counting, and most of the rest to measuring things. Of course, as the authors note, this method made it impossible for mathematical activities in the absence of speech to be recorded, and therefore "it is quite possible that activity without interaction was underestimated" (p. 96). Interestingly, although some of the parents were clearly trying to teach the child, and used a didactic style of language, and although others simply incorporated their mathematical language in the context of the games that the children were playing, most of the mathematical utterances came from the child and led to no comment on the part of anyone else.

This may seem surprising to those used to working in laboratory settings, in which mothers (particularly from middle-class backgrounds) tend to talk to their children a lot. Gelman, Massey, and McManus (1991) used an ingenious method to assess parent-child interactions around mathematics, by observing informally in a museum—a situation in which the observers appeared to be museum staff. Of particular interest was an exhibit set up by the actual museum staff specifically to help children with number, although the children who attended would be likely (most being pre-literate) to require adult help to read the signs (such as "how many headlights on a car?") that the exhibitors had displayed in order to encourage parents and children to talk about number. Gelman et al. (1991) found that the exhibit was popular, with approximately 400 visitors during a 3-month period. However, during the observational periods, only one-third of the parents actually read aloud the "how many" question, and only 19% counted or encouraged their children to count, while another third did not interact with their children at all. Gelman and her colleagues used these findings to point out that "adults—who surely are able to interact so as to encourage their children's interest in number activities—do not always choose to do so" (p. 237), particularly in situations in which they do not think that they are being observed for research purposes!

A number of scholars have also tried to determine the extent to which children are engaged in mathematics in some type of childcare or preschool setting. However, just as we know relatively little about children's naturally occurring mathematics at home, so too "very little is known about the nature and frequency of mathematical input in preschool classrooms" (Klibanoff et al., 2006, p. 59). As Baroody and his colleagues (2006) note, one should not expect a great deal of math to occur there, given many early childhood teachers' lack of comfort in providing mathematical instruction to young children.

This view certainly seems to have been born out by Tizard and Hughes' (1984) observations in the nursery school classrooms in which the three-year-olds in their study spent their mornings. The teachers, when interviewed, would talk about providing relevant materials with which the children could play, such as "the provision of vessels of different size and shape for water play [to help] the child to develop concepts of volume" (p. 182). Compared to the home setting, the children's likelihood of conversing with the teachers was far less, and the conversations themselves far more limited and, apparently, confusing to the children than Tizard and Hughes found at home. Very few instances were reported of a teacher communicating with a child about anything mathematical.

Klibanoff et al. (2006) examined hour-long transcripts of preschool teachers' talk in their classrooms, and found that on average the teachers provided some type of "math input" (the authors focused solely on number, rather than other aspects of mathematics) 28 times during the hour. However, the teachers varied widely in the extent of their input, ranging from one to 104 times, and also varied widely in the type of input, from counting and use of number symbols to ordering and calculation. Some of this mathematics is the sort of activity that parents or teachers, being asked about how they were spending their time, would have noted, such as when one of the teachers asked the children to help her count days on the calendar, or when another asked a child "Nine, what comes after nine?" (Klibanoff et al., p. 63). But other comments would almost certainly not have been noted in the same way, as for example a teacher said that three children could help her, or mentioned a story (*The three little pigs*) that they had read.

Although audiotape is a good means of picking up the sort of detail that is missed by live observation alone, we should be concerned by those studies that are based solely on audiotaped recordings, as they necessarily miss all examples of children's mathematical experiences that occur in the absence of conversation or verbal commentary, thus underestimating the extent to which children are involved in mathematics. This hypothesis seems to be clearly supported by those rather few studies that use videotape as a way of assessing children's involvement with things mathematical.

Videotaped Observations of Young Children's Everyday Mathematics

Aubrey and her colleagues (2003), whose analysis of Wells' audiotaped data was discussed earlier, also collected their own data in Coventry, using video to record the activities in and around the home for one hour, every four months, from the second year of life until the children started school (typically, in England, in the months before turning five years of age). They reported data on two of the nine children in the study, hoping that "the disturbance of the observer over time was minimal as parents and children appeared to ignore the video... [although] the parents admitted that they had probably paid more attention to their children during the observation period than was usual" (Aubrey et al., p. 97). Data analyses were based on five-minute segments, and dialog related to mathematics occurred in almost 50% of the segments of both girls when they were 30 months (the same age as with the data derived from Wells' transcripts). Obviously this is far higher than the extent of mathematics conversation found in Wells' data (2%). In part this difference may be due to the presence of a camera, but in addition the segments used in the analyses were well over three times longer, thereby allowing more mathematical language to be found per segment in the Aubrey et al. study.

The rate of monthly increase was far greater in the case of one child (3.6%) than the other (0.6%), and Aubrey and her colleagues (2003) explain that in part because of the different ways in which the mothers of the two children thought about encouraging mathematical understanding during the course of the children's play. However, it was also the case that the mother of only the first child participated in a lot of her child's imaginative games and was skilled "not only in capturing and holding the young child's interest, but in encouraging, supporting and even challenging her mathematically" (p. 101). These differences in practices led to the first child, when she had reached four years of age, being involved in mathematical dialog in close to all of the five-minute segments, compared to a little more than 50% of the segments in the case of the other girl.

Mathematical dialog, of course, is only a subset of mathematical experience and, as mentioned above, misses all nonverbal engagement in mathematics. It was thus a shame that Aubrey et al. (2003) used their videotape as others have used audiotape. By contrast Ginsburg and his colleagues (Ginsburg, Inoue, & Seo, 1999; Ginsburg et al., 2003; Seo & Ginsburg, 2004), in a series of studies using videotape, have made a powerful argument that "young children engage in a considerable amount of mathematical activity during their free play" (Seo & Ginsburg, 2004, p. 95). The methodology in each of these studies involved the videotaping of children, aged four and five, in their preschool classes, focusing on a single child for 15 minutes. The tapes were then analyzed, in one-minute segments, for the presence and type of mathematical experience. The codes for type of mathematical activity were not imposed in advance, but derived from the tapes, and included classification, magnitude, enumeration, dynamics, pattern and shape, and spatial relations. The study began with 30 children, from low-income Black and Latino families, in a childcare center in which Ginsburg and his colleagues had a long-standing working relationship, which allowed the children to be very comfortable with the researchers' presence (see Ginsburg et al., 1999). Seo and Ginsburg, however, reported on a total of 90 children, drawn from five different centers and encompassing equal numbers of low-income, middle-income, and high-income children, and similar numbers of Blacks (31), Latinos (25), and Whites (34, 30 of whom were from a single center and were classified as high income).

The results were striking in that 88% of the children engaged in at least one math-related activity during the course of the 15-minute videotaping, and on average the children engaged in at least one such activity in 43% of the one-minute segments. Seo and Ginsburg (2004) reported that there were no significant differences in the extent of involvement by income level (the range was approximately 40% to 44% across each group) or gender (boys 41.3%, girls 43.5%). Across all groups the children were most likely to be involved in activities using pattern or shape, followed by magnitude and enumeration.

Ginsburg et al. (2003) expanded on this study, drawing on a total of 24 children from Taipei, Taiwan and 60 children from four of the childcare centers in New York (the 30 upper-income White children did not feature in these analyses). The Chinese children were equally divided by social class, with middle-class families defined as those in which parents had professional occupations. As noted above, the American children were involved in mathematical activities in just under 45% of the one-minute segments; those from Taiwan, however, were involved in mathematics in about 70% of the segments (73% in the middle-class sample, 63% in the working-class sample). Although the children engaged in classifying, comparing size, and enumerating to quite similar extents in both countries, the Chinese children were far more likely to be involved with pattern and shape (49% vs. 21% of their activities) and in spatial relations (15% vs. 3%).

It thus appears that children are involved in mathematics once or twice a day when parents are asked to respond about their children's typically occurring activities, perhaps twenty times a day when observers study children's naturally occurring activities, or half the time when researchers videotape children's activities and then code for any type of involvement with mathematics, including cases when mathematics is not the focus of attention. We (Li, Kinney, & Tudge, 2005) wondered whether Ginsburg and his colleagues might have overestimated the extent to which children typically engaged in mathematics by filming in some childcare centers in which they had a long-standing relationship (Ginsburg et al., 1999). Our question was whether children would be as likely to engage in mathematics in their everyday lives outside of childcare.

As described above, Tudge and his colleagues (Tudge & Doucet, 2004; Tudge, 2008) collected 18 hours of data in the course of live coding in any of the settings in which the children in their samples were situated. They then observed for a further one to two hours, using videotape. The observational system was set up in such a way that the final two hours of direct (non-filmed) observation occurred outside of a childcare setting so that filming could immediately follow without the researchers needing to get additional permission to film within a childcare center. The great advantage of this approach was that the children, and those who interacted with them on a regular basis, were already used to the presence of the observer and, except in very isolated incidents, appeared to continue to behave as naturally as they had done previously.

We utilized the same coding scheme and methods that Ginsburg et al. (2003) had used, with the exception that we added one category (planning, or the idea that one thing is going to occur after another) which was derived inductively, as was the case with the original coding scheme, from examining our videos. We analyzed the tapes from 16 three-year-old children, evenly balanced by race/ethnicity (White and Black), social class (parents with and without professional occupations and higher education), and gender, dividing tapes into one-minute segments and coding whether or not mathematics occurred and the type of mathematics. Reliability was assessed on half the tapes, and kappas were consistently above 0.7.

Given the results of the live coding reported in Tudge and Doucet (2004), we were surprised to find that the children were involved in a good deal of mathematics. Overall it was less than that reported by Ginsburg et al. (2003), namely 36% rather than 44%, but this was perhaps to be expected given that the filming occurred in settings that were not specifically set up to help educate young children. Unlike Ginsburg and his colleagues, however, we also found some clear differences between the children based on their race/ethnicity and social class (but not gender). The working-class Black and middle-class White children were involved, on average, in about 45% of the minute-long segments, but the working-class White children were only involved in mathematics in approximately 33% of the segments and their middle-class Black counterparts in 17%. Given the small numbers of participants, some caution is clearly needed before interpreting these racial/ethnic and social class differences. The other major difference between our data and those of Ginsburg and his colleagues is that enumeration was the type of mathematics in which the children were most likely to be involved (more than 20% of the segments) and the White children were also quite likely to be involved in the mathematics of magnitude (about 12%); the children were not particularly likely to be involved in pattern and shape (less than 5%). It may of course be the case that childcare settings are more likely to have easier access to materials involving specific patterns and shapes than are the other settings in which children find themselves.

At and around the home, of course, many opportunities for mathematics present themselves in the course of typically occurring activities. For example, Georgina (a pseudonym), a middle-class White three-year-old is helping her mother bake cookies: "Hand me a little spoon," she says. "No," replies her mother, "You need a big spoon" and later tells her daughter that she needs to "mix it one more time." When it is time to pour the mixture into the containers it is clear that Georgina is occupied in estimating how much material is needed to fill the spaces, even though nothing is said explicitly about it. A little later, her mother helps her to plan her time by asking a couple of times whether Georgina wants to eat and then take a bath or bathe first and then, after her daughter has finished eating says that they can read "just one story" before taking a bath. Within the story itself there are various opportunities for Georgina to experience number and time, such as when her mother reads: "The hands [on the village clock] always pointed to 20 minutes to 4" (CEYC field notes 0107). For other children, experiencing mathematics, particularly number, occurred in very different ways. For example, a middle-class Black three-year-old, Kevin, spent a good deal of time playing with a computer at home, and among the games he played was one that required him to match the written number (on a turtle's back) with the number of eggs in a nest. A little later, he listened first to a computer-generated song involving numbers and then to one about shapes and then, for about five minutes, responded to computer-generated questions about "what number comes after...?" This was then followed by a game in which he created a picture by pressing on the number representing the correct answer to simple addition questions. Kevin's mother's role is restricted to suggesting that he might try the next level of difficulty, and then to explaining that he needs to wait while the computer loads. Kevin does wait, and while doing so plays with some blocks, helping his older sister fit them into the correct spaces (CEYC field notes 0302).

We were still somewhat surprised that the children were involved in as much mathematics as they appeared to be, despite the fact that the amount of mathematical activity was not much less than that reported by Ginsburg and his colleagues (2003). We wondered whether the specific method that has been used to identify the occurrence of some type of mathematical activity, namely its presence or absence during a one-minute period (five minutes, in the case of Aubrey et al., 2003) serves to overestimate the extent of children's involvement as the method does not tell us whether engaging in mathematics happened for the entire minute or only briefly within the minute. For this reason we decided to calculate the precise time each child was involved with something mathematical. These results cut by almost exactly half the amount of time that the children were actually engaged in mathematics, from approximately 40% of the minute-long segments to 20% of the time in the case of the White children, and from 32% of the minutes to 17% of the time in the case of the Black children (Li et al., 2005). It is also important to mention, however, that the average involvement in mathematics disguises rather large individual differences, as Aubrey and her colleagues found—some children are much more likely to be involved than are others. In our data, for example, some children were observed engaging in things mathematical during only 1% of the videotaped observations, and others as much as 48% of the time observed.

CONCLUSION

The methods that scholars have used to assess the extent to which young children are involved in mathematics in the course of their everyday activities are clearly implicated in the data that have been obtained. Relying on parents to report on how much mathematics their children are involved in is clearly inadequate. However, no greater reliance should be placed on methods that only attend either to mathematical discourse (in the case of those studies that rely on audiotape) or to the activities that appear to be the primary focus of the child's attention and which fail to take into account the extent to which one or other aspect of mathematics is being used to achieve some other, non-mathematical, goal. Parents' reports and these more general observational approaches seem to under-represent significantly children's informal engagement in mathematics given the extent to which it can be captured on videotape by researchers who have spent sufficient time with the participants to allow them to behave, insofar as can be ascertained, as they would have if the camera-wielding observer had not been present. It is also worth noting that only researchers who use videotapes can examine children's activities in sufficient detail to be able to describe the types and quality of children's mathematical experiences, and not simply the extent of that experience.

Contrasting even the most generous parental estimates or researchers' live observations of the extent to which children engage in mathematical activities with what can be seen when their everyday activities are video-taped is clearly supportive of Piaget's position that preschoolers' experiences with objects and shapes and the exploration of space and time without any explicit teaching by adults provide innumerable opportunities for children to build on as they develop their understanding of conservation of number, length, volume, and so on. As Piaget argued, young children do not learn mathematics by being taught; they learn in the course of their experiences in and of the world. These experiences by no means require adult support or teaching; Ginsburg's and our CEYC videotapes show children being involved in mathematics alone or in the company of other children. It may be the case, as Tizard and Hughes (1986), Munn and Schaffer (1993), and Baroody et al. (2006) point out, that both in Britain and in the United States teachers of preschool-aged children do not involve their children in much mathematics, but this clearly does not stop children from gaining potentially rich mathematical experiences without depending on adult support, contrary to what Munn and Schaffer had reported.

Nonetheless, one cannot downplay the role of adults. As is clear from much of the observational research as well as those studies that rely on parents' reports, other people (particularly mothers, at home, as noted by Tizard and Hughes, 1986) clearly support young children's learning of mathematics by involving them in mathematically-related activities, encouraging them to count, estimate, talk about time, and so much more. It is tempting to contrast Piaget's stress on the child as active experiencer with Vygotsky's emphasis on the critical role the sociocultural world plays in children's development. Nonetheless, this would be a mistake, given that Piaget clearly did not discount the role of parents and teachers but merely argued that they should spend their time questioning and encouraging curiosity rather than trying to impose understanding prematurely. Similarly, Vygotsky by no means ignored children's own active involvement in coming to understand the world they are living in. In our CEYC videotapes it is clear that much of the mathematics that young children are involved in occur, as we showed in the case of Kevin, because of the children's own initiation of the activity. In Kevin's case, of course, that interest was clearly mediated by technology that has been made available for him by his parents and by virtue of living in a society that has access to this type of technology. Thus, as Vygotsky's theory predicts, children's engagement in mathematics seems intimately related to the typical social practices in which they are involved.

In cases in which the surrounding social world not only provides mathematically-relevant objects and situations but also people who draw attention to them and encourage children to explore and think about them we should not be surprised that children develop mathematical skills to a greater extent than when those conditions are relatively lacking. It is thus not surprising that the "competence" that children subsequently demonstrate is remarkably variable. As Sophian (1999) argued, this might explain why children can apparently be shown to demonstrate more sophisticated mathematical reasoning than Piaget predicted once problems have been presented to them in ways that fit within a context that makes more sense to them, but who do not show such reasoning once the context has been altered. As Sophian wrote, "children's knowledge, especially in its earliest forms, is closely tied to their understanding of the real-world interactions and activities in which they take part" (pp. 16–17).

Children, clearly, are involved in a good deal of everyday mathematics; however, the evidence is most likely to be gained when one looks carefully for mathematics in everyday life. This has implications for scholars and their choice of methods, but also has implications for parents and for teachers of young children. There are plenty of opportunities to help children with their growing understanding, perhaps simply by attending more closely to what they are doing mathematically, perhaps by helping create a zone of proximal development, or perhaps (as Piaget said) by suggesting "such counterexamples that the child's new exploration will lead him to correct himself" (1973, p. 86). Parents and early childhood educators are happy to play a large role in young children's growing awareness and enjoyment of literacy; it is unfortunate that they appear to treat things mathematical as being a less important part of children's experience or something that should be left until children start formal schooling. No doubt children's understanding of mathematical principles is growing as they engage in the types of mathematical experiences that can be seen on videotape, but there is also no doubt that both parents and educators could do far more to encourage and extend these mathematical explorations. After all, as Vygotsky argued, the type of mathematics that children learn "naturally" needs to be culturally mediated, and this might best be achieved by adults taking a less didactic role and instead encouraging the creation of zones of proximal development in conjunction with young children.

NOTE

1.   We would like to express our thanks to the families who gave so generously of their time, and to Sarah Putnam, Judy Sidden, Fabienne Doucet, and Nicole Talley who collected the original data. Our thanks also to Herb Ginsburg, for sharing with us the coding scheme that we adapted for this study, and to him and to two anonymous reviewers for their helpful comments on previous drafts of this chapter. For providing the time to finish writing this chapter, the first author would also like to thank the University of North Carolina at Greensboro for the award of a year-long Research Assignment and the Psychology program of the Universidade Federal do Rio Grande do Sul, Brazil, for the invitation to spend a year as Visiting Professor with financial support generously provided by CAPES (Coordenação de Aperfeiçoamento de Pessoal de Nível Superior).

REFERENCES

Aubrey, C., Bottle, G., & Godfrey, R. (2003). Early mathematics in the home and out-of-home contexts. *International Journal of Early Years Education, 11*(2), 91–103.

Balfanz, R. (1999). Why do we teach young children so little mathematics? Some historical considerations. In J. V. Copley (Ed.), *Mathematics in the early years* (pp. 3–10). Reston, VA: National Council of Teachers of Mathematics.

Baroody, A. J. (2004). The developmental bases for earch childhood number and operations standards. In D. H. Clements, J. Sarama, & A.-M. Dibiase (Eds.), *Engaging young children in mathematics: Standards for early childhood mathematics education* (pp. 173–219). Mahwah, NJ: Erlbaum.

Baroody, A. J., Lai., M., & Mix, K. S. (2006). The development of young children's early number and ooperation sense and its implications for early childhood education. In B. Spodek & O. N. Saracho (Eds.), *Handbook of research on the education of young children* (2nd Ed., pp. 187–221). Mahwah, NJ: Erlbaum.

Baroody, A. J., & Wilkins, J. L. M. (1999). The development of informal counting, number, and arithmetic skills and concepts. In J. V. Copley (Ed.), *Mathematics in the early years* (pp. 48–65). Reston, VA: National Council of Teachers of Mathematics.

Berk, L. E., & Winsler, A. (1995). *Scaffolding children's learning: Vygotsky and early childhood education.* Washington, DC: National Association for the Education of Young Children.

Blevins-Knabe, B., & Musun-Miller, L. (1996). Number use at home by children and their parents and its relationship to early mathematical performance. *Early Development and Parenting, 5*(1), 35–45.

Bolger, N., Davis, A., & Rafaeli, E. (2003). Diary methods: Capturing life as it is lived. *Annual Review of Psychology, 54*, 579–616.

Carew, J. V. (1980). Experience and the development of intelligence in young children at home and in day care. *Monographs of the Society for Research in Child Development, 45* (6–7, Serial No. 187), 1–89.

Carew, J. V., Chan, I., & Halfar, C. (1976). *Observing intelligence in young children: Eight case studies.* Englewood Cliffs, NJ: Prentice-Hall.

Donaldson, M. (1978). *Children's minds.* London: Fontana.

Gelman, R., Massey, C. M., & McManus, M. (1991). Characterizing supporting environments for cognitive development: Lessons from children in a museum. In L. B. Resnick, J. M. Levine, & S. D. Teasley (Eds.), *Perspectives on socially shared cognition* (pp. 226–256). Washington, DC: American Psychological Association.

Ginsburg, H. P., Cannon, J., Eisenband, J., & Pappas, S. (2006). Mathematical thinking and learning. In K. McCartney & D. Phillips (Eds.), *Blackwell handbook on early childhood development* (pp. 208–230). Malden, MA: Basil Blackwell

Ginsburg, H. P., Inoue, N., & Seo, K.-H. (1999). Preschoolers doing mathematics: Observations of everyday activities. In J. Copley (Ed.), *Mathematics in the early years* (pp. 88–99). Reston, VA: National Council of Teachers of Mathematics.

Ginsburg, H. P., Klein, A., & Starkey, P. (1998). The development of children's mathematical thinking: Connecting research with practice. In I. E. Sigel & K.

A. Renninger (Volume Eds.) and W. Damon (Series Ed.), *Handbook of child psychology, Volume 4: Child psychology in practice* (pp. 401–476). New York: Wiley.

Ginsburg, H. P., Lin, C., Ness, D., & Seo, K.-H. (2003). Young American and Chinese children's everyday mathematical activity. *Mathematical thinking and learning, 5(4)*, 235–258.

Hannula, M. M. (2005). *Spontaneous focusing on numerosity in the development of early mathematical skills.* Annales Universitatis Turkuensis B, 282. Turku: Painosalama.

Hannula, M. M., Mattinen, A., & Lehtinen, E. (2005). Does social interaction influence 3-year-old children's tendency to focus on numerosity? A quasi-experimental study in day care. In L. Verschaffel, E. De Corte, G. Kanselaar, & M. Valcke (Eds.), *Powerful learning environments for promoting deep conceptual and strategic learning* (pp. 63–80). Studia Paedagogica. Leuven: Leuven University Press.

Hofferth, S. L., & Sandberg, J. F. (2001). How American children spend their time. *Journal of Marriage and Family, 63*(2), 295–308

Hughes, M. (1986). *Children and number: Difficulties in learning mathematics.* Oxford, UK: Basil Blackwell.

Hughes, M., Carmichael, H., Pinkerton, G., & Tizard, B. (1979). Recording children's conversations at home and at nursery school: A technique and some methodological considerations. *Journal of Child Psychology and Psychiatry, 20*(3), 225–232.

Juster, F. T., & Stafford, F. P. (1985). *Time, goods, and well-being.* Ann Arbor: Survey Research Center, University of Michigan.

Klibanoff, R. S., Levine, S. C., Huttenlocher, J., Vasilyeva, M., & Hedges, L. V. (2006). Preschool children's mathematical knowledge: The effect of teacher "math talk." *Developmental Psychology, 42*(1), 59–69.

Lave, J. (1988). *Cognition in practice: Mind, mathematics, and culture in everyday life.* New York: Cambridge University Press.

Li, L., Kinney, T., & Tudge, J. R. H. (2005, February). *Almost never or almost always? Young children's everyday mathematical experiences at childcare and at home.* Presented at the annual Symposium on Child and Family Development, Athens, GA.

Mix, K. S., Huttenlocher, J., & Levine, S. C. (2002). *Quantitative development in infancy and early childhood.* New York: Oxford University Press.

Munn, P., & Schaffer, H. R. (1993). Literacy and numeracy events in social interactive contexts. *International Journal of Early Years Education, 1*(3), 61–80.

Nourot, P. M. (2005). Historical perspectives on early childhood education. In J. L. Roopnarine & J. E. Johnson (Eds.), *Approaches to early childhood education*, 4th edition (pp. 3–43). Upper Saddle River, NJ: Pearson

Nunes, T., Schliemann, A.-L., & Carraher, D. (1993). *Street mathematics and school mathematics.* New York: Cambridge University Press.

Piaget, J. (1952). *The child's conception of number.* New York: Norton. (Original work published in 1941.)

Piaget, J. (1953). How children form mathematical concepts. *Scientific American, 189*(5), 74–79.

Piaget, J. (1970). *Science of education and the psychology of the child.* New York: Orion. (Original work published in 1935 and 1970.)

Piaget, J., (1973). *The child and reality: Problems of genetic psychology.* New York: Grossman. (Original work published in 1962.)

Piaget, J. (1973). Comments on mathematical education. In A. G. Howson (Ed.), *Developments in mathematical education: Proceedings of the Second International Congress on Mathematical Education* (pp. 79–87). Cambridge: Cambridge University Press.

Piaget, J. (1998). *Sobre a pedagogia: Textos inéditos [On education: Unedited texts].* (S. Parrat-Dayan & A. Tryphon, Eds., & C. Berliner, trans). São Paulo: Casa do Psicólogo. (Original work published between 1930 and 1976.)

Piaget, J., & Inhelder, B. (1967). *The child's conception of space.* New York: Norton. (Original work published in 1948.)

Plewis, I., Mooney, A., & Creeser, R. (1990). Time on educational activities at home and educational progress in infant school. *British Journal of Educational Psychology, 60*(3), 330–337.

Rogoff, B. (1987). Specifying the development of a cognitive skill in its interactional and cultural context. *Monographs of the Society for Research in Child Development, 52*, 153–159 (2, Serial No. 216).

Rousseau, J. J. (1969). *Émile.* London: Dent. (Originally published in 1762.)

Saxe, G. B. (1982). Developing forms of arithmetic operations among the Oksapmin of Papua New Guinea. *Developmental Psychology, 18*(4), 583–594.

Saxe, G. B. (1991). *Culture and cognitive development: Studies in mathematical understanding.* Hillsdale, NJ: Erlbaum.

Saxe, G. B., & Esmonde, I. (2005). Studying cognition in flux: A historical treatment of fu in the shifting structure of Oksapmin mathematics. *Mind, Culture, and Activity, 12*(3/4), 171–225

Saxe, G. B., Guberman, S. R., & Gearhart, M. (1987). Social processes in early number development. *Monographs of the Society for Reseach in Child Development, 52*(2, Serial No. 216).

Scribner, S. (1984). Studying working intelligence. In B. Rogoff & L. Lave (Eds.), *Everyday cognition: Its development in social context* (pp. 9–40). Cambridge, MA: Harvard University Press.

Seo, K.-H., & Ginsburg, H. P. (2004). What is developmentally appropriate in early childhood mathematics education? Lessons from new research. In D. H. Clements, J. Sarama, & DiBiase, A.-M. (Eds.), *Engaging young children in mathematics: Standards for early childhood mathematics education* (pp. 91–104). Mahwah, NJ: Erlbaum.

Sophian, C. (1995). *Children's numbers.* Madison, WI: Brown and Benchmark.

Sophian, C. (1999). Children's ways of knowing: Lessons from cognitive development research. In J. V. Copley (Ed.), *Mathematics in the early years* (pp. 11–20). Reston, VA: National Council of Teachers of Mathematics.

Starkey, P., Spelke, E. S., & Gelman, R. (1990). Numerical abstraction by human infants. *Cognition, 36*(2), 97–127.

Timmer, S. G., Eccles, J., & O'Brien, K. (1985). How children use time. In F. T. Juster & F. P. Stafford, *Time, goods, and well-being* (pp. 353–382). Ann Arbor: Survey Research Center, University of Michigan.

Tizard, B., & Hughes, M. (1984). *Young children learning: Talking and thinking at home and at school.* London: Fontana.

Tudge, J. R. H. (2008). *The everyday lives of young children: Culture, class, and childrearing in diverse societies.* New York: Cambridge University Press.

Tudge, J. R. H., & Doucet, F. (2004). Early mathematical experiences: Observing young Black and White children's everyday experiences. *Early Childhood Research Quarterly, 19*(1), 21–39.

Tudge, J. R. H., Doucet, F., Odero, D., Sperb, T., Piccinini, C., & Lopes, R. (2006). A window into different cultural worlds: Young children's everyday activities in the United States, Kenya, and Brazil. *Child Development, 77*(5), 1446–1469.

Tudge, J. R. H., Hayes, S., Doucet, F., Odero, D., Kulakova, N., Tammeveski, P., Meltsas, M., & Lee, S. (2000). Parents' participation in cultural practices with their preschoolers: A cross-cultural study of everyday activities. *Psicologia: Teoria e Pesquisa* [*Psychology: Theory and Research*], *16*(1), 1–11.

Tudge, J. R. H., Odero, D., Hogan, D., & Etz, K. (2003). Relations between the everyday activities of preschoolers and their teachers' perceptions of their competence in the first years of school. *Early Childhood Research Quarterly, 18*(1), 42–64.

Tudge, J. R. H., & Scrimsher, S. (2003). Lev S. Vygotsky on education: A cultural-historical, interpersonal, and individual approach to development. In B. J. Zimmerman & D. H. Schunk (Eds.), *Educational psychology: A century of contributions* (pp. 207–228). Mahwah, NJ: Erlbaum.

Vygotsky, L. S. (1994). The problem of the cultural development of the child. In R. Van der Veer & J. Valsiner (Eds.), *The Vygotsky reader* (pp. 57–72). Oxford: Blackwell. (Original work published in 1929.)

Vygotsky, L. S. (1997). *The collected works of L. S. Vygotsky: Vol. 4, The history of the development of higher mental functions* (R. W. Rieber, Ed., & M. J. Hall, trans.) New York: Plenum. (Originally written in 1931; chapters 1–5 first published in 1960, chapters 6–15 first published in 1997.)

Wells, C. G. (1984). Language development in the pre-school years. Cambridge, England: Cambridge University Press.

Wynn, K. (1998). Psychological foundations of number: Numerical competence in human infants. *Trends in Cognitive Sciences, 2*(8), 296–303.

CHAPTER 9

AN EXAMINATION OF THE ROLE OF STATISTICAL INVESTIGATION IN SUPPORTING THE DEVELOPMENT OF YOUNG CHILDREN'S STATISTICAL REASONING

Aisling Leavy

Statistics has assumed an increasingly central place in society. Children are being exposed to statistics from an early age partly through the use of complex data in the media and in children's texts, these texts provide less interpretation for the reader than do adult texts, thus posing a challenge for schools to educate children to make sense of data (Joram, Resnick, & Gabriele, 1995). As recently as a decade ago, however, statistics education in elementary and middle schools was identified as inadequate (Mosteller, 1988; NCTM, 1989; Posten, 1981) and instruction focused on the procedural and computational aspects of statistics rather than developing conceptual understanding (Garfield & Ahlgren, 1988; Shaughnessy, 1992). This identified neglect of data analysis and statistics lead to a call for investigations into children's statistical understanding by The Mathematical Sci-

Contemporary Perspectives on Mathematics in Early Childhood Education, pages 215–232 ences Advisory Committee of the College Entrance Examination Board (1984–1985) who stated "perhaps no other topics in mathematics surround and affect our lives as much and yet are so poorly understood as statistics and probability." In addition, two influential documents were published in the early 1990s which shaped the development of research and teaching related to statistics education. In April 1989, the National Council of Teachers of Mathematics released its *Curriculum and Evaluation Standards for School Mathematics*, which incorporated a strand focusing on data analysis and probability. In 1991, the American Statistical Association published *Guidelines for the Teaching of Statistics K–12* (Burrill, 1991). Both documents present perspectives which advocate statistics as an active discipline— requiring the collection and analysis of real data that leads to multiple avenues for making sense of and interpreting data arising from student-constructed questions.

The last decade has seen a growing movement to incorporate statistical concepts in elementary education and beyond, accompanied by copious and productive debate defining the means by which this should come about. Despite this increased attention to statistics in the research community, research examining young children's statistical thinking remains in its infancy.

FROM CONCEPT TO MODELS: THE EVOLUTION OF RESEARCH ON CHILDREN'S STATISTICAL THINKING

Research on children's understanding of statistics has focused predominately on the area of children's probability judgments, everyday inductive reasoning and heuristics (Shaughnessy, 1992). There has been less emphasis on the area of descriptive and inferential statistics and on how children understand key statistical concepts. Those studies carried out in the field of descriptive statistics have focused on specific elements of statistical thinking such as conceptions of central tendency and graphing rather than on broader concepts relating to data handling or more encompassing statistical concepts such as distribution. While a criticism of this kind of research is that it tends to address isolated components of students' statistical thinking, the information contributed by these studies has been important nonetheless in influencing the design of curricula and instructional programs.

A new research focus to emerge in statistics education is the development of cognitive models. The need for cognitive models of students' statistical thinking was identified in the '80s and '90s (Cobb et al., 1991; Resnick, 1983) leading to recent efforts to develop learning trajectories and models of statistical understanding. The development of cognitive models is critical as it can facilitate the identification of subcomponents and key concepts that contribute to understanding and thus lead to the design of tools and tasks which can support the development of such concepts. One such cognitive model that presents a focus on young children is the Jones et al. (2000) *Framework for Characterizing Student's Statistical Thinking*. This framework identifies and makes explicit students' patterns of thought while engaging in statistical activity, and represent such patterns as frameworks. The four-construct statistical thinking framework is based on the Biggs and Collis (1991) general cognitive development model (SOLO). Statistical thinking within each of the constructs (describing, organizing, representing, and analyzing and interpreting data) is characterized in terms of the four levels of cognitive thinking outlined in the SOLO model. Thus, performance at level 1: idiosyncratic corresponds to Biggs and Collis' prestructural thinking and is characterized by intuitive thinking and idiosyncratic imaging. A learner distracted by irrelevant aspects of statistical tasks is one feature that characterizes this level of cognitive thinking. Level 2: transitional relates to Biggs and Collis' unistructural thinking and represents learners that are transitioning between idiosyncratic and quantitative ways of thinking. This transitory state results in the tendency to pursue single aspects of tasks, the outcome being manifested in narrowly focused and incomplete attempts at representing and analyzing data. Level 3: quantitative displays characteristics of Biggs and Collis' multistructural thinking and is manifested in the ability of learners to focus on several relevant features of data and use informal quantitative thinking. Level 4: analytical compares to Biggs and Collis' relational thinking and incorporates the ability to make connections among features of a task and engage in quantitative and analytical reasoning about data, thus producing multiple perspectives on data and utilizing valid measures. The outcomes of research coming from this perspective provides frameworks within which an educator can situate an individual child's statistical practice and provide guidance in terms of evaluating that practice and setting a trajectory for future constructive experiences. While these frameworks are critical at this juncture for the field of statistics education, prudence should be applied to their use as assessment and placement tools until such as time as the field has had adequate time to engage in further examination and validation of the frameworks.

AN EXAMINATION OF YOUNG CHILDREN'S STATISTICAL THINKING

Consensus has been reached regarding the structural components that constitute the field of data analysis and statistics at the elementary level.

These components mirror the process of statistical investigation and reflect the recommendations of the American Statistical Association (Burrill, 1991) and the National Council of Teachers of Mathematics (1989, 2000). The NCTM document emphasizes a focus at the pre-K–2 level on: formulating questions, collecting, organizing, displaying data; analyzing data using appropriate methods; and developing inferences and predictions based on the data. Similarly, the ASA guidelines advocate a focus on data exploration at K–4 emphasizing a focus on five components of data exploration: Understanding the problem, gathering and exploring data, organizing and representing data, describing data, and interpreting data. The organization of the remainder of this paper is structured around the categories generated by NCTM and ASA.

Throughout the review of literature that follows, a situated cognitionist perspective is used to inform a critique of studies examining young children's statistical thinking in each of the components of statistical investigation: formulating questions, describing data, organizing and reducing data, representing data, analyzing and interpreting data. A situated perspective posits that 'Knowledge is situated in activity, context, and culture of which it is a part . . . learning is inseparable from and not ancillary to the content' (Brown, Collins, & Duguid, 1989). Drawing from this perspective, the assumption is made that any data analytic approach utilized by a child is influenced in part by the context used to represent the data and a child's familiarity with that context, and the authenticity of the task and the degree to which it engages a child in meaningful and purposeful activity.

Formulating a Statistical Question

It is commonly known that mathematics problems that are embedded in a context are more easily solved than those not embedded in context (Carraher & Schliemann, 1985). This notion of context has implications for school activities. Authentic activities are the ordinary activities of the culture, whereas school activities often do not reflect the practices of mathematicians. Hence, the activity in schools is "hybrid . . . implicitly framed by one culture, but explicitly attributed to another . . . limit[ing] students access to the important structuring and supporting cues that arise from the context" (Brown et al., 1989, p. 34). These issues are important ones for educators when considering the approaches used to engage children in data analysis and statistics and have resulted in a focus on children being involved in collecting and analyzing data that will be used for further analyses (Cockcroft, 1982; Curcio, 1987; Thompson, 1999; Tukey, 1977). Ownership of a statistical problem, then, becomes a critical first step in statistical problem solving. The problem must pose a real dilemma; otherwise the problem does not pose as a problem, rather as a constraint (Lave, 1997). One way to ensure that school statistical problems and activities are dilemma motivated is to engage children in the formulation of problems that have personal relevance.

The process of statistical investigation starts with defining a research question. For many children, transforming a real world question into a statistical question can be an arduous process. Young children often ask questions that require sampling entire populations (e.g., 'what height are all third graders in the United States?') and need to be supported in keeping the data collection process in mind when constructing questions. Young children also struggle posing questions that can be interpreted in the same way by different people (Konold & Higgins, 2002), while at the same time work hard to try and match a data collection method that generates the data required to answer their research question. Konold and Higgins illustrate the challenge involved when transforming general questions into statistical ones in their description of a pair of second graders interested in investigating 'How many States have you visited?' (p. 42). The children soon realized that the word 'visit' can connote a number of different meanings and finally settled on the question 'How many states have you ever set foot in?', despite one students' dissatisfaction that 'set foot in' didn't delineate sufficiently between those who traveled *through* versus *to* a state. The provision of support in guiding young children to revise their research questions into questions that support inquiry is rewarded by the interest and motivation generated through engaging children in collecting, analyzing and representing data that address questions of personal interest.

Describing Data

The act of describing data is referred to as *reading the data* (Curcio, 1987; Curcio & Artz, 1997) and involves a literal reading of data presented in graphical form. The skills required to describe data include (but are not limited to): understanding the problem situation from which the data are generated, making connections between the data as represented on the display and the original data, exposure to the representations used to display the data, and recognizing graphical conventions. The first two factors presuppose prior knowledge of the context and the last two call for knowledge of the displays, all four factors are particularly critical when considering the demands on K–3 children, as opposed to older children, when engaging in data analysis contexts.

An analysis of third grade students' performance on the Third International Mathematics and Science Study (TIMSS) indicates that more than 75% could read data from a bar graph and 40% from a pictogram (Beaton et al., 1996). The relative ease with which third grade children read data displays as indicated by the TIMSS study was supported by the classification by Jones et al. (2000) of 1–3 grade students. All grade 3 students exhibited level 3 thinking as demonstrated in part by the provision of complete descriptions of data, and the recognition of graphing conventions (see Table 9.1). Below third grade, however, difficulties arise for students when describing graphs. In the same study, Jones et al. found that while a small number of first and second students exhibited level 3 thinking, most students typically exhibited level 1 or level 2 thinking. When asked whether a line plot and bar graph represent the same data a grade 2 student exhibiting level 1 thinking stated 'No, because this one has writing [a reference to the story line on top of the line plot] and this one doesn't' (p. 292). An example of level 2 thinking in relation to the same task illustrates a student's focus on graphical conventions such as labeling as a justification for similarity, in this case the displays were considered analogous because they had identical labels. These difficulties focusing on relevant features of graphical representations are not surprising given first and second graders low exposure to bar graphs and line plots, but may be related in part to lack of familiarity with the problem context.

TABLE 9.1
Levels of Statistical Thinking Relating to the Statistical Construct *Describing Data Displays* (adapted from Jones et al., 2000)

Level 1: idiosyncratic	• Provides descriptions of the data which include idiosyncratic and irrelevant information; little awareness of graphing conventions • Does not recognize instances when graphical displays represent the same information (or provides idiosyncratic reasoning when describing relationship between displays) • When making determinations about the relative efficiency of different data displays, irrelevant features are taken into account
Level 2: transitional	• Provides an incomplete description of the data but demonstrates some recognition of graphing conventions • Recognizes instances when graphical displays represent the same information but the associated justification is based on conventions • When making determinations about the relative efficiency of different data displays, only one aspect is taken into account
Level 3: quantitative	• Provides a complete description of the data and demonstrates recognition of graphing conventions • Recognizes when different displays represent the same data and uses partial correspondences between elements in the display • When making determinations about the relative efficiency of different data displays, provides an explanation based on more than one aspect of the displays

A study carried out by Putt et al. (1999), examining eight first and second grade students' approaches to describing data displays, provides greater insight into the particular challenges faced when young children try to read the data off a display. Six of the eight students provided idiosyncratic responses that involved focusing on cosmetic features of graphs such as the title, the icons used to represent individual data values, and the names of categories of categorical data. Some students also demonstrated difficulties interpreting what the height of the bars on a bar graph and the scale represented, often assigning idiosyncratic meaning to these elements. For example, one first grade student who was examining a bar graph of the number of friends that came to visit on different days during the week (x axis indicating the categorical variables Monday-Sunday and the y axis representing the frequency of children who visited) described the height of the bars to mean the height of friends, and the numbers on the y-axis to indicate the age of the friends. These children also demonstrated difficulty, similar to that described by Jones et al. (2001), recognizing instances when graphical displays represent the same information. Another challenge faced by students when describing data is interpreting categorical data. A teaching experiment carried out with 2nd graders (Jones et al., 2000) indicated that children demonstrated difficulty interpreting categorical data especially in cases where the data were numerical identifiers (for example, a label '#2 ticket') and tended to interpret these as numbers or counts, indicating the need to invest time and resources in helping young children understand the meaning of individual data values and the contexts within which they are collected.

While an error analysis such as the one above is useful in identifying obstacles faced when describing data, it is important to examine the characteristics of the tasks used in the studies. None of the tasks presented data that were collected by the students, and neither did the students play a role in formulating the research questions. From a situated perspective, knowledge is viewed as co- produced by the learner and the situation. When mathematical activity is immersed in a context steeped in meaning, the authenticity of the context allows students to act on quantities and their relations 'in ways that make sense with ongoing activity' (Lave, 1997, p. 27). I argue that these tasks cannot be described as authentic activities because they do not represent the ordinary practice of the culture of statisticians, for example, statisticians aren't presented with semi-constructed graphical representations and asked to complete them. By requiring young children to engage in tasks that (a) are not endorsed by the cultures to which they are attributed, and (b) involve data collection procedures and contexts that students are not privy to, students do not have access to the important structuring and supporting cues that arise from the context. In such situations we are underestimating the statistical ability of young learners by not affording them the opportunity to engage in meaningful and authentic statistical activity.

Organizing and Reducing Data

Once data are collected, they need to be *organized* in a form that supports interpretation. This organization usually results in a spatial reorganization of the data, and quite often the questions we ask guide the way we organize the data. Given what we know about the importance of context and authentic activity in children's mathematics it is not unrealistic to expect that children who have been involved in formulating the research question and collecting the data around which the problem is posed, might have greater resources to draw from when asked to organize the data. In these situations, the main dilemma's for children are mathematical ones as compared to what Lave described as the 'performance dilemma's' associated with many school mathematical tasks.

The studies that follow examine the practices of young children when asked to organize data which they themselves have not collected. Difficulties organizing data were revealed in a study of second graders (Jones et al., 2001) which described the reorganization of data as 'torturous' (p. 127) for the children who did found it 'almost unnatural' to sort data into preassigned categories. Evidence to support the argument made in this paper about the importance of context is provided by the researcher's description of the need to engage students in conversations relating to real world contexts that involve sorting in order for students to begin to develop an understanding of a shared meaning for sorting. Again, the use of idiosyncratic responses by first and second graders when organizing data displays is reported by Putt et al. (1999) and Jones et al. (2000). For example, Jones et al. describe a second grade student who when asked to organize five different beanie babies© suggested that they all be put in a bag, and Putt et al. report a second grade students justification for their organizing strategy as 'I thought it up in my head' (p. 76).

The act of *reducing* data involves choosing value(s) that represent the data and serve as summaries thereby removing the need to represent each individual data value. Support for the need to use authentic contexts is found when examining the outcomes of studies involving young children in critically analyzing and reducing data that they themselves have collected, or studies that spend extensive amounts of time supporting children in understanding contexts within which data have been collected. Results from such studies reveal greater sophistication in young children's thinking about data than that posited by the previous studies. An interesting finding arising from the teaching intervention component of a teach-

TABLE 9.2
Levels of Statistical Thinking Relating to the Statistical Construct
Organizing and Reducing Data **(adapted from Jones et al., 2000)**

Level 1: idiosyncratic	• Does not group or order the data in non-idiosyncratic ways • Does not recognize when data reduction occurs • Cannot construct representative values for data sets • No indication of the presence of a sense of spread
Level 2: transitional	• Provides inconsistent groupings • Provides irrelevant explanations for when data reduction occurs • Provides poorly representative values for data sets • Constructs a measure to index spread – measure is usually invalid
Level 3: quantitative	• Can group into categories and provide explanations for categorizations • Can provide explanations for incidences when data reduction occurs • Provides measures of center as representational indices but reasoning is incomplete • Constructs a measure of spread but reasoning is usually incomplete

ing experiment with second graders (Jones et al., 2001) revealed multifaceted conceptions of average similar to those identified with upper elementary students (Cobb, 1999; Konold et al., 2002; Leavy & Middleton, 2001; Leavy, 2003; Lehrer & Schauble, 2002; Mokros & Russell, 1995). Children exhibited model, balance, close-to, and lowest bound conceptions of average. These measures, while not always implemented appropriately, provide some indication of understanding of typicality that draws upon conceptions of center and spread. Furthermore, students were found to demonstrate flexibility in moving between conceptions of average, indicating the potential for supporting the development of dynamic and flexible understandings of representativeness. The same study provides insight into young children's understanding of variability identifying that in data comparison situations students displayed two conceptions of spread: firstly, a "close-together or far-apart" schema, and secondly, a concept of range. Sophistication in thinking about variation was also found in a study of third graders following a 10-week instructional unit focusing on data and chance (Watson & Kelly, 2002). These studies demonstrate that there exists potential, currently untapped in our elementary classrooms, for developing young children's understanding of representativeness, and sources of variation and ways to model it. Evidence of this latent potential, however, seems to be revealed only in studies where statistical activity occurs in the context of meaningful statistical investigations.

There are factors, in addition to the provision of context, which may account for first and second graders construction of poorly representative values (Table 9.2). Firstly, measures of center are often not introduced until the later grades and it is frequently these measures that are used to construct representative values. Many children then do not have these tools at their disposal. Another explanation for the absence of quantitative (level 3) thinking in grades 1–2 is that understanding of representativeness is believed to be predicated on understanding of *data set as an entity* rather than a collection of individual data points (Mokros & Russell, 1995). This notion of data set as entity is a difficult concept given that many young children focus on individual data values—in particular, those values that represent their own selves in the data, rather than on global aspects of the data. Konold and Higgins (2002) describe the case of a kindergarten teacher engaging her students in recording their favorite colors, and she poses the question 'what does the graph tell us?'. Replies indicated that students were not focusing on global aspects of the data but focused instead on characteristics of individuals as indicated by responses such as 'my favorite color is red', 'my shirt is blue', and 'we learned English and Chinese colors' (p. 28). It seems that there is a large conceptual leap involved in moving from conceptualizations of data as a set of unique individual values to data as an aggregate, perhaps then accounting for the poor performance of younger children when constructing representational indices. A third reason is related to variability. Many of the representations used at the early grades (bar graphs and pie graphs, for example) may mask the variability of the data, thus reducing the measures that students may use to reduce data. Bar graphs and pie charts are commonly used representations with younger children.

There is evidence to indicate that by third grade children have greater resources at their disposal when organizing data and when generating representative measures. The Jones et al. framework categorized third grade students as demonstrating both level 2 and level 3 thinking. Other studies suggest that the *normalizing* activity of 8–9 year olds, in other words the ability to recognize anomalies in data displays and adjust data toward a perceived norm, results from children's ability to view the data set as an entity resulting in the identification of patterns or trends in data (Ainley, Pratt, & Nardi, 2001, p. 139). As discussed earlier, the ability to view data set as an entity is closely tied to and often a necessary condition for construction of representative values. This improved performance of third grade students as compared to their K–2 peers indicates that the obstacles that younger children face (developmental, lack of prior knowledge, for example) may begin to dissipate around the onset of third grade.

Representing Data

Studies examining data representation, a task involving the construction of visual displays that exhibit different organizations of the data, report different outcomes in terms of what we might expect younger children to be able to do. Examining the outcomes of studies involving students constructing representations for data they have not collected, against studies where students have been involved in all stages of the statistical investigation, reveals a pattern: When the data representation task relates to an authentic statistical investigation children appear to construct more appropriate and sophisticated graphical representations.

In data analytic contexts where children have not been privy to the data collection, a number of patterns in student responses may be expected. The provision of idiosyncratic responses that are not based on the represented data is a common finding from studies of first and second graders when asked to represent data (Jones et al., 2000; Putt et al., 1999). This type of thinking, akin to a level 1 classification (see Table 9.3), may result in the construction of an idiosyncratic graph that bears little or no relationship to the data presented, in difficulties completing a partially constructed graph, or in problems completing a bar graph using data from a table (Beaton et al., 1996). These difficulties may result from a lack of awareness of the function and purpose of data representation as evidenced in a teaching experiment carried out with 3rd grade students where students rearranged rather than represented data (Leavy, 2003). Not all children produce idiosyncratic responses, some first and second graders demonstrated the ability to complete graphs, and while the resulting graph was not entirely valid it was accurate in some dimensions. At this point it is also important keep in mind that a number or combination of variables or factors, in addition to lack of access to the data collection phase of statistical inquiry, may contribute to the difficulties outlined above.

These studies do not present a particularly positive picture relating to young children's flexibility in representing data. In contrast, studies examining children representing data they themselves have collected provide

TABLE 9.3
Levels of Statistical Thinking Relating to the Statistical Construct *Representing Data* (adapted from Jones et al., 2000)

Level 1: idiosyncratic	• Unable to accurately complete partially constructed graphical displays
	• When presented with data in a graphical display, could not reorganize the data and represent on an alternative display
Level 2: transitional	• Could complete a partially constructed graphical displays that was valid in some aspects
	• When presented with data in a graphical display, could not reorganize the data and represent on an alternative display
Level 3: quantitative	• Completed partially constructed graphical displays
	• When presented with data in a graphical display, constructs a valid display

different expectations for what we may expect. Indeed, a study carried out by Curcio and Folkson (1996) demonstrated that kindergarten children even with no formal instruction can invent their own representations as a means to organize and display data. The important aspect of this study was that these representations arose from situations involving children in constructing questions of interest, and gathering and representing data to answer these questions, thus highlighting the importance of engaging young children in all stages of statistical investigation. Another case of young students constructing representations of data, in this case categorical data, is provided by Konold and Higgins (2002) in their description of a group of first graders who used a grid of rows and columns to represent categorical data describing the games they liked to play at recess. They also describe a group of second graders who ordered numerical data relating to the number of lost teeth in tabular form, resulting in a highly detailed representation that recorded student names, frequencies of teeth lost, and a pictorial representation of the number of teeth lost.

This aspect of the *meaningfulness* of the activity has been referred to by Roth and McGinn (1997) who support a focus on the study of graphing as practice whereby there is a focus on 'participation in meaningful practice and experience' (p. 92). They argue that in school-based graphing activities the production of the graph often constitutes the end rather than the means for meaning-making. If students had greater opportunities to make graphs to achieve certain ends then they may demonstrate greater competence in doing so, a hypothesis supported by the findings of Curcio and Folkson (1996).

Analyzing and Interpreting Data

The analysis and interpretation of data represent one component of what Friel, Curcio, and Bright (2001) term *graph comprehension*. They define graph comprehension as a 'graph readers' abilities to derive meaning from graphs created by others or by themselves' (p. 132). This interpretation of a graph requires that the reader distinguish important from less important features of the data (Wood, 1968) in addition to examining relationships between visual dimensions and structural components of graphical representations. Arising from an analysis of the pertinent literature, Friel et al. (2001) characterized three levels of graph comprehension that relate to Curcio's (1987) earlier characterization of the tasks of comprehension: reading the data, reading between the data, reading beyond the data (Curcio, 1987, p. 384). The first level, an elementary level, focuses primarily on extracting information from a graph and corresponds to 'reading the data'; the second intermediate level requires finding relationships in the data and is compatible with 'reading between the data'; and, the final advanced level, involving reading 'beyond the data', requires extrapolating from the data.

Given that large scale assessments, most notable NAEP and TIMSS, examining 4th graders' performance on analyzing graphs indicate difficulty interpreting graphs and drawing conclusions (Lindquist et al., 1983; Zawojewski & Heckman, 1997), it is not surprising to find that younger students demonstrate difficulties analyzing and interpreting graphs. When assessed on their ability to analyze and interpret data, grade 1 students demonstrated primarily level 1 thinking and grade 2 students were evenly split between levels 1 and 2 thinking when classified using the Jones et al. (2000) framework for characterizing children's statistical thinking (see Table 9.4). Level 1 thinker's presented invalid or irrelevant responses when asked to (a) make comparisons or read 'between the data', and (b) extend, predict or make inferences to 'read beyond the data' (p. 384). This often resulted in the provision of idiosyncratic responses when trying to make conclusions that required more than literal reading of the data. Level 2 thinkers were better able to read between the data than read beyond the data, and were also able to identify certain aspects of the data set that were not illuminated by the graphical representation. In contrast children classified as level 3, all of whom were third graders, demonstrated more sophisti-

---

TABLE 9.4
Levels of Statistical Thinking Relating to the Statistical Construct
Analyzing and Interpreting Data **(adapted from Jones et al., 2000)**

Level 1: idiosyncratic	• Unable to accurately identify aspects of the data not illuminated by the display • Invalid and inappropriate responses when asked to 'read between the data' • Invalid and inappropriate responses when asked to 'read beyond the data'
Level 2: transitional	• Presented incomplete references to aspects of the data not illuminated by the display • Valid response to some aspects of the data when asked to 'read between the data' • Valid response to some aspects of the data when asked to 'read beyond the data'
Level 3: quantitative	• Identified multiple relevant aspects of the data not illuminated by the display • Provides multiple valid responses when asked to 'read between the data' • Provides some valid responses when asked to 'read beyond the data' but reasoning is incomplete

cated analysis and interpretation abilities. They could readily identify aspects of the data absent from the representations, demonstrated ease in reading between the data, and were better able to make predictions based on the data (reading beyond the data).

Examination of first- and second-graders attempts to analyze data presented on line plots and bar graphs highlighted that 80% gave incomplete or superficial responses (Putt et al., 1999). However, the study used a number of probes to assess skills in data analysis, and performance across these probes varied. Students were successful on tasks involving identifying the highest frequency data values (mode) and the lowest frequency data values thus demonstrating skill in 'reading between the data'. However, analysis tasks involving the construction of typical or representative values resulted in idiosyncratic responses. This is not surprising given similar findings of fourth graders constructing idiosyncratic representative values (Leavy & Middleton, 2001).

A number of characteristics identified as important for graph comprehension may contribute to young students' performance on analysis and interpretation tasks. *Characteristics of graph readers* (Friel et al., 2001), in particular the prior knowledge that students bring to a comprehension task, is one such characteristic of particular relevance to young children. An examination of the effect of prior knowledge on elementary students' comprehension of a number of graphical representations concluded that prior knowledge of mathematical content was the most important of the three aspects of prior knowledge, and emphasized the need for "children to be involved in graphing activities to build and expend the relevant schemata needed for comprehension" (Curcio, 1987). In addition to prior knowledge relating to number concepts and relations and operations contained in the graph, mathematics knowledge relating to counting, measuring and classifying have also been identified as essential to data analysis activities with young children (Russell, 1991).

A second characteristic that may account for performance on the Jones et al. tasks is *characteristics of the discipline*, in particular the data reduction (Ehrenberg, 1975) that takes place when data are presented in particular displays. Certain graphical representations support the display of individual data values, such as in a line plot. Other displays, such as bar graphs and pie graphs, do not present raw data—they present grouped data. The Jones et al. study contained a bar graph representation, thus the low performance on this task may be accounted for in part by absence of visible data points on the bar graph.

Friel et al. identify another factor that influences graph comprehension: *the purposes for using graphs*. They present the possibility that 'graph instruction within a context of data analysis may promote a high level of graph comprehension that includes flexible, fluid, and generalizable understanding of graphs and their uses' (p. 133). One example of this arose from a study of 8–9 year-old children who identified patterns in data, and data values that did not fit the patterns, thus demonstrating the ability to read between the data (Ainley et al., 2000). The activity involved children constructing paper bridges with different numbers of folds and testing how much weight the bridge could hold by placing weights on the bridge until it collapsed. One pair of students began to deduce a mathematical pattern from the activity and predict the weight that an x-fold bridge could hold. This predicting, or reading beyond the data, was supported by cues inherent in the activity, cues that would not have been available had children not been engaged in the investigation. This ability to read beyond the data has also been evidenced when children work with bivariate data. Three 8–9 year-old children engaged in investigating how wing-length influences length of flying time of a helicopter (Pratt, 1995) recognized a linear pattern in a scatterplot of the data. The investigational context, and use of a computer tool to represent the data, supported children in continuing to test the influence of variables and come to an appreciation of linear trend. These studies provide insight into how pedagogical settings involving data investigations changes our expectations for the types of analyses a third grade student might be expected to carry out on a graph. The authors posit that the sense of regularity regarding a phenomenon that was developed during a data collection activity provided norms that supported children in making assertions about the data presented in graphs.

WHERE SHOULD WE GO FROM HERE?

This review of research examining young children's statistical thinking highlights aspects of statistical reasoning that may be classified as idiosyncratic or transitional thinking (Jones et al., 2000). Children demonstrating idiosyncratic statistical thinking frequently draw from their own experiences when trying to make sense of data and arrive at conclusions that regularly are not supported by the data. These students demonstrate high levels of engagement in the task but are often distracted by irrelevant aspects of the data display. While transitional thinkers attend more closely to aspects of the data, these same students often cannot focus on relationships within the data thus presenting a non-connected view which may result in invalid and incomplete measures. However, the categorization of younger children as idiosyncratic or transitional thinkers should not be considered a permanent and stable assessment of cognitive ability. These categorizations which are based on the SOLO taxonomy (Biggs & Collis, 1991) assist in the evaluation of the quality of a students response on a particular item, and place a focus on the response rather then on the cognitive structure of a particular student. Use then of this framework produces a description of performance at a specific point in time but does not assume that a particular response predicts performance on similar activities nor does it assume that the response represents the maximum potential of the student. Correspondingly, the level of response is not considered an invariable property of the learner rather it is determined by the learners experience with and understanding of the situation (Biggs & Collis, 1991). This focus on the potential of experience with the situation to influence the level of response on a particular task may account for some of the disparities in level of statistical reasoning, i.e., those students who possess greater familiarity of the statistical investigation display more sophisticated statistical reasoning. Other factors are presumed to influence performance on any one task (e.g., motivation, previous educational experiences, etc.) thus supporting the premise that specific instruction strategies can promote learning beyond currently observed levels. This allows a focus on the outcomes of instruction—generating the possibility of supporting younger students' development of statistical reasoning through the use of well-designed contexts which support statistical inquiry and thoughtfully implemented instruction.

REFERENCES

Ainley, J., Pratt, D., & Nardi, E. (2001). Normalising: Children's activity to construct meanings for trend. *Education Studies in Mathematics Special Issue: Constructing meanings from data, 45,* 131–146.

Beaton, A., Mullis, I., Martin, M., Gonzalez, E., Kelly, D., & Smith, T. (1996). *Mathematics achievement in the middle school years: IEA's Third International Mathematics and Science Study (TIMSS).* Chestnut Hill, MA: Boston College, TIMSS International Study Center.

Biggs, J. B., & Collis, K. F. (1991). Multimodal learning and quality of intelligent behavior. In H. A. H. Rowe (Ed.), *Intelligence: Reconceptualization and measurement* (pp. 57–76). Hillsdale, NJ: Erlbaum.

Brown, J. S., Collins, A., & Duguid, P. (1989). *Situated cognition and the culture of learning.* In Yazdani & Lawler (Eds.), *Artificial intelligence and education* (Vol. 2). Norwood, NJ: Ablex.

Burrill, G. (Ed.). (1991). *Guidelines for the Teaching of Statistics.* Alexandria, VA: American Statistical Association.

Carraher, T. N., & Schliemann, A. D. (1985). Computation routines prescribed by schools: Help or hindrance? *Journal for Research on Mathematics Education, 16,* 37–44.

Cobb, P. (1999). Individual and collective mathematical development: The case of statistical data analysis. *Mathematical Thinking and Learning, 1*(1), 5–43.

Cobb, P., Wood, T., Yackel, E., Nicholls, J., Wheatley, G., Trigatti, B., & Perlwitz, M. (1991). Assessment of a problem-centered second-grade mathematics project. *Journal for Research in Mathematics Education, 22,* 3–29.

Cockcroft, W. H. (1982). *Mathematics counts.* London: HMSO.

Curcio, F. (1987). Comprehension of mathematical relationships expressed in graphs. *Journal for Research in Mathematics Education, 18*(5), 382–393.

Curcio, F. R., & Artz, A. F. (1997). Assessing students' statistical problem-solving behaviors in a small-group setting. In I. Gal & J. B. Garfield (Eds.), *The assessment challenge in statistics education* (pp 123–138). Amsterdam: IOS Press.

Curcio, F. R., & Folkson, S. (1996). Exploring data: Kindergarten children do it their way. *Teaching Children Mathematics, 2,* 382–385.

Ehrenberg, A. S. C.(1975). *Data reduction.* New York: Wiley.

Friel, S. N., Curcio, F. R., & Bright, G.W. (2001). Making sense of graphs: Critical factors influencing comprehension and instructional implications. *Journal for Research in Mathematics Education, 32,* 124–158.

Garfield, J., & Ahlgren, A. (1988). Difficulties in learning basic concepts in probability and statistics: Implications for research. *Journal for Research in Mathematics Education, 19*(1), 44–63.

Jones, G. A., Langrall, C. W., Thornton, C. A., Mooney, E. S., Wares, A., Jones, M. R., Perry, B., Putt, I. A., & Nisbet, S. (2001). Using students' statistical thinking to inform instruction. *Journal of Mathematical Behavior, 20,* 109–144.

Jones, G. A., Thornton, C. A., Langrall, C. W., Mooney, E. S., Perry, B., & Putt, I. J. (2000). A framework for characterizing children's statistical thinking. *Mathematical Thinking and Learning, 2,* 269–307.

Joram, E., Resnick, L. B., & Gabriele, A. J. (1995). Numeracy as cultural practice: An examination of numbers in magazines for children, teenagers, and adults. *Journal for Research in Mathematics Education, 26,* 346–361.

Konold, C., & Higgins, T. (2002). Highlights of related research. In S. J. Russell, D. Schifter, & V. Bastable (Eds.), *Developing mathematical ideas: Working with data* (pp. 165–201). Parsippany, NJ: Dale Seymour Publications.

Konold, C., & Higgins, T. (2003). Reasoning about data. In J. Kilpatrick, G. Martin, & D. Schifter (Eds.), *A research companion to NCTM's Standards* (pp. 193–215). Reston, VA: NCTM.

Konold, C., & Pollatsek, A. (2002). Data analysis as the search for signals in noisy processes. *Journal for Research in Mathematics Education, 33,* 259–289.

Lave, J. (1997). The culture of acquisition and the practice of understanding. In D. Kirschner & J. Whitson (Eds.), *Situated cognition: Social, semiotic and psychological perspectives* (pp. 17–35). Mawah, NJ: Lawrence Erlbaum Associates.

Leavy, A. M. (2003). Gifted students' understanding of statistics: Analysis of data arising from a small group teaching experiment. *Gifted and Talented International, 18*(1), 17–26.

Leavy, A. M., & Middleton, J. A. (2001). *Middle grade students understanding of the statistical concept of distribution.* Paper presented at the Annual Meeting of the American Educational Research Association, Seattle, WA.

Lehrer, R., & Schauble, L. (2002). Inventing data structures for representational purposes: Elementary grade students' classification models. *Mathematical Thinking and Learning, 2,* 51–74.

Lindquist, M. M., Carpenter, T. P., Silver, E. A. & Matthews, W. (1983). The third national mathematics assessment: Results and implications for elementary and middle schools. *Arithmetic Teacher, 31,* 14–19.

Mathematical Sciences Advisory Committee, 1984–1985. *Academic preparation in mathematics: Teaching for transition from high school to college.* Cited in: Beres, R. J. (1988). Statistics for college bound students: Are the secondary schools responding? *School Science and Mathematics, 88*(3), 200–209.

Mokros, J., & Russell, S. J. (1995). Children's concept of average and representativeness. *Journal for Research in Mathematics Education, 26*(1), 20–39.

Mosteller, F. (1988). Broadening the scope of statistics and statistical education. *The American Statistician, 42(2),* 93–99.

National Council of Teachers of Mathematics (2000). *Principles and Standards for School Mathematics.* Reston, VA: Author.

National Council of Teachers of Mathematics Commission on Standards for School Mathematics. (1989). *Curriculum and evaluation standards for school mathematics.* Reston, VA: Author.

Posten, H. (1981). Review on statistical materials for 11- 16-year-olds. *The American Statistician, 35*(4), 258–259.

Pratt, D. (1995). Young children's active and passive graphing. *Journal of Computer Assisted Learning* 11, 157–169.

Putt, I. J., Jones, G. A., Thornton, C. A., Langrall, C. W., Mooney, E. S., & Perry, B. (1999). Young students' informal statistical knowledge. *Teaching Statistics, 21*(3), 74–78.

Resnick, L. B. (1983). Toward a cognitive theory of instruction. In S. G. Paris, G. M. Olson, & W. H. Stevenson (Eds.), *Learning and motivation in the classroom* (pp. 5–38). Hillsdale, NJ: Erlbaum.

Roth, W.-M., & McGinn, M. K. (1997). Graphing: A cognitive ability or cultural practice? *Science Education, 81,* 91–106.

Russell, S. J. (1991). Counting noses and Scary things: Children construct their ideas about data. In D. Vere-Jones (Ed.), *Proceedings of the third international conference on teaching statistics* (Vol. 1, pp. 158–164). Voorburg, The Netherlands: International Statistical Institute.

Shaughnessy, J. M. (1992). Research in probability and statistics: Reflections and directions. In D. A. Grouws (Ed.), *Handbook of research on mathematical teaching and learning* (pp. 465–494). New York: Macmillan.

Thompson, W. B. (1999). Making data analysis realistic: Incorporating research into statistics courses. In M. E. Ware & C. L. Brewer (Eds.), *Handbook for teaching statistics and research methods.* Hillsdale, NJ: Erlbaum.

Tukey, J. W. (1977). *Exploratory data analysis.* New York: Addison-Wesley.

Watson, J. M., & Kelly, B. A. (2002). *Can grade 3 students learn about variation?* Proceedings of the Sixth International Conference on Teaching Statistics, Cape Town, South Africa.

Wood, R. (1968). Objectives in teaching of mathematics. *Educational Research, 10,* 83–98.

Zawojewski, J. S., & Heckman, D. J. (1997). What do students know about data analysis, statistics, and probability? In P. A. Kenney & E. A. Silver (Eds.), *Results from the sixth mathematics assessment of the National Assessment of Educational Progress* (pp. 195–223). Reston, VA: National Council of Teachers of Mathematics.

CHAPTER 10

RESEARCH ON SPATIAL SKILLS AND BLOCK BUILDING IN GIRLS AND BOYS

The Relationship to Later Mathematics Learning

Joanne Kersh, Beth M. Casey, and Jessica Mercer Young

Spatial skills are connected to mathematics competency in a variety of areas of early mathematics (Pre-K to Grade 2) including geometry, measurement, and graphing. The National Council of Teachers of Mathematics (NCTM, 1989, 2000) has stressed the critical role of developing "spatial sense" as well as "number sense" from the start of young children's formal mathematics learning. Indeed, the NCTM Standards recommend a shift away from a primary concentration on number sense in the early childhood curriculum, instead recommending equal weight be given to geometry and number sense (see NCTM, 2000). Furthermore, Clements (2004) emphasizes the importance of developing early spatial reasoning skills within the domain of geometry in his overview of the 2000 Conference on Standards for Pre-kindergarten and Kindergarten Mathematics Education. The development of spatial reasoning needs to be nurtured in the early years so that students can effectively apply spatial strategies later when approaching complex mathematical problems.

Contemporary Perspectives on Mathematics in Early Childhood Education, pages 233–251
Copyright © 2008 by Information Age Publishing
All rights of reproduction in any form reserved.

THE RELATIONSHIP BETWEEN SPATIAL SKILLS
AND MATHEMATICS

Spatial skills involve an individual's capacity to mentally compare, manipulate, and transform visual, nonlinguistic information. Mental rotation and spatial visualization are two domains of spatial ability that are of particular importance to mathematics learning (Linn & Petersen, 1985). Mental rotation is defined as the ability to quickly and accurately visualize the appearance of two- and three-dimensional figures when they are rotated in space. Spatial visualization involves the multi-step processing of spatial information, such as the ability to hold a shape in one's mind and then search for the same shape hidden within a more complex figure (e.g., embedded figures), or to combine two shapes to create a new design (e.g., pattern blocks). These spatial skills not only impact specific content areas in mathematics, such as geometry and measurement, but also can be applied to mathematical problem solving across content areas (Battista, 1990). Spatial thinking is contrasted with an alternative mode of information processing that is language-based, drawing on analytical, logical-deductive reasoning (Baddeley, 1986). To illustrate, a spatial approach to solving a math problem might involve drawing a diagram or mentally manipulating shapes, while a verbal, logical-deductive approach might involve working through a step-by-step algorithm or making deductions from propositions or rules.

The connection between spatial skills and mathematics achievement has been most conclusively shown in the later years of schooling when the mathematics content is less focused on numerical learning and problem solving requires a wider range of solution strategies (e.g., Battista, 1990; Casey et al., 1995; Casey, Nuttall, & Pezaris, 1997, 2001; Delgado & Prieto, 2004; see review by Friedman, 1995). Generally, geometry and problem solving are the domains of mathematics in which the spatial/math relationship is most visible. For example, Battista (1990) found that among high school students, scores on a test of mental rotation were significantly correlated with geometry performance, and related to students' choice of geometry problem-solving strategies. Delgado and Prieto (2004) found that, in a sample of 13-year-old students, mental rotation ability added significant unique variance to performance on geometry and word problems, but not to arithmetic performance. Finally, in a sample of sixth grade boys, Hegarty and Kozhenikov (1999) found moderately high correlations between math achievement and scores on two measures of spatial ability, one a measure of spatial visualization and the other, mental rotation.

Although the spatial-math relationship has rarely been investigated in early education, one study did address this question with a large sample of mathematically precocious preschool and kindergarten students (Robinson et al., 1996). The investigators found strong correlations between spatial and math tasks for both boys and girls. Certainly, more research is warranted to document this relationship at the preschool and kindergarten levels, and among more typical samples. Nevertheless, based on the research with older students, an early emphasis on teaching spatial reasoning skills may ultimately help students solve mathematics problems more effectively by applying spatial strategies.

GENDER, SPATIAL SKILLS, AND MATHEMATICS

There is some indication that girls may benefit more from spatial interventions, as researchers have found that the association between spatial skills and mathematics achievement is more robust in females (Battista, 1990; Casey et al., 1995; Friedman, 1995; Halpern, 2000). In a detailed study of this association, Fennema and Tartre (1985; also see Tartre, 1990) examined middle-school boys and girls who had large discrepancies between their verbal and spatial abilities (high verbal/ low spatial or low verbal/ high spatial), and found that spatial skill level was more important in mathematics achievement for females. Females who scored high on the spatial test did as well as or better than the males on math problems. However, the low spatial/high verbal girls were the group who consistently performed most poorly. Additionally, there is evidence that in high school and college students, gender differences in mathematics achievement are mediated in part by gender differences in spatial ability (Casey et al., 1995; Casey et al., 2001). Further, the mediating effects of spatial ability appear to be stronger than the mediating effects of either mathematics anxiety or self-confidence (Casey et al., 1997). Finally, the types of items that show a male advantage on the Quantitative section of the Graduate Records Exams (GRE) include those that can be solved using a spatial strategy (Gallagher et al., 2000). In her meta-analysis, Friedman (1995) concluded that while overall correlations between verbal and math skills were higher than those between spatial and math skills, the relationship between spatial skills and mathematics achievement was strongest in girls, particularly those with higher cognitive abilities.

Gender Differences in Spatial Skills

There is clear evidence of a female disadvantage in different types of spatial tasks across a wide range of ages (e.g., Johnson & Meade, 1987; Levine, Huttenlocher, Taylor, & Langrock, 1999; Linn & Petersen, 1985; McGuinness & Morley, 1991). In adolescents and adults, this male advantage is particularly evident on mental rotation tasks (Linn & Petersen,

1985; Voyer, Voyer, & Bryden, 1995) and has been documented across diverse cultures (Flaherty, 2005).

It was previously thought that gender differences in spatial ability did not emerge until adolescence (e.g., Maccoby & Jacklin, 1974). However, more recently there is evidence of a male advantage in spatial skills at much earlier ages, even at the preschool level (e.g., Cronin, 1967; Fairweather & Butterworth, 1977; Levine et al., 1999; Rosser et al., 1984; Vasilyeva & Bowers, 2006). For example, Johnson and Meade (1987) found a male advantage in overall spatial ability as early as the first grade, when they controlled for reading ability. Rosser and colleagues (Rosser et al., 1984) reported a strong male advantage in a group of 4- and 5-year-olds on a two-dimensional mental rotation task. Finally, Levine and colleagues (1999) found that by age four, gender differences favoring males were evident on spatial transformation tasks that tapped both spatial visualization and two-dimensional mental rotation skills. In contrast, they reported no evidence of a male advantage in verbal skills.

Gender Differences in Mathematics

The male advantage in mathematics has been well documented (e.g., Halpern, 2000; Maccoby & Jacklin, 1974). However, gender differences favoring males are found more often on mathematics achievement tests than in school grades (Hyde, Fennema, & Lamon, 1990). In fact, when mathematics grades are considered rather than test scores, females often outperform males (Dwyer & Johnson, 1997; Kimball, 1989). Nonetheless, Hyde and colleagues (1990), in their meta-analysis, concluded that males, particularly in older and higher achieving samples, do appear to excel in critical areas, especially on mathematical problem-solving tasks. For example, among high-ability students taking the Mathematics Scholastic Aptitude Test (SAT-M), males were more successful at applying intuitive or innovative solutions to solve unconventional items (Gallagher et al., 2000; Gallagher & De Lisi, 1994). Thus, the gender differences favoring males appear most evident when problems require solution strategies that go beyond the application of conventional algorithmic methods. This may place females at a disadvantage in later years, as problem solving ability is essential to career success in the fields of mathematics and science.

Research has failed to find consistent evidence of gender differences when examining overall mathematics performance before age 12 (Hyde et al., 1990). However, patterns of gender differences do occur within different mathematical domains. For example, girls demonstrate superior computation skills during elementary and middle school (Hyde et al., 1990), while recent national and international math assessments show that boys outperform girls on measurement skills (a spatial domain of mathematics) at fourth, eighth, and twelfth grades (Mullis et al., 2000).

In a finer-grained investigation, Carr and Jessup (1997) focused on young children's problem-solving *processes* instead of test scores or grades and discovered gender differences in mathematics as early as first grade. Girls tended to use concrete manipulatives to calculate solutions to basic mathematics problems, while boys used mental representations of numbers and retrieval strategies for solving these problems. A follow-up investigation of these differences showed that first-grade boys could use manipulatives as well as the girls. However, the reverse was not true; the girls could not use retrieval of mathematics facts as well as boys, even when specifically instructed to use that approach (Carr & Davis, 2001).

A longitudinal study of young children in the first- through third-grades found similar differences in strategy use (Fennema et al., 1998). Throughout the three years of the study, girls were more likely to use concrete solution strategies like modeling and counting, while boys tended to apply abstract solution strategies to a range of math problems, reflecting deeper conceptual understanding. By third grade, boys were more successful at solving problems that required them to be more flexible and extend their knowledge of standard algorithms. For both girls and boys, the ability to solve these "extension problems" in the third grade was related to a more creative, flexible approach to problem solving in the earlier grades. These findings of early gender differences in strategy-use are provocative, as they indicate that the gender gap in mathematics may be evident at a much earlier age than is commonly believed. These early differences may mark the beginning of the educational pipeline that leads students either toward or away from eventual careers in mathematics or science. Thus, it is essential to investigate the experiential factors that potentially contribute to these initial differences.

THE RELEVANCE OF BLOCK BUILDING FOR DEVELOPING MATH AND SPATIAL SKILLS

The early childhood classroom provides an important context for the development of spatial and math skills. Anybody who has set foot in a preschool or kindergarten classroom knows that block play, a key spatial activity, is a fundamental aspect of the early learning environment. Certainly, many young children spend a great deal of time playing with blocks and other construction materials, but what do they gain from these experiences? Engaging in block play helps children acquire a diverse range of valuable competencies and knowledge, from social skills (e.g., Rogers, 1985) to the foundations for later math achievement (Wolfgang, Stannard,

& Jones, 2001). Yet, block play often remains on the periphery of the curriculum. Blocks are usually considered only a free-play choice in early childhood classrooms, and rarely do teachers plan activities for the block area or incorporate blocks into their curriculum plans.

It is easy to grasp the intuitive connection between block play and the development of spatial and geometry concepts. When building with blocks, young children are actively engaged in activities that promote spatial awareness, spatial reasoning skills, and beginning geometry concepts. For example, a child who purposefully rotates a block 90 degrees in order to construct the corner of an enclosure has engaged in mental rotation and spatial visualization before any physical manipulation of the block has occurred. During block building, children create mental images of geometric shapes, combine parts to make wholes, predict the effects of transformations on shapes, and recognize and describe the spatial relationships between the blocks (using words like inside, outside, top and bottom).

Block building and spatial skills. What empirical evidence is there to support a connection between early block play experiences and the development of spatial skills? There has long been the suggestion that differences in *early spatial experiences* may contribute to gender differences in spatial skills and mathematics (e.g., Newcombe, 1982; Sherman, 1967). Specifically, it has been hypothesized that the types of play materials and activities that are traditionally considered masculine (e.g., blocks and other manipulative play) may encourage the development of spatial ability. The existing evidence does provide support for such a relationship in young children. Serbin and Connor (1977, 1979) investigated this mechanism in preschoolers. They found a correlational relationship between amount of "masculine play" (which included play with blocks and other construction toys) and performance on the Block Design subtest of the WPPSI (Wechsler, 1967), a test of spatial visualization skills. In a later study, Sprafkin, Serbin, Denier, and Connor (1987) used an experimental design to investigate whether differences in performance on visual-spatial tests might be attributable to differential play experiences. Preschool boys and girls were randomly assigned to an intervention group in which they received explicit instruction and encouragement around the use of constructive play materials (including blocks). Performance on spatial visualization tasks was significantly improved at post-test for children in the training group, while there were no differences in the pre- and post-test scores for children in a control group. This study provides some evidence supporting a causal relationship between play with construction toys and spatial competency.

Other research has examined the relationship between block building *competency* and spatial skills. Caldera and colleagues (1999) conducted perhaps the most in-depth study to date addressing this question with preschool children. Block building skill was measured in two ways: first, in level of complexity of block structures built during an open-ended, unstructured task, and second, in children's accuracy in reproducing a model of a block structure. Spatial ability was measured by a variety of standardized tests that tap spatial visualization, including: the Block Design subtests for the WPPSI (Wechsler, 1967) and the Wechsler Intelligence Scale for Children-Revised (Wechsler, 1974), the Children's Embedded Figures Test (Karp & Konstadt, 1971), and the Copying Blocks subscale of the Stanford-Binet Intelligence Scale (Thorndike, Hagen, and Sattler, 1986). After controlling for age, the complexity of the structures built by the children significantly predicted performance on Block Design and was marginally related to the Embedded Figures test. Furthermore, accuracy of block placement during the structured block-building task predicted children's performance on both Block Design and Copying Blocks tests. Thus, preschoolers' block-building skills appear to be related to their spatial visualization skills, as measured by their ability to analyze and reproduce abstract patterns, to abstract a geometric figure embedded within a more complex picture, and to reproduce constructions made from small cubes.

Furthermore, several studies have demonstrated a relationship between success at block reproduction tasks and mental rotation ability among primary school children. Brosnan (1998) found that the performance of 9-year-olds on a mental rotation task was a strong predictor of their ability to accurately complete a reproduction of a complex Lego model. Jahoda (1979) also found significant correlations between mental rotation and reproduction tasks using small wooden cubes among Scottish youth ranging in age from 7- to 11-years. Collectively, these studies suggest a link between block building activities and the development of spatial competency in boys and girls. Nonetheless, more research is needed to better understand and document the mechanisms involved in this relationship.

Block building and mathematics. There is almost no research on the relationship between early block building skills and mathematics. A recent longitudinal study showed that block-building skills in preschool predicted for mathematics achievement in middle school and high school (Wolfgang et al., 2001). Although the sample size was very small, the researchers collected achievement scores from this intact sample at third, fifth, and seventh grades, and mathematics grades from elementary, middle, and high school. In preschool, children's block play was assessed using a global score that included a measure of complexity (integration of blocks). Block building performance predicted mathematics achievement at the seventh grade and high school levels, but not at the elementary level. The results from this block-building study are consistent with other finding that the spatial/mathematics relationship is strongest for students at the higher grades (e.g., Battista, 1990; Casey et al., 1997; Delgado & Prieto, 2004).

Gender differences in block building. Much of the interest and research on block building has centered on gender differences. Early childhood teachers often report the striking differences between boys and girls in terms of their interest and engagement in block building. This observation by teachers has long been supported by the research literature (Connor & Serbin, 1977; Farrell, 1957; Farwell, 1930; Margolin & Leton, 1961; Saracho, 1994, 1995; Tracy, 1987). While girls appear to prefer non-block play activities when given a choice of activities in their classrooms, boys demonstrate an equal preference for playing with blocks and engaging in nonblock play, (Farwell, 1930; Margolin & Leton, 1961). Boys have also been observed to spend more time in the block area (Farrell, 1957). Efforts to foster gender equity in the block area may be critical, as Hanline, Milton, and Phelps (2001) found that over a three-year period, amount of time spent in the block area was key to developing block-building skills.

Above and beyond the well-documented difference between boys' and girls' *preference* for block play, some work has addressed the qualitative differences in the *types of structures* built by boys and girls when given openended block-building tasks (Erikson, 1951; Goodfader, 1982; Pezaris et al., 1998). In this body of research, students have been rated on the characteristics of the structures they built; specifically, whether they tended to build towers or enclosures. This distinction might have important implications, as boys and girls may be learning very different lessons about their spatial world if they are interacting with blocks in substantially different ways.

In perhaps the most well known study of its kind, Erikson (1951) explored gender differences in the styles of block building exhibited by adolescents (age 11 to 13). Using a combination of blocks and toys as props, 468 adolescent students were individually asked to build "an exciting scene out of an imaginary moving picture." A higher percentage of 12- and 13-year-old boys than girls built towers that were at least twice as high as they were wide and had at least half of the height above the rest of the construction. The girls, on the other hand, were more likely to build enclosed scenes of everyday life, often using only the non-block props, such as furniture, to create inside enclosures. Observing that boys built tall structures, while girls built enclosures, Erikson reasoned from a psychoanalytic perspective that males and females experience and organize space differently based on differences in their genital morphology. Many have since dismissed Erikson's findings because of the difficulty in replicating his work (Budd, Clance, & Simerly, 1985; Karpoe & Onley, 1983; McKay, Pyke, & Goranson, 1984). His methodology has also been critiqued; for example, he included sex-biased props and toys that may have confounded the results (Caplan, 1979). Still, subsequent studies have suggested that boys are more likely to build tall towers than are girls (Goodfader, 1982; Pezaris et al., 1998). Additionally, when toys and furniture are provided, girls are more likely to make non-block indoor configurations (e.g., Cramer & Hogan, 1975).

Goodfader (1982) studied preschoolers and kindergartners to determine whether the same gender differences in style of block building in older children could be found at an earlier age. She provided only blocks, with no props, and asked judges, blind to the gender of the block builder, to rate the "towerness" and "enclosureness" of the blocks from photographs. Her results supported Erikson's findings that boys showed a greater degree of "towerness" in their structures, and girls were more apt to build enclosures.

Several studies have contributed greater insight into why the block constructions of boys and girls seem to differ in structural style. In one study, suburban middle school students were asked simply to build "something interesting" using different types of wooden blocks, with no additional toys or props (Pezaris et al., 1998). Results again replicated Erikson's findings that boys build taller structures than girls. In this study, however, an additional scoring component was developed to assess the structural aspects of block building. Developed in consultation with architects, mathematics educators, and psychologists, this scoring system incorporated a balance rating that reflected the extent to which a large number of blocks were balanced on a small base. A gender difference was also found on this measure; boys were more likely than girls to balance a large number of blocks on a small base. A similar study with high school students (Bassi, 2000) showed the same effect.

In both these studies, differences in the structural element of balance mediated the statistical relationship between gender and height of the constructions. Thus, boys' greater focus on the structural properties of their constructions may be the explanatory factor for why they tend to build higher. It appears that boys create higher, tower-like structures, in part, because they are more likely to incorporate sophisticated structural elements of balance in their block constructions than girls. In other words, boys are more likely than girls to approach block building as an engineering task, balancing a complex edifice upon a risky base. It is not clear whether this difference in preference is based on inherent differences or on differential experiences with blocks, or both, but it does suggest that even if boys and girls are given equal access and exposure to the block area, they may not gain the same spatial knowledge. Thus, teachers may want to design block-building activities that address the structural and spatial elements of block building.

In addition to investigating gender differences in terms of *interest* in block play and *style* of block building, other studies have compared boys and girls in term of the *competency of the block structures* (as measured by the spatial complexity of the structures). These findings are not as clear-cut.

Generally speaking, studies that have found evidence supporting gender differences in block building competence have used *unstructured, open-ended block-building tasks* (Goodfader, 1982; Sluss, 2002). In these tasks, the children were given a large number of blocks, and asked simply to build something nonspecific; their structures were then rated for complexity. Both Goodfader (1982) and Sluss (2002) found a male advantage in the complexity of structures built. Sluss (2002) observed a small sample of same-sex dyads engaged in open-ended block play in a laboratory setting. All children attended private preschools that served middle- and upper-class families. Boys demonstrated greater complexity in their block building techniques, including greater use of symbolism. Goodfader (1982) examined block building in a small group of middle-class children, aged 4- through 6- years old. She also found that boys, in addition to building taller, incorporated more complexity in their structures than girls. However, Caldera and colleagues (1999) failed to find a gender difference in block-building competence among a group of middle-class preschoolers attending university affiliated early childhood programs.

When using *semi-structured tasks* that posed specific block-building problems to the young children, two studies failed to find any gender differences in the complexity of block building. In Reifel's work (e.g., Reifel & Greenfield, 1982), children were read a story (a version of Little Red Riding Hood) and asked, individually, to represent the story with blocks. The children were observed in a university-affiliated laboratory school at ages 4- and 7-years. Complexity was measured in terms of the dimensionality of their structures (e.g., constructed in 1-, 2-, or 3-dimensional space) and the degree of integration between the different components of the structure. No gender differences in complexity were observed at either age (Reifel & Greenfield, 1982).

Casey, Erkut, and Andrews (2005) presented a different semi-structured task in their research with low-income urban kindergarteners. Children were asked to build a school out of blocks and instructed to provide a roof to keep the students inside dry when it rains. The children were rated using a developmental rating scale, based in part on the earlier work of Reifel and Greenfield (1982). The rating scale consisted of a composite of the highest dimensional level incorporated into the structure, presence versus absence of internal space (vertical or horizontal enclosure), and presence versus absence of a roof covering the internal space. This study also failed to find any gender differences.

A recent longitudinal study provides some insight into a possible explanation for discrepancies in findings. Hanline and colleagues (2001) conducted an analysis of developmental changes in block building among a group of preschoolers (both with and without disabilities) over three years in a community-based program. The amount of time spent in the block area was carefully controlled so that, over the three-year period, boys and girls had equal time to play with blocks. Each week, the children were given 10 minutes of block-building and geometry instruction, followed by an opportunity to play with blocks for 80 minutes. The 65 children were observed a total of 421 times. No gender differences in block-building complexity were observed, and the amount of involvement in block building over time was associated with the level of complexity of the block structures for both girls and boys. These findings suggest the possibility that gender differences can be reduced or eliminated when girls and boys are given equitable quality time in the block area. The inconsistencies in results for studies examining gender differences may have occurred in part due to wide variations in the amount of time boys vs. girls spent in the block area across the preschool and kindergarten classrooms that were included in these different studies. This hypothesis remains to be tested.

To summarize, research has been inconsistent regarding gender differences in block building. Thus, it is essential to consider other possibly confounding variables. For example, age and socioeconomic status (SES) of the children in the study may be related to the amount (or lack of) experience that children have had with blocks. Although middle-class children enrolled in private preschools and community centers did show a male advantage (Goodfader, 1982; Sluss, 2002), no similar gender differences were found in a three-year longitudinal early childhood study that was carefully designed to expose boys and girls equally to block building activities (Hanline et al., 2001). Furthermore, no gender differences were found in a study conducted within a university-based childcare program (Caldera et al., 1999). Perhaps university-based programs are more likely to make a concerted effort to include girls in the block area. Moreover, research conducted with lower SES children did not reveal gender differences (Casey et al., 2005). Perhaps this is due, in part, to the limited experiences with blocks for both boys and girls in lower SES environments. Because prior block-building experience and regular classroom exposure to block play were not variables in the cross-sectional studies discussed above, it is possible that these factors might explain the discrepancies regarding gender differences in the complexity of block play. These results, taken collectively, suggest that equal access to block-building experiences may be important in order to equalize girls' and boys' block-building skills, but this hypothesis needs to be tested more fully.

Methodological considerations may also contribute to discrepant findings, as the types of tasks and assessment techniques used in various studies may tap quite different skill sets. For example, gender differences are more evident in open-ended, unstructured block-building tasks, than in semi-structured tasks that pose more specific problem-solving challenges (Casey et al., 2005; Reifel & Greenfield, 1982). Furthermore, when *structural style characteristics* are assessed, boys have generally been shown to build taller during unstructured block-building activities. Gender differences in this domain have been observed as early as preschool (Goodfader, 1982), and appear to extend into adolescence (Bassi, 2000; Erikson, 1951; Pezaris et al., 1998). Thus, while young boys and girls do not consistently differ in the *complexity* of their block structures, they may well be acquiring different types of knowledge about the *structural properties* of blocks through divergent building styles. Furthermore, anecdotal evidence from preschool and kindergarten teachers, as well as from research findings (e.g., Erikson, 1951), suggest that young girls may spend a lot of time in the block area using the blocks as props in their dramatic play. If this is true, it may be useful to consider designing more formal block building interventions in order to provide both boys and girls with the opportunity to explore the structural properties of blocks.

FUTURE DIRECTIONS IN RESEARCH AND PRACTICE RELATING TO BLOCK BUILDING

Research recommendations. First of all, in order to make further progress in understanding block-building skills, consistent operationalizing of terms (e.g., "complexity") and methods of assessment are necessary. Otherwise, research in this area will continue to be scattered rather than systematic. Further exploration of the relationship between block building and spatial and mathematical skills is also needed. Block building will not be taken seriously as a valid and important component of early mathematics education until the efficacy of block building as a foundation for later cognitive and academic development has been more fully documented. There is some initial evidence that engaging in block building may provide a foundation for later math achievement (Wolfgang et al., 2001), though much more research is needed to substantiate this relationship. One of the challenges that accompany this goal is that it involves extended longitudinal research, following students from preschool into middle and high school, and possibly beyond. This may be expedited by the extensive collection of achievement data over time due to the 'No Child Left Behind' legislation. Until such longitudinal research is undertaken, the educational benefits of block building are most clearly demonstrated through their association with the improvement of spatial skills. These findings alone suggest that a more systematic integration of block building into the early childhood curriculum may have advantageous repercussions for all students over time, but especially for girls.

Finally, more intervention-based research is essential to inform the design of block-building programs to facilitate spatial and mathematical thinking. For, even if early childhood teachers acknowledge that block-building skills are an important link to the development of mathematics ability, many may not know how to "teach" in the block area or how to nurture spatial awareness and mathematics competency through block building activities. Thus, it behooves researchers and curriculum developers in the field to disseminate information and materials to teachers.

Classroom applications. We conclude by making some recommendations on how block-building skills can be developed systematically in preschool and kindergarten classrooms. A recent evaluation study found that block-building skills improved more when small groups of kindergartners experienced systematic interventions over a number of block-building sessions (Casey et al., 2005). The intervention conditions were based on the block-building activities in a book entitled, *Sneeze Builds a Castle* (Casey, Paugh, & Ballard, 2002). The performance of the children in the interventions was compared to performance in the control condition in which the students received the equivalent amount of block-building experiences during unstructured free-play sessions. In the interventions, the block-building activities were structured around specific problems that were designed to encourage spatial/mathematical thinking, and were sequenced over extended lessons, building on the spatial content in the prior construction activities, and providing the knowledge necessary for subsequent activities. The first problem involved the construction of an enclosure with walls that were at least two blocks high and required the building of a simple arch, thereby introducing the concept of bridging. Bridging skills require that children apply not only the concept of balance, but also measurement and estimation skills, as they figure out how far apart the uprights must be to support the horizontal. The children were then asked to build more complex bridges, extending further the concepts of balance, measurement, and estimation. For example, they were challenged to construct a complex bridge with multiple arches. The children also had to design their bridge to include ramps or stairs at either end. Building stairs requires children to apply advanced spatial planning and problem solving skills and nurtures development of the understanding of seriation. Next, they were challenged to construct a complex tower of at least two levels (floors). To aid them in this task, they were given cardboard ceilings to place between the levels. The children had to figure out how to make the walls fit within the confines of the length and width of the cardboard ceiling, thereby reinforcing skills required for estimating area. Thus, the block-building activities described above were designed to enable children to systematically develop the types of spatial skills that are related to math achievement.

Children's maturational age and their experiences are both important in the development of block building competency (Hanline et al., 2001). In free play, young children are often observed to build the same structure repeatedly (Johnson, 1984). Practice and repetition help them achieve mastery of the materials by strengthening neural pathways and achieving automaticity, which increase their learning potential (Wellhousen & Kieff, 2001). Observation of other more experienced block builders also appears to be a critical component of young children's block building development. In a longitudinal investigation conducted in partnership with the Froebel Blockplay Research Group, Gura (1992) noted that 3-year-olds entering a classroom of more experienced block builders (4- and 5-year-olds) evidenced more rapid development than the 3-year-olds in their "pioneer group," who had no reference group of more experienced peers. Furthermore, Gregory, Kim, & Whiren (2003) found that preschool-aged children showed significant increases in the complexity of their block building when adults provided them with verbal scaffolding. These findings suggest that children may benefit from more considered, systematic teaching practices focused on block building activities. Clearly, children acquire skill in block building through a combination of individual and shared experiences that serve to create and reinforce cognitive structures.

As such, we strongly recommend that caregivers and teachers nurture the development of block-building skills by providing children with lots of opportunity to explore the structural properties of blocks, by posing semi-structured problem-solving tasks, and by providing supportive scaffolding to young children in their block play. Block building provides a rich context for spatial and mathematical thinking. The inherent geometric properties of blocks encourage the development of the understanding of space and the physical properties of objects. This, in turn, leads to foundational math concepts. When playing with blocks, most children spontaneously engage in activities such as sorting, classifying, and seriating based on the blocks' geometric properties. When young children stack blocks of the same shape and size to make towers, they not only sort and classify, they apply their emerging understanding of concepts such as congruence and equivalence. They use concepts integral to measurement and estimation as they determine which block is needed to complete a tower or decide whose tower is taller and by how much. As they become more proficient, children become acquainted with geometric principals, such as the concepts of two- and three-dimensional space (area and volume) and demonstrate increasing understanding of part-whole relationships. Finally, as children build progressively more complex and elaborate structures, they may incorporate elements of symmetry and patterning. Additionally, the representational quality of blocks provides an ideal platform for developing problem solving skills (e.g., challenging students to build a school). Blocks are a natural medium for integrating mathematics into the early childhood classroom. We propose that a more systematic, planned approach to this critical component of the early childhood classroom is essential to the future of early childhood math education. Additionally, encouraging young girls to spend more time on the structural aspects of block building may be particularly helpful in reducing the gender gap in math and science achievement by promoting and nurturing the development of spatial skills and mathematical competency.

REFERENCES

Baddeley, A. D. (1988). Imagery and working memory. In M. Denis, J. Engelkamp, & J. T. E. Richardson (Eds.), *Cognitive and neuropsychological approaches to mental imagery. NATO ASI series: Series D. Behavioral and social sciences, No. 42* (pp. 169–180). Dordrecht, Netherlands: Martinus Nijhoff Publishing.

Bassi, J. (2000). *Block play: Exposing gender differences and predicting for math achievement.* Unpublished Doctoral Dissertation, Northeastern University, Boston, MA.

Battista, M. T. (1990). Spatial visualization and gender differences in high school geometry. *Journal of Research in Mathematics Education, 21,* 47–60.

Brosnan, M. J. (1998). Spatial ability in children's play with Lego blocks. *Perceptual and Motor Skills, 87,* 19–28.

Budd, B. E., Clance, P. R., & Simerly, D.E. (1985). Spatial configurations: Erikson reexamined. *Gender Roles, 12,* 571–577.

Caldera, Y. M., Culp, A. M., O'Brien, M., Truglio, R. T., Alvarez, M., & Huston, A. C. (1999). Children's play preferences, construction play with blocks, and visual-spatial skills: Are they related? *International Journal of Behavioral Development, 23,* 855–872.

Caplan, P. J. (1979). Erikson's concept of inner space: A data-based reevaluation. *American Journal of Orthopsychiatry, 49,* 100–108.

Carr, M., & Davis, H. (2001). Gender differences in arithmetic strategy use: A function of skill and preference. *Contemporary Educational Psychology, 26,* 330–347.

Carr, M., & Jessup, D. L. (1997). Gender differences in first-grade mathematics strategy use: Social and metacognitive influences. *Journal of Educational Psychology, 89,* 318–328.

Casey, B., Erkut, S., & Andrews, N. (2005). *Early spatial interventions are particularly beneficial for girls.* Paper presented at the Society for Research in Child Development meetings in Atlanta.

Casey, M. B., Nuttall, R., Pezaris, E., & Benbow, C. P. (1995). The influence of spatial ability on gender differences in mathematics college entrance test scores across diverse samples. *Developmental Psychology, 31,* 697–705.

Casey, M. B., Nuttall, R. L., & Pezaris, E. (1997). Mediators of gender differences in mathematics college entrance test scores: A comparison of spatial skills with internalized beliefs and anxieties. *Developmental Psychology, 33,* 669–680.

Casey, M. B., Nuttall, R. L., & Pezaris, E. (2001). Spatial-mechanical reasoning skills versus mathematics self-confidence as mediators of gender differences on mathematics subtests using cross-national gender-based items. *Journal for Research in Mathematics Education, 32,* 28–57.

Casey, B., Paugh, P., & Ballard, N. (2002). *Sneeze builds a castle.* Chicago: The Wright Group/McGraw-Hill.

Clement, D. H. (2004). Major themes and recommendations. In D. H. Clements & J. Sarama (Eds.), *Engaging young children in mathematics: Standards for early childhood mathematics education* (pp 7–72). Mahwah, NJ: Lawrence Erlbaum Associates.

Connor, J. M. & Serbin, L. A. (1977). Behaviorally based masculine- and feminine-activity-preference scales for preschoolers: Correlates with other classroom behaviors and cognitive tests. *Child Development, 48,* 1411–1416.

Cramer, P., & Hogan, K. A. (1975). Gender differences in verbal and play fantasy. *Developmental Psychology, 11,* 145–154.

Cronin, V. (1967). Mirror-image reversal discrimination in kindergarten and first grade children. *Journal of Experimental Child Psychology, 5,* 577–585.

Delgado, A. R., & Prieto, G. (2004). Cognitive mediators and sex-related differences in mathematics. *Intelligence, 32,* 25–32.

Dwyer, C. A., & Johnson, L. M. (1997). Grades, accomplishments, and correlates. In W. W. Willingham & N. S. Cole (Eds.), *Gender and fair assessment* (pp. 127–156). Mahwah, NJ: Erlbaum.

Erikson, E. H. (1951). Gender differences in the play configurations of preadolescents. *American Journal of Orthopsychiatry, 21,* 667–692.

Farrell, M. (1957). Gender differences in block play in early childhood education. *Journal of Educational Research, 51,* 279–284.

Farwell, L. (1930). Reactions of kindergarten, first- and second-grade children to constructive play materials. *Genetic Psychology Monographs, 8,* 431–562.

Fairweather, H., & Butterworth, G. (1977). The WPPSI at four years: A sex difference in verbal-performance discrepancies. *British Journal of Educational Psychology, 47,* 85–90.

Fennema, E., Carpenter, T. P., Jacobs, V. R., Franke, M. L., & Levi, L. W. (1998). A longitudinal study of gender differences in young children's mathematical thinking. *Educational Researcher, 27,* 6–11.

Fenema, E., & Tartre, L. A. (1985). The use of spatial visualization in mathematics by girls and boys. *Journal of Research in Mathematics Education, 16,* 184–206.

Flaherty, M. (2005). Gender differences in mental rotation ability in three cultures: Ireland, Ecuador, and Japan. *Psychologia, 48,* 31–38.

Friedman, L. (1995). The space factor in mathematics: Gender differences. *Review of Educational Research, 65,* 22–50.

Gallagher, A. M., De Lisi, R. (1994).Gender differences in Scholastic Aptitude Test—Mathematics problem solving among high ability students. *Journal of Educational Psychology, 86,* 204–211.

Gallagher, A. M., De Lisi, R., Holst, P. C., McGillicuddy-De Lisi, A., Morely, M., & Cahalan, C. (2000). Gender differences in advanced mathematical problem solving. *Journal of Experimental Child Psychology, 75,* 165–190.

Goodfader, R. A. (1982). Gender differences in the play constructions of preschool children. *Smith College Studies in Social Work, 52,* 129–144.

Gregory, K. M., Kim, A. S., & Whiren, A. (2003). The effect of verbal scaffolding on the complexity of preschool children's block constructions. In D. E. Lytle

(Ed.), *Play and educational theory and practice: Play and culture studies, Vol. 5.* West-port, CT: Praeger.

Gura, P. (1992). Developmental aspects of blockplay. In P. Gura (Ed.), *Exploring learning: Young children and block play* (pp. 48–74). London: Paul Chapman Publishing Ltd.

Halpern, D. F. (2000). *Sex differences in cognitive abilities* (3rd ed.). Mahwah, NJ: Erlbaum.

Hanline, M. F., Milton, S. & Phelps, P. (2001). Young children's block construction activities: findings from 3 years of observation. *Journal of Early Intervention, 24,* 224–237.

Hegarty, M., & Kozhevnikov, M. (1999). Types of visual-spatial representations and mathematical problem-solving. *Journal of Educational Psychology, 91,* 684–689.

Hyde, J. S., Fennema, E., & Lamon, S. J. (1990). Gender differences in mathematics performance: A meta-analysis. *Psychological Bulletin, 107,* 139–155.

Jahoda, G. (1979). On the nature of difficulties in spatial-perceptual tasks: Ethnic and gender differences. *British Journal of Psychology, 70,* 351–363.

Johnson, E. S. & Meade, A.C. (1987). Developmental patterns of spatial ability: An early gender differences. *Child Development, 58,* 725–740.

Johnson, H. (1984). The art of block building. In E. S. Hirsch (Ed.), *The block book* (pp. 8–23). Washington, DC: National Association for the Education of Young Children.

Karp, S. A., & Konstadt, N. (1971). *Children's embedded figures test.* Palo Alto, CA: Consulting Psychologists Press.

Karpoe, K. P. & Onley, R. L. (1983). The effect of boys' or girls' toys on gender-typed play in preadolescents. *Gender Roles, 9,* 507–518.

Kimball, M. M. (1989). A new perspective on women's math achievement. *Psychological Bulletin, 105,* 198–214.

Levine, S. C., Huttenlocher, J., Taylor, A., & Langrock, A. (1999). Early gender differences in spatial skills. *Developmental Psychology, 35,* 940–949.

Linn, M. C., & Petersen, A. C. (1985). Emergence and characterization of gender differences in spatial ability: A meta-analysis. *Child Development, 56,* 1479–1498.

Maccoby, E. E., & Jacklin, C. N. (1974). *The psychology of sex differences.* Stanford, CA: Stanford University Press.

Margolin, E. G. & Leton, D. (1961). Interest of kindergarten pupils in block play. *Journal of Educational Research, 55,* 13–18.

McGuinness, D., & Morley, C. (1991). Gender differences in the development of visual-spatial ability in pre-school children. *Journal of Mental Imagery, 15,* 143–150.

McKay, J., Pyke, S. W. , & Goranson, R. (1984). Whatever happened to inner space? A failure to replicate. *International Journal of Women's Studies , 7,* 387–396.

Mullis, I. V., Martin, M. O., Fierros, E. G., Goldberg, A. L., & Stemler, S. E. (2000). *Gender differences in achievement: IEA's Third International Mathematics and Science Study.* Chestnut Hill, MA: TIMSS International Study Center, Boston College.

National Council of Teachers of Mathematics. (1989). *Curriculum and evaluation for school mathematics.* Reston, VA: Author.

National Council of Teachers of Mathematics. (2000). *Principles and standards for school mathematics.* Reston, VA: Author.

Newcombe, N. (1982). Gender-related differences in spatial ability: Problems and gaps in current approaches. In M. Poegal (Ed.), *Spatial abilities*. New York: Academic Press.

Pezaris, E., Casey, M. B., Nuttall, R. L., Bassi, J., Trynski, M. Averna, S. et al. (1998, June). *Style of block building in boys and girls and its relationship to their spatial and mathematical skills*. Presentation to the International Neuropsychology Society Meetings, Budapest, Hungary.

Reifel, S., & Greenfield, P. M. (1982). Structural development in a symbolic medium: The representational use of block constructions. In G. Forman (Ed.), *Action and thought: From sensorimotor schemes to symbolic operations* (pp. 203–233). New York: Academic Press.

Robinson, N. M., Abbott, R. D., Berninger, V. W., & Busse, J. (1996). The structure of abilities in math-precocious young children: Gender similarities and differences. *Journal of Educational Psychology, 88*, 341–352.

Rogers, D. L. (1985). Relationships between block play and the social development of young children. *Early Child Development and Care, 20*, 245–261.

Rosser, R. A., Ensing, S. S., Gilder, P. J., & Lane, S. (1984). An information-processing analysis of children's accuracy in predicting the appearance of rotated stimuli. *Child Development, 55*, 2204–2211.

Saracho, O. N. (1994). The relationship of preschool children's cognitive style to their play preferences. *Early Child Development and Care, 97*, 21–33.

Saracho, O. N. (1995). Preschooler's cognitive style and their selection of academic areas in their play. *Early Child Development and Care, 97*, 21–33.

Serbin, L. A., & Connor, J. M. (1977). Behaviorally based masculine and feminine activity preference scales for preschoolers: Correlates with other classroom behaviors and cognitive tests. *Child Development, 48*,1411–1416.

Serbin, L. A., & Connor, J. M. (1979). Gender-typing children's play preferences and patterns of cognitive performance. *The Journal of Genetic Psychology, 134*, 315–316.

Sherman, J. A. (1967). Problem of gender differences in space perception and aspects of intellectual functioning. *Psychological Review, 74*, 290–299.

Sluss, D. J. (2002). Block play complexity in same-gender dyads of preschool children. In J. L. Roopnarine (Ed.), *Play and culture studies: Vol. 4. Conceptual, social-cognitive, and contextual issues in the fields of play* (pp. 77–91). Westport, CT: Ablex.

Sprafkin, C., Serbin, L. A., Denier, C. & Connor, J. M. (1983). Gender-differentiated play: Cognitive consequences and early interventions. In M. B. Liss (Ed.), *Social and cognitive skills: Gender roles and children's play* (pp. 167–192). New York: Academic Press.

Tartre, L. A. (1990). Spacial orientation skill and mathematical problem solving. *Journal for Research in Mathematics Education, 21*, 216–229.

Thorndike, R., Hagen, E., Sattler, J., (1986). *Stanford-Binet Intelligence Scale, fourth edition*. Chicago: Riverside.

Tracy, D. M. (1987). Toys, spatial ability, and science and mathematics achievement: Are they related? *Sex Roles, 17*, 115–138.

Vasilyeva, M., & Bowers, E. (in press). Children's use of geometric information in mapping tasks. *Journal of Experimental Child Psychology*.

Voyer, D., Voyer, S., & Bryden, M. P. (1995). Magnitude of sex differences in spatial abilities: A meta-analysis and consideration of critical variables. *Psychological Bulletin, 117*, 250–270.

Wechsler, D. (1967). *Wechsler Preschool and Primary Scale of Intelligence (WPPSI)*. New York: Psychological Corporation/Harcourt, Brace, Jovanovich.

Wechsler, D. (1974). *Wechsler Intelligence Scale for Children-Revised (WISC-R)*. New York: Psychological Corporation/Harcourt, Brace, Jovanovich.

Wellhousen, K., & Kieff, J. (2001). *A constructivist approach to block play in early childhood*. Canada: Delmar/Thomson Learning.

Wolfgang, C. H., Stannard, L. L., & Jones, I. (2001). Block play performance among preschoolers as a predictor of later school achievement in mathematics. *Journal of Research in Childhood Education, 15*, 173–180.

CHAPTER 11

SOCIOCULTURAL INFLUENCES ON YOUNG CHILDREN'S MATHEMATICAL KNOWLEDGE

Prentice Starkey and Alice Klein

All members of society need a broad range of basic mathematical knowledge to make informed decisions in their work, households, and communities (Glenn Commission, 2000). Careers, in particular, require an increasing level of proficiency (U.S. Department of Labor, Bureau of Labor Statistics, 2000). A series of assessments of mathematics achievement by American students has revealed an overall level of proficiency well below what is desired and needed (Kilpatrick, Swafford, & Findell, 2001; Mullis et al., 1997; Mullis et al., 2000). Several research studies have found that mathematics achievement by American students compares unfavorably with achievement by students from several other nations at the middle- and high-school levels (LaPointe, Mead, & Phillips, 1989; McKnight et al, 1987; Peak, 1996; Takahira et al., 1998). Moreover, cross-cultural differences in mathematics achievement have been found in the elementary school grades (Frase, 1997; Stevenson, Chen, & Lee, 1993; Stevenson, Lee, & Stigler, 1986), including kindergarten (Stevenson, 1987). Within the United States, students from low-income families or who are members of linguistic or ethnic minority groups are especially at risk for underachievement in mathematics (National Research Council, 1989). This pattern of under-

Contemporary Perspectives on Mathematics in Early Childhood Education, pages 253–276
Copyright © 2008 by Information Age Publishing

253

achievement is evident not just in middle and high school (e.g., Dorsey et al., 1988), but also in the earliest grades of elementary school (Bowman, Donovan, & Burns, 2001; Denton & West, 2002; Entwisle & Alexander, 1990; Natriello, McDill, & Pallas, 1990).

Children's early achievement in mathematics is now known to be far more important than was previously thought. Mathematics achievement trajectories of children are already established early in elementary school and tend to persist in later grades (Entwisle & Alexander, 1989). Consequently, children who are academically behind their peers in mathematics early in elementary school tend to fall further behind over time. A recent meta-analysis linking children's mathematical knowledge, literacy skills, and socioemotional development at school entry with later school achievement found that mathematical knowledge was the strongest predictor of later achievement in general (Duncan et al., 2004). Thus, there is now ample evidence that close attention should be paid to children's early learning and development of mathematics.

We will first examine early theories of mathematical learning and development that claimed that mathematical knowledge first develops during the elementary school years. We will then review research showing that these theories were fundamentally incorrect. Mathematical competence is present from an early point in life and undergoes rapid development during early childhood. More recent theories of mathematical learning and development have acknowledged that a form of mathematical knowledge is present during early childhood, but claim that this knowledge develops naturally with little intervention by society and has little influence on mathematics achievement that occurs during the elementary school years or beyond. In this chapter, we argue that recent theories of mathematical learning and development (1) have underestimated the importance of the informal mathematical knowledge that develops during early childhood, and (2) are incorrect in assuming that this early form of mathematical knowledge will naturally and fully develop without deliberate support. To the contrary, some cross-cultural and within-cultural differences in mathematics achievement stem from the foundation of informal mathematical knowledge children develop during early childhood. Early childhood education programs in some other countries have taken a systematic approach to supporting early mathematical development. We will argue that preschool programs in the United States should likewise take a more deliberate approach to helping children, especially economically disadvantaged children, develop a good foundation of informal mathematical knowledge.

EARLY THEORIES OF MATHEMATICAL LEARNING
AND DEVELOPMENT

For many years, theories of learning and cognitive development asserted that young children are devoid of mathematical knowledge before entry into elementary school. Learning theorists (e.g., Bereiter & Engleman, 1966; Clapp, 1924; Knight & Behrens, 1928) believed that mathematical knowledge begins when children are exposed to the abstract notation of written arithmetic such as the written numerals (1, 2, 3, etc.) and arithmetic symbols (+, −, =, etc.). Since formal arithmetic instruction usually commences in elementary school, young children were thought to enter school as mathematical blank slates.

Likewise, Piaget's theory of cognitive development held that mathematical knowledge is not present until children enter the period of concrete operations at around age 6–7 years (Piaget, 1952). During the preschool years pre-operational children were said to be developing knowledge of classes and relations that will be used as cognitive building blocks for the construction of children's first numerical structures at the onset of the period of concrete operations. Piaget believed that mathematical learning followed, rather than preceded, the onset of the period of concrete operations. In the absence of mathematical knowledge, mathematics instruction during the preschool years would be contrary to Piagetian principles.

These early learning and Piagetian theories had the effect of diverting basic research away from a search for the origins of mathematical knowledge in early childhood. This began to change when researchers became dissatisfied with Piaget's negative characterization of young children as "pre-operational." Researchers wanted a better understanding of the cognitive abilities that were present in the preoperational period, and they began designing tasks to study this knowledge. A feature of Piaget's research method proved to be especially useful in designing tasks used to investigate children's knowledge of mathematical features of their world. Piaget had disagreed with learning theorists about the primacy of formal arithmetic notation in children's mathematical development. He believed instead that children's earliest mathematical knowledge was concerned with physical objects, which can be added, subtracted, or put into one-one correspondence with other objects. The insight that mathematical knowledge is first seen in children's activities with concrete objects instead of in their use of written mathematical symbols was a major advance in understanding how mathematical knowledge originates and develops early in life.

Researchers began to use tasks involving concrete objects in order to study the development of children's informal mathematical knowledge— knowledge that depends upon the presence or mental representation of sets of concrete objects. Researchers designed new tasks that could be administered to young children. As they studied younger and younger children, and eventually toddlers and even infants, they continued finding mathematical competence, albeit less extensive and less abstract knowledge than that of older children. This research, conducted by a generation of researchers over the past 25 years, has revealed that mathematical knowledge begins during infancy (Geary, 2006; Haith & Benson, 1998) and undergoes extensive development over the first five years of life (see Ginsburg, Klein, & Starkey, 1998, and Bisanz, et al., 2005 for reviews). This knowledge includes enumerative abilities such as subitizing (Starkey & Cooper, 1995) and counting (Cordes & Gelman, 2005), arithmetic problem solving (Bisanz et al., 2005), spatial reasoning and geometric knowledge (Newcombe & Huttenlocher, 2000, 2006), and pre-algebraic pattern knowledge (Klein & Starkey, 2004a). This knowledge undergoes considerable development during the preschool years and provides a necessary foundation for the acquisition of formal mathematical knowledge in elementary school (Geary, 1994; Ginsburg, 1989). In sum, this highly successful program of research has changed the view of young children as premathematical. It is now believed that it is just as natural for children to acquire and use knowledge of mathematics as it is for them to acquire and use language.

SOCIOCULTURAL INFLUENCES ON EARLY MATHEMATICAL DEVELOPMENT

Contemporary learning theorists now recognize that some mathematical knowledge is present before entry into elementary school (Stevenson, 1987). They have continued to argue, however, that attention should be focused on mathematics learning during the elementary school years. The theoretical position taken is that differences in mathematics achievement stem solely from classroom and home practices during the elementary school years (Stevenson & Stigler, 1992). Likewise, contemporary Piagetian theorists have acknowledged that young children possess informal mathematical knowledge (Ginsburg & Russell, 1981). However, they too have continued to argue that attention should be focused on the elementary school years (e.g., Kamii, 1985). The theoretical position taken is that young children from different sociocultural contexts develop few, if any, differences in informal mathematical knowledge, and that early achievement differences are the result of classroom practices during the elementary school years instead of any experiential deprivation during early childhood (Ginsburg & Allardice, 1984).

A continuing theoretical focus on the elementary school years has diverted attention from the study of differences in mathematical knowledge in early childhood and the potential causes of these differences. The argument that differences in mathematics achievement are solely attributable to practices during the elementary school years removed a potential rationale for investigating sociocultural differences in children's early mathematical knowledge and their home and preschool learning environments. Piagetian researchers focused instead on the age at which specific mathematical abilities first appeared and on broad patterns of mathematical development. Piagetian cross-cultural research (Dasen, 1977) was concerned with universal sequences of development. Researchers found that both schooled and unschooled children appeared to develop the same number concepts in the same sequence (Davis & Ginsburg, 1993; Ginsburg, Posner, & Russell, 1981). Some findings suggested that the rate of development of universal types of mathematical abilities varied among cultures (Price-Williams, Gordon, & Ramirez, 1969), but rate of development was a peripheral topic in Piaget's theory. This theory also ignored the learning environments of young children. Although Piagetian theory acknowledged the importance of both biological and environmental factors in cognitive development, it assumed that all children are exposed to the necessary and sufficient environmental inputs that play a role in the development of mathematical cognition. This lack of attention to child-environment interactions that play a role in mathematical development was an underdeveloped aspect of Piaget's theory.

In contrast, Vygotsky's theory (e.g., Vygotsky, 1978) and work in this tradition raised questions about the influence of cultural variables such as economic specialization, schooling, and number-word systems on mathematical knowledge (Lave, 1988; Scribner, 1986). Originally this line of research focused on mathematical thinking used by adults to solve problems that arise in a customary activity such as their work (see Schliemann, Carraher, & Ceci, 1997 for a review). Subsequent research has focused on the mathematical thinking used by children to solve problems, the intellectual tools children acquire from their culture, and other supports parents and teachers provide that help children develop mathematical knowledge (Carraher, Carraher, & Schliemann, 1985; Radziszewska & Rogoff, 1991). Since Vygotsky's theory made learning and child-environment interactions central topics in the study of cognitive development, it brought a focus on sociocultural influences to studies of early mathematical development.

Over the past decade or so, research on sociocultural influences on early mathematical development has rapidly expanded. Theories have been developed to try to explain how mathematical knowledge originates and develops in children, and researchers have begun to investigate children's early mathematical development and learning environments within and across cultures. Here we focus on three sets of issues.

Issue 1.   Do young children from different cultural or socioeconomic groups differ in the extent of their informal mathematical knowledge, and if so, at what age do knowledge gaps emerge, how wide are the gaps, and do they change over time?

Issue 2.   What is known about the causes for cultural and SES-related differences in early mathematical knowledge? Are early cross-cultural differences in mathematical thinking caused primarily by differences in number word systems, or by a more complex set of factors such as the amount or effectiveness of support for early mathematical development provided in children's home and preschool learning environments?

Issue 3.   If young children from different cultural or socioeconomic groups differ in the extent of their informal mathematical knowledge, do preschool curricula have the potential to close this gap and help all young children enter school ready to learn school mathematics? Can curricula be used effectively to enrich both the home and preschool classroom learning environments of economically disadvantaged children?

CROSS-CULTURAL DIFFERENCES IN INFORMAL MATHEMATICAL DEVELOPMENT

A small body of research has addressed questions of whether cross-cultural differences in informal mathematical knowledge emerge during early childhood. A few cross-cultural studies have compared aspects of children's mathematical knowledge prior to entry into elementary school (e.g., Geary et al., 1993; Ginsburg et al., 1997; Miller et al., 1995). Most studies compared East Asian (Chinese, Japanese, or Korean) and American children on an individual numerical ability or a small set of numerical abilities, such as children's counting or strategies used in solving concrete addition problems. The findings indicate that at least some informal numerical abilities are more developed in 4- to 5-year-old East Asian children than in American children.

Starkey et al. (1999) used the Child Math Assessment (CMA)(Klein & Starkey, 1999) to compare Chinese and American 4-year-olds on a broader set of mathematical concepts and skills. It was found that numerical and spatial/geometric knowledge was significantly more extensive in Chinese preschoolers than in American children of the same age (Table 11.1).

This research was recently expanded to include Chinese, Japanese, and American children and to track children's mathematical development longitudinally (Starkey & Klein, 2006). These longitudinal studies were conducted (1) to compare the development of informal mathematical cognition in 3- to 6-year-old children attending preschool in China, Japan, and the United States, and (2) to investigate how these cultures support

TABLE 11.1
Mean Proportion Correct on Child Math
Assessment by American and Chinese 4-Year-Olds

Problem type	Nationality	
	American	Chinese
Number, arithmetic	.44	.59
Space/geometry	.55	.84

children's early mathematical development in home and preschool learning environments. The sample included children from families representing different socioeconomic strata to ensure that variation within cultures as well as variation between cultures was addressed in the research. Young children's mathematical learning environments were examined to determine the nature and extent of support for informal mathematical development that children received at home and in preschool classroom environments across diverse socioeconomic and cultural contexts. Several converging methodologies were employed to study each of these subsystems in the home and classroom so as to yield a more comprehensive account of the support provided for children's early mathematical development in China, Japan, and the United States. The investigations included video ethnographies, observations, and self-reports of practices that parents and preschool teachers follow to support children's mathematical development, and information on parents' and teacher's ethno-theories about school readiness and children's mathematical development. Significant cross-cultural differences in mathematical development were evident (in CMA scores) during the preschool years. More extensive knowledge had developed in Chinese and Japanese preschool children than in their American peers. Cross-cultural differences were evident in all areas assessed, including number (counting and arithmetic operations), space/geometry, pattern knowledge, and measurement, and were already present in 3-year-olds near the beginning of the preschool year.

Findings consistent with those just described were obtained in a recent cross-cultural study of number word knowledge in Chinese and American children (Miller, Kelly, & Zhou, 2005). Cross-cultural differences, in favor of Chinese children, were found to appear at age 3 years and to grow larger across the preschool years. Thus, several studies have revealed cross-cultural differences in informal mathematical knowledge during the preschool years.

Socioeconomic Differences in Informal Mathematical Development

Research has revealed early socioeconomic status- (SES-) related differences in children's informal mathematical knowledge. An SES-related difference in the extent of economically disadvantaged children's numerical knowledge has been found at kindergarten age (Griffin, Case, & Siegler, 1995; Jordan, Huttenlocher, & Levine, 1992) and during the preschool years (e.g., Ginsburg & Russell, 1981; Hughes, 1986; Jordan, Huttenlocher, & Levine, 1994; Saxe, Guberman, & Gearhart, 1987; Starkey & Klein, 1992; Starkey, Klein, & Wakeley, 2004). This knowledge gap is apparent even among children attending Head Start, the American public preschool program for economically disadvantaged children (Starkey et al., 2004). Furthermore, the gap is broad and encompasses informal numerical knowledge, spatial/geometric abilities, knowledge of patterns, and measurement skills (Starkey et al., 2004).

When in early childhood do SES-related differences in mathematical knowledge first appear? Are these early differences a distinctly American phenomenon or do they occur in other cultures as well? Our recent cross-cultural research provides answers to both of these questions (Starkey & Klein, 2006). In China, Japan, and the United States, SES-related differences were found on the CMA, and in all cases these differences favored children from higher SES families. This finding helps disentangle the influence of SES and race or ethnicity on early mathematical development. Both China and Japan are far more homogeneous ethnically than the United States, yet early SES-related differences are present in all three countries. This pattern of findings indicates that variables associated with SES play a role in early mathematical development. It remains an open question whether or how ethnicity per se plays a role in early mathematical development. The mathematical knowledge gap appeared surprisingly early, by age 3 years, and it was most pronounced in the United States. Since most 3-year-old children in all three countries had recently entered preschool, the initial source of the SES-related gap is likely the home environment prior to preschool entry. What happened to this early gap as children progressed through preschool depended on the country in which children were being reared. In the United States, the gap widened over the preschool years, such that economically disadvantaged children finished preschool significantly further behind their more privileged peers than when they had entered preschool (Figures 11.1 and 11.2). This pattern of change, however, did not prove to be inevitable. In China and Japan, the gap narrowed and was no longer significant by the end of children's second year of preschool.

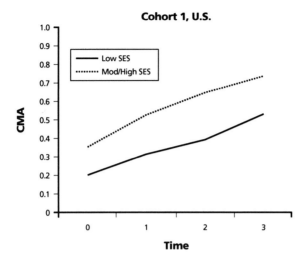

Figure 11.1.   Mean composite score on Child Mathematics Assessment by low- and middle-SES American children over the final two years of preschool.

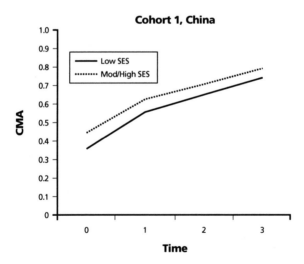

Figure 11.2.   Mean composite score on Child Mathematics Assessment by low- and middle-SES Chinese children over the final two years of preschool.

Findings on child outcomes in mathematics from the recently completed Head Start Impact Study (Administration for Children and Families, 2005) shed some light on why the gap grows in the United States. In this large study, economically disadvantaged young children were randomly assigned to either a Head Start condition or a control condition in which enrollment was denied. Children in the Head Start group experienced no gains in math knowledge relative to that of the control group. It indicates that preschool attendance per se by economically disadvantaged children is not enough to ensure that economically disadvantaged children will catch up or become ready for mathematics in elementary school.

In summary, cross-cultural and cross-SES differences in informal mathematical development are present by three years of age. American preschool children have less extensive mathematical knowledge than their East Asian peers. Within the United States as well as within China and Japan, preschool children from lower SES families have less extensive mathematical knowledge than their more advantaged peers. Consequently, children from different cultures and socioeconomic backgrounds enter elementary school at different levels of readiness for school mathematics. Cross-cultural and SES-related differences in mathematics achievement stem, in part, from the foundation of informal mathematical knowledge that is laid down during early childhood.

Sociocultural Differences in Support for Early Mathematical Development

In order to understand how group (cross-cultural or cross-socioeconomic) differences in informal mathematical knowledge come about, it is necessary to examine the ecological context of young children's mathematical development. The two principal environments that can support early mathematical development are the home and the preschool.

The home learning environment. Consider first research on the mathematical learning environment in American homes. Research with middle-class parents (Blevins-Knabe & Musin-Miller, 1996) and from a mixed sample of working-class and low-income parents (Saxe et al., 1987) has documented that low-income parents provide significantly fewer and less complex number activities than middle-class parents. Starkey et al. (1999) conducted surveys of low- and middle-SES American parents and of mixed-SES Chinese parents to provide data on the types and frequency of math-related activities that 4-year-old children engaged in at home (Table 11.2). Some types of math-related activities (activities during the home routine, made-up and purchased games, and math books) were engaged in more often by Chinese children than by American children. The converse was true for other types of math-related activities (TV shows with math content, number songs, and computers with math software) (Table 11.2). Within the United States, mathematics support was provided more often and in more types of activities by middle-class parents than by low SES parents. The relative frequency of some activities, such as math-related books, purchased games, and computers with math software may result from differences in families'

TABLE 11.2
Percent of Parents Reporting Weekly or Monthly Occurrence of Math Activity at Home

Activity	American		Chinese
	Low-SES	Mid-SES	Mixed SES
Activity during home routine	60%	86%	87%
Made-up games/activities	66%	79%	92%
Number/shape books	63%	74%	76%
Purchased games	37%	54%	85%
TV shows with math content	79%	63%	31%
Number songs	65%	63%	61%
Computer with math software	23%	42%	12%

financial resources. Other differences, however, cannot be explained in this way. Consider the relative frequency of math activities integrated into the home routine and made-up math games. These activities cost nothing financially, yet they occur more frequently in middle SES homes. Further research and theoretical analysis is needed to understand why economically disadvantaged families appear to provide less support of this kind for mathematical development. One possible explanation is related to educational differences that are often found between low- and middle-SES parents. Middle-SES parents are more likely than low-SES parents to have completed high school and college, and therefore to have taken more mathematics courses. It is possible that the experience of taking more math courses leads parents to value math more highly and hence to seek out or create mathematical learning opportunities more often for children at home. Close study of parental values and home practices is needed to shed light on this important set of issues.

The preschool learning environment. Next, we consider the few studies that have examined the mathematical learning environment in preschool classrooms. Surveys have revealed that many preschool teachers in the U.S. and China believe that the preschool learning environment supports mathematical development more than the home learning environment (see Table 11.3, adapted from Starkey et al., 1999). Many teachers, however, report that they did not know how to support children's developing numerical abilities (Farran, Silveri, & Culp, 1991), and that they are unfamiliar with school mathematics curricula for which they are expected to prepare children.

Observational studies likewise reveal a paucity of support for mathematics in American preschool classrooms. As part of a larger study of overall classroom quality in a North Carolina Head Start program, Bryant, Lau,

TABLE 11.3
Percent of Parents and Teachers who Rated the Relative Contribution of Home and Preschool Environment in Preparing Children for School Mathematics

	Parents			Teachers	
	American				
Relative Contribution	Low-SES	Mid-SES	Chinese	American	Chinese
Home > Preschool	15%	36%	10%	9%	5%
Home = Preschool	37%	31%	26%	17%	39%
Preschool > Home	48%	33%	64%	71%	56%

Burchinal, and Sparling (1994) found little developmentally appropriate support for early mathematical development. Starkey and Klein (2006) used an instrument, the Early Mathematics Classroom Observation (EMCO), designed to measure the amount of math support provided by preschool teachers. Specifically, the EMCO measured the amount of time children engaged in mathematical activity with their teacher present to provide scaffolding as needed. Chinese teachers provided, on average, 36 minutes of math support to 4-year-old children per day. In contrast, American teachers provided only 21 minutes of math support, most in whole-group activities such as calendar time. American teachers in programs for children from economically disadvantaged families provided children even less math support, less than 10 minutes per day. This pattern of findings indicates that preschool learning environments are less rich mathematically in the United States than in China. Within the United States, preschool learning environments are less rich mathematically in programs for economically disadvantaged children than in programs serving predominantly middle-class children. Thus, the amount of math support provided in preschool classrooms in China and the United States is correlated with the extent of preschool children's mathematical development.

Explanations for sociocultural differences in informal mathematical knowledge. In regard to the cross-cultural differences in children's informal mathematical knowledge, how can we explain the superior mathematics performance by young Japanese children? In Asian languages, including Japanese and Mandarin, the number-word system is highly regular and the base structure is coded clearly by number names (e.g., the teens are counted, "ten-one, ten-two, ten-three," etc.). Most European languages, including English, have a less regular number-word system and the base structure is more opaque (e.g., the teens are counted, "eleven, twelve, thirteen," etc.). Some theorists and researchers have used the number-word system as an explanation for cross-national differences in both informal and formal mathematical development (e.g., Fuson & Kwon, 1992; Miller et al., 1995; Miller et al., 2005). This explanation, however, does not seem plausible in regard to informal mathematics. Although the Japanese number words are regular both in the order of reference (always from the largest) and in their indication of the base-ten system (ten-one, ten-two), and may have some facilitative effect, this explanation must be discounted due to the presence of the double counting systems and the use of numerical classifiers. Japanese children are often taught another enumeration system of original Japanese words—up to ten—before the Chinese-derived system of number words that is used in elementary school (Imagaki & Hatano, 1999). There are no similarities between the corresponding number words in the two systems. In addition, children are taught to count objects with numerical classifiers, which vary depending on the category of objects and may change euphonically. For example, whereas candies are counted, "hitotsu, futatsu, mittsu," dogs are counted, "ippiki, nihiki, sanbiki," and sheets of paper, "ichimai, nimai, sanmai." The orderly verbal expression of numerical operations would be advantageous only for symbolic problems, which do not occupy a very significant place for preschoolers.

Ecological explanations thus seem more tenable. One study (White, 1987) has reported that Japanese mothers teach their preschool-age children to count to high numbers and to memorize the sums and remainders of single-digit addition and subtraction problems. This finding conflicts with other studies that have shown that parents do not in general teach young children large numbers or formal mathematics (Inagaki & Hatano, 1999). It is possible that White's sample of mothers may have included a disproportionate number of "education mothers," members of what is thought to be a small minority of mothers who attempt to greatly accelerate their young children. Although a few studies have collected data on parental support for formal mathematics in older children, there has been no research on Japanese parents' support for the development of informal mathematics in preschool children.

Survey results as well as our informal observations strongly suggest that most Japanese preschool teachers are rather reluctant to teach formal mathematics. A survey by the National League of Institutes for Educational Research (1971) found that almost no day-care center teachers thought that the teaching of formal mathematics was important. What preschool teachers do is prepare materials that are likely to induce "quantitative" (i.e., informal mathematical) activities, such as counting, and to enhance such activities often by participating in them by themselves or by inviting a child who reveals more advanced skills or understanding to stimulate other children. Early education is much less centrally controlled than elementary and secondary school education. Furthermore, the Ministry of Education discourages the teaching of math in an elementary school-like way. Indirect teaching and inducing children, for example, by arranging environmental settings, are encouraged. Teachers are encouraged to cultivate an interest in quantity in children. Little is known about specifically how parents or teachers support informal mathematical development and the effect it has on specific aspects of children's mathematical development. Studies of home and classroom support for informal mathematical development in Japan would be an important addition to the research literature.

Now consider the superior mathematics performance of young Chinese children. Here too, a sociocultural explanation seems more tenable. Early childhood educators in China have developed a preschool mathematics curriculum (Liang & Pang, 1992) as part of their national curriculum, and it has been used for several years in urban areas such as Beijing. Although the regular number-word system appears to have some facilitative effect on number word knowledge as Miller et al. (2005) have reported, this system does not play a central role in spatial tasks or geometric reasoning. Chinese children, nonetheless, had more extensive knowledge of these concepts than their American peers had (Table 11.1). Thus, it is more likely that the preschool math curriculum, comprising both teacher-directed activities and math learning-center activities, is fostering the development of early mathematical knowledge in young Chinese children. Further support for this view comes from our survey of Chinese parents and teachers (Starkey et al., 1999). Most Chinese parents and teachers indicated that the preschool learning environment was more responsible than the home for preparing their children for the elementary school mathematics curriculum (Table 11.3).

In conclusion, by the time children enter preschool, cross-cultural and SES-related differences in mathematical knowledge are already present. Early SES-related gaps in mathematical knowledge are present in Chinese and Japanese children as well as American children. This presence of gaps prior to preschool entry is consistent with the view that SES-related variables in children's early environments prior to preschool entry are the source of the gap. The gap widens during the preschool years in the United States but not in China or Japan. Our research suggests that early differences in children's mathematical knowledge are the result of differential levels of support for mathematics provided in children's home and preschool learning environments. In the United States, neither the home nor preschool learning environments of low-SES children provide sufficient enrichment to close or even maintain early SES-related differences in mathematical knowledge. We close with a discussion of the reasons that American preschool classrooms are relatively impoverished with respect to mathematics and what can be done to rectify this situation.

IMPLICATIONS OF THEORY AND RESEARCH
FOR EARLY CHILDHOOD CURRICULA AND PRACTICE

Early theories of mathematical learning and development also had an impact on the treatment of mathematics in early childhood curricula and pedagogy. Curricula founded on learning theory (e.g., Bereiter & Engleman, 1966; preschools' use of math workbooks) attempted to "push down" formal mathematical curricula from elementary school into preschool. This provoked a sharp anti-math reaction from the child development community. For example, Bredekamp (1987) highlighted the use of math workbooks in examples of inappropriate practice. In curricula and pedagogy based on Piagetian theory (e.g., Weikart, 1971), mathematics was excluded on theoretical grounds, and activities such as classification that were thought to support the later development of a number concept were included. To illustrate, Copeland (1974) reprints a lengthy quote from a Piagetian scholar, "Average children of 4–5 years may be able to count readily up to perhaps eight or ten...But the illuminating sequence of experiments of Piaget and his collaborators show that behind this verbal façade these self same children have in reality not a glimmering of the idea of number." (p. 354). Weikart's original High/Scope curriculum has been the most widely adopted curriculum in Head Start programs (Weikart, 1971). This curriculum included support for a variety of cognitive abilities but not mathematical abilities, which recent research has found in preschool-age children. Many preschools still utilize these curricula or other curricula derived from them. Consequently, mathematics is not a well-developed content area in many preschool curricula.

Another reason that mathematics is not prominent in early childhood curricula is due to the well-recognized time lag between when research discoveries are made, such as the discovery that young children possess a variety of mathematical concepts, and when these findings impact educational practice. Recently, research discoveries about early mathematical development have begun to be utilized in early childhood programs through the advent of intervention research aimed at helping preschool programs and parents better prepare young children, especially economically disadvantaged children, for school mathematics (e.g., Starkey & Klein, 2000; Klein et al., 2006; Starkey et al., 2004). This research involves the development of curricular activities for teachers or parents to use with preschool children to support the acquisition of mathematical concepts and skills that research has shown are within the capacity of young children to acquire. Creation of developmentally appropriate mathematics curricula requires detailed knowledge of cognitive developmental research on children's early mathematical thinking. Delivery of curricula requires knowledge of the home or classroom settings in which the curricula will be implemented as well as a training model for teaching preschool teachers or parents to implement the curricula with fidelity. We will use two of our recent intervention experiments to illustrate the efficacy of early childhood curricula to enrich children's learning environments and to enhance the development of early mathematical knowledge.

Mathematics Interventions for Young Children

One math intervention was directed toward the home environment of children enrolled in Head Start programs in California (Starkey & Klein, 2000). The intervention design included a group of predominantly African-American families and a group of Latino families. Within both groups, families were randomly assigned to intervention or control conditions, with intervention families receiving the experimental math curriculum and control families not receiving it. The curriculum consisted of a series of parent-child math activities. In each activity, a parent presented his or her child with math problems or tasks involving concrete manipulatives and scaffolded, or assisted, that child as needed. Parent-child dyads initially attended a series of family classes at their Head Start program. In a class, teachers first demonstrated an activity in English for African-American families or in English and Spanish for Latino families, and then distributed materials for families to use. Parents presented the math activities to their children and received assistance from teachers as needed. At the end of class, parents took the materials for the activities home and used them to support the development of their preschoolers' informal mathematical knowledge until the next scheduled class. Assessments of all children's mathematical knowledge were made before (pretest) and after (posttest) families participated in the series of classes. Analyses revealed that intervention children developed significantly more extensive informal mathematical knowledge than control children whose families did not participate in the classes. This intervention experiment demonstrated that a home mathematics curriculum, when delivered by parents who were taught to implement it, produced positive child outcomes in mathematics. The curriculum and training provided low-income families with concrete mathematics materials and experience in using them, and thus empowered these parents to enrich mathematically their children's home learning environment.

Another math intervention was directed toward the preschool learning environment of economically disadvantaged children (Klein et al., 2006). A pre-kindergarten mathematics intervention was implemented in two types of preschool programs, Head Start and state-funded preschools, serving low-income families in California and New York. Forty classrooms (10

Head Start and 10 state-funded preschool classrooms per state) were randomly assigned to the intervention condition or the control condition. In intervention classrooms, teachers learned to implement a pre-kindergarten mathematics curriculum and were monitored for fidelity of implementation. In control classrooms, no change was made. The curriculum, *Pre-K Mathematics* (Klein & Starkey, 2004b), consisted of small-group math activities with concrete manipulatives for teachers to use in the classroom and home math activities and materials for parents to use with their preschool-age child. *DLM Express* mathematics software (Clements & Sarama. 2003) was also used by children in intervention classrooms. Eight pre-kindergarten children were randomly selected from each classroom to participate in the research study; all children were in the age range eligible for entrance into public kindergarten the following year. The sample size was 278 children. Teachers in the intervention classrooms received training (workshops and on-site training) in how to implement the curriculum with fidelity. They learned pedagogical content in early childhood mathematics and classroom management techniques for conducting small-group activities. Children's mathematical knowledge was assessed by the Child Math Assessment (CMA) and the Woodcock Johnson III (WJIII) Applied Problems. Assessments were conducted in fall (pretest) and spring (posttest) of the pre-kindergarten year.

Intervention and control children's CMA scores in the fall and spring were compared in a 2 (group) × 2 (time of testing) mixed model ANOVA with children nested within classrooms. The Time × Group interaction was significant ($F(1,274) = 39.57$, $p < .0001$), which indicated a steeper increase in CMA scores across the year for intervention children than for control children. The effect size (Cohen, 1988) for the change in CMA scores from fall to spring was .89 for the control group and 1.43 for the intervention group, with the .55 difference representing the effect size for the curriculum. Compared to the gain in the control group over the preschool year, these effect size values show that the curriculum produced a 62% increase in math knowledge over what children would have otherwise experienced. Furthermore, the results show a significant difference between the math intervention and control groups across the two states on WJIII Applied Problems ($F(1,64) = 3.92$, $p < .05$). These findings indicate that the Pre-K Mathematics Curriculum was quite effective at enhancing low-income children's informal mathematical knowledge. In conclusion, our intervention research has demonstrated that high quality, pre-kindergarten curricula can significantly enhance mathematical knowledge in economically disadvantaged children.

In conclusion, American preschool children, especially economically disadvantaged children, do not receive enough support for informal mathematical development to be able to enter elementary school ready to learn a formal mathematics curriculum. Cross-cultural research in China and Japan has shown that it is possible to reduce a SES-related gap in mathematical knowledge during the preschool years. Furthermore, intervention research has shown that quality mathematics activities provided through home and preschool curricula can significantly close the SES-related gap in mathematical knowledge in young children in the United States. These findings have implications for early childhood education policy, especially policy governing programs for economically disadvantaged children.

Some Implications for Policy Governing Public Preschool Programs

Cross-cultural, cross-socioeconomic, and intervention research on early mathematical development has implications for policy governing public preschool programs. Most fundamentally, policy makers and program providers are advised to note that economically disadvantaged children begin to fall behind in mathematical knowledge well before they enter school. Due to differences in children's home environments, economically disadvantaged children enter preschool with less extensive mathematical knowledge than their peers from middle-SES families. If sufficient mathematical enrichment is not provided during the preschool years, this knowledge gap grows wider. By the time disadvantaged children complete preschool, they may be as much as one year behind their middle-class peers and almost two years behind children in China. Public preschool programs in the United States, by and large, are yet to act on these research findings. Chinese preschools we have studied use an extensive mathematics curriculum in preschool classrooms, but American public preschools do not. Intervention research has shown that it is possible for low-income parents and public preschool teachers, when provided with an effective mathematics curriculum and training in how to use it, can significantly enhance young children's mathematical knowledge. We advise that public preschool programs take steps necessary to mathematically enrich their classrooms and provide activities for parents to use at home to support children's early mathematical development. By helping teachers and parents provide early enrichment in mathematics, an important step can be taken toward ensuring an equal educational opportunity for all children, regardless of the circumstances into which they are born.

REFERENCES

Administration for Children and Families. (2005). *Head Start Impact Study: first year findings.*   www.acf.hhs.gov/programs/opre/hs/impact_study/reports/first_yr_finds/first_yr_finds.pdf

Bereiter, C., & Engleman, S. (1966). *Teaching disadvantaged children in the preschool.* Englewood Cliffs, NJ: Prentice-Hall.

Bisanz, H., Sherman, J.L., Rasmussen, C., & Ho, E. (2005) Development of arithmetic skills and knowledge in preschool children. In J. I. D. Campbell (Ed.). *Handbook of mathematical cognition* (pp. 143–162). New York: Psychology Press.

Blevins-Knabe, B., & Musun-Miller, L. (1996). Number use at home by children and their parents and its relationship to early mathematical performance. *Early Development and Parenting, 5*, 35–45.

Bowman, B. T., Donovan, M. S., & Burns, M. S. (Eds.). (2001). *Eager to learn: Educating our preschoolers.* Washington, DC: National Academy Press.

Bredekamp, S. (Ed.). (1987). *Developmentally appropriate practice in early childhood programs serving children from birth to age eight.* Washington, DC: National Association for the Education of Young Children.

Bryant, P. (1995). Children and arithmetic. *Journal of Child Psychology and Psychiatry, 36*, 3–32.

Carraher, T. N., Carraher, D. W., & Schliemann, A. D. (1985). Mathematics in the streets and in schools. *British Journal of Developmental Psychology, 3*, 21–29.

Clapp, F. L. (1924). The number combinations: Their relative difficulty. *Bureau of Educational Research Bulletin (No.2).*

Clements, D. H., & Sarama, J. (2003). *DLM Express Math Resource Package.* Columbus, OH: SRA/McGraw-Hill.

Cohen, J. (1988). *Statistical power for the behavioral sciences* (2nd ed.). Hillsdale, NJ: Erlbaum.

Copeland, R.W. (1974). *How children learn mathematics: Teaching implications of Piaget's research* (2nd ed.). New York: Macmillan.

Cordes, S., & Gelman, R. (2005). The young numerical mind: When does it count? In J. I. D. Campbell (Ed.), *Handbook of mathematical cognition* (pp. 127–142). New York: Psychology Press.

Dasen, P. R. (1977). *Piagetian psychology: Cross-cultural contributions.* New York: Gardner.

Davis, J. C., & Ginsburg, H. P. (1993). Similarities and differences in the formal and informal mathematical cognition of African, American, and Asian Children: The role of schooling and social class. In J. Altarriba (Ed.), *Cognition and culture: A cross-cultural approach to cognitive psychology* (pp. 343–360). Amsterdam: Elsevier.

Denton, K., & West, J. (2002). *Children's reading and mathematics achievement in kindergarten and first grade.* National Center for Education Statistics. Available: http://nces.ed.gov/pubsearch/pubsinfo.asp?pubid=2002125 [2002.

Dorsey, J. A., Mullis, I. V. S., Lindquist, M. M., & Chambers, D. L. (1988). *The mathematics report card: Are we measuring up?* NAEP Report No. 17-M-01. Princeton, NJ: Educational Testing Service.

Duncan, G. J., Dowsett, C. J., Claessens, A., Magnuson, K., Huston, A. C., Klebanov, P., Pagani, L., Feinstein, L., Engel, M., Brooks-Gunn, J., Sexton, H., Duckworth, K., & Japel, C. (2004). *School readiness and later achievement.* [on-line]. Available: www.northwestern.edu/ipr/publications/papers/2004/duncan/SchoolReadiness.pdf.

Entwisle, D. R., & Alexander, K. L. (1989). Early schooling as a "critical period" phenomenon. *Research in the Sociology of Education and Socialization, 8,* 27–55.

Entwisle, D. R., & Alexander, K. L. (1990). Beginning school math competence: Minority and majority comparisons. *Child Development, 61,* 454–471.

Farran, D. C., Silveri, B., & Culp, A. (1991). Public preschools and the disadvantaged. In L. Rescorla, M. C. Hyson, & K. Hirsh-Pasek (Eds.), *Academic instruction in early childhood: Challenge or pressure?* (No. 53, pp. 65–73). *New directions for child development,* W. Damon (editor-in-chief).

Frase, M. (1997). *Pursuing excellence: A study of U.S. fourth-grade mathematics and science achievement in international context. Initial findings from the Third International Mathematics and Science Study.* (GPO#065-000-00959-5). Washington, DC: Government Printing Office. (ERIC No. ED410098).

Fuson, K. C., & Kwon, Y. (1992). Learning addition and subtraction: Effects of number words and other cultural tools. In J. Bideau, C. Meljac, & J.-P. Fischer (Eds.), *Pathways to number* (pp. 283–302). Hillsdale, NJ: Erlbaum.

Geary, D. C. (1994). *Children's mathematical development.* Washington, DC: American Psychological Association.

Geary, D. C., Bow-Thomas, C. C., Fan, L., & Siegler, R. S. (1993). Even before formal instruction, Chinese children outperform American children in mental addition. *Cognitive Development, 8,* 517–529.

Ginsburg, H. P. (1989). *Children's arithmetic* (2nd ed.). Austin, TX: Pro-Ed.

Ginsburg, H. P., & Allardice, B. S. (1984). Children's difficulties with school mathematics. In B. Rogoff & J. Lave (Eds.), *Everyday cognition: Its development and social context* (pp. 194–219). Cambridge, MA: Harvard University Press.

Ginsburg, H. P., Choi, Y. E., Lopez, L. S., Netley, R., & Chi, C.-Y. (1997). Happy birthday to you: The early mathematical thinking of Asian, South American, and U.S. children. In T. Nunes & P. Bryant (Eds.), *Schools, mathematics, and the world of reality* (pp. 237–262). Boston: Allyn & Bacon.

Ginsburg, H. P., Klein, A., & Starkey, P. (1998). The development of children's mathematical thinking: Connecting research with practice. In W. Damon, I. E. Sigel, & K. A. Renninger (Eds.), *Handbook of child psychology, Vol. 4: Child psychology in practice* (5th ed., pp. 401–476). New York: Wiley.

Ginsburg, H. P., Posner, J., K., & Russell, R. L. (1981). The development of mental addition as a function of schooling and culture. *Journal of Cross-Cultural Psychology, 12,* 163–178.

Ginsburg, H. P., & Russell, R. L. (1981). Social class and racial influences on early mathematical thinking. *Monographs of the Society for Research in Child Development, 46,* (6, Serial No. 193).

Glenn Commission. (2000). *Before it's too late: A report to the nation from the National Commission on Mathematics and Science Teaching for the 21st Century.* U.S. Department of Education.

Griffin, S., Case, R., & Siegler, R. S. (1995). Rightstart: Providing the central conceptual prerequisites for first formal learning in arithmetic to students at risk for school failure. In K. McGilly (Ed.), *Classroom lessons: Integrating cognitive theory and classroom practice.* Cambridge, MA: MIT Press.

Haith, M. M. & Benson, J. B. (1998). Infant cognition. In W. Damon (Series Ed.), D. Kuhn, & R. S. Siegler (Vol. Eds.), *Handbook of child psychology: Vol. 2: Cognition, perception and language* (5th ed., pp. 199–254). New York: Wiley.

Holloway, S. D., Rambaud, M. F., Fuller, B., & Eggers-Pierola, C. (1995). What is "appropriate practice" at home and in child care?: Low-income mothers' views on preparing their children for school. *Early Childhood Research Quarterly, 10,* 451–473.

Hughes, M. (1986). *Children and number: Difficulties in learning mathematics.* Oxford: Blackwell.

Inagaki, K., & Hatano, G. (1999). Early childhood mathematics in Japan. In J. Copley (Ed.), *Mathematics in the early years.* Reston, VA: National Council of Teachers of Mathematics.

Jordan, N. C., Huttenlocher, J., & Levine, S. C. (1992). Differential calculation abilities in young children from middle- and low-income families. *Developmental Psychology, 28,* 644–653.

Jordan, N. C., Huttenlocher, J., & Levine, S. C. (1994). Assessing early arithmetic abilities: Effects of verbal and nonverbal response types on the calculation performance of middle- and low-income children. *Learning and Individual Differences, 6,* 413–432.

Kamii, C. (1985). *Young children reinvent arithmetic: Implications of Piaget's theory.* New York: Teachers College Press.

Kilpatrick, J., Swafford, J., & Findell, B. (2001). *Adding it up: Helping children learn mathematics.* Washington, DC: National Academy Press.

Klein, A. & Starkey, P. (1999). *Child Math Assessment.* Berkeley, CA: Author.

Klein, A., & Starkey, P. (2004a). Fostering preschool children's mathematical knowledge: Findings from the Berkeley Math Readiness Project. In D. H. Clements & J. Sarama (Eds.), *Engaging young children in mathematics* (pp. 343–360). Mahwah, NJ: Erlbaum.

Klein, A., & Starkey, P. (with Ramirez, A.) (2004b). *Scott Foresman – Addison Wesley Mathematics: Pre-K, Teachers Edition* (Rev. ed.). Glenview, IL: Pearson Scott Foresman.

Klein, A., Starkey, P., Clements, D., & Sarama, J. (June, 2006). *A longitudinal study of the effects of a pre-kindergarten mathematics curriculum on low-income children's mathematical knowledge.* Paper presented at the Institute of Education Sciences 2006 Research Conference, Washington, DC.

Knight, F. B., & Behrens, M. S. (1928). *The learning of the 100 addition combinations and the 100 subtraction combinations.* New York: Longmans, Green.

LaPointe, A. E., Mead, N. A., & Phillips, G. W. (1989). *A world of differences: An international assessment of mathematics and science.* Princeton, NJ: Educational Testing Service.

Lave, J. (1988). *Cognition in practice: Mind, mathematics, and culture in everyday life.* Cambridge: Cambridge University Press.

Liang, Z., & Pang, L. (1992). Early childhood education in the People's Republic of China. In G. A. Woodill, J. Bernhard, & L. Prochner (Eds.), *International handbook of early childhood education*. New York: Garland.

McKnight, C. C., Crosswhite, F. J., Dossey, J. A., Kifer, E., Swafford, J. O., Travers, K. J., & Cooney, T. J. (1987). *The underachieving curriculum: Assessing U.S. school mathematics from an international perspective*. Champaign, IL: Stipes.

Miller, K. F., Kelly, M., & Zhou, X. (2005). Learning mathematics in China and the United States. In J. I. D. Campbell (Ed.), *Handbook of mathematical cognition* (pp. 163–178). New York: Psychology Press.

Miller, K. F., Smith, C. M, Zhu, J. J., & Zhang, H. C. (1995). Preschool origins of cross-national differences in mathematical competence: the role of number-naming systems. *Psychological Science, 6*, 56–60.

Mullis, I. V. S., Martin, M. O., Beaton, A. E., Gonzalez, E. J., Kelly, D. L., & Smith, T. A. (1997). *Mathematics achievement in the primary school years: IEA's third international mathematics and science study (TIMSS)*. Chestnut Hill, MA: Center for the Study of Testing, Evaluation, and Educational Policy, Boston College.

Mullis, I. V. S., Martin, M. O., Gonzalez, E. J., Gregory, K. D., Garden, R. A., O'Connor, K. M., Chrostowski, S. J., & Smith, T. A. (2000). *TIMSS 1999 international mathematics report*. Boston, MA: The International Study Center, Boston College, Lynch School of Education.

National League of Institutes for Educational Research. (1971). *Opinion survey for the improvement of compulsory education*. Tokyo: Author (in Japanese).

National Research Council. (1989). *Everybody counts: A report to the nation on the future of mathematics education*. Washington, DC: National Academy Press.

Natriello, G., McDill, E. L., & Pallas, A. M. (1990). *Schooling disadvantaged children: Racing against catastrophe*. New York: Teachers College Press.

Newcombe, N. S., & Huttenlocher, J. (2000). *Making space: the development of spatial representation and reasoning*. Cambridge, MA: MIT Press.

Newcombe, N. S., & Huttenlocher, J. (2006). Development of spatial cognition. In W. Damon & R. M. Lorner (Series Ed.) & D. Kuhn & R. S. Siaglar (Vol. Ed.), *Handbook of child psychology: Vol. 2. Cognition, perception, and language* (6th ed., pp. 734–776). Hoboken, NJ: Wiley.

Peak, L. (1996). *Pursuing excellence: a study of U.S. eighth-grade mathematics and science teaching, learning, curriculum, and achievement in international context. Initial findings from the Third International Mathematics and Science Study*. (GPO #065-000-01018-6). Washington, D.C.: Government Printing Office. (ERIC No. ED400209)

Piaget, J. (1952). *The child's conception of number*. London: Routledge & Kegan Paul Ltd.

Price-Williams, D. R., Gordon, W., & Ramirez, M. (1969). Skill and conservation: A study of pottery-making children. *Developmental Psychology, 1*, 769.

Radziszewska, B., & Rogoff, B. (1991). Children's guided participation in planning imaginary errands with skilled adults or peer partners. *Developmental Psychology, 27*, 381–389.

Saxe, G. B., Guberman, S. R., & Gearhart, M. (1987). Social processes in early number development. *Monographs of the Society for Research in Child Development, 52*, (2 Serial No. 216).

Schleimann, A. D., Carraher, D. W., & Ceci, S. J. (1997). Everyday cognition. In J. W. Berry, P. R. Dasen, & T. S. Saraswathi (Eds.), *Handbook of cross-cultural psychology, Vol. 2: Basic proceses and human development* (2nd ed., pp. 177–216).

Scribner, S. (1986). Thinking in action: Some characteristics of practical thought. In R. Sternberg & R. K. Wagner (Eds.), *Practical intelligence: Nature and origins of competence in the everyday world* (pp. 13–60). Cambridge, MA: Harvard University Press.

Starkey, P., & Cooper, R. G. (1995). The development of subitizing in young children. *British Journal of Developmental Psychology, 13*, 399.

Starkey, P., & Klein, A. (1992). Economic and cultural influence on early mathematical development. In F. L. Parker, R. Robinson, S. Sombrano, C. Piotrowski, J. Hagen, S. Randoph, & A. Baker (Eds.), *New directions in child and family research: Shaping Head Start in the 90s* (pp. 440). New York: National Council of Jewish Women.

Starkey, P., & Klein, A. (2000). Fostering parental support for children's mathematical development: An intervention with Head Start families. *Early Education and Development, 11*, 659–680.

Starkey, P., & Klein, A. (2006). *The early development of mathematical cognition in socioeconomic and cultural contexts.* Paper presented at the Institute for Education Sciences Research Conference, Washington, DC.

Starkey, P., Klein, A., Chang, I., Dong, Q., Pang, L., & Zhou, Y. (1999). *Environmental supports for young children's mathematical development in China and the United States.* Paper presented at the meeting of the Society for Research in Child Development, Albuquerque, NM.

Starkey, P., Klein, A., & Wakeley, A. (2004). Enhancing young children's mathematical knowledge through a pre-kindergarten mathematics intervention. *Early Childhood Research Quarterly, 19*, 99–120.

Stevenson, H. W. (1987). The Asian advantage: The case of mathematics. *American Educator, 47*, 26–31.

Stevenson, H. W., Chen, C. S., & Lee, S. Y. (1993). Mathematics achievement of Chinese, Japanese, and American children—10 years later. *Science, 259*, 53–58.

Stevenson, H. W., Lee, S. Y., & Stigler, J. W. (1986). Mathematics achievement of Chinese, Japanese, and American children. *Science, 231*, 693–699.

Stevenson, H. W., & Stigler, J. W. (1992). *The learning gap.* New York: Simon & Schuster.

Takahira, S., Gonzales, P., Frase, M., & Salganik, L. H. (1998). *Pursuing excellence: a study of U.S. twelfth-grade mathematics and science achievement in international context. Initial findings from the Third International Mathematics and Science Study.* (National Center for Educational Statistics No. 98-049). Washington, DC: Government Printing Office. (ERIC No. ED419717)

U.S. Department of Labor Bureau of Labor Statistics. (2000, Spring). The Outlook for College Graduates, 1998–2008. In *Getting ready pays off!*, U.S. DOE, October 2000, and BLS Occupational Employment Projections to 2008, in NAB, *Workforce Economics, 6*(1).

Vygotsky, L. S. (1978). *Mind in society: The development of higher psychological processes.* Cambridge, MA: Harvard University Press.

Weikart, D. P. (1971). *The cognitively oriented curriculum: A framework for preschool teachers*. Washington, DC: National Association for the Education of Young Children.

White, M. (1987). *The Japanese educational challenge*. New York: The New Press.

CHAPTER 12

PARENTAL GUIDANCE OF NUMERACY DEVELOPMENT IN EARLY CHILDHOOD

Maureen Vandermaas-Peeler

The purpose of this chapter is to highlight the importance of parent-child interactions during play activities for preschoolers' learning, and to review the extent research on parent-child activities that support preschoolers' emergent numeracy. A sociocultural framework is utilized to demonstrate that parent-child interactions and parental beliefs must be considered within the context of the family ecology as well as the broader societal and cultural expectations for preschoolers' development. Numeracy has been defined as knowledge and mastery of mathematics, and as the use of mathematics to meet various challenges in the individual's environment (Botha, Maree, & de Witt, 2005). In preschoolers, concepts that constitute *emergent* numeracy tend to include a focus on number, measurement, space, and shape (Botha et al., 2005). Although the development of literacy has been widely examined in the context of both home and school-related activities, very little research and practice have focused on the development of numeracy (Warren & Young, 2002). This review encompasses parent-child play in cultural context, parental support of structured activities related to mathematics, and home-school connections in literacy and numeracy development.

Contemporary Perspectives on Mathematics in Early Childhood Education, pages 277–290
Copyright © 2008 by Information Age Publishing
All rights of reproduction in any form reserved.

PARENTAL SCAFFOLDING AND USE OF ZONES OF PROXIMAL DEVELOPMENT DURING PLAY

In the following exchange, a mother and her four-year-old child have been playing with toys related to the post office after reading a story about a postman who delivers mail to fairy tale characters. They have just made a birthday card, and put it in the pretend mailbox for the mail carrier to pick up and deliver to a friend.

> **Mother:** What do you think we do with this machine (points to cash register)? Do you know what to do with that?
> **Child:** Mailmen do something with it. They just do that (points to scanner).
> **Mother:** Does that tell them where to send it?
> **Child:** Yeah.
> **Mother:** I think it tells them how much postage they put on it (pushes register buttons). Do you need to weigh it?
> **Child:** Yes (pushes the 7). Seven.
> **Mother:** Seven?
> **Child:** Yep.
> **Mother:** Seven dollars or seven cents?
> **Child:** Seven cents.
> **Mother:** Oh thank goodness, I thought you meant seven dollars, that would be expensive!

This exchange illustrates the way parents and their children incorporated talk and activities related both to numeracy and literacy in a free play session with toys that encouraged pretend, literacy and numeracy-related play. The mother supported the child's understanding of what happens in a post office by asking the child questions, offering suggestions for play, and providing information about the value of money in their culture. In the rest of the play session, they created more letters to send and spent the majority of the time writing and reading their "mail." Discussions related to numeracy and especially the exchange of money occurred naturally throughout their interactions, although they were never the primary focus of the play. The play session was very child-directed, though the mother supported his play with her suggestions and comments. The next example illustrates mother-child talk related to numeracy, with more direct talk about numbers and counting, observed in the same study. The mother and child have just finished addressing an envelope.

> **Mother:** Now you have to bring it to the post office. I am open.
> **Child:** Okay.

Mother: But here are my charges. I don't think you have enough postage on there, ma'am. This is how much. I have stamps, envelopes, paper, and a box if you're mailing large items, and these are my costs. How much are my stamps? (she is asking the child to read the sign that lists the prices)

Child: (shrugs shoulders)

Mother: One penny. We'll pretend this is a scale.

Child: (presses the number one on the cash register)

Mother: Oh, you figured it out. Push it again. Mmm, they gave you a credit card. Kind of like the Barbie cash register.

The child pushes the register open, and they play with it for a few minutes.

Mother: Let's see if the credit card works. (runs the card through the scanner) Credit approved. I'd like to mail that please.

Child: Mail that?

Mother: Can you, let's weigh it (takes envelope from the child and pretends to weigh it) Hey, it says you need three stamps. So how many do we have on there?

Child: Two.

Mother: So how many more do you need? If you have two . . .

Child: You need one more.

The dyad continued playing post office for a few minutes, eventually deciding that the child would deliver the mail. As the child reached for letters to put in her bag, the mother began a counting sequence.

Mother: How much do you have? You have one. Do you want to count them? Just count them as you put them in. You have a lot.

Child: Mom, you count them.

Mother: No, you count them.

Mother and child proceed to count the mail, with the child responding to mothers' prompts to count. They counted 9 letters.

The second mother employed a more didactic style than the mother in the first example. She incorporated more direct teaching into the play, with a focus on the mechanics of letter writing and number counting interjected into pretend play scenarios. Although they differed in their style of interaction, both mothers engaged their children in the play activity and offered valuable conceptual and cultural information to their preschoolers within the context of play.

These parent-child interactions illustrate the importance of children's learning within the social context, and in particular with adults from whom they learn much about the rules and expectations for participation in culturally relevant routines. Rogoff (1990) referred to these interactions as components of a process called guided participation, in which parents and others share knowledge with children during every day, culturally important activities such as making dinner, folding the laundry, or counting the change the cashier gave back at the store. Vygotsky (1967, 1978, 1990) proposed that play is one of the most important sources of learning for young children, and that learning occurs primarily through observations and interactions with highly skilled members of the culture. Bodrova and Leong (1996) highlighted the utility of play for establishing a zone of proximal development or ZPD, in which adults provide support for children to play with more complexity than they would achieve on their own. In Vygotsky's theory, one important goal of the learning process is that the learner uses the information gained through social collaboration to *internalize* the new knowledge. Thus, important aspects of providing instruction within the ZPD include the adult's recognition of the child's ability level and contingent responses. The use of scaffolding, or the provision of structured assistance at a level that encourages the child to progress, has been studied in many tutorial and play situations (e.g., Farver, 1993; Vandermaas-Peeler et al., 2002; Wood, Bruner, & Ross, 1976). Optimally, scaffolding should encourage the learner's future competencies by gradually lessening the level of intervention and allowing the learner to take ownership of the situation. Sensitive guidance involves provision of adequate support to encourage this transfer of responsibility combined with ample leeway for the child to make and learn from their own mistakes (Rogoff, 1990).

Vandermaas-Peeler et al. (2002) described U.S. middle-class parents' use of guided participation to create zones of proximal development during pretend play with their preschool-aged child. Of the various types of scaffolding employed by parents during play, including teaching the child, commenting on play, making suggestions, and directing the ongoing activities, teaching was by far the most common. Parents frequently used the context of play to teach their children conceptual knowledge (e.g., "this is how the doctor takes your blood pressure" when playing doctor), as well as the use of objects in the real world (e.g., "this is a credit card machine" when playing store). Vandermaas-Peeler et al. (2002) found that the majority of parents' teaching in pretend play consisted of sharing conceptual knowledge about the world. Parents varied widely in the types of guidance employed and how they integrated teaching into play. Some parents were able to maintain both high rates of play and teaching, and others completely halted the play in order to focus on instruction. Thus, some parents are more successful than others at using play as a time for teaching as well as fostering imagination and fun.

In the free play scenarios described above, parental scaffolding was not as goal-oriented as in many prior studies that used structured tasks such as block building and games. Nonetheless, these highly educated, Western middle-class parents generally showed sensitivity in their responses to their children and supported their efforts with regard to both numeracy and literacy, appearing to value those activities over "just" pretend play.

SOCIAL AND CULTURAL CONTEXTS OF PARENTAL INVOLVEMENT IN PLAY

Parents' involvement in play and the nature of their activities during dyadic play with a young child differs widely by culture and depends in large part on the belief systems associated with the importance of play for development (Roopnarine et al., 3003; Vandermaas-Peeler, 2002). Gaskins' (1999) research on a Maya community in the Yucatan, for example, has attributed parents' lack of structured support and involvement in young children's play to their beliefs that child development is largely innate. Play is just one of many activities that enable nature to take its course and there is no real reason for adults to get involved, except to ensure the physical safety of young children and to keep them busy so adults can work (Gaskins, 1999). Prior research with East Indian, Guatemalan (Goncu & Mosier, 1991) and Mexican mothers (Farver, 1993) supported the conclusion that when mothers did not consider themselves appropriate play partners for their children, they were much less involved and engaged in playing with their children than U.S. mothers, who considered play culturally appropriate behavior (Farver & Wimbarti, 1995; Haight, Parke, & Black, 1997).

The frequency and nature of parent-child play is thus dependent in part on the cultural context of parental values. Haight et al. (1997) found that European American parents in their study viewed play as important for creativity and cognitive development, and engaged frequently in pretend-play activities with their toddlers. In a review of the literature on caregiver-child interactions during play, O'Reilly and Bornstein (1993) emphasized the importance of supportive interactions with parents for the development of the child's cognitive abilities. In the context of play with their parents, children have been found to play with more complexity and be receptive to parental suggestions (O'Reilly & Bornstein, 1993). Studies examining parental guidance of play have found that parents in higher socioeconomic brackets in the United States tend to be highly responsive and didactic in their play interactions with young children (e.g., Farver, 1993; Vandermaas-Peeler et al., 2002).

Parental support of children's play is not limited to their own involvement in the play activities, however. The arrangement of children's time, the physical environment and materials, and allowing for other social play partners are important considerations (Vandermaas-Peeler, 2002). Research has shown that children around the world play in creative ways despite constraints of time, work and space (Schwartzman, 1986), and that various play partners support their development (e.g., Farver, 1993). Farver and her colleagues (e.g., Farver, 1993; Farver & Wimbarti, 1995) have documented the importance of the role of older siblings in guiding children's play. Farver (1993) found that in Mexican families, the older siblings' guidance of play and tendency to involve their younger siblings in complex pretend play was very similar to the way American mothers behaved with their young children. This was in contrast to sibling play in the United States, which tended to be more discordant (Farver, 1993). In Mexico, older siblings are much more likely to be younger children's play partners and there is a highly nurturing relationship between the older and younger siblings. Similarly, Farver and Wimbarti (1995) reported that in Indonesia, parents respond to their young infants' needs but encourage older siblings to take a more active role once the infants are mobile. Dependency on the adult is thus lessened and the siblings play together. Farver and Wimbarti (1995) found that the older siblings tended to scaffold and encourage younger children's play whereas Indonesian mothers used more directives and corrections of children's behavior. Cultural beliefs and practices are thus important determinants of optimal play partners for children's development.

As noted by Roopnarine et al. (2003), the real challenge for early childhood educators lies in the potential discord between philosophical beliefs and empirical support for the importance of play for child development, and parental belief systems to the contrary. If parents' goals for their children both in the home and preschool contexts do not match those of the educators, how well do parents and teachers work together to encourage or at least allow play interactions that foster positive growth, and what is the impact on the children's learning? Research is needed to address these questions.

LITERACY AND NUMERACY DEVELOPMENT IN HOME AND SCHOOL CONTEXTS

The connections between home- and school-based literacy and numeracy practices were examined by Warren and Young (2002) in elementary school programs in Australia. Warren and Young (2002) noted that schools deem the home-literacy connection to be a very important one, and parents are often asked to read with their child at home. The connection between home and numeracy development also is important, but little is known or discussed with regard to parental support of mathematics, science or technology (Warren & Young, 2002). Their survey uncovered an important discrepancy. While parents viewed their own role as supporting and encouraging both literacy and numeracy development at home, teachers viewed the parents' role as supporting school learning only. Parents reported being more comfortable with literacy learning, and frequently read aloud to their young children. They were much less positive about numeracy, citing their own lack of knowledge and interest in numeracy and especially mathematics. Teachers generally asked parents to focus on rote learning (e.g., number facts) rather than conceptual understanding.

How often do parents and childcare providers incorporate number-related activities into preschool children's activities and routines? Blevins-Knabe et al. (2000) examined the frequency and type of mathematical activities provided by parents and family day care providers. Their findings indicated that mathematical activities were ranked as less important than social skills, reading and language, occurred relatively infrequently, and were not linked with preschool math achievement scores. However, there were some interesting correlations between provision of math activities and frequency of engaging in literacy activities. Parents and providers who enjoyed math and reading and who provided the most literacy activities also provided the most math activities. Blevins-Knabe et al. (2000) concluded that math activities were not a high priority in the children's daily settings, a concern given the children's low mathematics scores. They suggested that child care providers be given information about possible activities that support mathematics concept development. They also emphasized the need for positive affect about math in the adults themselves. Parental negative affect about mathematics is an important component of the social context of numeracy learning that has been mentioned in several research findings (Blevins-Knabe et al., 2000; Warren & Young, 2002), but rarely addressed directly in investigations of parent-child interactions related to numeracy. Adult motivation and interest in the topic may be a very important influence on the nature of their guidance of numeracy in both home and school contexts.

In recent research examining maternal support of literacy and numeracy activities in the context of reading and play with their preschool-aged child at home, Vandermaas-Peeler and colleagues (Vandermaas-Peeler et al., in press; Vandermaas-Peeler, Nelson, & Bumpass, 2007) supported prior research findings that European American mothers valued these activities for child development and provided high levels of guidance during both reading and play. The play materials were related to the story that was read by mother-child dyads in the experimental group, and included pretend, literacy, and numeracy-related play props (e.g., a large stuffed bear, a mail carrier shirt, a cash register, play money, pens, envelopes, stamps and paper). Literacy activities were observed most frequently in the videotaped play session, with no apparent differences in play due to the nature of the story read just prior to the play session. Parents and children also discussed topics related to numeracy in the context of both literacy and pretend play. There were approximately 21 number-related interactions per dyad in 15 minutes of play, with parents initiating most of the interactions but children initiating about 20%. Few dyads engaged in mathematical operations (such as counting the money in the example with the second mother in the beginning of the paper). Instead, the large majority of parents engaged in teaching conceptual information about the use of money for buying and selling goods. In their talk related to numeracy concepts, children focused most often on the quantity and the comparison of the materials (e.g., "one really big envelope" and "some small stamps").

It was interesting that parents seldom engaged their children in counting or discussions of number facts. This may be related to the free play context of the present study, rather than a structured activity that was clearly designed to investigate numeracy as in most prior research, and also to the children's fascination with the literacy-related materials (real stamps, markers, note cards and envelopes). It is noteworthy that parents and children spontaneously included concepts related to numeracy in their play, especially as few studies have focused on numeracy-related interactions during parent-child play sessions.

In another study that examined the nature of parent-child interactions during activities at home, Anderson (1997) audio-taped parents and four-year-olds interacting with four different sets of materials (a book, blocks, paper, and a mathematics workbook for preschoolers) in four 15-minute play sessions. Unlike parents in Vandermaas-Peeler's research, the families in Anderson's research (1997) were aware that the research focused on mathematical events. One interesting difference is that Anderson (1997) found that many parents engaged the children in counting activities, whereas very few parents counted with their children in the study described above. Perhaps parents automatically turn to counting when asked to engage their child in mathematical learning, because this is a rudimentary skill within preschoolers' zone of proximal development, or because of the influence of the school context on rote learning of number facts (Warren & Young, 2002). Anderson (1997) also reported that most of the mathematics events were parent-initiated and that parents supported math in questions and comments during the activities. There were a variety of parent–child interaction styles in her study as well, with some parents focusing on math for nearly the entire time, and others interjecting it into the context of other activities periodically. Anderson (1997) concluded that parents were important mediators of children's early mathematics learning and that more research on parent-child interactions in everyday activities is needed to understand the importance of the home context for children's numeracy.

Studies of the specific processes by which parents encourage or teach number development are relatively rare (Benigno & Ellis, 2004). One of the seminal studies designed to investigate the social context of parent-child interactions during number-related activities was conducted by Saxe, Guberman and Gearhart (1987). The researchers assessed low-income and middle-income 2- and 4-year-old children's understanding of numeracy, interviewed their mothers about their involvement in numeracy-related activities with their children at home, and examined the ways that mothers taught them within the context of a game. Saxe et al. concluded that there was a reciprocal dependency between the children's abilities and the opportunities that were afforded them. Younger children and children from low-income backgrounds who showed less competence in numeracy were also engaged in less complex number activities at home. Mothers adjusted their assistance to the children according to their successes and failures in the task, showing sensitive scaffolding in accord with Vygotskian theory.

Recent research on mathematics learning in the context of games and children's use of mathematics strategies supported the findings of Saxe et al. (1987) and Anderson (1997), that parents provide sensitive and contingent instruction during tasks at home. Bjorklund, Hubertz, and Reubens (2004) conducted a microgenetic study of 5-year-olds playing a board game with a parent over the course of three weeks. Children's and parents' behaviors during the game situation were compared to a math context in which children solved arithmetic problems. Bjorklund et al. (2004) found that parents engaged their children more in the math context than in the board game, with most of the cognitive directives they provided being related to counting in that context. Despite differences in the dyads and in individual child improvement over time, Bjorklund et al. (2004) concluded that parents tended to provide appropriate levels of support to their children, with more guidance provided to children who needed it according to their ability levels. Interestingly, parents often provided assistance during their own turn during the board game, a finding supported by Benigno and Ellis (2004) in their study of parental teaching during a board game.

Parents' abilities to provide sensitive assistance to young children are affected by the social context of the interactions. Benigno and Ellis (2004) found that parental teaching while playing a board game was impeded by the presence of an older sibling. When no older sibling was present, parents were more likely to use their own turns in the game to teach the child about counting, and provided more sensitive responses to the younger child. Benigno and Ellis (2004) suggested that these differences can be attributed in part to cognitive resources allocated to help one child instead of two, and/or to different motivational constraints when two children are present (e.g., moving the game along to keep both happy). It would be interesting to observe both parents and siblings in a less structured situation such as free play where there is no clear goal or outcome and the motivation to "finish" is not a constraint. It is possible that in some play contexts older siblings would provide additional scaffolding and encourage more complexity in the play of their young siblings, as Farver (1993) and others have demonstrated in other cultures. Given that most parents juggle many demands for their attention in everyday interactions, more research on parent-child interactions in complex social situations is needed.

How important is parental support of numeracy development for subsequent involvement in numeracy-related activities? Simpkins, Davis-Kean, and Eccles (2005) examined the relationship between parental encouragement and joint participation in elementary children's out-of-school math, science and computer activities, and how frequently children participated in those activities. They found that the parental behaviors were significant predictors of children's rate of participation, more for computer than math and science activities. There were few gender differences overall, although mothers appeared to provide more encouragement to boys and boys reported engaging in more computer-related activities and fewer math activities than girls.

Given the relatively poor mathematics performance of children in the United States, as compared to Asian and European students (e.g., Geary, 1996; Stevenson, Chen, & Lee, 1993), investigations of the impact of early numeracy activities on subsequent mathematical abilities are critical. The nature of parent involvement in young children's activities differs by culture and parental beliefs, as noted above. Parent-child interactions in preschool and elementary school should thus illuminate cultural differences in parenting practices contributing to these findings. Longitudinal research conducted by Huntsinger and colleagues (e.g., Huntsinger, Jose & Larson, 1998; Huntsinger et al., 2000) seems to contradict traditional European American beliefs that didactic instruction for preschoolers is not optimal for learning, and especially not for social adjustment. Their research comparing European American children to Chinese American children showed that the formal, structured and academically focused teaching style employed by Chinese American parents led to higher scores in mathematics and equally positive social development outcomes in the short-term assessment (Huntsinger et al., 1998) and several years later (Huntsinger et al., 2000). Chinese American parents emphasized the importance of hard work and discipline over ability, believed strongly in homework and encouraged it at home, were rated as more didactic in a counting game, and helped their children more at home. Interestingly, Huntsinger et al. (2000) reported that European American parents in their study who employed more didactic methods also had children who performed well in math. The results of these studies highlight the importance of parental beliefs, the home environment, and the nature of the parent-child activities for children's early numeracy and subsequent mathematical abilities.

In order to generalize the results of these findings, the sociocultural context of parental teaching must be considered. The Chinese American parents employed a teaching style consistent with their beliefs and within a complex family ecology. The European American parents held different beliefs and may have had different goals for their children. It is quite possible, therefore, that many European American parents could not or would not use didactic strategies as effectively as Chinese American parents. Huntsinger et al. (1998) reported that European American parents tended to provide support and assistance embedded in real-world contexts and games, which may be associated with other positive outcomes not measured in the studies. Further research is needed to examine the links between parental support of mathematical activities, the family ecology, and children's achievement.

CONCLUSIONS AND CONSIDERATIONS FOR FUTURE RESEARCH

The connections between play and literacy have been examined frequently in early child development research, but seldom have connections between numeracy and parent-child play been the focus of investigations. Research investigating the nature of parental guidance to children in structured activities at home has confirmed the importance of parental support of children's numeracy learning by the provision of sensitive assistance during the task (e.g., Bjorklund et al., 2004; Saxe et al., 1987). Parental support and joint participation in numeracy-related activities was shown to be an important predictor of elementary school children's subsequent participation (Simpkins et al., 2005), and parental support and teaching related to math activities at home have been linked to children's achievement in school (Huntsinger et al., 1998, 2000). As demonstrated in this chapter, a greater emphasis and focus on the importance of parent-child interactions related to numeracy at home is needed, both in practice and in research. The mathematics education community has not embraced and fostered parental involvement in numeracy-related activities at home in the same way that literacy has been promoted. Most parents in countries that emphasize the importance of early formal schooling have received copious amounts of information about the importance of literacy, through media reports, teacher emphasis and their own education. The review of the extant research suggests that numeracy should be partnered with literacy more often.

Consideration of the sociocultural context of parent-child interactions is critical to the success of any programs focused on early childhood and numeracy. Parents from cultural backgrounds in which play is believed to be essential for children's learning, and for whom direct involvement in children's play is typical and highly valued, would be most likely to embrace suggestions to include numeracy in their interactions with young children during play and conversations at home. For parents from cultural backgrounds that do not emphasize the importance of play, or the importance of parents as play partners, teachers can suggest that parents incorporate numeracy concepts into everyday activities (e.g., making dinner), and can also involve older siblings and others in the family in suggested numeracy-related interactions at home. For all communities, guidance of emergent numeracy can include informal talk and play as well as more deliberate and structured activities.

In conclusion, there are several important questions for future research on early numeracy in home and school contexts (see also Warren & Young, 2002). We need more information about parental beliefs concerning the importance of emergent numeracy and how early learning is supported in the home and the cultural context more broadly. Future research should also address the question of parents' efficacy regarding their own mathematics abilities. If parents have low self-efficacy for mathematics, how likely are they to include numeracy-related concepts in their interactions with their children, and how successful are they in providing guidance to their children? Future studies should also investigate what teachers believe about the importance of parent–child interactions at home, and their willingness and abilities to suggest activities and provide support for parental involvement with their young children for both literacy and numeracy. These are critical avenues for future research and practice, especially given the dearth of research and lack of focus on early numeracy development within the education community. Investigations of parents' and teachers' beliefs and practices concerning the intersections of play, literacy and numeracy are needed to design culturally appropriate programs that enrich young children's development.

REFERENCES

Anderson, A. (1997). Families and mathematics: A study of parent-child interactions. *Journal for Research in Mathematics Education, 28,* 484.

Benigno, J. P., & Ellis, S. (2004). Two is greater than three: Effects of older siblings on parental support of preschoolers' counting in middle-income families. *Early Childhood Research Quarterly, 19,* 4–20.

Bjorklund, D. F., Hubertz, M. J., & Reubens, A. C. (2004). Young children's arithmetic strategies in social context: How parents contribute to children's strategy development while playing games. *International Journal of Behavioral Development, 28,* 347–357.

Blevins-Knabe, B., Austin, A. B., Musum, L., Eddy, A., & Jones, R. M. (2000). Family home care providers' and parents' beliefs and practices concerning mathematics with young children. *Early Child Development and Care, 165,* 41–58.

Bodrova, E., & Leong, D. (1996). *Tools of the mind.* Englewood Cliffs, NJ: Merrill.

Botha, M., Maree, J. G., & de Witt, M. W. (2005). Developing and piloting the planning for facilitating mathematical processes and strategies for preschool learners. *Early Child Development and Care, 175*(7–8), 697–717.

Bronfenbrenner, U. (1979). *The ecology of human development.* Cambridge, MA: Harvard University Press.

Farver, J. (1993). Cultural differences in scaffolding pretend play: A comparison of American and Mexican mother-child and sibling-child pairs. In K. MacDonald (Ed.), *Parent-child play: Descriptions and implications.* Albany: SUNY Press.

Farver, J., & Wimbarti, S. (1995). Indonesian children's play with their mothers and older siblings. *Child Development, 66,* 1493–1503.

Gaskins, S. (1999). Children's daily lives in a Maya village. A case study of culturally constructed roles and activities. In A. Goncu (Ed.), *Children's engagement in the world* (pp. 25–61). Cambridge: Cambridge University Press.

Geary, D. C. (1996). International differences in mathematical achievement: Their nature, causes, and consequences. *Current Directions in Psychological Science, 5,* 133–137.

Goncu, A., & Mosier, C. (1991). *Cultural variations in the play of toddlers.* Presented at the Society for Research in Child Development, Seattle, WA.

Haight, W. L., Parke, R. D., & Black, J. E. (1997). Mothers' and fathers' beliefs about and spontaneous participation in their toddlers' pretend play. *Merrill-Palmer Quarterly, 43*(2), 271–290.

Huntsinger, C. S., Jose. P.E., & Larson, S. L. (1998). Do parent practices to encourage academic competence influence the social adjustment of young European American and Chinese American children? *Developmental Psychology, 34*(4), 737–756.

Huntsinger, C. S., Jose, P. E., Larson, S. L., Krieg, D. B., & Shaligram, C. (2000). Mathematics, vocabulary, and reading development in Chinese American and European American children over the primary school years. *Journal of Educational Psychology, 92*(4), 745–760.

O'Reilly, A. W., & Bornstein, M. H. (1993). Caregiver-child interaction in play. In M. H. Bornstein & A. W. O'Reilly (Eds.), *The role of play in the development of thought* (Vol. 59), *New directions for child development.* San Francisco: Jossey-Bass.

Rogoff, B. (1990). *Apprenticeship in Thinking: Cognitive development in social context.* New York: Oxford University Press.

Roopnarine, J., Shin, M., Jung, K., & Hossain, Z. (2003). Play and early development and education. The instantiation of parental belief systems. In O. N. Saracho & B. Spodek (Eds.), *Contemporary perspectives on play in early childhood education* (pp. 115–132). Greenwich, CT: Information Age Publishing.

Saxe, G. B., Guberman, S. R., & Gearhart, M. (1987). Social processes in early number development. *Monographs of the Society for Research in Child Development, 52* (Serial No. 216).

Schwartzman, H. B. (1986). A cross-cultural perspective on child-structured play activities and materials. In A. W. Gottfried & C. C. Brown (Eds.), *Play interactions. The contribution of play materials and parental involvement to children's development.* Lexington, MA: Heath.

Simpkins, S. D., Davis-Kean, P. E., & Eccles, J. S. (2005). Parents' socializing behavior and children's participation in math, science, and computer out-of-school activities. *Applied Developmental Science, 9,* 14–30.

Stevenson, H. W., Chen, C., & Lee, S. Y. (1993). Mathematics achievement of Chinese, Japanese, and American children: Ten years later. *Science, 259,* 53–58.

Vandermaas-Peeler, M. (2002). Cultural variations in parental support of children's play. In W. J. Lonner, D. L. Dinnel, S. A. Hayes, & D. N. Sattler (Eds.), *Online readings in psychology and culture* (Unit 11, Chapter 3), (http://www.wwu.edu/~culture), Center for Cross-Cultural Research, Western Washington University, Bellingham, WA.

Vandermaas-Peeler, M., King, C., Clayton, A., Holt, M., Kurtz, K., Maestri, L., Morris, E., & Woody, E. (2002). Parental scaffolding during joint play with preschoolers. In J. L. Roopnarine (Ed.), *Conceptual, social-cognitive, and contextual issues in the fields of play* (Vol. 4, pp. 165–181). *Play and Culture Studies.*

Vandermaas-Peeler, M., Nelson, J., von der Heide, M. & Kelly, E. (in press). Parental guidance with four-year-olds in literacy and play activities at home. *Play and Culture Studies.*

Vandermaas-Peeler, M., Nelson, J., & Bumpass, C. (2007). Quarters are what you put into the bubblegum machine: Numeracy interactions during parent–child play. *Early Childhood Research & Practice, 9*(1), Retrieved from http://ecrp.uiuc.edu/v9n1/vandermaas.html.

Vygotsky, L. S. (1967). Play and its role in the mental development of the child. *Soviet Psychology, 5,* 6–18.

Vygotsky, L. S. (1978). The role of play in development. In M. Cole, V. John-Steiner, S. Scribner, & E. Souberman (Eds.), *Mind in Society. The development of higher psychological processes.* Cambridge, MA: Harvard University Press.

Vygotsky, L. S. (1990). Imagination and creativity in childhood. *Soviet Psychology, 28,* 84–96.

Warren, E., & Young, J. (2002). Parent and school partnerships in supporting literacy and numeracy. *Asia-Pacific Journal of Teacher Education, 30*(3), 217–228.

Wood, D., Bruner, J., & Ross, G. (1976). The role of tutoring in problem-solving. *Journal of Child Psychology and Psychiatry, 17,* 89–100.

CHAPTER 13

DO PARENTS COUNT?

The Socialization of Children's Numeracy

Joann P. Benigno and Shari Ellis

By the start of kindergarten, there is wide individual variation in children's proficiency in mathematics. While some children can enumerate small sets, match sets on the basis of cardinality, and carry out simple calculations, others' skills and understandings are far more limited (Baroody, 1987; Brannon & Van de Walle, 2001; Clements, 2004; Huttenlocher, Jordan, & Levine, 1994; Mix, Huttenlocher, & Levine, 2002). On average, children of middle-income backgrounds begin school with higher levels of mathematical achievement than do their less privileged peers (Case, Griffin, & Kelly, 2001, Griffin, Case, & Siegler, 1994; Jordan, Huttenlocher, & Levine, 1992). Striking cross-national differences in children's numerical skills are also apparent by the time children begin formal schooling (Miller et al., 1995; Starkey et al., 1999).

It is widely accepted that experience is a key contributor to individual differences in early mathematical understanding. The goal of the present chapter is to examine how variability in children's mathematical cognition is accounted for, in part, by children's experiences in the family environment. In our view, the development of numeracy skills in the family context is best understood within the framework of the sociocultural approach.

Contemporary Perspectives on Mathematics in Early Childhood Education, pages 291–308
Copyright © 2008 by Information Age Publishing

SOCIOCULTURAL APPROACHES TO NUMERACY

According to the sociocultural approach, children become mathematically competent by participating in mathematical activities practiced in their communities. Sociocultural research on emerging numeracy has been guided by three core ideas: (1) mathematics is a cultural tool, (2) mathematical understanding is social in origin, and (3) mathematical practices can only be understood within a cultural-historical context. We discuss these tenets in more detail below.

Mathematics as a Cultural Tool. Mathematical tools include the words and notations used to represent number, material artifacts that embody mathematical knowledge such as currency and clocks, and social practices such as routines and rituals that organize and structure mathematical activity. These tools and artifacts are part one's cultural inheritance and have evolved over the course of the culture's social history. Children's mastery of mathematical tools begins with the acquisition of words to represent number. Number naming systems and other mathematical tools mediate the biologically-based capacity for quantification. As their competency with the mathematical tools of their culture grows, children's mathematical thinking is fundamentally transformed.

Evidence that the words used to represent number do indeed influence children's mathematical thinking can be found in studies that compare the development of counting among children who speak languages with different number naming structures. For example, base-10 number naming systems vary in how the base structure is represented (Miura et al., 1993). In Chinese, number names beyond ten are composed of the same words used for numbers of ten or less. The numbers between 10 and 20 consist of the word for ten plus the ones value (e.g., eleven or "shi-yi" is the equivalent of "ten one"). And number words for decades are formed with the word for the number of decades, plus the word for ten. (e.g., 20 is the equivalent of two ten). Number names within the decades are formed by appending the appropriate number name (e.g., 25 is "two ten five"). In English and other Indo-European languages, in contrast, the "teen" number names are irregular. Not surprisingly, young English speakers have greater difficulty learning to count than their Chinese counterparts. While English and Chinese speakers show comparable counting skill at 3 years of age when few children can count above 10, a large difference favoring Chinese speakers emerges between the ages of 3 and 4 years (Miller et al., 1995). English-speaking American preschoolers also produce idiosyncratic number names (e.g., "twenty-eight, twenty-nine, twenty-ten, twenty-eleven, twenty-twelve"). Young Chinese speakers never make these kinds of mistakes (Miller & Stigler, 1987).

The length of words used to represent number may also influence children's early proficiency with counting and arithmetic (Geary et al., 1993). Chinese number words are short and can be articulated more quickly than English number names. The speed with which number names can be pronounced influences memory span for numbers. When number names are shorter, more numbers can be stored in working memory. This, in turn, affects the ease with which one can perform mental arithmetic (i.e., "count in the head). And, indeed, young Chinese children are more likely to solve simple addition problems by counting verbally, whereas young English-speaking American children are more likely to count using their fingers (Geary et al., 1996).

Of course, the structure of the number naming system is just one of many factors that shape children's emerging numeracy. Parents' beliefs, attitudes, and practices related to mathematics determine the type and extent of exposure that young children have to number words. The relative contributions of the structure of the number naming system and parenting practices related to learning were nicely illustrated in a study that compared the early number skills of French- and English-speaking Canadian children (LeFevre, Clarke, & Stringer, 2002).

As in English, the French words for 11 and 12 are irregular. At 13, however, the English system becomes somewhat more predictable with all words ending in "teen" and most formed by combining the unit word with teen (e.g., fourteen, sixteen). In French, the number names are irregular through the number 16 while the number names for 17, 18, and 19 are formed by adding a unit word to ten as in the Chinese system.

As expected, young French-speaking children acquire the correct sequence of number names more slowly than English-speaking children. However, the home experiences of the children also differed. French-speaking parents held lower expectations for their children's early numeracy skills and they also reported teaching their children about numbers, words, and letters less frequently than the English-speaking parents. These findings highlight the importance of examining children's acquisition of early number skills in its social context. This is the topic to which we turn next.

Social Origins of Numeracy. Children are introduced to their culture's mathematical tools—including number words and procedures for counting things—through participation in activities structured by and involving other people. Children initially use mathematical tools—and the new modes of thinking that the tools afford—with the guidance and support of others.

There has been considerable interest among theorists and researchers alike in the nature of the interactions likely to foster mathematical understanding. Vygotsky (1978) proposed that the most productive interactions occur in what he termed the *zone of proximal or potential development* (ZPD).

The *zone of proximal development* is the gap between what a child can accomplish on his or her own and what the child can accomplish with aid. Scholars have used the metaphor of a scaffold to describe how more advanced partners support children's development in the zone of proximal development. The metaphor was originally used to describe moment-to-moment adjustments in the level of help that effective tutors provide during didactic exchanges (Wood, Bruner, & Ross, 1976). During these interactions, skilled teachers calibrate the level of help provided in response to the learner's level of performance, offering more direct, explicit assistance if the learner falters and less direct forms of help as the learner develops mastery. According to Berk and Winsler (1995), effective scaffolding involves collaborative problem-solving (two individuals working toward a goal), intersubjectivity (shared understanding between the two individuals jointly participating), warmth and responsiveness, remaining in the child's ZPD, and supporting the child's autonomy and self-regulatory capacities.

Much of young children's exposure to mathematics does not occur during explicitly didactic interactions, but rather while participating in routine cultural activities such as mealtime, shopping, household chores, and play. Although parents may not interpret these activities as opportunities to teach children about number, participation in the activities can provide children access to and involvement with the mathematics used in their community. As in scaffolded teaching interactions involving formal mathematical instruction, parents support children's learning about number in everyday activities by regulating the level of children's involvement. In this way, parents build a bridge between children's existing skills and new understandings for applying this knowledge (Rogoff, 1990, 2003).

The Cultural-Historical Context of Mathematical Development. Every child develops his or her mathematical skills and knowledge in a particular cultural/historical context. This context defines what constitutes mathematical thinking and practice, norms regarding when it is appropriate to use mathematics to solve problems and values related to the solutions and strategies (e.g., using arithmetic rather than using one's fingers to count at the store). The context also specifies beliefs about the underlying sources of mathematical skills, as well as attitudes regarding the importance and enjoyment of mathematical skills and activities (Goodnow, 1990; Street, Baker, & Tomlin, 2005). In industrialized societies, mathematics is primarily defined by "school" or formal mathematics and, as such, largely involves the mastery and manipulation of symbol systems.

Sociocultural researchers have long been interested in the similarities and differences between numeracy practices in school and those that occur in the home or other settings (Lave, 1988; Nunes, Schliemann, & Carraher, 1993; Saxe, 1991). For some individuals—typically those with more schooling—there is considerable overlap between the numeracy practices used in different settings. Many people, however, engage in very different practices in different settings. Greater understanding of cultural norms, beliefs, and values that shape the practices used in different settings is critical in building bridges between mathematical practices used in the home and those taught in school (Civil & Bernier, 2006; González, Moll, & Amanti, 2005; Street et al., 2005).

Street et al. (2005) adopted the *ideological model of numeracy* to understand the similarities and discrepancies between home and school numeracy practices. Their model includes four, unique, but interrelated dimensions: (1) *content*, (2) *context*, (3) *values and beliefs*, and (4) *social and institutional relations*. *Content* includes the types of numeracy activities and procedures (e.g., number knowledge) that people engage in—the decontextualized aspect of mathematics. *Context* refers to the *framing* and purpose of the numeracy activities. Even though similar mathematical problems can be solved at both home and school, the implementation of the problems will vary according to the different contexts. For example, number knowledge may be embedded in word problems at school and in shopping at home. Further, contexts that might be legitimate or viable at home may not be legitimate or viable at school or vice versa. *Values and belief systems* refer to the ideological and epistemological aspects of numeracy practices. That is, this component deals with what is considered the best or right way to do mathematics within a particular setting. For example, using arithmetic rather than counting on one's fingers to determine the correct amount of change when purchasing an item at the store. Finally, *social and institutional relations* are the overarching factors that control or regulate the implementation of the content, context, and the values that are espoused by individuals regarding numeracy practices. Specifically, the content, context, values/beliefs, social and institutional relations components of numeracy practices are determined by power relations. In this sense, numeracy practices are affected by the prevailing social and cultural context rather than neutral or value-free practices.

The idea of numeracy as a cultural practice has been further developed through the work on *ethnomathematics* (Bishop; 1991) and *funds of knowledge* (González et al., 2005). *Ethnomathematics* is an approach to mathematics concerned with how the culture, society, and the individual construct numeracy practices. *Funds of knowledge* represents an approach that capitalizes and transfers preexisting numeracy practices within the home and community environment to the classroom environment. From this perspective, the goal is not to transfer knowledge only from the classroom to the street, but rather from the street to the classroom. One manifestation of this approach is the placement of teachers within the home environment as observers and learners of naturally occurring numeracy practices.

Thus, the goal is not to instruct parents on how to teach their children, but to instruct educators on how parents already teach their children.

In the next section, we review empirical studies of emerging numeracy within the family context. We reviewed these studies with three questions in mind: (1) To what extent do parents engage their young children in mathematical practices during early childhood?; (2) What do those practice entail?; and (3) Does engagement in mathematical practices in the home promote early numeracy skills?

PARENTAL SUPPORT OF EMERGENT NUMERACY: EMPIRICAL FINDINGS

Parent Report. Clearly, opportunities abound for children to explore and develop counting and other mathematical concepts in their daily routines and activities. Mealtimes and cooking, sports and games, book reading, television and shopping excursions outside of the home potentially expose children to a variety of number concepts. Do parents of young children take advantage of these opportunities to foster their children's mathematical competence?

Many parents report that they do. Parents cite a considerable range of activities including reciting number rhymes, counting while climbing stairs, reading numbers on license plates, measuring while cooking, as well as those explicitly designed to teach children about number concepts such as playing computer games and completing worksheets (Aubrey, Bottle, & Godfrey, 2003; Blevins-Knabe & Musun-Miller, 1996; Fluck, Linnell, & Holgate, 2005; Guberman, 2004; Huntsinger et al., 2000; Saxe, Guberman, & Gearheart, 1987).

The kinds of activities that parents report they engage in with their children varies across cultural communities as well as families. Chinese and Korean parents, for example, report that they engage their children in didactic exchanges involving counting and number concepts (Hutsinger et al., 2000; Guberman, 2004). Many Latin American parents, in contrast, are more likely to report that they offer their children opportunities to engage in instrumental transactions involving money—both real and pretend (Guberman, 2004).

Reported participation in these early encounters with counting and number concepts does appear related to children's mathematical development. Young children who reportedly participate in number activities with their parents at greater frequency exhibit a more advanced understanding of number than peers who have fewer opportunities (Blevins-Knabe & Musun-Miller, 1996; Hutsinger et al., 2000; LeFevre et al., 2002; Young-Loveridge, 1989). Moreover, children tend to perform best on problems that resemble those that they engage in with their families (Guberman, 2004).

Naturalistic Observations. Although many parents report that they frequently engage young children in activities involving number, evidence from naturalistic studies is mixed. Among some families, exposure to number names and concepts begins as early as the first year of life. One longitudinal study of language development among middle-income British families found that mothers began using number words in conversational exchanges when their infants were as young as nine months (Durkin et al., 1986). As the children entered the toddler years, mothers introduced increasingly complex number concepts. Mothers recited number words embedded in nursery rhymes, stories, games, and songs, they used numbers when requesting items from their children during conversation, and they recited number strings when they attempted to teach their children to count.

Other observational studies suggest that parents do little to support the mathematics learning of young children. Tudge and Doucet (2004) observed three-year-olds as the children went about their daily routines in their own and others' homes, childcare centers, and public settings. Strikingly, 60% of children were never observed engaged in a mathematical activity. There was, however, large individual variation among the ethnically and economically diverse sample. Both Caucasian and Black children, irrespective of social class, engaged in few number activities. When they did, the activities occurred outside of childcare settings and focused primarily on counting objects in the environment in response to questions such as "how many?" and interacting with number-oriented toys, games, or books.

Researchers also observed disappointingly low levels of support for mathematics learning at a popular exhibit "1-2-3-Go!" at a children's museum (Gelman & Massey, 1987). Nearly one-third of the parents did not interact at all with the display or their children. Only one-third of the parents asked the question, "how many?" (despite the large sign that read "HOW MANY...") and only 25% of parents used the exhibit as a teaching opportunity to model counting for their children, ask their children to count, or announce the target number of items. None of the children who explored the exhibit on their own visibly attempted to count.

The studies reviewed so far focus primarily on activities that involve explicit instruction on mathematics. Findings from a unique diary study of one child's activities from 12 to 38 months of age reveals that home environments can support children's emerging mathematical understanding in subtle ways that may have been overlooked in previous investigations. In this study (Mix, 2002), a mother and expert on children's quantitative reasoning, kept track of instances in which her son, Spencer, engaged in activities that involved one-to-one correspondence. Her observations were limited to activities initiated by Spencer and did not include teaching interactions or situations in which the child may have been imitating her actions.

One interesting finding was the myriad of ways in which everyday practices common to many home environments such as matching up objects, playing simple kissing games, and taking turns might foster the development of one-to-one correspondence. Interestingly, the most frequent one-to-one correspondence activity, and the earliest observed, involved distributing objects to people—and pets! Mix suggests that the act of distributing objects to living things (in particular, treats to dogs) scaffolds the use of one-to-one correspondence in ways that interactions with inanimate objects might not. First, parents, playmates, and pets are easily distinguishable from one another thereby reducing the likelihood of making mistakes. Second, the task makes sense; there is a reason that each adult would get a spoon or each pet a treat. Third, and perhaps most important, people and pets can be active participants in the interaction, providing both motivation and feedback.

Structured Observations. Studies that utilize structured interactions in which researchers provide parents with a set of materials and observe how they use the materials to teach their children counting and other number concepts generally paint a positive portrait of parents' role in children's emerging numeracy. Using this approach, Anderson and her colleagues (Anderson, 1997; Anderson, Anderson, & Shapiro, 2004) demonstrated that middle-income parents readily incorporate mathematics instruction into a wide variety of activities such as block play, paper crafts, and storybook reading. As was true among the families observed by Tudge and Doucet (2004), however, the most common activity involved counting objects while other kinds of mathematical understandings were largely neglected.

Other researchers have used structured observations to examine not only *what* parents teach young children about number, but *how* they do so. This work has been grounded in the Vygotskian theoretical framework (Vygotsky, 1978). In an early study, Saxe and colleagues (1987) found middle- and working income mothers to be quite skilled at adjusting the level of support for two aspects of counting—the count word sequence and one-to-one correspondence. To illustrate, when young children made errors while counting an array of dots (e.g., failing to represent each dot with a number or reciting numbers out of order), mothers provided aid specific to the kind of error that was made. Mothers' support—such as modeling counting for their children—provided children with an opportunity to adjust their counting behaviors. Mothers also adjusted the goal of the task when it appeared too difficult for their children to complete—even with assistance. For example, a mother with a child unable to count to an array of 13 dots might cover up a portion of the array to reveal the number of dots their child was capable of counting. Thus, mothers capitalized on the opportunity to teach their children about number by adjusting the goals of a complex task into a simpler form.

Evidence from a series of recent studies by Fluck and colleagues (Fluck et al., 2005; Linnell & Fluck, 2001) suggests that parental support of emerging numeracy is greatest for learning counting procedures and less so for learning counting principles. In these studies, parents were asked to predict how their three-year-olds would respond to number tasks that require a variety of different understandings. Parents were also observed as they helped their children perform two kinds of number tasks—counting and cardinality. In the counting task, children were to count the number of toys in a set; in the cardinality task, children were to "give 'x'" (e.g., "the toy clown can have x cars; put x cars in his basket"). Parents were more likely to adjust their support in the counting task than in the cardinality task. So although parents were able to accurately predict their children's ability to count objects and their understanding of the *how to count* principles, they were not as accurate in estimating or effectively supporting their children's understanding of cardinality.

Why do parents fail to recognize their children's limited grasp of cardinality? One possibility is that parents rarely observe their children behave in ways that reveal confusion (Fluck et al., 2005). Even young children may appear to grasp the concept when working with very small numbers (e.g., "I got 2!"). And, if parents do not follow a successful count of larger sets with "So how many are there?" they have no evidence that their children fail to make the connection between the last word recited and the total number of items in the set.

Parents are also likely to intervene when children begin to exhibit difficulty when completing a task that requires an understanding of cardinality, especially when the "give x" exchanges occur in the context of ongoing, everyday activities (e.g., "Please give your brother four of those blocks."; "Will you bring me five spoons?"). In these circumstances, parents are more likely focused on achieving the end goal than teaching number concepts. They may also misinterpret failure in terms of misbehavior rather than misunderstanding. Linnell and Fluck (2001) also suggest that parents in their study did not seem to interpret the "give 'x'" task as one that required the precision of simple counting activity. Indeed, in everyday exchanges, particularly between siblings and other playmates, giving *some* amount—rather than a precise amount—may be an adequate response.

How parents support young children's emerging numeracy in the context of everyday exchanges was the focus of an investigation by Benigno and Ellis (2004). Of interest was whether parents would support their children's early counting as skillfully when interacting with two children as they do when working with one, especially in the absence of explicit encouragement to use the interaction as a teaching opportunity. In this study, we observed middle-income families as they played a board game. Some of the family groups were composed of a parent and a preschooler, while the remaining family groups included a parent, preschooler, and a school-age sibling within two years of age of the preschooler. The board game occurred at the end of a 75-minute session that included an assortment of activities including fantasy play, beanbag toss, coloring, and a snack. During the second session, children completed mathematical reasoning and language assessments (TEMA-2, Ginsburg & Baroody, 1990; EOWPVT-R, Gardner, 1990). As noted above, parents were not explicitly instructed to teach their children about number. Rather, we told parents that the focus of the study was on sibling interaction and children's learning.

To solicit a maximum amount of counting and to reduce the effects of prior experience with a particular board game, we created a game for the study. *The Picnic Game* is a board game that resembles manufactured games such as Monopoly®. The object of the game is to collect items for a picnic. Players take turns moving among squares placed around the perimeter of the game board. On each square, there are between one and six examples of a single picnic item to be retrieved (e.g., one hotdog, six drinks). Movement from square to square is determined by drawing a card from a stack. Players count the number of ants on each card (again, ranging from one to six) to determine the number of squares to move (see Benigno & Ellis, 2004 for a full description of the game).

We assessed parent support of children's counting using a variety of measures. These included the frequency of help offered before or after an error, and on small counts (one, two, and three) versus large counts (four, five, and six); the number of times parents checked the accuracy of the preschoolers' counts; and the number of times parents used their own turns as teaching opportunities. We also assessed the relationship between the amount of help parents provided and children's errors during the game and their performance on the standardized mathematics assessment.

There were many similarities across the two conditions in the amount and type of support parents provided. Parents in both conditions provided significantly more aid following a counting error than before an error occurred, and when the preschooler drew a larger rather than a smaller number. Parents in both conditions were also more likely to check the accuracy of the preschoolers' count when they drew a large versus a small number. Parents in both conditions also used their own turns as teaching opportunities, especially when they drew a larger number. However, parents playing the game with only a preschooler did so more often than those playing the game with two children.

Overall, parents in dyads and triads provided comparable amounts of assistance to the preschooler during the game. However, differences emerged in the sensitivity of the parental intervention provided. Although preschoolers in dyadic and triadic conditions were—on average—of equal mathematical ability, differences existed in the relations between parental intervention and preschoolers' counting and mathematical abilities. Specifically, among dyads, the amount of parental intervention was strongly related to both preschoolers' counting errors and their scores on the mathematical assessment. Among triads, in contrast, amount of parental intervention was unrelated to preschoolers' counting errors and only weakly related to their mathematical assessment scores.

These findings highlight the importance of placing parent-child interactions around number in the broader family context. Many of the opportunities that parents have to foster their children's mathematical development are going to arise "on the fly" and outside of one-on-one didactic exchanges. To accurately evaluate the impact of parenting practices on children's emerging numeracy and to design effective programs to enhance those practices requires that researchers look beyond dyadic interactions.

INTERVENTION STUDIES

Recognizing the importance of young children's early participation in everyday activities, researchers have recently developed interventions designed to increase parent–child engagement in mathematics within the home environment. In one such program parents and children from low-income African-American and Latino communities attended a family math class biweekly over the course of four months (Starkey & Klein, 2000). The classes were organized around a series of mathematically oriented units such as number concepts, logical reasoning, and patterns. During the classes, teachers demonstrated an activity to the class and helped parents learn how to teach their children about the various mathematical concepts. Children who participated in the intervention with their parents were better able to solve numerical and spatial reasoning tasks than those who did not participate in the intervention. The findings suggest that providing parents with opportunities to learn and implement effective domain-specific instructional strategies can enhance their children's mathematical skills during early childhood.

In conjunction with Head Start classrooms, researchers at the University of Hawaii developed an intervention that also included both classroom experiences and a home component (DeBaryshe & Gorecki, 2005; Sophian, 2004). The home component consisted of weekly activities that paralleled the classroom curriculum. Parents were provided a simple description of the activity and any needed materials. In most cases, parents were asked to help the children make something to be brought back to the center. A mentor visited each classroom on a biweekly basis and described the upcoming activities to parents, answered their questions, and offered guidance. Children in classrooms with the mathematics intervention demonstrated higher levels of mathematical understanding than children in control classrooms, although it is unknown how much either the home or classroom components alone contributed to the improved performance.

IMPLICATIONS FOR EVIDENCE-BASED PRACTICE AND FUTURE RESEARCH

Early interventions in the domain of literacy aimed at increasing both awareness and the use of instructional strategies are widespread (see Hall, Larson, & Marsh, 2003; Purcell-Gates, 2000; Wasik, 2004 for reviews). Until recently, however, far less energy has been devoted to children's early numeracy skills. The increasing concern of both educational practitioners and policy makers alike is reflected in the new standards of early mathematics education for the pre-kindergarten (age 3–5) years (Neuman & Roskos, 2005) and school-age children. The standards specify that mastery goals in the domain of numeracy (in addition to literacy and language) be established according to the children's developmental level. The shift to specific learning goals has led to revisions of mathematical curriculums and increased training opportunities for teachers to address these goals in their classrooms. Although the implementation of standards varies from state to state, most states incorporate base their standards on the category of learning, domain-specific instruction within the category, and indicators of performance.

Future intervention research should continue to conduct systematic program evaluations to determine which instructional approaches or activities best facilitate learning that interfaces school instruction with home-based practice (Starkey, et al., 2004) and that transfers home-based practice to school instruction (e.g., Gonzalez et al., 2005). Standards emphasize the importance of engaging children in concrete, meaningful, and enjoyable activities, but there is little understanding of how to do this in practice. Training programs have emphasized one-on-one didactic interactions on isolated "lessons" rather than helping parents find ways to incorporate math into their actual everyday experiences. Further, the long-term implication of such intervention programs incorporating school and family-based learning must be studied in order to fully unpack the long-term success of such intervention strategies and how parental involvement shifts and can be maintained once children enter grade school.

Some evidence reviewed regarding parental involvement in homework with their school-age children suggests that the quality, not quantity of time spent working on homework related to student achievement (Balli, Wedman, & Demo, 1997). Clearly, other factors such as characteristics of the dyad in question (e.g., parent education level and child ability) impact the success of the dyadic experience. In order to fully understand the impact of social experiences on mathematical learning from a Vygotskian perspective, factors influencing the quality of the interchanges in both dyadic and multi-child learning contexts must be further considered.

There is, without question, a developmental shift that influences the parents' ability to provide assistance that coincides with their children's abilities. For instance, during the preschool years, mathematics can be embedded in a range of everyday activities that do not explicitly target number (e.g., book reading). However, during middle childhood, math is increasingly equated with "school math." As mathematics becomes more formalized (and an end in itself via tests), engaging in mathematics with their children may become more difficult for some parents. Although it may be challenging for parents to incorporate complex mathematical in everyday interactions, there are still numerous opportunities to reinforce their children's learning, such as in relation to sports statistics (e.g., batting averages) and economic transactions (e.g., shopping, fund raising). Empowering parents to participate in math and parent partnerships, such as those suggested by Marta Civil and her colleagues (e.g., *Math and Parent Partnerships in the Southwest*), will enhance parents' involvement not only as facilitators, but also as learners and leaders who can impact their children's mathematical learning (Civil & Bernier, 2006).

Overall, children's use of mathematics outside of school with or without their parents is understudied and perhaps undervalued—except among those interested in cultural differences (Civil, 2002; Civil & Bernier, 2006; Guberman, 2004; Nunes et al., 1993; Saxe, 1991). Because the belief and value systems espoused by parents vary as a function of their cultural background, the belief and value systems adopted by their children are also subject to the same influences. Upon entry into formal schooling, parents, for instance, may believe that their children's education rests in the hands of their teachers or that their children should be independently responsible for completing their homework. As a result, much of what homework researchers find—that parental engagement in homework does not strongly correspond to their children's mathematical skills—may not be that surprising. Perhaps, more strong relations between parental support and young children's emerging numeracy exist because parents are able to build mathematics within everyday activities their children enjoy. If parents adopt a similar approach once children enter the grade-school years and broaden their involvement beyond the context of homework, more positive benefits, particularly the extent to which parental involvement influences mathematical competence, may result.

The work on cultural differences reveals that children can be quite sophisticated in their mathematical reasoning outside of school, but demonstrate difficulty in solving the exact same problems when they are presented in the scholastic context (e.g., Nunes et al., 1993). Perhaps increasing parental engagement in numeracy activities that bridge home and school may result in greater transfer of learning between the contexts (e.g., Moll et al., 1992).

CONCLUSIONS

The goal of this chapter was to orient the reader to the state of research on parental socialization of numeracy in children. There are numerous opportunities for parents to involve their children in meaningful mathematics activities outside of school. However, wide variation exists in the extent to which families support children's mathematics learning in everyday contexts. Even when parents do make active attempts to engage in numeracy activities, they tend to focus on basic procedures such as rote counting to the relative neglect of more complex concepts. Although intervention studies have successfully increased the frequency as well as the breadth of activities with which parents engaged in mathematics activities with their children, developing skill sets that also reinforce positive attitudes about mathematics in the context of everyday activities, might lead to greater gains in other contexts, such as school.

Intervention studies which enlist parents to play a significant role in their children's learning of numeracy in everyday contexts will lead to partnerships among families, educators, and researchers (Civil & Bernier, 2006; Gonzalez et al., 2005). These partnerships will provide parents and educators alike with the tools they need in order to *fund* children's numeracy across a variety of learning contexts, thereby supporting students' ability, success, and confidence in the domain of mathematics.

REFERENCES

Anderson, A. (1997). Families and mathematics: A study of parent-child interactions. *Journal for Research in Mathematics Education, 28*(4), 484–511.

Anderson, A., Anderson, J., & Shapiro, J. (2004). Mathematical discourse in shared storybook reading. *Journal for Research in Mathematics Education, 35*(1), 5–33.

Aubrey, C., Bottle, G., & Godfrey, R. (2003). Early mathematics in the home and out-of-home contexts. *International Journal of Early Years Education, 11*, 91–103.

Baroody, A. J. (1987). *Children's mathematical thinking: A developmental framework for preschool, primary, and special education teachers*. New York: Teachers College Press.

Balli, S., Wedman, J., & Demo, D. H. (1997). Family involvement with middle-grades homework: Effect of differential prompting. *The Journal of Experimental Education, 66*(1), 31–48.

Benigno, J. P., & Ellis, S. (2004). Two is greater than three: Effects of older siblings on parental support of preschoolers' counting in middle-income families. *Early Childhood Research Quarterly, 19*, 1–20.

Berk, L. E., & Winsler, A. (1995). *Scaffolding children's learning: Vygotsky and early childhood education*. Washington DC: National Association for the Education of Young Children.

Bishop, A. J. (1991). *Mathematical enculturation: A cultural perspective on mathematics education*. Dordrecht: Kluwer.

Blevins-Knabe, B., & Musun-Miller, L. (1996). Number use at home by children and their parents and its relationship to early mathematical performance. *Early Development and Parenting, 5*, 35–45.

Brannon, E. M., & Van de Walle, G. A. (2001). The development of ordinal numerical competence in young children. *Cognitive Psychology, 43*, 53–81.

Case, R., Griffin, S., & Kelly, W. M. (2001). Socioeconomic differences in children's early cognitive development and their readiness for schooling. In S.L. Golbeck (Ed.), *Psychological perspectives on early childhood education: Reframing dilemmas in research and practice* (pp. 37–63). Mahwah, NJ: Erlbaum.

Civil, M. (2002). Culture and mathematics: A community approach. *Journal of Intercultural Studies, 23*, 133–148.

Civil, M., & Bernier, E. (2006). Exploring images of parental participation in mathematics education: Challenges and possibilities. *Mathematical thinking and learning, 8*, 309–330.

Clements, D. H. (2004). Major themes and recommendations. In D. H. Clements, J. Sarama, & A.-M. DiBiase (Eds.), *Engaging young children in mathematics: Standards for early childhood mathematics education* (pp. 7–72). Mahwah, NJ: Erlbaum.

Cooper, H. (1989). Synthesis of research on homework. *Educational Leadership, 47*, 85–91.

DeBaryshe, B. D., & Gorecki, D. M. (2005). Learning connections; A home-school partnership to enhance emergent literacy and emergent math skills in at-risk preschoolers. In A. E. Maynard & M. I. Martini (Eds.), *Learning in cultural context: Family, peers, and school* (pp. 175- 198). New York: Kluwer Academic/Plenum Publishers.

Durkin, K., Shire, B., Riem, R., Crowther, R. D., & Rutter, D. R. (1986). The social and linguistic context of early number development. *British Journal of Developmental Psychology, 4*, 269–288.

Fluck, M., Linnell, M., & Holgate, M. (2005). Does counting count for 3- to 4-year-olds?: Parental assumptions about preschool children's understanding of counting and cardinality. *Social Development, 14*, 496–513.

Gardner, M. F. (1990). *Revised early one word picture vocabulary test.* Navato, CA: Academic Therapy Publications.

Gauvain, M. (1995). Thinking in niches: Sociocultural influences on cognitive development. *Human Development, 38,* 25–45.

Geary, D. C., Bow-Thomas, C. C., Liu, F., & Siegler, R. S. (1993). Even before formal instruction, Chinese children outperform American children in mental addition. *Cognitive Development, 8,* 517–529.

Geary, D. C., Bow-Thomas, C. C., Liu, F., & Siegler, R. S. (1996). Development of arithmetical competencies in Chinese and American children: Influence of age, language, and schooling. *Child Development, 67,* 2022–2044.

Gelman, R., & Massey, C. (1987). The cultural unconscious as contributor to the supporting environments for cognitive development. Commentary on social processes in early number development. *Monographs of the Society for Research in Child Development, 52*(2, Serial No. 216).

Ginsburg, H. P., & Baroody, A. J. (1990). *Test of early mathematical ability* (2nd ed.). Austin, TX: ProEd.

Ginsburg, H. P., Choy, Y. E., Lopez, L. S., Netley, R., & Chao-Yuan, C. (1997). Happy birthday to you: Early mathematical thinking of Asian, South American, and U.S. children. In T. Nunes & P. Bryant (Eds.), *Learning and teaching mathematics: An international perspective* (pp. 163–207). East Sussex, U.K: Psychology Press.

Ginsburg, H. P., Klein, A., & Starkey, P. (1998). The development of children's mathematical thinking: Connecting research with practice. In W. Damon, I.E. Sigel, K.A. Renniger (Eds.), *Handbook of child psychology: Vol. 4, Child psychology in practice* (5th ed., pp. 404–476). New York: Wiley.

González, N., Moll, L. C., & Amanti, C. (2005). *Funds of knowledge: Theorizing practices in households, communities, and classrooms.* Mahwah, NJ: Lawrence Erlbaum.

Goodnow, J. J. (1990). The socialization of cognition: What's involved? In J. W. Stigler, R. A. Shweder, & G. Herdt (Ed.), *Cultural psychology: Essays on comparative human development* (pp. 259–286). New York: Cambridge University Press.

Griffin, S. A., Case, R., & Siegler, R. S. (1994). Rightstart: Providing the central conceptual prerequisites for first formal learning of arithmetic to students at risk for school failure. In K. McGilly (Ed.), *Classroom lessons: Integrating cognitive theory and classroom practice* (pp. 25–49). Cambridge, MA: MIT Press.

Guberman, S. R. (1999). Cultural aspects of young children's mathematics knowledge. In J. V. Copley (Ed.), *Mathematics in the early years* (pp. 30–36). Reston, VA: National Council of Teachers of Mathematics.

Guberman, S. R. A. (2004). Comparative study of children's out-of-school activities and arithmetical achievements. *Journal for Research in Mathematics Education, 35,* 117–150.

Hall, N., Larson, J., & Marsh, J. (2003). *Handbook of early childhood literacy.* London: Sage.

Huntsinger, C. S., Jose, P. E, Larson, S. L., Balsink Krieg, D., & Shaligram, C. (2000). Mathematics, vocabulary, and reading development in Chinese American and European American children over the primary school years. *Journal of Educational Psychology, 92*(4), 745–760.

Huttenlocher, J., Jordan, N. C., & Levine, S. C. (1994). A mental model for early arithmetic. *Journal of Experimental Psychology: General, 123,* 284–296.

Jordan, N. C., Huttenlocher, J., & Levine, S. C. (1992). Differential calculation abilities in young children from middle- and low-income families. *Developmental Psychology, 28,* 644–653.

Klibanoff, R. S., Levine, S. C, Huttenlocher, J., Vasilyeva, M., Hedges, L. V. (2006). Preschool children's mathematical knowledge: The effect of teacher "math talk." *Developmental Psychology, 42,* 59–69.

Lave, J. (1988). *Cognition in Practice.* New York: Cambridge University Press.

LeFevre, J., Clarke, T., & Stringer, A. P. (2002). Influences of language and parental involvement on the development of counting skills: Comparisons of French- and English-speaking Canadian children. *Early Child Development and Care, 172,* 283–300.

Linnell, M., & Fluck, M. (2001). The effect of maternal support for counting and cardinal understanding in pre-school children. *Social Development, 10,* 202–220.

Miller, K. F., Smith, C. M., Zhu, J., & Zhang, H. (1995). Preschool origins of cross-national differences in mathematical competence: The role of number naming systems. *Psychological Science, 6,* 56–60.

Miller, K. F., & Stigler, J. W. (1987). Counting in Chinese: Cultural variation in a basic cognitive skill. *Cognitive Development, 2,* 279–305.

Miura, I. T., Okamoto, Y., Kim, C. C., Steere, M., & Fayol, M.(1993). First graders' cognitive representation of number and understanding of place value: Cross-national comparisons-France, Japan, Korea, Sweden, and the United States. *Journal of Educational Psychology, 85,* 24–30.

Mix, K. S. (2002). The construction of number concepts. *Cognitive Development, 17,* 1345–1363.

Mix, K. S., Huttenlocher, J., & Levine, S. C. (2002). *Quantitative development in infancy and early childhood.* New York: Oxford University.

Moll, L. C., Amanti, C., Neff, D., & Gonzalez, N. (1992). Funds of Knowledge for teaching: Using a qualitative approach to connect homes and classrooms, *Theory into Practice, 31,* 132–141.

Neuman, S. B., & Roskos, K. (2005). The state of state pre-kindergarten standards. *Early Childhood Research Quarterly, 20,* 125–145.

Nunes, T., Schliemann, A. D., & Carraher, D. W. (1993). *Street mathematics and school mathematics.* New York: Cambridge University Press.

Purcell-Gates, V. (2000). Family literacy. In M. L. Kamil, P. B. Mosenthal, D. O. Pearson, & R. Barr (Eds.,) *Handbook of Reading Research,* Vol. III. (pp. 853–870). Mahwah, NJ: Erlbaum.

Rogoff, B. (1990). *Apprenticeship in thinking: cognitive development in social context.* New York: Oxford University Press.

Rogoff, B. (2003). The cultural nature of human development. New York: Oxford.

Saxe, G. B. (1991). *Culture and cognitive development: Studies in mathematical understanding.* Hillsdale, NJ: Erlbaum

Saxe, G.B., Guberman, S. & Gearheart, M. (1987). Social and developmental processes in children's understanding of number. *Monographs of the Society for Research in Child Development, 52,* 100–200.

Shumow, L. (1998). Promoting parental attunement to children's mathematical reasoning through parent education. *Journal of Applied Developmental Psychology, 19,* 109–127.

Sophian, C. (2004). Mathematics for the future: developing a Head Start curriculum to support mathematics learning. *Early Childhood Research Quarterly, 19,* 59–81.

Starkey, P., & Klein, A. (2000). Fostering parental support for children's mathematical development: An intervention with Head Start families. *Early Education and Development, 11,* 659–680.

Starkey, P., Klein, A., Chang, I., Dong, Q., Pang, L., & Zhou, Y. (1999). *Environmental supports for young children's mathematical development in China and the United States.* Paper presented at the meeting of the Society for Research in Child Development, Albuquerque, NM.

Starkey, P., Klein, A., & Wakeley, A. (2004). Enhancing young children's mathematical knowledge through a pre-kindergarten mathematics intervention. *Early Childhood Research Quarterly, 19,* 99–120.

Street B. V., Baker D. A., & Tomlin, A. (2005). *Navigating numeracies: Home/school numeracy practices.* London: Kluwer.

Stevenson, H. W., Chen, C., & Lee, S. (1993). Mathematics achievement of Chinese, Japanese, and American children: Ten years later. *Science, 259,* 53–58.

Tudge, R. H., & Doucet, F. (2004). Early mathematical experiences: observing young Black and White children's everyday activities. *Early Childhood Research Quarterly, 19,* 21–39.

Vygotsky, L. S. ([1960] 1981). The genesis of higher mental functions. In J. V. Wertsch (Ed.), *The concept of activity in Soviet psychology* (pp. 144–188). Armonk, NY: Sharpe.

Vygotsky, L. S. (1978). *Mind in society: The development of higher psychological processes.* Cambridge, MA: Harvard University Press.

Wasik, B. H. (2004). *Handbook of Family Literacy.* Mahwah, NJ: Erlbaum.

Wood, D. J., Bruner, J., & Ross, G. (1976). The role of tutoring in problem solving. *Journal of Child Psychology and Psychiatry, 17,* 89–100.

Young-Loveridge, J. M. (1989). The relationship between children's home experiences and their mathematical skills on entry into school. *Early Child Development and Care, 43,* 43–59.

CHAPTER 14

RESEARCH PERSPECTIVES IN EARLY CHILDHOOD MATHEMATICS

Olivia N. Saracho and Bernard Spodek

Recently, researchers have developed an increasing interest in the mathematics education of young children. Over time researchers have discovered that as early as infancy young children are able to discriminate numbers (Antell & Keating, 1983) and occupy themselves in topological explorations during block play (Leeb-Lundberg, 1996). Studies suggested that mathematics education could develop children's mathematical knowledge if it was initiated in the early years (Hinkle, 2000). Current research and other developments have impelled those involved directly and indirectly with young children to focus their attention in mathematics in early childhood education. Clements, Sarama, and DiBiase, (2004) identified the following explanations for the vast increase in mathematics research in early childhood education:

- *The number of children enrolled in early childhood education has increased.* The United States Department of Education (2000) reported that in1999, 70% four-year-olds and 93% five-year-olds attended an early childhood education program. In 1999 one million children were enrolled in state early childhood education programs. This number continues to increase (Hinkle, 2000). Both federal and state agencies have funded pre-kindergarten programs that can increase the chil-

Contemporary Perspectives on Mathematics in Early Childhood Education, pages 309–320
Copyright © 2008 by Information Age Publishing
All rights of reproduction in any form reserved.

dren's mathematics academic achievement, especially in low-income children.

- *The importance of mathematics has been acknowledged* (Kilpatrick, Swafford, & Findell, 2001). Presently, the world's economy requires that most occupations employ individuals who have sophisticated skills, which has increased an international preoccupation for the children's knowledge of mathematics (Mullis et al., 1997). Unfortunately, students' mathematics achievement (including kindergarten children) in the United States is lower than those students from other countries. Klein and Starkey (2004) also found significant cross-national differences in the four- and five-year-old children's informal mathematics knowledge.

- *Differences in students' mathematics achievement have also been found within the United States* (Klein & Starkey, 2004; Starkey &Klein, in this volume; Young-Loveridge, in this volume). Klein and Starkey (2004) have shown that preschool children from different sociocultural heritages vary in their readiness levels for a standards-based mathematics curriculum (Klein & Starkey, 2004). This raises serious concerns about equity in relation to the pre-kindergarten children's lack of readiness for mathematics instruction in the elementary schools. Most of these children later have trouble with mathematics. Several government agencies have funded programs for low-income children who have trouble with mathematics and are considered to be at-risk of school failure (Bowman, Donovan, & Bruns, 2001). In order to assure that these children experience long-term success in their learning and development, they need to have a foundation for learning and be provided with high quality educational experiences during their early years (Carnegie Corporation, 1998, 1999). These children need to gain informal mathematics knowledge to provide the foundation to learn mathematics.

- *Research indicate that mathematics education initiated in the early years and better quality mathematics education programs could lead into valuable learning benefits as prerequisites for the elementary school mathematics.* Regrettably, most programs are not of high quality (Hinkle, 2000). Preschool children become spontaneously interested in mathematics. Early childhood education programs need to nurture and meet their intellectual needs, including mathematics learning (Bowman et al., 2001; Kilpatrick et al., 2001).

The aforementioned explanations have stimulated both researchers and practitioners to develop an interest in mathematics education for preschool children. In the report titled, *Before it's too late: A report to the nation from the National Commission on Mathematics and Science Teaching for the 21st century*, the Glen Commission (2000) reported:

> at the daybreak of this new century and millennium . . . the future well-being of our nation and people depends not just on how well we educate our children generally, but on how well we educate them in mathematics and science specifically. (p. 6)

STANDARDS AND EXPECTATIONS

A high-quality mathematics education for young children begins with a set of standards for early childhood based on knowledge of young children's mathematical knowledge, which includes acting, thinking, and learning. These guidelines need to be flexible to consider the children's individual needs (Clements, 2004). The National Council of Teachers of Mathematics (2000–2004a-c) developed and published the *Principles and Standards for School Mathematics*, which included education from preschool through the twelfth grade. Although each of these Standards relates to all these grades, the proportional focus on specific *Principles and Standards* differs for each grade (National Council of Teachers of Mathematics, 2000–2004c). The *Principles and Standards* for preschool through second grade children can be found in their website under *Overview: Standards for school mathematics: Prekindergarten through Grade 12*.

The National Council of Teachers of Mathematics (2000–2004a) believes that a solid mathematical foundation needs to be developed for children who are in preschool through the second grade. These children are generating beliefs about (a) the meaning of mathematics, (b) the functions of mathematics, and (c) the benefits of mathematics to them as mathematics learners. Such beliefs contribute to their (1) thinking about, (2) performance in, (3) attitudes toward, and (4) effects in mathematics in their later years.

In the future, all students must have access to rigorous, high-quality mathematics instruction. They need to learn to use mathematics in their personal life, in the workplace, and in further studies. Students must be provided with opportunities to understand the power and beauty of mathematics. They need to acquire a new repertoire of the mathematics basic skills that allows them to compute fluently and to solve problems creatively and resourcefully. This suggests that students need to have opportunities to learn important mathematical concepts and procedures with understanding. Students need to have access to technologies that broaden and deepen their understanding of mathematics. More students are pursuing educational paths that prepare them for lifelong work as mathematicians, statisticians, engineers, and scientists. In the *Principles and Standards for School Mathematics*, the National Council of Teachers of Mathematics (2000–2004a,c) suggests that in the future all students should have access to rigorous, high-quality mathematics instruction and learn essential mathematical concepts and procedures with understanding. The use of technology can help the students expand and intensify their understanding of mathematics.

Young children develop many mathematical concepts, beginning in an intuitive way. Infants instinctively recognize and distinguish among small numbers of objects, while preschool children have a considerable body of informal mathematical knowledge. Even the youngest children can develop their mathematical knowledge in an environment that is rich in quantitative experiences and language; thus, when their thinking is stimulated, uniqueness is valued, and exploration is encouraged (National Council of Teachers of Mathematics, 2000–2004a). When young children attend a formal school setting, they typically have a range of mathematical understanding. Initial assessments can provide information to plan their mathematics instruction and early interventions (National Council of Teachers of Mathematics, 2000–2004a).

Interventions that are provided to the children at an early age can prevent them from later having learning difficulties in school (Clements et al., 2004; Griffin, 2004). To determine the effectiveness of interventions, appropriate assessment instruments are needed. Unfortunately, a limited number of reliable and appropriate measures of early childhood mathematics achievement have been developed (Ginsburg & Golbeck, 2004). Several researchers use Ginsburg and Baroody's (2003) *Test of Early Mathematics Ability* (TEMA-3), which is a nationally normed and theoretically-based assessment. Unfortunately, the TEMA-3 only assesses numbers. It is essential that instruments also assess meaningful elements that include shape, space, measurement, and logic. Propitiously, a number of researchers (e.g., Sarama & Clements, 2004; Sophian, 2004; Starkey, Klein, & Wakeley, 2004) are developing similar instruments. In addition, instruments should assess characteristics of scientific reasoning, including recording systematic observations (Gelman & Brenneman, 2004). Furthermore, measurement instruments must be developmentally appropriate for young children who have difficulty with tests, especially with standardized measures. Standardized measures require that all children be treated the same way. Although standardized measures can be used to compare groups of children, they fail to motivate young children. Young children usually become parsimonious in the testing situation, have difficulty maintaining attention, exhibit a variable interest in the activity, and find the testing situation to be unfamiliar (Bowman et al., 2001) and strange. The outcomes of these types of testing conditions usually become unreliable, misleading, and useless. Appropriate assessment procedures need to be developed such as clinical interviews and observations that are responsive to the young children's needs and distinctive features (Ginsburg & Golbeck, 2004).

All students benefit from high-quality programs where instruction in mathematics is presented in a way that honors both the nature of mathematics and the nature of young children by building on their intuitive and informal mathematical knowledge. Such programs need to rely on principles and practices of child development in an environment where children are motivated to be active learners and to respond to new challenges. In addition, the programs need to use a strong conceptual framework that encourages and develops the children's mathematical skills and their natural disposition to solve problems (National Council of Teachers of Mathematics, 2000–2004a).

MATHEMATICAL COMPETENCE

During the last three decades, researchers emphasized young children's competence in their cognitive abilities, especially in young children's mathematical thinking. Results from their studies have introduced new insights of the young children's capabilities. However, Ginsburg and Golbeck (2004) warn researchers of the following dangers inherent in a strong emphasis on competence.

- *Reducing the limits on young children's mathematical understanding.* Young children can informally add and subtract, but they have difficulty representing the operations symbolically or verbally describing them in words (Pappas, Ginsburg, & Jiang, 2003). They can understand principles that form the base for whole numbers, but young children seriously misunderstand rational numbers (Hartnett & Gelman, 1998). Preschoolers can follow a map of their classroom if the map is drawn at one azimuth (an oblique angle), but they have difficulty if the map is drawn directly from an overhead (Liben & Yekel, 1996) projector. Similarly, children are able to locate clusters of model furniture items in a scale model of their classroom, but they become confused if they have to position the furniture items themselves (Golbeck, Rand, & Soundy, 1986).
- *Overestimating young children's mathematical competence.* Overestimating young children's mathematical competence can set them up for failure. Instruction may be accelerated with advanced topics. It is important to consider the risks involved when young children are pushed to learn concepts beyond their cognitive limits.

- *Disregarding the complexity of young children's competence.* Young children's competence is determined by the context (Vygotsky, 1978) and on the precise nature of the activities (Donaldson, 1978). It is a complicated domain (Sophian, 1997) that involves various elements (Gelman & Greeno, 1987). Young children develop their mathematical and scientific thinking in a social and emotional environment (Ginsburg & Golbeck, 2004).

Researchers need to consider the importance of accurately assessing the young children's early competence. They need to examine young children's actions, abilities, and the environment (Ginsburg & Golbeck, 2004). It is important that mathematical research and instruction be established based on the knowledge of young children's mathematical acting, thinking, and learning (Clements, 2004). Communication among researchers, educators, and policy makers is essential to understand mathematics that is developmentally appropriate for young children.

MATHEMATICAL ASSUMPTIONS AND RECOMMENDATIONS

Attempts were initiated to develop standards for preschool and kindergarten mathematics education in a conference that was funded by grants from the National Science Foundation and the Exxon Mobil Foundation to the State University of New York at Buffalo. *The Conference on Standards for Prekindergarten and Kindergarten Mathematics Education* included a comprehensive group of experts from diverse fields, including representatives who were developing standards for young children's mathematics in almost every state; federal government officials; mathematicians, mathematics educators, researchers from mathematics education, researchers from early childhood education, and psychology researchers; curriculum developers; teachers; policy makers; and representatives from national organizations such as the National Council of Teachers of Mathematics (NCTM) and the National Association for the Education of Young Children (NAEYC). According to Clements (2004), the participants in this conference generated the following assumptions and recommendations:

Assumptions

- Knowledge of what young children can do and learn as well as specific leaning goals, are necessary for teachers to realize any vision of high-quality, early childhood education (p. 9).
- Pre-kindergarten children have the interest and ability to engage in significant mathematical thinking and learning (p. 11).

Recommendations

- The children's individual differences need to be considered in mathematics education. Children differ developmentally and socioculturally, which will affect their later achievement in mathematics. Such sociocultural and developmental differences indicate "what children know" and "what they bring to the educational situation."
- Early childhood teaching and assessment standards need to be flexible with developmentally appropriate guidelines that are based on current research and practice of young children's mathematical learning.
- The young children's mathematics experiences need to be related to their everyday life.
- High-quality mathematics programs for young children need to incorporate mathematical content, general mathematical processes (e.g., problem solving, reasoning, proof, communication, connections, representation), specific mathematical processes (e.g., organizing information, patterning, composing), and habits of mind (e.g., curiosity, imagination, inventiveness, persistence, willingness to experiment, sensitivity to patterns).
- Curriculum development and teaching need to be based on research and practice. Educators and policymakers need to require teaching, learning, curriculum, and assessment approaches that have been developed and widely tested with young children.
- Young children learn mathematics through play because it relates learning to life in their daily experiences, interests, and questions.
- Teachers need to provide young children with a mathematical environment and with frequent opportunities that allow them to reflect and extend their knowledge of mathematics into their everyday experiences, conversations, and play. Teachers need to use practical experiences to introduce mathematical concepts, methods, and vocabulary.
- Teachers need to use a combination of teaching strategies and planned sequences of experiences that are integrated throughout the day to promote children's learning. Teachers need to consider the children's informal knowledge, everyday experiences, cultural background, langauge, mathematical ideas and strategies.
- Children's learning can be facilitated through appropriate types of technology, particularly computer tools that enrich and extend mathematical experiences.
- Teachers need to understand each child's own mathematical ideas and strategies and use them to adapt their instruction in the curriculum.

- Teachers need to develop children's conceptual foundation to help understand the relationships between concepts and skills.
- Assessment should be used to understand young children's thinking and to plan instruction for the young children's mathematical learning. Practical and information forms of assessment consist of interview, performance task, and continuous observations.
- Sustained and coherent professional development needs to integrate research and expert practice. It needs to use multiple strategies and a variety of professional development models that focus on the importance of teacher leaders and collegial support groups.
- To improving teaching, pre-service and professional development programs need to include a profound knowledge of the (a) mathematics to be taught, (b) children's thinking, and (c) methods to develop the young children's mathematical skills and understandings.
- Professional development programs need to address high quality of mathematics curriculum materials and programs.
- An interpretation of the information from *The Conference on Standards for Prekindergarten and Kindergarten Mathematics Education* needs to be disseminated to different audiences using a variety of forms.
- State agencies across all states need to join forces to develop clear and related state mandates and guidelines to teach mathematics to young children. Governments need to offer appropriate funding and frameworks to provide high quality mathematics education for all children and high quality professional development for their teachers.

RECOMMENDATIONS IN TECHNOLOGY

Recommendations were also made about the use of technology in the learning and teaching of mathematics. Many researchers believe that technology increases children's opportunities for learning, increases their opportunity to solve problems in the real world, and increases their orientation to the future (Ball & Stacey, 2005). In their book, *Principles and standards for school mathematics,* the National Council of Teachers of Mathematics (2000–2004c) includes recommendations from their October 2003 position statement in technology. Masalski and Elliot (2005) selected the following recommendations from the National Council of Teachers of Mathematics position statement.

- Every school mathematics program should provide students and teachers with access to tools of instructional technology, including appropriate calculators, computers with mathematical software,

Internet c connectivity, handheld data-collection devices, and sensing problems.

- Pre-service and in-service teachers of mathematics at all levels should be provided with appropriate professional development in the use of instructional technology, the development of mathematics lessons that take advantage of technology-rich environments, and the integration of technology into day-to-day instruction.
- Curricula and courses of study at all levels should incorporate appropriate instructional technology in objectives, lessons, and assessment of learning outcomes.
- Programs of pre-service teacher preparation and in-service professional development should strive to instill dispositions of openness to experimentation with every-evolving technological tools and their pervasive impact on mathematics education.
- Teachers should make informed decisions about the appropriate implementation of technologies in coherent instructional program (p. 2).

CONCLUSION

Toward the end of the last century, researchers from a variety of disciplines focused on research related to different perspectives in mathematics. A range of research trends surfaced in the area of mathematics including (a) the growth of research, (b) growing diversity in research methods, (c) a shift in epistemology, (d) a shift in learning psychology, and (e) growth of political awareness that are related to the study of teaching and learning in school settings and to determine how those trends have influenced the study of mathematics in schools. To provide an understanding of the basis of these trends, researchers have (1) described some features of mathematical sciences education as a field of study, (2) drafted the researchers' activities, (3) summarized the array of research methods that are presently used (Romberg, 1992), which may have prompted the surge on research in mathematics education. Presently there is a recognizable body of research that extends beyond the realm of mathematics. Studies differ in the degree to which they explore and are sensitive to the area of mathematics education. Nevertheless, sufficient data are available to characterize research on mathematics education as a distinct field and to identify those researchers who focus on the mathematics education research community. This volume has provided a synthesis and reconceptualization of past research, has offered guidelines for future research, and has identified educational implications.

REFERENCES

Antell, S., & Keating, D. (1983). Perception of numerical invariance in neonates. *Child Development, 54,* 695–701.

Ball, L., & Stacey, K. (2005). Teaching strategies for developing judicious technology use. In W. J. Masalski & P. C. Elliot (Eds.), *Technology-supported: mathematics learning environments.* (pp. 3–15). Reston, VA: National Council of Teachers of Mathematics.

Bowman, B. T., Donovan, M. S., & Bruns, M. S. (Eds.). (2001). *Eager to learn: Educating our preschoolers.* Washington, DC: National Academy Press.

Carnegie Corporation (1998). *Years of promise: A comprehensive learning strategy for America's children.* Retrieved from http://www.carnegie.org/exesum.html on November 24, 2006.

Carnegie Corporation of New York. (1999). *America's promise: The Alliance for Youth, Annual Report 1999.* Alexandria, VA. Retrieved from http://www.carnegie.org/sub/about/ar1999.pdf on November 18, 2006.

Clements, D. H. (2004). Major themes and recommendations. In D. H. Clements, J. Sarama, & A-M. DiBiase (Eds.). *Engaging young children in mathematics: Standards for early childhood mathematics education* (pp. 7–72). Mahwah, NJ: Erlbaum.

Clements, D. H., Sarama, J., & DiBiase, A.-M., (Eds.). (2004). *Engaging young children in mathematics: Standards for early childhood mathematics education.* Mahwah, NJ: Erlbaum.

Donaldson, M. C. (1978). *Children's minds.* New York: Norton.

Gelman, R., & Brenneman, K. (2004). Science learning pathways for young children. *Early Childhood Research Quarterly, 19,* 150–158.

Gelman, R., & Greeno, J. G. (1987). On the nature of competence: Principles for understanding in a domain. In L. B. Resnick (Ed.), *Knowing and learning: Issues for a cognitive science of instruction* (pp. 125–186). Hillsdale, NJ: Erlbaum.

Ginsburg, H. P., & Baroody, A. J. (2003). *The test of early mathematics ability* (3rd ed.). Austin, TX: Pro Ed.

Ginsburg, H. P., & Golbeck, S. L. (2004). Thoughts on the future of research on mathematics and science learning and education. *Early Childhood Research Quarterly, 19,* 190–200.

Glen Commission. (2000). *Before it's too late: A report to the nation from the National Commission on Mathematics and Science Teaching for the 21st century.* Washington, DC: United States Department of Education.

Golbeck, S.L., Rand, M., & Soundy, C. (1986). Constructing a model of a large scale space with the space in view: Effects of guidance and cognitive restructuring. *Merrill Palmer Quarterly, 32,* 187–203.

Griffin, S. (2004). Number worlds: A research-based mathematics program for young children. In D. H. Clements, J. Sarama, & A-M. DiBiase (Eds.). *Engaging young children in mathematics: Standards for early childhood mathematics education.* (pp. 325–342). Mahwah, NJ: Erlbaum.

Hartnett, P.M., & Gelman, R. (1998). Early understandings of number: Paths or barriers to the construction of new understandings?. *Learning and Instruction: The Journal of the European Association for Research in Learning and Instruction, 8,* 341–374.

Hinkle, D. 2000). *School involvement in early childhood.* Washington, DC: United States Department of Education.

Kilpatrick, J., Swafford, J., & Findell, B. (2001). *Adding it up: Helping children learn mathematics.* Washington, DC: National Academy Press.

Klein, A., & Starkey, P. (2004). Fostering preschool children's mathematical knowledge: Findings from the Berkeley math reading project. In D. H. Clements, J. Sarama, & A-M. DiBiase (Eds.), *Engaging young children in mathematics: Standards for early childhood mathematics education.* (pp. 343–360). Mahwah, NJ: Erlbaum.

Leeb-Lundberg, K. (1996). The block builder mathematician. In E. S. Hirsch (Ed.), *The block book* (pp. 34–60). Washington, DC: National Association for the Education of Young Children.

Liben, L.S., & Yekel, C.S. (1996). Preschoolers' understanding of plan and oblique maps: The role of geometric and representational correspondence. *Child Development, 67,* 2780–2796.

Masalski, W. J., & Elliot, P. C. (2005). Prologue NCTM position paper on technology. The use of technology in the learning and teaching of mathematics. In W. J. Masalski & P. C. Elliot (Eds.) *Technology-supported: mathematics learning environments.* (pp. 1–2). Reston, VA: National Council of Teachers of Mathematics.

Mullis, I. V. S., Martin, M. O., Beaton, A. E., Gonzales, E. J., Kelly, D. L., & Smith, T. A. (1997). *Mathematics achievement in the primary school years: IEA's third international mathematics and science study (TIMSS).* Chestnut Hill, MA: Center for the Study of Testing, Evaluation, and Educational Policy, Boston College.

National Council of Teachers of Mathematics. (2000–2004a). *Overview: Prekindergarten through Grade 2.* Retrieved from http://standards.nctm.org/document/chapter4/index.htm on November 21, 2006.

National Council of Teachers of Mathematics. (2000–2004b). *Overview: Standards for school mathematics: Prekindergarten through Grade 12.* Retrieved from http://standards.nctm.org/document/chapter3/index.htm on November 21, 2006.

National Council of Teachers of Mathematics. (2000–2004c). *Principles and standards for school mathematics.* Reston, VA: National Council of Teachers of Mathematics.

Pappas, S., Ginsburg, H.P., & Jiang, M. (2003). SES differences in young children's metacognition in the context of mathematical problem solving. *Cognitive Development, 18*(3), 431–450.

Romberg, T. A. (1992). Perspectives on scholarship and research methods. In D. A. Grouws (Ed.). *Handbook of research on mathematics teaching and learning.* (pp. 49–64). New York: Macmillan.

Sarama, J., & Clements, D. H. (2004). Building Blocks for early childhood mathematics. *Early Childhood Research Quarterly, 19,* 181–189.

Sophian, C. (1997). Beyond competence: The significance of performance for conceptual development. *Cognitive Development, 12,* 281–303.

Sophian, C. (2004). Mathematics for the future: Developing a Head Start curriculum to support mathematics learning. *Early Childhood Research Quarterly, 19,* 59–81.

Starkey, P., Klein, A., & Wakeley, A. (2004). Enhancing young children's mathematical knowledge through a pre-kindergarten mathematics intervention. *Early Childhood Research Quarterly, 19*, 99–120.

United States Department of Education, National Center for Educational Statistics. (2000). *The condition of education 2000.* Washington, DC: U. S. Government Printing Office.

Vygotsky, L. S. (1978). *Mind in society: The development of higher psychological processes.* Cambridge, MA: Harvard University Press.

ABOUT THE CONTRIBUTORS

Ann Anderson is a professor in the Department of Curriculum Studies at the University of British Columbia where she teaches and conducts research in the areas of preschool children's mathematics learning and problem solving in the primary grades. Recent publications include Supporting multiliteracies: Parents' and children's mathematical talk within storybook reading in *Mathematics Education Research Journal* (2005) and Mathematical discourse in storybook reading in *Journal for Research in Mathematics Education* (2004).

Jim Anderson is a professor in the Department of Language and Literacy Education at the University of British Columbia where he teaches and conducts research in the areas of early literacy and family literacy. Prior to joining UBC, he worked for 15 years in the public education system as a classroom teacher, reading specialist, school principal, language arts coordinator and assistant superintendent of curriculum and instruction. Recent publications include the edited volume, *Portraits of Literacy Across, Families, Communities and Schools: Intersections and Tensions* (Erlbaum).

William M. Bart received the Ph.D. degree from the University of Chicago. He is presently a Professor of Educational Psychology at the University of Minnesota. His research areas are learning, cognition, and testing. His main interest is the improvement of cognitive skills among learners.

Joann P. Benigno is currently a faculty member in the School of Hearing, Speech, and Language Sciences at Ohio University in Athens, OH. She received her Ph.D. in psychology from the University of Florida in 2004. She completed an NIMH postdoctoral research traineeship at the Institute of Child Development at the University of Minnesota, Twin Cities. Her research program addresses the role of sociocultural influences on children's cognitive and language development.

Contemporary Perspectives on Mathematics in Early Childhood Education, pages 321–326
Copyright © 2008 by Information Age Publishing
All rights of reproduction in any form reserved.

Beth Casey is a Professor of Applied Developmental and Educational Psychology at Boston College, and previously coordinated the Early Childhood Education Program at the School of Education for many years. She has recently received two NSF grants to study the relationship between spatial and mathematical skills.

Douglas H. Clements is Professor of Education at University of Buffalo, SUNY, where he was granted the Chancellor's Award for Excellence in Scholarship and Creative Activities. His primary research interests lie in the areas of the learning and teaching of geometry, computer applications in mathematics education, and the early development of mathematical ideas. He has published over 90 refereed research studies, 6 books, 50 chapters, and 250 additional publications. His recent book is, Clements, D. H., Sarama, J., & DiBiase, A.-M. (Eds.). (2004). *Engaging young children in mathematics: Standards for early childhood mathematics education.*

Shari Ellis is at the Center for Informal Science Education, Florida Museum of Natural History, University of Florida. She received her Ph.D. from the University of Utah in 1987. Her research focuses on the development of scientific and mathematical understanding in social contexts. She currently directs an early childhood science curriculum expansion project in Head Start classrooms.

Barbrina Ertle is a research associate at Teachers College, Columbia University where she earned her Ed.D. in Cognitive Studies. She earned her M.A. from Johns Hopkins University in Elementary Education and her B.S. in Marine Sciences from Long Island University. She has served as a middle school teacher. She is currently involved in curriculum evaluation research and the design of professional development for early childhood and elementary mathematics teachers.

Herbert P. Ginsburg is the Jacob H. Schiff Professor of Psychology and Education at Teachers College, Columbia University, where he teaches in the departments of Human Development and Mathematics Education. For many years, he has conducted research on cognitive development, particularly the development of children's mathematical thinking, both nationally and internationally. He has developed several kinds of educational applications, including a mathematics program for young children, *Big Math for Little Kids,* and a test of mathematical thinking.

Joanne Kersh is a doctoral candidate in Educational and Developmental Psychology at Boston College. She has a broad interest in research that informs policy and practice that enhances the well-being of children with developmental disabilities, such as investigating the development of spatial ability in children in order to inform more accessible, inclusive teaching practices. Her primary focus is currently on relationships within families of children with disabilities.

Alice Klein is a research psychologist in the Institute of Human Development at the University of California, Berkeley. Dr. Klein's research activities focus on socioeconomic and cultural influences on young children's mathematical thinking and how early mathematical development impacts children's later achievement in mathematics. Her current research involves the development and evaluation of large-scale math interventions for preschool children who are at-risk for underachievement in school mathematics. Dr. Klein has published numerous articles on early mathematical development and education, and is co-author of an early childhood mathematics curriculum, *Pre-K Mathematics.*

Aisling Leavy is a mathematics educator focusing on the teaching of mathematics at the elementary level. Her research interest is children's mathematical thinking with a focus on statistical reasoning. She is faculty member at Mary Immaculate College at the University of Limerick and is affiliate faculty at the Center for Mathematics Education at the University of Maryland.

Linlin Li is a doctoral student in the Department of Human Development and Family Studies at the University of North Carolina at Greensboro, having worked on the Cultural Ecology of Young Children project for two years. She completed her MS in educational and developmental psychology in China. Her research focuses on inclusive environments for young children and cultural study in early childhood education.

Olivia N. Saracho is a professor of education in the Department of Curriculum and Instruction at the University of Maryland. Her areas of scholarship include family literacy, cognitive style, play, and teaching and teacher education in early childhood education. She is widely published in the field of early childhood education. Olivia N. Saracho is coeditor, with Bernard Spodek, of the *Handbook of Research on the Education of Young Children,* 2/ed. (2006, Erlbaum). They are also coeditors of the *Contemporary Perspectives in Early Childhood Education* series (Information Age).

Julie Sarama is an Associate Professor of Mathematics Education at the University at Buffalo (SUNY). She conducts research on the implementation and effects of her own software environments in mathematics classrooms, young children's development of mathematical concepts and competencies, implementation and scale-up of educational reform, and professional development, published in more than 35 refereed articles, 15 chapters, and 50 additional publications.

Catherine Sophian is a professor in the Department of Psychology at the University of Hawaii. She is the author of the 2007 book, *The Origins of Mathematical Knowledge in Childhood* (Erlbaum)and a member of the writing team for the *Number and Numeration* volume in the NCTM Essential Understandings series.

Bernard Spodek is Professor Emeritus of Early Childhood Education at the University of Illinois at Urbana-Champaign where he has taught since 1965. He received his doctorate in early childhood education from Teachers College, Columbia University, then joined the faculty of the University of Wisconsin-Milwaukee. He has also taught nursery, kindergarten and elementary classes in New York City. His research and scholarly interests are in the areas of curriculum, teaching and teacher education in early childhood education. Dr. Spodek has lectured extensively in the United States, Australia, Canada, China, England, Greece, Hong Kong, Israel, Japan, Korea, Mexico, Portugal, and Taiwan. From 1976 to 1978 he was President of the National Association for the Education of Young Children, and from 1981 through 1983 he chaired the Early Education and Child Development Special Interest Group of the American Educational Research Association. Currently, he is president of the Pacific Early Childhood Educational Research Association (PECERA). He is widely published in the field of early childhood education.

Tiffany Kinney Stanley recently completed her BS in Psychology at the University of North Carolina at Greensboro, having worked for two years as a research assistant on the Cultural Ecology of Young Children project.

Prentice Starkey is a professor of human development and early childhood education at the University of California, Berkeley. He received his doctorate in developmental psychology from the University of Texas at Austin and was a postdoctoral scholar at the University of Pennsylvania and the Medical Research Council's Cognitive Development Unit in London. He has studied children's early mathematical development for more than 20 years and published the first paper on the origins of numerical knowledge in infants in *Science*. His recent research focuses on socioeconomic and cultural influences on early mathematical development and education. Prof. Starkey has co-authored (with H. Ginsburg and A. Klein) a review of research on mathematical development for the *Handbook of Child Psychology* and a curriculum, *Pre-K Mathematics*, published by Scott Foresman-Addison Wesley.

Carolyn Thauberger is a doctoral candidate in Language and Literacy Education at the University of British Columbia. Carolyn has taught reading and mathematics to students with special needs in both elementary and high schools in Saskatchewan as well as in a clinical setting. Her masters degree was completed at the University of Regina in 1995. Her academic and research interests are primarily in teaching academic support, in reading fluency instruction, and in developing self-regulated learning.

Jonathan Tudge is a professor in the Department of Human Development and Family Studies at the University of North Carolina at Greensboro and a visiting professor at the Institute of Psychology, Federal University of Rio Grande do Sul, Brazil. He completed his Ph.D. in Human Development and Family Studies at Cornell University. His research examines young children's initiation of and engagement in everyday activities both within and across a number of different societies, particularly focusing on the years prior to and immediately following the entry to school.

Maureen Vandermaas-Peeler is a professor of psychology at Elon University with a PhD in Developmental Psychology from North Carolina State University. Her research interests include parental guidance of children's learning in informal contexts such as play and activities at home related to literacy and numeracy, and other topics related to child development in sociocultural context. She has taught lifespan development, cultural psychology, and many other courses related to development and culture in the past decade. She has also been involved in community education and intervention efforts on behalf of young children and families.

Jennifer Young-Loveridge is an Associate Professor at the University of Waikato in the School of Education in Hamilton, New Zealand. After a brief period teaching 6-year-olds in New Zealand, she was awarded a Commonwealth Scholarship at the University of Toronto to complete a Ph.D. in Applied Psychology. She returned to New Zealand to an academic position at the University of Canterbury in Christchurch. Her interest in children's mathematical thinking began with a longitudinal study of 5-year-olds in Christchurch, following the children over their first four years at school. After moving to Hamilton to take up a position at the University of Waikato, she set up several intervention programs, including school-based and home-based intervention with 5-year-olds, and a project with 4-year-olds. She developed *Checkout*, a shopping game to assess numeracy on entry to school at five, which was included in a *School Entry Assessment* kit distributed to all schools in New Zealand. Her most recent research has involved analysis of the data on students' number knowledge and strategies gathered by teachers involved in New Zealand's numeracy initiative, and a study of students' perspectives on their mathematics learning.

Jessica Mercer Young is a former Early Childhood Teacher and a Doctoral Candidate at Boston College in Developmental and Educational Psychology. Her current research interests include the development of cognitive and social processes in early childhood for children with developmental disabilities.

Masamich Yuzawa graduated from Tokyo University in Japan in 1985, and received the Ph.D. degree in Psychology at Hiroshima University in 1992. He is presently Professor in Psychology at Hiroshima University. His research areas are developmental psychology and educational psychology, and his main interest is in development of mathematical and scientific concepts.

Miki Yuzawa graduated from Nagasaki University in Japan in 1994, and received Ph.D. in Psychology at Hiroshima University in 2002. She is presently a Lecturer at Notre Dame Seishin University. Her research area is developmental psychology, and her research interests include the development of working memory and the acquisition of words.

LaVergne, TN USA
10 December 2009

166649LV00002B/144/A